AF754744

# Zero Poverty Society

# Zero Poverty Society

*Ensuring a Decent Income for All*

Sarah Marchal and Ive Marx

OXFORD
UNIVERSITY PRESS

OXFORD
UNIVERSITY PRESS

Great Clarendon Street, Oxford, OX2 6DP,
United Kingdom

Oxford University Press is a department of the University of Oxford.
It furthers the University's objective of excellence in research, scholarship,
and education by publishing worldwide. Oxford is a registered trade mark of
Oxford University Press in the UK and in certain other countries

© Sarah Marchal and Ive Marx 2024

The moral rights of the authors have been asserted

All rights reserved. No part of this publication may be reproduced, stored in
a retrieval system, or transmitted, in any form or by any means, without the
prior permission in writing of Oxford University Press, or as expressly permitted
by law, by licence or under terms agreed with the appropriate reprographics
rights organization. Enquiries concerning reproduction outside the scope of the
above should be sent to the Rights Department, Oxford University Press, at the
address above

You must not circulate this work in any other form
and you must impose this same condition on any acquirer

Published in the United States of America by Oxford University Press
198 Madison Avenue, New York, NY 10016, United States of America

British Library Cataloguing in Publication Data
Data available

Library of Congress Control Number: 2024932675

ISBN 9780192871527

DOI: 10.1093/9780191967771.001.0001

Pod

Links to third party websites are provided by Oxford in good faith and
for information only. Oxford disclaims any responsibility for the materials
contained in any third party website referenced in this work.

# Acknowledgements

This book is a result of many years of work on the topic of minimum income protection.

We thank our colleagues at the Centre for Social Policy Herman Deleeck. Working there remains one of the great privileges of our lives. Elise Aerts, Henri Haapanala, and Alessandro Nardo contributed directly to this book and deserve special mention here. We want to give a special thanks to some CSB colleagues with whom we have worked particularly closely over the past years: Bea Cantillon, Jeroen Horemans, Dries Lens, Julie Janssens, Sarah Kuypers, Ninke Mussche, Julie Vinck, and Gerlinde Verbist.

That also applies to many former colleagues who have ventured onto other walks of life. Natascha Van Mechelen and Tim Goedemé laid many of the foundations of our work on minimum income protection and deserve special mention, as do Marjolijn De Wilde and Bérénice Storms.

There is a long list of colleagues and friends of many years to whom we owe intellectual gratitude and in more than a few cases a drink or two. Many of you will find yourselves cited and thus acknowledged in this book! Our special thanks to Daniel Dumont, Werner Eichhorst, Michael Förster, Janet Gornick, Anton Hemerijck, Herwig Immervoll, Henning Lohmann, Lane Kenworthy, Kenneth Nelson, Rense Nieuwenhuis, Brian Nolan, Bruno Palier, Zach Parolin, Wiemer Salverda, Julia Shu-Huah Wang, Tim Smeeding, Istvan Toth, Wim Van Lancker, and Frank Vandenbroucke. A special mention to five great scholars who have left us far too early. Tony Atkinson, Rebecca Blank, John Hills, Martin Ravallion, and Chris Whelan. All giants in our profession. Sharp minds, generous people, and good company.

In addition to all the people listed here, and we are sure we have omitted more than a few, we want to thank people who have commented at seminars or as (anonymous) referees. Referees may not always be our favourite people but they do help us forward!

We regularly give talks to non-academic audiences of all walks of life. That constant 'touch with reality' has influenced our thinking in a more substantial way than may be apparent from the mostly academic references in this book. Chapter 5, on the political economy of minimum income protection, is particularly reflective of the (sometimes quite forthright) comments we have received over the past years.

That brings us to some more personal reflections.

*For Ive:*
Sarah, it has been such a pleasure seeing you blossom into the scholar you are today. It has been a joy writing this book together.

I thank Philip Kasinitz, Director of ARC at CUNY's Graduate Center, and Janet Gornick, Director of the Stone Center on Socio-Economic Inequality at CUNY's Graduate Center, for generously hosting me on various occasions. Thank you, Kay Powell, for making those stays so pleasant.

I thank the AIPRIL team for indulging me—I know this book took a lot of time and focus.

Academic work does not get done without support, especially with three daughters to raise. My thanks to Martine Cools for her continued support. I extend the same thanks to our families, old and new.

Which brings me to my lovely daughters Inés, Esther, and Rachel, to Darius, and of course to Laurie. Thank you all for your love and support, and for all the joy and fun you bring.

*For Sarah:*
I thank my co-author for his vision and enthusiasm in writing this book. Ive, thank you for encouraging me, as co-author, previously as supervisor and ever as mentor, to more often 'think big'.

Writing this book was a long-term effort. Luckily, and as always, I could count on my unparalleled sisters, in-laws, and parents, both for support and for distraction.

Most importantly: dear Kris, thank you for your love and support on so many levels. Not in the least keeping the house running in the mad end sprint in the vain attempt to finish this book before the centre of our world would fundamentally shift forever.

Which brings me to you, darling Tuur. Welcome.

# Contents

# List of Tables, Figures, and Boxes

## Tables



## Figures

## Boxes

# What This Book Is About

The notion that every person living amidst the relative affluence of the rich world has a right to minimum means of existence enabling at least physical survival and preferably also a modicum of social participation, be it frugally and soberly, holds as a fundamental matter of social justice to most people.

We say most. Some people will indeed dispute that any such right exists in meritocratic societies as long as equality of opportunity prevails and a wealth of opportunities present themselves. That is a valid argument yet it is also true that a streak of bad luck may derail the most assiduous of people. And so much of the real discussion is about the specifics of how to guarantee a shelter against poverty. People disagree for example on the question of who qualifies for a guaranteed minimum income. Should it be restricted to law-abiding citizens with a longstanding attachment to the society granting and funding such a right or should it be given to everyone, including newly arrived or even irregular immigrants? People also differ on the role personal responsibility and effort towards self-reliance play in determining or modulating the (continued) right to a minimum income. In the eyes of some, chronic bad life choices or continued lack of effort to regain self-reliance are grounds for disqualification. People also differ on how much any minimum income guarantee may cost and how it may impact on work effort and economic dynamism. And people disagree, of course, on how much is enough.

Yet the general principle that provisions should exist ensuring adequate minimum incomes to those deemed deserving is widely accepted. Indeed, it is codified into international and in many cases also national law.

This book is about such minimum income provisions. How can we make sure that every person has a decent minimum income allowing for a life in dignity and free of poverty in a society rich enough to afford such a right? Should we modulate the right to minimum income support by characteristics and behaviours that people deem relevant, and if so, how can we do it? How can we ensure that minimum income support is cost-effective and compatible with other goals such as promoting work effort, self-reliance, and upward mobility? How can political support for such schemes be fostered and made robust?

We see this book as a contribution to the real-world policy debate, not as an exercise in utopian thinking, however intellectually satisfying that may be. This book is not about how we think the world should look like but how we think it could realistically look like.

Not that we lack ambition or a healthy dose of idealism, as we hope the aspirational title of this book conveys. Our conviction is that things can be made much better, especially for people most in need of help. We genuinely believe that better poverty prevention and poverty relief is possible in many places, without the cost having to be prohibitive. We are convinced, as we hope to demonstrate convincingly here, that effective poverty relief can be compatible with having a thriving, dynamic economy and a well-functioning labour market yielding high levels of employment and low levels of chronic unemployment. Many countries could do a lot better.

Our message, however, is also that there is no 'silver-bullet' approach to this. It is not a matter of getting one scheme or policy right. It is a matter of getting a lot of things right, in the right in proportions and configuration, depending on the national and perhaps even local context. The economic context, socio-demographic context and indeed the political context. That, again, may be less appealing and visionary than grand proposals like a universal basic income but we believe that incremental, context-conscious expansion of minimum income provisions is the way forward if we really care about the most vulnerable.

We think this book comes at a good time for various reasons. The COVID-19 crisis drove home the crucial importance of adequate minimum income support in sheltering people from material deprivation in times of existential threat. Adequate minimum income provisions, where such existed, helped to stabilize societies, prevent costly loss of human capital and in containing the pandemic itself. People, after all, had to be able to afford to stay home and self-isolate. Before COVID-19, the Great Recession had already demonstrated the crucial stabilizing importance of social safety nets in times of major and unexpected disruption.

All this has happened against the background of structural shifts in mainstream thinking in the rich world, all strengthening the case for improving minimum income provisions. We have come to realize that economic growth is not enough if we care about poverty, even if it means that more people move into work. In-work poverty was an unknown term in much of Europe 20 years ago. Now it is common currency.

At the same time the world has been hit by a (benevolent) tsunami of high-quality inequality and poverty research. We have all become fully aware of how massively unequal rich societies really are, especially if wealth is drawn into the picture. We know for a fact that rich societies are more than rich enough to fund decent social safety nets, especially if those living in great affluence do their part to allow the less fortunate minimal means of existence.

We also know for a fact now that poverty harms. It harms those affected and it harms society at large. There is an economic cost. Rich societies increasingly depend on educated talent. We cannot afford to let some of it go to waste. Child poverty prevention in particular has been demonstrated to have significant societal and economic pay-offs. Research also shows that there is no trade-off between adequate poverty prevention and economic dynamism. On the contrary, the evidence sides with the view that both are increasingly complementary, if done right.

Finally, social rights have become more firmly entrenched in law. In national law in many cases, but also in international law. The European Pillar of Social Rights, to which each and every EU Member State subscribed in 2017, explicitly recognizes the right to an adequate minimum income, whether a person is in work or not. The adoption of the truly groundbreaking Minimum Wage Directive in 2022 can be seen as evidence that EU Member States are actually serious about making real progress towards better minimum incomes.

A word about the scope of this book. The prime focus is on minimum income schemes. Of course, income support may be provided through a host of channels, with social insurance playing a very important role in most countries. Indeed, the brunt of social transfer spending tends to be channelled through social insurance schemes. But social insurance has another primary rationale: income maintenance and not poverty prevention. For the sake of focus and feasibility our book is about the arrangements whose primary focus is to prevent poverty.

We also restrict ourselves to the rich world—basically the countries that the OECD classifies as high-income countries. In part that is a choice of principle. We want to look at countries that have the economic and budgetary capacity to ensure everybody a decent minimum if there is the political will. For another part the choice is pragmatic. We have the best comparable data for Europe. The purpose here is not to make rankings of countries for the sake of it. The purpose is to identify the cases from which we can potentially learn. For that reason we will also draw on evidence from other rich countries. We may have less comparable data for those countries, but we cannot ignore relevant studies for non-European countries that are highly informative. Some of the best and most sophisticated studies relevant for this book pertain for example to the United States even if this country can hardly be seen as a lodestar when it comes to providing people with adequate minimum incomes. But it is a country where radical and innovative change has taken place that is truly informative.

The organization of this book is as follows.

We first set out why we think minimum income protection is more relevant than ever. We also address the key issue of how much is enough. What constitutes an adequate minimum income?

We then move on to document the state of affairs in the field of minimum income protection in Europe. A first chapter deals with minimum income protection for people (mostly) not in work, a second focuses on people mostly reliant on work for their income. In both chapters we draw lessons from the best performing countries.

The next two chapters deal in more detail with crucial policy design choices, particularly the role and limits of pro-poor targeting in minimum income provision. These chapters deal with more technical design issues, but also with issues of political feasibility.

We dedicate a separate chapter to universal basic income as the ultimate minimum income guarantee. Not because we ourselves believe that a universal basic income is the best way to guarantee a minimum economic right but because so many people seem to think it offers a way to a zero poverty society.

A final chapter sketches what we see as the way forward. A zero poverty society will not happen overnight. If it is ever achieved, it will happen through incremental, well-coordinated, careful tweaks to multiple policy levers. That is perhaps not as immediately appealing as a 'Grand Solution', but it might just do the trick.

# 1

# Why Minimum Income Protection, What Is It, and How Much Is Enough?

## 1.1 Why Minimum Income Protection?

Minimum income protection is there to protect people from poverty. With the recent implementation of rights-based minimum income schemes in Italy, Spain, and Greece, every EU Member State currently has some form of minimum income protection for the non-elderly. Similar provisions have proliferated in the rest of the world. Moreover, the number of countries with a minimum wage has steadily risen. All but a few rich countries have a minimum wage today. The watershed EU Directive on Adequate Minimum Wages should provide an additional boost towards more adequate minimum wages in Europe. At the very least the ambition to lift income floors significantly is clearly there.

However, the reality is that minimum income protection levels—especially those targeted at the non-working population—still remain highly inadequate in Europe and elsewhere in the rich world. Currently guaranteed minimum protections fall well below widely accepted poverty standards and this is the case just about everywhere. Poverty rates among the working age population have remained stagnant almost everywhere, or even increased in a number of countries (Vandenbroucke & Diris, 2014; Gábos et al., 2019; Cantillon, 2022; Akarçeşme et al., 2023).

This really should come as a surprise. Countless governments all across the rich world have declared the elimination of poverty a top priority. Some have been doing so for decades. 'Europe has to be "Triple A" on social matters', Jean-Claude Juncker declared when he became president of the European Commission (Lecerf, 2016). In 2017, European leaders solemnly signed up to a European Pillar of Social Rights, detailing 20 rights and principles to be aspired to in the European Union. Principle 14 states 'Everyone lacking sufficient resources has the right to adequate minimum income benefits ensuring a life in dignity at all stages of life, and effective access to enabling goods and

*Zero Poverty Society*. Sarah Marchal and Ive Marx, Oxford University Press. © Sarah Marchal and Ive Marx (2024).
DOI: 10.1093/9780191967771.003.0001

services.' Earlier, in 2010, the European Parliament had already passed a Resolution calling for adequate minimum incomes. In January 2023, the Council adopted the European Commission's proposal for a Council Recommendation on minimum incomes (European Parliament, 2010; Aranguiz, 2022; European Commission and Social Protection Committee, 2022; Council, 2023).

Principle 14 is far from a reality. Not in Europe, not anywhere really. But what is the best way forward? Is it incremental progress? That is to say, higher minimum wages, more generous social assistance and social security benefits? Or is it time for radically new approaches? Is an unconditional, universal income—a basic income—the answer?

At any rate, the question of ***how*** to guarantee adequate minimum incomes has more urgency than ever, we believe.

*First*, because poverty harms. It harms not just those directly affected, and perhaps in some measure responsible for their plight, but it also impacts on those who cannot be held responsible in any way. Children growing up in poverty see their life chances affected in profound ways. That is not just an injustice at their own cost. In advanced economies where we can ill afford to let talent go to waste, the cost may well be much wider. It affects their development and their ability to put to use the talents they have. Research shows that children growing up in poverty are more likely to have poor physical health, experience mental health problems, have a low sense of well-being, experience stigma and bullying, underachieve at school, have employment difficulties in adult life, and experience social deprivation (Attree, 2004; Attree, 2006; Duncan et al., 2012; Cooper & Stewart, 2021; Parolin & Van Lancker, 2021). Of course, it is hard to isolate the causal effects of low (parental) income from other compounding factors. But some of the causal channels through which low incomes affect children are pretty straightforward. If a child grows up in a crowded home in a low-quality structure with a lot of noise, that child is much more likely to suffer mental and cognitive developmental debilitation than one who grows up in better quality surroundings. As economies become more dependent on optimally nurtured creative and intellectual talent, such losses in realized talent extend beyond the individuals concerned.

*Second*, because we know so much more about inequality today. The first comparative studies of inequality came out three decades ago (Atkinson et al., 1995). These brought to light substantial levels of inequality across the rich world. But the Gini coefficients in such studies told only a partial and in effect rather abstract story. A Gini of 0.42 is not a great igniter of indignation. Even an increase of 0.05, massive as such an increase is in the case of the Gini, is unlikely to bring the crowds to the street. It is only when researchers started to focus and gather data on top incomes and wealth that the full and far more disconcerting picture became clear (OECD, 2008, 2011, 2015; Atkinson et al., 2011; Atkinson & Bourguignon, 2014; Piketty, 2014; Atkinson, 2015; Milanovic, 2016). We now know that the top levels of society accumulate vast richness in terms of income and wealth, in some countries extremely so. Work by Gabriel Zucman (2015) shows with ever greater certainty and clarity what many long suspected, i.e., that even such staggering numbers of 'official' wealth inequality may well understate its true extent. A lot of wealth is shipped off-shore, it turns out. The truly rich are not just very wealthy, they are stratospherically wealthy. In a world of such vast, highly concentrated wealth, the idea that everybody deserves at least some minimum economic rights has enormous appeal. It is not hard to see how all the recent research on inequality is fuelling growing public affection and even support for proposals like universal basic income. Chapter 6 is for that reason entirely devoted to basic income.

*Third*, the notion made popular by Arthur Okun in the 1970s that there is such a thing as a trade-off between 'equity' and 'efficiency', between economic equality and economic growth, has been shattered by most empirical research. Somewhat of a tenet of faith in the more neoliberal 1980s and 1990s and espoused by influential organizations like the OECD and the IMF, few still attach much credence to it in its simplest form. Somewhat ironically, both organizations have been at the forefront of this research. They have brought out papers over recent years that are very critical of the simple trade-off idea. On the contrary, an OECD (2015) study concluded 'that income inequality has a *negative* and statistically significant impact on subsequent growth. In particular, what matters most is the gap between low income households and the rest of the population.' It goes on to argue that increased income disparities depress skills development among individuals with poorer parental education background, both in terms of the quantity of education attained (e.g., years of schooling), and in terms of its quality (i.e., skill proficiency). Policies to reduce income inequalities 'should [then] not only be pursued to improve social outcomes but also to sustain long-term growth. Redistribution policies via taxes and transfers are a key tool to ensure the benefits of growth are more broadly distributed and the results suggest they need not be expected to undermine growth' (Cingano, 2014, p. 6).

*Fourthly*, there now is more political urgency than ever to actually do something about poverty. The European Union and its Member States have not just made declarations; they have actually committed themselves to bringing down poverty and ensuring better minimum rights. Already in 2000, leaders of the European Union had proclaimed that 'steps must be taken to make a decisive impact on the eradication of poverty by setting adequate targets to be agreed by the Council by the end of the year' (European Parliament, 2000). Later that year, they backtracked from the promise to set clear goals. But they re-iterated the need for decisive action and they agreed on the need for a social monitoring instrument to track progress. Ten years later then, all EU leaders signed the Europe 2020 Agenda, which did include clear poverty reduction targets (European Council, 2010). In 2017, European leaders signed up to the European Pillar of Social Rights, a document that stresses the importance of (among others) the right to adequate minimum incomes. In 2021, the main principles of this pillar were reconfirmed by the Von der Leyen Commission (European Commission, 2021). Both the Minimum Wage Directive of 2022 and the 2023 Council Recommendation on minimum income ensuring active inclusion constitute significant steps towards better minimum incomes (The European Parliament and the Council of the European Union, 2022; Council, 2023).

*Fifth*, it has become abundantly clear that effective poverty reduction requires better minimum income protection. For decades the dominant doctrine was that 'the best protection against poverty is a job' (Cantillon, 2011; Cantillon & Vandenbroucke, 2015) The slogan can still be heard. Work is obviously important for a host of reasons. Getting a job often does bring an improvement in living standards, especially in the longer run. But it is also true that even episodes of very strong employment growth have not always resulted in commensurate drops in the number of people in poverty. On the contrary, employment growth in many instances has gone accompanied with increases in relative poverty. This is abundantly documented (Cantillon, Goedemé, & Hills, 2019). Essentially, there are two reasons for this. First, people who need work most for financial reasons often fail to move into work even when demand for workers is very strong. People who have long been absent from the labour market suffer from loss of skills, work habits, and social ties to potential employers. A long absence from work often brings stigma (Machin & Manning, 1999; Filomena, 2023). If an economy booms, and wages and living standards rise, those failing to secure jobs fall further behind, unless income support keeps pace, which it rarely does. A second reason why more people in work does not always bring fewer people in poverty is simply because getting a job does not always bring an escape from poverty. The so-called 'working poor' were long seen as essentially an American phenomenon. The reality is that they are found everywhere in the rich world, including in Europe (Lohmann & Marx, 2018; Hick & Marx, 2022). European governments acknowledge this now, as does the European Commission. The European Pillar of Social Rights explicitly acknowledges the problem under Principle 6: 'Workers have the right to fair wages that provide for a decent standard of living. [...] In-work poverty shall be prevented.'

*Finally*, there is the role of several major crises in the (re-)appreciation of adequate social safety nets and minimum income provisions. The worldwide financial crisis of 2008 brought the Great Recession and resulted in massive numbers of people losing the jobs upon which they and their families relied for their economic survival. That crisis happened at a time when even much of the political left—once defenders of robust market regulation and generous welfare states—was going along with the notion that market liberalization and 'making work pay' policies (read lower and less accessible benefits) would bring economic growth, jobs, and eventually higher living standards for all. In fact, employment growth was not bringing the hoped for drops in poverty but that awareness was still nascent at the time. But the Great Recession did shatter the notion that the state standing out of the way of the market offered a glorious path to greater prosperity for all. It ended the notion that unfettered market economies do not really require safety nets, let alone generous safety nets. That realization was definitively driven home by the COVID-19 crisis. This was perhaps an even more unexpected and even more dramatic shock, because of its magnitude and its suddenness. Many countries took rapid crisis measures to shelter citizens from the economic impact of COVID-19. Short-time work schemes and unemployment insurance benefits were of paramount importance for workers forced to stay home. Yet it rapidly became clear that there were 'forgotten' groups of vulnerable workers having to turn to means-tested, minimum-income-protection benefits, such as workers with non-standard contracts, freelancers, and self-employed individuals.

The COVID-19 crisis also put into stark light some of the longer-standing problems with existing social safety net provisions, not in the least the fact that guaranteed minimum incomes tend to fall well below widely used poverty thresholds. They are simply inadequate in many cases, as this book will document in detail. Also highlighted was the fact that people often find it difficult to gain access to the benefits to which they are entitled, as we will also document here Application procedures tend to be complicated, cumbersome, lengthy, intrusive, and stigmatizing. Access conditions can be quite stringent. Strict income tests apply and assets are usually taken into account.

In short, we believe that arguments for more adequate minimum income floors have more traction these days than they have ever had. This book asks how we can do better. However, before we do so, we address the question of how much is enough? What is an adequate minimum income floor?

## 1.2 A Working Definition of Minimum Income Floors

Minimum income protection is sometimes used as a synonym to social assistance (Frazer & Marlier, 2016; Crepaldi et al., 2017). But it goes broader than that: it refers to all the provisions that in combination provide a minimum income floor. Think for example of the potential role of minimum wages, refundable tax credits, or child benefits.

This book is about what governments do and can do to *guarantee minimum cash resources to households.* Throughout the book, we will discuss minimum income protection for two important target groups, and how these minimum income arrangements relate to one another. Mainly, we will focus on minimum income protection for the able-bodied non-working of active age, who, as they are generally least well protected (Bahle et al., 2011), usually coincide with the absolute floor of the welfare state. In the broader sense, we also focus on the alternative guarantees for the working able-bodied of active age. In Chapter 3, we describe the specific difficulties related to identifying the minimum income floor guaranteed to workers.

In the fight against poverty, policy makers have—increasingly—stressed the importance of ensuring access to work. Ever since the activation turn, a job is deemed to be the best protection against poverty. Whereas it is true that poverty rates among the employed are far lower than poverty rates among the unemployed, non-negligible, and often increasing, rates of in-work poverty, make it essential to also ask what kind of income protection is guaranteed to workers, and how this compares to out-of-work minimum income protection.[1]

Our general definition hinges on three main characteristics: minimum income protections ensure *minimal resources* in *cash* and are *guaranteed by the government.*

*Minimal resources* refer to the main aim of the social provision: to provide beneficiaries with an income that protects against poverty. Clearly, different countries define 'poverty' or hardship in different ways (see also Section 1.3.4). For some, minimal resources should cover a frugal lifestyle, whereas elsewhere the focus is more on preventing severe destitution or, in contrast, ensuring a life in line with human dignity. Still, the common denominator is that, for that specific target group, it is the lowest guaranteed income level.

*Cash* refers to the way in which these minimal resources are ensured. One can think of different ways of ensuring a minimal living standard, including the provision of social housing, free medical care and education, or free public transport. In this book, we focus on the cash benefits awarded to citizens. For one, these reflect the choice citizens actually have in prioritizing certain expenses. In this regard, one should question the value of vouchers awarded to beneficiaries that can be solely used to buy specific goods, such as food (e.g., Whitmore, 2002). Whereas these rank above in-kind food packages, in the sense that claimants can tailor their groceries more to their own needs (Hermans, Cantillon, Bernat, et al., forthcoming), they still severely limit the budgeting capacities of claimant households. In addition, cash benefits are also easier to guarantee by the government, as the value of other in-kind protection measures lies in the (different) use made of them by different beneficiaries.

Last but not least, the fact that these provisions are *legally guaranteed* is crucial. This is what minimum income protection ultimately distinguishes from old-school charity relief (Leibfried, 1992; Panican & Ulmestig, 2016; Heggebø & West Pedersen, 2022). With legally guaranteed we mean that the right to a minimal social protection is ultimately described and laid out in law.[2] The exact legal basis can however differ. Most welfare states have in their constitution a reference to ensuring a life in dignity or a right to social security, but this is only rarely a subjective right. Rather, it should be read as a duty of the state to take steps in order to ensure a life in dignity (Leijten, 2015; International Labour Organization, 2016). The exact policy instruments and conditions (i.e., the exact legal guarantee) still need to be made explicit in specific legislation,[3] that can leave more or less room for discretion to the implementation level (Frazer & Marlier, 2016; Panican & Ulmestig, 2016; De Wilde & Marchal, 2019). For instance, article 23 of the Belgian constitution states that everyone is entitled to a life in human dignity, and as such has a right to social security, social and material aid, and work that offers a fair remuneration. However, the same article states explicitly that secondary law is needed in order to actually establish social rights,[4] that should also define the obligations that citizens need to fulfil in order to be entitled (Schoukens, 2016). Belgian minimum wages, that can be considered one of the means to guarantee fair remuneration and minimum income protection for working adults, even only have a quasi-statutorily legal basis.

Similarly, many states have subscribed to international treaties that call for adequate income protection. The International Labour Organization has created social security rights standards, with a declaration for adequate income floors in 2012 (International Labour Organization, 2012). Within the EU, the (Revised) European Social Charter was established, which has led to increased monitoring of national policy changes (Pennings, 2016). Often, such supranational or international covenants give rise to later changes in national law or are referred to in interpretative case law (Chemla, 2016; Eichenhofer, 2016; Palmer, 2016; Pennings, 2016; Schoukens, 2016). In 2017, the European institutions have jointly proclaimed the European Pillar of Social Rights, that lists 20 principles that ought to define and further guide the development of a Social Europe. Several of these principles refer to an adequate income protection for different target groups, not least in article 6 on adequate and fair wages, and article 14 of adequate minimum incomes (Cantillon, 2019). The exact impact of the pillar is still unclear and will also depend on how future commissions and councils will let it guide their policies (Vandenbroucke, 2019). The 2021 Porto declaration on the implementation of the pillar by the European Council is promising in that regard (European Council, 2021), as is the adoption of the Minimum Wage directive and the Council Recommendation on adequacy minimum income (Aranguiz, 2022; European Commission and Social Protection Committee, 2022; Council Recommendation, 2023).

What is conspicuously absent from our definition in comparison to other scholars is a reference to the conditionality of minimum income protection. Bahle et al. (2011) explicitly include a means-test in their definition of a minimum income in their book *The Last Safety Net*. Effectively, this will most often be the case when governments aim to guarantee minimal resources. However, in our view of minimum income protection, it is the combination of different provisions that ensure an actual floor under the welfare state. For families with children, such a floor can just as well be made up of the combination of universal child benefits with some form of social assistance, as from a very strictly means-tested all-encompassing social assistance benefit. Perhaps more clearly, in a society in which all provisions are abolished in favour of a basic income, such a basic income will effectively provide a minimum income guarantee, without any conditionality. Alternatively, some scholars hold that behavioural conditionality has increased to such an extent that it is in some countries hard to speak of guaranteed minimum income provisions (Moreira, 2008; Leibetseder et al., 2017). This is not to say that we negate the importance of eligibility and behavioural conditions in minimum income provisions but rather that we are agnostic on their importance for the definition of minimum income protection. Section 2.8.3 describes the conditionality that is effectively inherent in contemporary European minimum income protection schemes in more detail.

## 1.3 What Is an Adequate Minimum?

A large part of this book will look into the adequacy of minimum income protection arrangements in order to learn best practices and likely effects of specifically designed benefits. An important question is then what the yardstick is against which we assess the adequacy of minimum income protection.

### 1.3.1 Commonly Used Relative Poverty Measures in Cross-national Comparative Research

For cross-national comparative research we still mainly rely on the same workhorse measures that have been in use for decades. The OECD, the Luxembourg Income Study as well as the European Union favour the use of a relative income-based poverty threshold. The exact technical operationalization differs, but in essence, all three organizations assess an individual's poverty status by comparing the equivalized income of the household in which he or she lives to a poverty threshold that is defined as a percentage of the median or mean equivalized net disposable household income. The OECD favours a poverty threshold equal to 50% of the median household income (OECD, 2020), LIS employs a range of cut-off percentages for its key figures (https://www.lisdatacenter.org/data-access/key-figures/), whereas the EU uses 60% as the threshold to determine one's poverty status and general poverty rates. To account for the fact that poverty experiences are both individual and multidimensional, this indicator is commonly referred to as the at-risk-of-poverty threshold, used to calculate the at-risk-of-poverty rate.

### 1.3.2 Advantages

The relative poverty measure, defined as some percentage (first 50%, then increasingly 60%) of median or average equivalent disposable household income, became the de facto standard measure for international comparisons during the 1980s. It was 'officially' adopted as a prime EU social inclusion measure at the EU Laeken summit in 2001. Arguably facilitating its widespread adoption was the fact that the measure happened to produce country rankings and differences that—among the Member States of the EU at that time—were more or less consistent with general perception and intuition. The broad picture was that of the Nordic and Northern Continental countries enjoying comparatively low poverty and of poverty being highest in the Southern European countries: Italy, Spain, Portugal, and Greece. A similar reasoning goes for the OECD relative poverty indicator.

In addition, these internationally comparable relative poverty indicators are easily applicable to a wide range of national and international data sets, which has no doubt helped their ubiquitous adoption. Specifically for the EU at-risk-of-poverty threshold, the general availability of the EU SILC (Statistics on Income and Living Conditions) survey, which is explicitly designed to facilitate cross-nationally comparable relative income poverty measurement, has further fostered its adoption.

Also, the 60% (or 40, or 50) at-risk-of-poverty threshold very explicitly aligns with the relative view of poverty that is commonly accepted in most advanced Western welfare states. It means that, broadly speaking, 'poverty has to be seen in terms of the standard of living of the society in question' (Callan & Nolan, 1991, p. 252). The relative view is contrasted with the absolute definition of poverty, which is couched in terms of 'the minimum necessaries for the maintenance of merely physical efficiency', i.e., surviving and being able to earn one's living (Rowntree, B.S., 1901, cited in Townsend, 1979, p. 33).[5]

### 1.3.3 Drawbacks

The common-sense consistency is, however, no longer evident in an enlarged EU (or OECD) setting. The fact that Romania, one of the poorest EU countries, counts relative to its population only marginally more people at risk of financial poverty by the 60% of median threshold than Luxembourg may appear baffling, especially since the difference in the share of the population affected by severe material and social deprivation is tenfold.

While a purely relative operationalization of poverty measurement may be appropriate when comparing countries of more or less similar economic prosperity, the failure to track more 'absolute' differences in living standards raises interest in alternative measures.

Amartya Sen (1983) famously argued that poverty is an absolute notion in terms of a person's capabilities, even though it may be relative in terms of commodities or incomes. According to Sen (1983), there is 'an irreducible absolutist core in the idea of poverty [. . .] if there is starvation and hunger, then—no matter what the relative picture looks like—there clearly is poverty' (p. 159). Sen proposes that poverty is best conceptualized in terms of capabilities. The list would include such basic capabilities as to be sheltered, to be clothed and to have enough food, but also the capability to live without shame and the ability to participate in the activities of the community. The resource requirements of the latter type of capability are particularly likely to vary tremendously from one community to another.

In the first place, local circumstances and social conventions influence what you need to obtain certain functionings. To a large extent, what is conventional is determined by what most people actually do or have, and thus by the average standard of living. Secondly, resource requirements may also be relative in a more direct or stronger sense (cf. Goodin & Ware, 1990). The usefulness of a certain commodity may depend directly on how many others have the same commodity.

In practical terms, however, the implications of a relative and an absolute conception of poverty may not differ that much. Sen probably would agree to the statement that, because resource requirements for many basic functionings are relative, the poverty line must be put at a higher level in rich countries than in poor ones; also, as a country gets more prosperous, the poverty line is likely to increase in real terms. What he does not accept is that the poverty line should necessarily rise by x per cent, each time median income rises by x per cent (and even more strongly, that if median income would happen to drop by y per cent, the poverty line should decrease by the same percentage). However, the same may well be true for proponents of the relative view on poverty.

Believing that poverty is about not having the resources to fully participate in society, does not imply believing that the level of the resources needed to reach that goal always moves immediately and proportionally whenever there is a change in median income. In other words, despite the theoretical differences of opinion, there may well be broad consensus that any credible income poverty line should be relative to some extent, but not fully so.

During the 2008–2013 financial and economic crisis, the relative 60% at-risk-of-poverty threshold did indeed garner a lot of criticism as it failed to pick up the severe worsening of living conditions in Greece. The poverty threshold, expressed as a percentage of median income, decreased, leading to a drop in the share of people falling under the threshold. This led to the more widespread use of anchored poverty thresholds at the time.

### 1.3.4 Alternative Measures

In its essence, poverty is commonly regarded as a multifaceted issue. Many therefore argue that there is not just one 'perfect' indicator, but that policy makers and researchers should keep track of relevant aspects using a dashboard of indicators.

The European Union has adopted the 60% at-risk-of-poverty threshold (i.e., a poverty threshold defined at 60% of the national median equivalized household income) as an official indicator, incorporated in its Social Scoreboard that tracks socio-economic developments in the EU Member States. Alternative poverty thresholds (most commonly the 40% threshold), as well as poverty gap measures and poverty rates that zoom in on specific population groups, are used to further contextualize the depth and extent of poverty. Other outcome indicators included in the Social Scoreboard of the European Union are—most importantly—the number of people living in jobless households and the material deprivation rate. The union of these measures renders the share of the population that is considered to be at risk of poverty and social exclusion.[6]

Material deprivation rates show the share of the population that (by necessity) fails to possess three or four out of nine items that are considered desirable or necessary by most people to lead an adequate life. There is only weak correspondence between a country's level of relative poverty and the extent and depth of material deprivation experienced by the population. Material deprivation levels are a magnitude higher in Hungary than in Denmark or the Netherlands, despite the fact that the countries have similar poverty rates. While clearly informative, we should not simply replace the at-risk-of-poverty threshold with the material deprivation index. Also here, there are important problems of cross-country comparability, as the meaning of any item will differ greatly, depending on social, economic, and climate circumstances (Russell & Whelan, 2004). In addition, as it is not an income-based measure, a direct comparison of income support policies and material deprivation levels is far from evident.

An alternative avenue to incorporate a more absolute core in relative measures is through the design of reference budget standards. Such reference budgets list the goods and services that are minimally needed to fully participate in a given society, based on expert opinions, focus groups, and information from surveys (Storms et al., 2014). Their monetary value, obtained through specific pricing strategies, can then be used to assess incomes against, in order to determine one's poverty status. While reference budget standards are developed in a number of EU member states (each with their own specific methodology), this is only rarely with the express purpose to act as a poverty measure. In fact, their use as a poverty threshold raises new issues regarding the broader applicability of the assumptions that will—implicitly or explicitly—underlie the composition of the basket of goods and services (such as the inclusion of specific medicines, that will ultimately depend on the assumptions regarding health status). Nonetheless, a number of countries do employ more needs-based poverty thresholds and operationalizations in their national social monitoring. The Netherlands, for instance, use, complementary to their official poverty threshold,[7] such reference-budget based measures, that aim to capture a minimum living standard. Based on minimum budgets for a typical single person household, and taking account of a number of non-avoidable costs (mainly child care and health-related expenses), they estimate the share of the population who has an income below the 'not much, but adequate' threshold (Hoff et al., 2010; Goderis et al., 2018). According to Menyhert et al. (2021), Italy is the only EU Member State that uses and measures an absolute poverty indicator. Their approach builds mainly on survey data (in particular the Italian Household Budget Survey), coupled with national (legislative) information on minimal standards for specific goods and services, such as housing (ISTAT et al., 2009). Somewhat atypically, this threshold is used to assess household's monthly expenses, rather than used to evaluate incomes. Nonetheless, this approach is not one-on-one transferable to other EU Member States (Menyhert et al., 2021).

Efforts have been made to develop similar needs-based poverty measures in a comparable fashion for all the EU Member States. The ImPrOve project found for instance that the task of developing comparable budget standards for all EU Member States, at very different levels of economic development and with substantially different patterns of consumption is a daunting one (Goedemé et al., 2019).

Recently, the Joint Research Centre of the European Commission published the results of the ABSPO pilot project. The aim of this project was to design, develop, and pilot a more absolute poverty measure suitable for EU-wide measurement, to be scaled up in the future (Menyhert et al., 2021). The project explored a number of options in order to design a more absolute poverty measure.[8] For one, it built further on the reference-budget based approach initiated by Goedemé et al. (2019). Alternatively, it developed a survey-based approach to the operationalization of a more absolute poverty measure. Finally, it developed a food-based statistical approach to absolute poverty measurement. Overall, it found that regardless of the precise method, resulting poverty thresholds were relatively similar. Poverty rates however differed. Importantly, the resulting poverty rates were more cyclical, sensitive to changes in prices, and reflected larger differences between Eastern and Western EU Member States than are commonly found with the AROP and AROPE measures. The project concluded that the design and operationalization of an additional complementary 'absolute' poverty measure to monitor the social situation in the EU is definitely possible but requires additional efforts.

Overall, while this approach may be a promising avenue to assess the adequacy of minimum income protection packages in the future, for now, the data collection efforts required remain prohibitive. In conclusion, it looks very likely that the relative poverty threshold is here to stay for some time to come. Consequently, this is the threshold we use in this book.

# 2
# The State of Means-Tested Minimum Income Protection for People Not in Work

## 2.1 Introduction

This chapter is about the adequacy and design of minimum income protection arrangements for those out-of-work. We focus, as a minimal case, on those who are at the same time out-of-work and able to work, but ineligible for social insurance.

People can be ineligible for social insurance for a variety of reasons. For one, prospective claimants may not have secured a sufficiently long employment history to fulfil the contributory requirements to enter social insurance protection. There are indications that securing access to contributory unemployment insurance is getting harder for some: access conditions to unemployment insurance are tightening, as the link between contributions and benefits is strengthened (Van Lancker et al., 2015; Knotz, 2018). At the same time, new forms of flexible labour are on the rise, at least in some places (Nautet & Piton, 2019). Evidently, for those with more patchy or less secure labour market attachment, meeting tightened contributory requirements will be a challenge, even in light of the accommodations some welfare states recently made to tally also more piecemeal work experiences in individual contribution records (Eichhorst et al., 2023). This stresses the importance of out-of-work minimum income protection also in a different way: the role of social assistance may well change to support in-work incomes, or to cover temporal income gaps between successive interrupted employment spells.

But there is perhaps an even more important reason to look at this. Minimum income protection for the non-working offers an easily understandable reference point of the absolute minimum that contemporary welfare states guarantee to their citizens, when they find themselves in a specific situation. In most countries under analysis here, this target group is catered for by a combination of means-tested social assistance benefits, topped up with

*Zero Poverty Society.* Sarah Marchal and Ive Marx, Oxford University Press. © Sarah Marchal and Ive Marx (2024).
DOI: 10.1093/9780191967771.003.0002

benefits that have more specific purposes, such as housing allowances or child benefits.

We first discuss the role of means-tested minimum income protection in national welfare states, and their historical development. We then present and discuss in-depth the adequacy and design of cash minimum income protection packages, using model family simulations. This method allows us to take account of the interplay of various means-tested benefits, and to capture in an accurate way the minimal legally guaranteed social floor for the target group of the non-working able-bodied of active age. We find that for most model families included in our analysis, minimum income protection packages fall well short of the 60% at-risk-of-poverty line. We then ask whether minimum income protection packages in their current form can be expected to combat poverty, and we identify several hurdles in this regard. In particular, we highlight the role of minimum income protection coverage and eligibility. Finally, we identify a number of 'best practice' country cases and assess what policy mixes guarantee adequate minimum income protection packages there.

## 2.2 Benefits and Adequate Incomes as Core Businesses of the Welfare State

Modern welfare states have developed an entire arsenal of income support instruments. Not all of these, nor, in fact, the majority, are primarily intended to prevent hardship. Cantillon and Van Mechelen (2014) distinguish three distinct functions of the welfare state: predistribution, horizontal redistribution, and vertical redistribution.

Predistribution refers to direct government intervention on the market income distribution through regulations that limit ex ante income inequality: obvious examples are education and health care, but also vocational training for the unemployed, as well as labour market regulations that directly impact on market incomes such as minimum wages. The rationales behind these different predistribution instruments do not necessarily refer to income protection. Minimum wages may for instance just as much—or even more so—stem from a desire for fair remuneration or to prevent wage inequality, as to provide workers with adequate incomes (International Labour Organization, 2008; Vaughan-Whitehead, 2010; European Parliament, 2017b).

Horizontal redistribution refers to welfare states redistributing incomes over different phases of the lifecycle: from active aged to elderly, from people without children to people with children, from the healthy to the ill, etc. Horizontal redistribution is most clearly present in the grand social insurance schemes, where people pay contributions so that they can maintain their living standards when they are confronted with a social risk (Barr, 2001; Cantillon & Buysse, 2016). Similarly, child benefits, which are presented as (partial) cost compensations for families with children, are effectively a redistribution from people without children to people with children.

Vertical redistribution then explicitly refers to the redistribution over the income distribution, from the rich to the poor. It is here that we categorize means-tested minimum income protection schemes that have as express raison-d'être the prevention of severe poverty. Still, it should be clear from the above that they are aided in this by other schemes, even though these may be primarily designed in line with the other functions of the welfare state. Social assistance benefits can be supplemented by universal child benefits, and they may have an easier job preventing poverty in countries with more well-functioning labour markets and in-work income protection (Collado et al., 2019).

After all, most welfare state programmes combine these different elements. Even classic social insurance schemes such as pensions or unemployment insurance have provisions built-in that deviate from a clear insurance logic to (comparatively speaking) 'overcompensate' the poor. Obvious examples are minimum pensions and benefit ceilings. In addition, unemployment benefits can be made conditional upon participation in active labour market programmes, to ultimately re-affect the predistribution. Other programmes, such as means-tested social assistance schemes, are more explicit in their vertical redistribution logic. At the same time, such minimum benefits can be further supplemented by universal benefits, or additional means-tested social allowances that can be more (or less) broadly targeted, for instance through housing allowances or single-parent supplements to a child benefit. Similarly, means-tested social assistance can function as a top-up to the income of people with insufficient employment records for full contributory benefits, with too low wages (for instance due to precarious work) or with too low unemployment assistance benefits.

Throughout this book, we assess the social floors guaranteed by the interplay of these different redistribution logics to the specific target groups of the non-working and the working active aged. Our interest in the absolute minimum means that we will focus on means-tested social assistance for the non-working, and minimum wages for the working population, as these are generally the main provisions in each country. However, we do devote ample attention to how these measures are further boosted (or not) by other non-contributory social support measures relevant to these target groups.

## 2.3 The Spread of Social Safety Nets

Most Western welfare states now have safety nets of last resort: means-tested benefits that aim to ensure a minimal living standard.[1] These benefits have as express purpose to mitigate experiences of poverty or destitution. In this sense, they have a lot in common with old-school charity relief. However, a crucial difference is that benefit levels and eligibility criteria are now—to substantial extent—laid down in law: people can exercise a right to financial support.

The shift from charity relief to rights-based minimum income protection for those of active age who are able to work is one of the more recent accomplishments of the 'old' welfare states: while most other social security branches and categorical social assistance schemes, including those for the elderly and the disabled, already took shape before the Second World War, the first social assistance schemes also covering the 'less deserving' working age population with no work or access to contribution-based social insurance, date from the 1960s (Germany, Netherlands, United Kingdom), 1970s (Belgium, Denmark, Ireland), and 1980s (Sweden, Finland, France, Luxembourg) (Cantillon, Van Mechelen, & Schulte, 2008).

In the countries of Central and Eastern Europe universal social assistance systems appeared from the 1990s onwards. Before, in the communist era, these countries relied on full employment, strong subsidization of basic goods and services, and adequate social insurance provisions to prevent poverty (Standing, 1997). Evidently, their transition to capitalist societies changed the situation tremendously. High unemployment growth and rampant inflation caused a steady increase in poverty (Ferge & Juhász, 2004).

In the Southern European countries, minimum income guarantees developed even later. In Portugal, the Rendimento Mínimo Garantido was introduced in 1997 (Matsaganis et al., 2003), whereas Spain's first regional social assistance schemes (in Basque Country and Catalonia) date from the late 1980s. Other Spanish regions followed suit only from the 1990s onward. Even then, major differences between the regional benefit schemes remained, both in terms of design and poverty fighting effectiveness (Ayala et al., 2021; Eichhorst et al., 2023; Hernández, Picos, & Riscado, forthcoming). In addition, in a limited number of regions, minimum income protection did not gain the status of a subjective right, but access depended on budget availability (Hernández, Picos, & Riscado, forthcoming). It is only in 2020, in full coronavirus lockdown turmoil, that a national rights-based general social assistance scheme was implemented. While the coalition government agreed upon the introduction of a nation-wide minimum income scheme throughout its mandate, they initially prioritized a reform of the child benefit system. However, the COVID-19 shock pushed forward the introduction of the Minimum Vital Income to June 2020, as a top-up benefit of household incomes up to a guaranteed minimum. Importantly, the national minimum income benefit does not replace regional minimum income benefits, rather it lays a common floor that regional government can choose to raise further (Badenes Plá & Gambau-Suelves, 2020). Hernández, Picos, and Riscado (forthcoming) highlight the risk of cost-shifting that may arise from this set-up.

Italy and Greece only very recently introduced a guaranteed minimum income scheme.

In Greece, this process started in April 2015 with the trial of a food stamps programme that was in place until January 2017, which provided households with a prepaid debit card for food purchases, scaled according to their composition and need. Initially intended as a one-year trial, the programme was extended and eventually replaced by the guaranteed minimum income scheme currently in place since February 2017 (Matsaganis, 2018). This followed a significant increase in poverty and deprivation in post-Recession Greece (Perez & Matsaganis, 2017). The establishment of a general minimum income scheme, to replace the previous kaleidoscope of categorical minimum income schemes for sometimes exceedingly small target groups (e.g., the blind) was a recommendation made by the IMF in the aftermath of the financial and budgetary crisis (International Monetary Fund, 2012).

While the Greek pilot minimum income protection programme came relatively suddenly—lacking support among politically and socially strong actors made earlier trials or reforms politically unpalatable and inhibited the political alliance-building which brought about minimum income schemes in the other Southern European countries (Lalioti, 2015)—Italy's (bumpy) trajectory started earlier. In 1998, the centre-left Prodi government introduced a national-level 'minimum insertion income'. This was however discontinued by the incoming right-wing government (Natili, 2018). Afterwards, some regions and municipalities retained their own schemes, leading to the veritable patchwork of regional social assistance benefits that existed in Italy in the 2000s (Madama, Jessoula, & Natili, 2014). In the aftermath of the Great Recession in 2009, the government introduced a heavily means-tested 'social card' for certain household purchases (Marchal, Marx, & Van Mechelen, 2014). Nevertheless, a nationally present minimum income scheme remained absent until the 2018 implementation of the *Reddito di Inclusione* (ReI), a means-tested, non-categorical social assistance scheme available in the whole country (Baldini et al., 2018). From March 2019 the Five Star Movement and

Lega replaced this with the 'citizen's income', or *Reddito di Cittadinanza*. In its new conception the benefit is more generous than the *ReI*, but also restricts receipt to long-term legal residents only (Jessoula & Natili, 2020).

With Italy and Greece joining the ranks, now all EU Member States provide guaranteed minimum income protection to the non-working of active age. This is not to say that all the non-working of active age have access to this support, nor that protection levels are similar throughout the union. Previous research has conclusively demonstrated the large (and persistent) variation in minimum income benefit levels (Gough et al., 1996; Marchal & Siöland, 2019). All countries apply strict (but varied) access conditions, including citizenship and residence criteria (such as the Reddito di Cittadinanza, see above) and means-tests that also include savings, other assets, and incomes from other household members. Continued receipt requires efforts from claimants to improve their financial situation through work or participation in active labour market programmes (see, e.g., Marchal & Van Mechelen, 2017; Marchal et al., 2021). We discuss each of these issues in more depth in the following sections of this chapter.

It is noteworthy here that the EU has taken an active role in the promotion of both the spread and the quality of means-tested minimum income protection schemes. However, as the EU does not hold binding competences in the field of minimum income protection (Aranguiz, 2022),[2] these efforts have generally taken the form of recommendations or resolutions, calling for the Member States to recognize the importance of adequate minimum income protection (e.g., Council of the European Communities, 1992; European Commission, 2008; European Parliament, 2010; European Parliament, 2017a). More recently, the European institutions proclaimed the European Pillar of Social Rights, of which the 14th principle stresses 'the right to adequate minimum income benefits ensuring a life in dignity at all stages of life, and effective access to enabling goods and services. For those who can work, minimum income benefits should be combined with incentives to (re)integrate into the labour market' (European Commission, 2017). In addition, in the framework of the European Semester, minimum income schemes have come under increased scrutiny. The Social Protection Committee has outlined a benchmarking framework on minimum income, which is now used to regularly monitor countries' performance in the Joint Employment Report and the Country Reports. It includes outcome indicators that track poverty rates among the population, in line with minimum income's preoccupation with reducing poverty; performance indicators that focus on specific aspects of unmet needs, as well as benefit coverage; and finally, also on policy input indicators. The latter focus on the design of minimum income protection and track the adequacy of benefits (operationalized among others as the benefit level for a single person household relative to the at-risk-of-poverty threshold), eligibility rules and take-up of benefits as well as activation elements and access to services (European Commission and Social Protection Committee, 2022). This benchmarking framework was also used in a recent Social Protection Committee report that prepared the 28 September Commission proposal for a renewed Council recommendation on adequate minimum incomes ensuring active inclusion, and hence ultimately the resulting 2023 Council Recommendation. This recommendation supports Member States' policies to alleviate poverty and prevent social exclusion (European Commission, 2022b; European Commission and Social Protection Committee, 2022). It refers to (admittedly broadly defined) reference values of adequate minimum incomes and highlights the importance of access to income support. While the Commission initially proposed a three-yearly progress monitoring, the final recommendation only asks for monitoring at regular intervals (European Commission, 2022b; Council Recommendation, 2023).

It is hard to pinpoint the exact impact previous recommendations have had on the spread of safety nets throughout the EU Member States, and their precise characteristics. For instance, Van Mechelen and Marchal (2013b) state that the 1992 European Council recommendation may have reaffirmed an ongoing trend, rather than increased enthusiasm for nation- or region-level initiatives. Also, evaluations by the European institutions do not always find evidence for a decisive impact, for instance regarding the 2008 Commission active inclusion recommendation (European Commission, 2022b; European Commission and Social Protection Committee, 2022). At the same time, Van Mechelen and Marchal (2013b, p. 19) nuance that 'some authors feel that the 1992 recommendation effectively contributed to the introduction of universal social assistance schemes in Southern Europe during the 1990s' (Arriba & Ibáñez, 2002; Matsaganis et al., 2003). Between 1990 and 1995, one Spanish region after another adopted general social assistance programmes. Nonetheless, in some of these regions, social assistance is still provided on an ad hoc basis and there is little evidence of a subjective right to assistance (Arriba & Moreno, 2005; Rodríguez Cabrero, 2009). Also, there are stark indications that the introduction of the Greek minimum income schemes, as well as a far-reaching reform of the Cypriot minimum income scheme, were at least partially driven by the European Union, but in those cases in its binding role as a lender of last resort (International Monetary Fund, 2012; Koutsampelas, 2016), rather than through the more soft-policy instruments of recommendations and public performance monitoring.

In this chapter, we also investigate minimum income protection packages in the United States, as an interesting reference case. Minimum income protection in the United States is different. On the one hand, programmes to support specific groups of needy people appeared relatively early, in the 1930s. On the other hand, in-kind benefits play a significant role in securing a social floor for the able-bodied of active age. The federal scheme SNAP (Supplemental Nutritional Assistance Program) provides vouchers (in the form of a debit card) that can be used for food purchases for needy claimants (Institute of Medicine & National Research Council, 2013). The cash value of these vouchers is usually included in international comparisons of minimum income benefit generosity (Van Mechelen & Marchal, 2013a; Aerts, Marx, & Parolin, 2022), as the programme is both highly relevant (and big) in the US context, and legally guaranteed. Other support schemes are organized at the state level. Of relevance are general social assistance for childless adults in several states and, more importantly, the Temporary Assistance for Needy Families (TANF) for households with children, designed and implemented by the states, but (co-)financed by block grants from the federal government (Parolin & Luigjes, 2019). TANF was introduced in 1996 by the Personal Responsibility and Work Opportunity Reconciliation Act, replacing the previous Aid to Families with Dependent Children (AFDC) (Scott et al., 2004). Also different to what is common across the European countries, both SNAP and TANF employ lifetime time limits to benefit receipt (Van Mechelen & Marchal, 2013a).

## 2.4 The Adequacy of Minimum Income Protection Packages

Figure 2.1 shows the level of minimum income protection packages for a hypothetical single person household and a lone parent with two children relative to the at-risk-of-poverty threshold. The white diamonds show the final net disposable household income relative to the 60% at-risk-of-poverty threshold in each country (indicated by the black reference line), and as such provide an indication of the adequacy of the guaranteed minimum income protection package for a typical family in each country. Box 2.1 contains more detailed information on the calculation of and the assumptions underlying these indicators of minimum income protection package adequacy. Box 2.2 discusses some of the features that we do not, and cannot, take account of, including non-monetary benefits, discretion and local variation.

## Box 2.1 Measuring guaranteed minimum income protection levels with model family simulations

We use hypothetical household simulations to assess the generosity of minimum income protection *packages*. As the rules for combining means-tested minimum income support with other benefits, such as child benefits and housing allowances, differ between countries, hypothetical household simulations are elementary to compare like with like. They allow to assess the generosity of actual policy rules in combination in a comparable fashion over time and across countries, eliminating confounding elements distorting assessments of policy generosity such as the underlying demography or economy. In addition, such simulations allow to assess policies for specific groups—such as lone parents or minimum income beneficiaries—that are theoretically interesting but may be underrepresented in surveys. For these reasons, hypothetical household simulations are often used to comparatively assess the institutional design of minimum income protection. Famous examples are the seminal study by Eardley et al. (1996), the OECD Benefits and Wages model (OECD, 2023a) and Kenneth Nelson's SaMIP dataset (Nelson, 2007; OECD, 2023a).

At the University of Antwerp, Cantillon et al. (2004) and Van Mechelen et al. (2011) established the CSB MIPI dataset, that collected hypothetical household calculations made by national experts, and that allowed to assess the generosity of minimum income protection for the working, the non-working, and the elderly at specific moments in time. This dataset focused on the minimally guaranteed standard by functionally equivalent minimum income provisions selected through a risk-type approach. It contains minimum income protection packages that are relevant when certain risks manifest: unemployment while being uninsured but able to work, or low-wage employment. This database was later continued and improved using the hypothetical household function HHoT (Hypothetical Household Tool) of the EUROMOD microsimulation model (Hufkens et al., 2016), under the moniker MIPI-HHoT (available at https://zenodo.org/record/2533898) (Marchal, Siöland, & Goedemé, 2018).

We mainly build on CSB MIPI and the newly developed MIPI-HHoT database as these data reflect *minimal* situations, adopting carefully balanced and empirically grounded country-specific and general assumptions that allow to gauge a minimal situation while simultaneously including the full scope of rights-based benefits in a country (see Marchal, Siöland, & Goedemé, 2018 for a full discussion). The indicators are calculated for the following hypothetical households: a single person household, a married couple, a married couple with two children and a divorced lone parent with

*continued*

**Box 2.1** *continued*

two children. Adults are 35 years old; children are aged 7 and 14. The households have no assets and no incomes other than that explicitly assumed or the income that is guaranteed by the tax benefit system. Housing costs are assumed to be equal to the median housing costs for the respective household type according to the 2015 EU SILC numbers (uprated to the relevant price levels for other years). The household lives in a private rented dwelling that confirms to the eligibility rules for housing allowances. We furthermore assume that out-of-work adults are looking for work, and that the children regularly attend school. The other parent of the children living in the lone parent household is known, but unable to pay alimony. The households live in the largest non-capital city or urban region in each country. The data were validated against the OECD Benefit and Wages data, and against the SaMIP data (see Van Mechelen et al., 2011, and Marchal & Goedemé, 2018 for a thorough comparison of the three available datasets), and were used in multiple peer-reviewed publications (e.g., Chzhen & Bradshaw, 2012; Marchal & Van Mechelen, 2017; Marchal & Marx, 2018).

Hypothetical household simulations are self-evidently highly reliant on the assumed characteristics of the selected households. Seemingly small parameters of the household, such as the age of the children, the housing costs, or the willingness to work of the adults present in the household, may have a large effect on overall assessments of generosity (see Van Mechelen et al., 2011). Also, the assumed location matters: in some countries benefit levels are defined at the regional or municipal level. Headline indicators may obfuscate substantial intranational variation in some countries (Ayala & Rodriguez, 2013; Marchal & Cantillon, 2022). In addition, the hypothetical household types may be more or less representative for individual country experiences. It is clear that the more assumptions we must make (and the more conditional benefits are), the less representative the indicator of the generosity of minimum income protection will be. Hence, it is of paramount importance to be aware of the impact of the assumptions made, and to contextualize the indicators with additional information, on eligibility criteria, but also on the reach of minimum income protection and its effectiveness.

Two remarks are especially relevant in terms of assessing guaranteed minimum income protection packages. For one, hypothetical household simulations show the system as it is *supposed to* work. It is assumed that the hypothetical households actually receive all the different income components they are entitled to, whereas empirical research has indicated this is for some—mainly means-tested—benefits quite unlikely, due to issues of non-take-up (Eurofound, 2015) and non-compliance (Ryckx & Kampelmann, 2012; Eurofound, 2019a). In addition, for some benefits, the legislator explicitly leaves room for discretion. A government official should then take account of the claimant's situation to tailor support to the specific needs. Additional support for exceptional circumstances is usually provided on a discretionary basis. In this book, we specifically focus on benefits that have a legal basis, i.e., where (guidelines for) level and basic admission criteria are legally defined. Even then, discretionary elements may be relevant, such as work willingness conditions or an individual assessment of assets in minimum income protection for the non-working (Marchal et al., 2018, 2021; De Wilde & Marchal, 2019). Hypothetical households will then possibly provide an overly positive picture. One of the first large quantitative studies into the impact of discretion, found however that the discretionary assessment of work willingness by Belgian social workers was an important criterion for the continuing of the benefit, but not from the start (De Wilde & Marchal, 2019). At a first awarding, social workers tend to give prospective claimants the benefit of the doubt, or even see stabilization of the living situation through the benefit receipt as a condition sine qua non to later start looking for work. Of course, whether this finding also holds in other cultural, socio-economic, and legal contexts is unclear. On the other hand, we do not include fully discretionary benefits for more specific expenses or situations, which are likewise possible in some countries and municipalities.

The image apparent from Figure 2.1 is in line with conclusions elsewhere: minimum income protection packages for the non-working active aged are not sufficient to protect against poverty (Van Mechelen & Marchal, 2013a; Cantillon & Vandenbroucke, 2015). They fall short of the at-risk-of-poverty threshold in each country included in Figure 2.1, although the gap is negligible for single person households in the Netherlands, and relatively limited for families with children in Denmark (for couples with children, not shown), the Netherlands, Austria, the United Kingdom and Luxembourg. Overall guaranteed minimum incomes are higher for lone parents with children: lone parent-households see the smallest relative gap to the poverty threshold.

The continental welfare states of Austria, Belgium, Luxembourg, the Netherlands, France, and Germany are among the better-performing nations, together with the Scandinavian Finland, Denmark and Sweden, and Anglo-Saxon United Kingdom. In these countries incomes are generally over 70% of the poverty threshold, although exceptions exist: couples with children in Belgium and France are closer to the middle of the spectrum, as are single-person households in Germany. Cyprus stands out as a lone Mediterranean country consistently among the top performers, even though Italy provides—since the last reform—relatively high benefits to single-person households. Also in Malta, we observe generous minimum income protection packages for single-person households, whereas protection levels for families with children are rather at the lower end of the spectrum.

In general, however, minimum income packages guaranteed by the Mediterranean countries find themselves in the 50–70% range of the national at-risk-of-poverty thresholds, placing this group among the middle performers. Here we also find the Czech Republic and Estonia. Ireland and Slovenia find themselves among the better performing ones of this middle group, for specific family types even surpassing the 70% threshold. Lithuania, Poland, and Portugal find themselves well established in the group of middle performs for families with children but show far lower protection levels for single-person households.

Central and Eastern European countries Bulgaria, Hungary, and Romania consistently provide minimum income protection packages well below 50% of the at-risk-of-poverty threshold. As Goedemé et al. (2019) show that reference budgets are in Eastern European levels generally far higher than the at-risk-of-poverty threshold, the adequacy of minimum income protection benefits for those out-of-work will be even more inadequate against such an alternative measure. Croatia also guarantees minimum income packages lower than 50% of the at-risk-of-poverty threshold, although the shortfall is less pronounced, and benefit levels for a lone parent with two children are more generous. Compared to the European countries, the United States consistently provides the least generous minimum income protection packages.

We should highlight that the general inadequacy of minimum income protection is no recent phenomenon. Over the last three decades, we have intermittently seen gradual erosion and catch-up growth of minimum income protection benefit levels in most of the included countries. Whereas in the 1990s, the observed erosion was a shared characteristic of minimum income protection trends in the majority of the Western European Member States (Van Mechelen & Marchal, 2013a), in the early 2000s trends were far more varied. Some countries issued large scale reforms, resulting in a boost in the guaranteed protection levels. This was for instance the case in Austria and Slovenia in 2010 and 2012. Elsewhere, reforms were more inspired by a desire to make work pay by reducing out-of-work benefits. This resulted for instance in a substantial decrease in Slovakia. Right after the financial and economic crisis, most European countries saw a slight increase in benefit levels, partially because of supportive crisis measures, partially because of ongoing indexation efforts (Marchal, Marx, & Van Mechelen, 2014, 2016; Marchal & Siöland, 2019). With the austerity shift in later years these efforts were not sustained. The recent reforms in the Mediterranean countries have

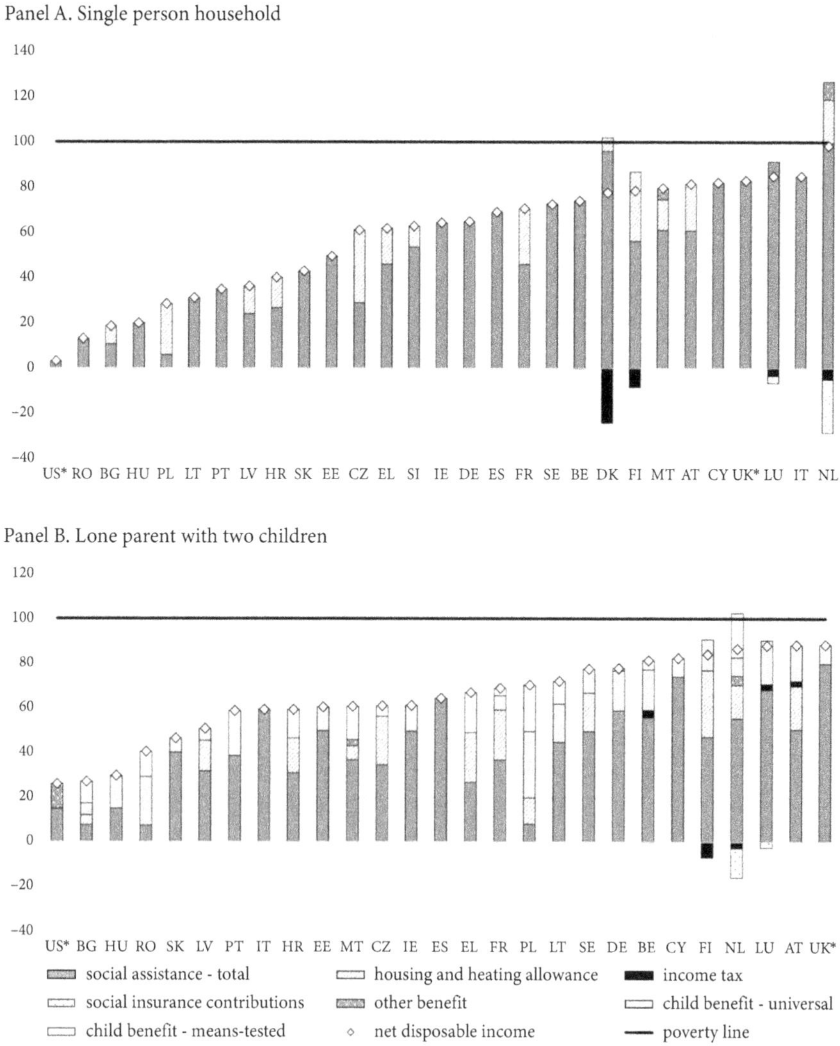


**Figure 2.1** Minimum income protection packages for the non-working of active age, 2021

*Note*: see Box 2.1 for more information on the method used. Data for the US are based on the figures reported in Aerts et al. (2022). Data for the UK represent the situation in 2020. We exclude temporary measures specifically linked to the COVID crisis. For more information on this, see Box 2.3.
*Source*: MIPI-HHoT (see Marchal et al. 2018). We thank Elise Aerts for valuable assistance in updating this dataset.

however provided a boost in their minimum income protection package generosity, establishing this group now among the middle (rather than the worst) performers. In Box 2.4, we zoom in on the reaction of out-of-work minimum income protection to the COVID-19 pandemic.

## 2.5 The Make-up of Minimum Income Protection Packages

It is clear from Figure 2.1 that means-tested minimum income benefits (the grey bars in Figure 2.1) constitute a large share of guaranteed minimum income packages for those out of work. In some countries, the means-tested minimum income benefit can be combined with housing or heating allowances (the dashed bars) or other benefits. Child benefits are common for families with children, even though the balance between universal and means-tested child benefits can differ greatly between countries. Income taxes and social insurance contributions are only relevant in some countries, as the benefits important to our hypothetical households are usually not taxed. Self-evidently, in these countries the 'gross' minimum income benefit is defined at a higher level. Below, we discuss each of these components in more detail.

### Box 2.2 Non-monetary benefits, discretion, and local variation

This book investigates the design and adequacy of minimum income protection packages, that we defined in Chapter 1 as cash-based minimal resources guaranteed by the government. In our analysis, we hence focus on the non-discretionary income components of minimum income protection packages, as they are applicable to hypothetical households with specific characteristics, living in a large city in each country (see Box 2.1).

Consequently, our indicators of minimum income protection packages do not capture certain elements. For one, we do not look in-depth into the importance of in-kind benefits and other non-monetary income components. Second, we do not consider discretionary income components. And finally, we ignore the intra-national variation that may exist regarding minimum income protection package adequacy, conditionality, and implementation practices. These issues are to considerable extent related to one another. In this box, we shortly contextualize the likely impact of these choices.

We should note that beneficiaries of means-tested minimum income benefits may be entitled to certain in-kind benefits or can have access to specific services. Whereas some of these may be universally provided, such as education, often means-tested minimum income benefits can be tied towards the provision of additional discretionary or non-discretionary support. In 2015, the ESPN country reports synthesized in Frazer and Marlier (2016) indicated that minimum income recipients *could* benefit from education or vocational training, free school meals, childcare, in-kind benefits for education and participation, social counselling and psychological services, social services, social assistance services, funeral expenses, energy tariffs, compensation for renovation, state legal assistance, and support for higher school students. In addition, minimum income beneficiaries are in many countries eligible for basic health care, or their contributions to the general health insurance scheme are (explicitly or implicitly) covered by the local welfare agency (European Commission and Social Protection Committee, 2022). A recent study by Hermans, Cantillon, and Marchal (forthcoming) furthermore showed for four European countries that municipal welfare agencies may cooperate with local food banks, in order to smooth access to this type of in-kind support for welfare beneficiaries. In Spain, Belgium, and Hungary, this cooperation may include explicit formal referrals by local welfare agencies. Importantly, not all these services are provided in all countries, or even in all localities of a certain country. The study by Hermans, Cantillon, and Marchal (forthcoming) demonstrated major differences in both cooperation with the local welfare agency, as in the value of the food packages provided, even between different food bank organizations located in the same city. Also, the different types of non-monetary support are not necessarily exclusively meant to improve the situation of minimum income beneficiaries specifically.

Quantifying the relative importance of these benefits is hard.

For one, the value of certain cost compensations, tariff reductions, and vouchers for minimum income beneficiaries depends on their actual use and on the utility derived from this use. For instance, social tariffs for energy may have a larger beneficial impact on the living standards of those having high energy bills, whereas reduced tariffs for culture outings will be worth more to culture afficionados who regularly participate in such events. Reduced or free public transport is only relevant for minimum income beneficiaries living near public transport stops, and to the extent that they are mobile enough to use this transport mode. This is even more relevant regarding the valuation of very specific benefits, which compensate for expenses that one only rarely needs to make, such as vouchers to buy new household appliances, or support in covering funeral expenses.

Hermans, Cantillon, Bernat, et al. (forthcoming) assess the value of the monthly food parcels included in their study to raise the minimum income package on average (for different family types and taking the average per city) by 7% in Belgium, 3.8% in Finland, 5.2% in Hungary, and 11.2% in Spain. The high percentages for Hungary and Spain should be understood in the context of inadequate minimum income protection packages. The gap with the at-risk-of-poverty threshold decreases with respectively 5, 3.1, 1.3, and 7.3 percentage points, and overall remains substantial. In addition, these values are based on a snapshot in each country, and by no means

*continued*

**Box 2.2** *continued*

mean that the same family will each week or month again have access to this food package. Availability indeed partially depends on the specific donations that were received. In addition, the monetary values cited above are derived from a direct market pricing, without taking into account the marginal utility of these parcels for the beneficiaries (Whitmore, 2002; Hermans, Cantillon, Bernat, et al., forthcoming).

A number of studies have specifically aimed to quantify the value of less charity-based cost compensations in Belgium (Cantillon et al., 2014; Penne, Cornelis, & Storms, 2019; Marchal et al., 2022, forthcoming), i.e., of those cost-compensations that are subject to standardized rules, and therefore generally accessible to minimum income beneficiaries if they face certain expenses. These studies built on a scientifically derived normative minimum use to link the reduced tariffs to a valid consumption profile. Cantillon et al. (2014) estimate that for such a minimum use, social tariffs would reduce the necessary expenses by 58% for water, 31% for energy, 29% for mobility and 13% for health expenses. In a more recent study, Penne, Cornelis, and Storms (2019) find that including the value of nine social cost reductions for necessary expenses would increase the net minimum income protection package by 10% of a couple with two children relying on social assistance. However, since these social tariffs usually need to be applied for at different administrations, it is by no means certain that a family will have access to all nine compensations. Moreover, the overall minimum income protection package remains far off the at-risk-of-poverty threshold. While the percentage reductions are substantial, they are based on relatively limited values, as the expenses fit into a minimal lifestyle. In the Belgian context, however, there is one type of in-kind benefit that does have the potential to substantially raise the adequacy of a minimum income protection package. The value represented by living in a dwelling rented on the social housing market, rather than on the private market, brings net disposable incomes very close (or even above) the minimum income necessary for a decent participation to society. Within a Belgian context, it is however difficult to consider social housing a non-monetary benefit commonly accessible for minimum income beneficiaries. The social rent sector is exceedingly small, and access is governed by waiting lists spanning several years, also for minimum income beneficiaries. Social housing is therefore not usually included in cross-national comparisons of benefit adequacy. Also in this book, we look at the income support provided to those who rent on the private market, at median rent levels, and only include the value of housing allowances in our assessment of minimum income protection packages.

So far, we have discussed the value of non-monetary benefits that are either discretionary and charity-based, or alternatively, rights-based cost-compensations.

A different type of non-monetary support is personal support, tailored to the individual and local situation. Some countries explicitly award benefits in case of pressing need, also outside the general social assistance scheme (European Commission and Social Protection Committee, 2022). These types of benefits are almost by definition discretionary, since the assessment of the specific need, and the required actions are taken by social workers. Other countries also foresee highly individualized social assistance services, such as legal assistance, debt consolidation support, and counselling. In terms of actual benefits, Belgian local welfare agencies have the mandate to ensure the capacity of citizens to fully participate in society. Social workers and local welfare agencies have to interpret themselves which actions are required for specific situations (De Wilde et al., 2016). For instance, they can cooperate with various local partners, which likely impacts the accessibility of both integrated social services and the minimum income protection benefit itself (Janssens & Marchal, 2022). Another instrument they have at their disposal is the additional discretionary support, financed from local budgets. In the past, Van Mechelen and Bogaerts (2008) have used model families to assess the extent to which different localities aimed to support in specific situations, for instance in coping with high school invoices in atypical educations (specifically, an expensive knife set to obtain a cook's diploma). They found large local variation in the value of these additional discretionary benefits. A more recent large-scale quantitative study, building on a D-efficient experimental design, found on the other hand that most of the variation in discretionary assessments can be found at the level of the individual beneficiary situations, and, in second order, at the level of individual social workers. At the same time, large part of the variation in assessment remains unexplained (De Wilde, 2018). Clearly, when differences are already pronounced at the subnational (and even individual) level, a cross-nationally comparative valuation of the importance of non-monetary benefits and discretionary treatment would obfuscate rather than further enlighten the situation of means-tested benefits.

Finally, the issue of individual and local discretion is also relevant considering those services and practices that are available for minimum income beneficiaries to facilitate (or force) their re-entry onto the labour market. Various training as well as labour market experience services that aim to shorten the distance between social assistance beneficiaries and the labour market are organized at the local level or depend on local interaction with third-sector organizations. It has been well studied that activation measures, especially those targeted at persons on a large distance from the labour market, are often designed and implemented at the local level, in order to better align with the needs of the local labour market, and the target population (Sabatinelli, 2010; Bothfeld, Eydoux, & Leibetseder, 2022).

### 2.5.1 Means-Tested Minimum Income Protection Benefits

The main element of minimum income protection packages is the means-tested social assistance benefit available to non-working active age households, which has as first and foremost purpose to provide a minimal living standard. Usually, this benefit of last resort is not taxed, with the exception of Denmark, Finland, the Netherlands, and Luxembourg.

In most countries, the non-working of active age are catered for by the general social assistance scheme. However, specific categorical schemes do exist. Hungary has for instance an 'employment substituting benefit' for those who are able to work, with more stringent activity requirements and lower (yet individual) benefit levels than applicable in the social assistance scheme. Since the Hartz IV reform in 2004, Germany caters for those able to work, but ineligible to social insurance, under the categorical Arbeitlosengeld II.[3] Similarly, Finland has the labour market subsidy as main means-tested minimum income support scheme for those able to work, whereas Ireland caters for this target group with its non-contributory jobseeker's allowance. Malta makes a similar distinction. The United Kingdom on the other hand has grouped various means-tested benefits under the recent Universal Credit scheme (Immervoll & Knotz, 2018).

Within Europe, a wide range of practices exists in determining the level of the minimally guaranteed income floor. Based on a systematic review of country reports on minimum income protection, Frazer and Marlier (2016, p. 15) found that only a small majority of European countries bases their minimum income benefit levels on an objective measure, that either serves to guarantee a specific level of living standards, or, more often, to safeguard the relationship between the minimum income benefit and alternative benefits or minimum wage levels.

In some of the Scandinavian countries, minimum incomes are based on the value of a basket of goods and services deemed necessary by the government. In Sweden, for instance, the government sets each year a national norm (*riksnorm*) that covers food, clothes and shoes, hygiene and health, leisure and hobbies, child insurance, consumer goods, newspapers, and telephone costs. This amount should at the very least be covered by municipalities. In addition, the norm also states expenses related to housing, energy, commuting, home insurance, and professional fees that municipalities may additionally cover (directly, or by applying for other benefits, such as housing allowances) (Nelson & Fritzell, 2015). Every now and then, the underlying basket is revised, to keep benefit levels in line with living standards. Still, municipalities may decide whether they guarantee all the different elements of the basket or not (Panican & Ulmestig, 2016; Leibetseder et al., 2017). Elsewhere, living standards are operationalized through a comparison with consumption patterns of the lowest income groups. This is for instance (partially) the case in Germany. Every five years, the benefit level is recalculated based on the expenditure of lower-income groups included in the Income and Consumption Sample. Intermittently, benefits are uprated in line with a weighted index combining trends in prices and net average wages (European Commission and Social Protection Committee, 2022). Other countries that rely on the calculation of a basket of goods and services to determine the benefit level are Cyprus, Estonia, Lithuania, Luxembourg, Poland, and Slovenia (European Commission and Social Protection Committee, 2022).

In other countries, including the Netherlands, Spain, Luxembourg, Hungary, Denmark, Malta, and Portugal, benefit levels are defined in relation to the minimum wage, pension, or other social benefit indicators (Van Mechelen & Marchal, 2013a; Frazer & Marlier, 2016; MISSOC, 2022).

Yet in nearly half of the EU Member States, there does not appear to be an explicit rationale behind minimum income benefit levels, rather benefit levels are arbitrarily set by policy makers. For instance the actual benefit levels provided by some Italian municipalities before the introduction of the Reddito di Inclusione and the subsequent Reddito di Cittadinanza were more determined by the available budget than by clear considerations on what beneficiaries should be able to afford (Arlotti & Sabatinelli, 2017). Elsewhere, if there ever was a clear link, it has long since disappeared through erosion or ad-hoc changes (Van Mechelen & Marchal, 2013a; Frazer & Marlier, 2016). Leibetseder et al. (2017) for instance describe the development of minimum income protection levels in Switzerland: these were originally tied to the income thresholds and consumption patterns of the lowest 10% income groups. This practice was however abandoned in 2002, and since then, ad hoc increases in line with the cost of living, or one-off cuts have effectively obfuscated the previous link. A similar development occurred in Romania, though far more outspokenly. Where initially the guaranteed minimum income level was tied to the minimum wage, the minimum wage as benchmark value for the definition and uprating of a set of social benefits was abolished in 2008, as part of a tripartite agreement that foresaw to gradually increase the minimum wage over the following years. As an alternative, a social reference indicator was introduced to replace the minimum wage as a reference value. While this social reference indicator was initially set at the same level as the gross minimum wage, it has since been left to erode, with its first indexation only taking place in 2022 (Rat, 2022).

A simple comparison of guaranteed minimum income protection benefit levels and their underlying rationale may give an idea of the aspirations of welfare states, but such a comparison is not informative on the actual guaranteed protection level. Minimum income benefits can be designed to cover housing costs, or alternatively to be combined with separate housing allowances. Similarly, higher supplementary amounts can be awarded for children at the cost of child benefits. Indeed, minimum income protection is—at the moment—everywhere a means-tested benefit. The details of this means-test vary between countries (see Box 2.3). Hence, it is possible that housing allowances, child benefits or other benefits lower the value of the social assistance benefit. This explains the relatively low minimum income benefit levels in combination with a housing allowance in, e.g., Poland and France. Therefore, it is of utmost importance to assess the level of the minimum income protection provisions in combination, and to look at the overall guaranteed minimum income protection package, as we do in Figure 2.1.

### Box 2.3 Minimum income protection: a means-tested benefit

Minimum income benefits are a protection measure of last resort: means-tested minimum income protection schemes only cater to those that have no sufficient means of living, despite their best efforts to acquire these. Clearly, countries can be more or less stringent in defining 'no sufficient means'. As a general rule, minimum income is only relevant after all rights to social insurance benefits are extinguished: only those who are not (sufficiently) covered by social insurance will need to rely on (top-ups from) the means-tested minimum income schemes (Bahle, Hubl, & Pfeifer, 2011).

The means-tests of these safety nets of last resort usually include a broad range of income sources, reducing the benefit level one on one with every income the beneficiary household acquires. This can be taken quite literally: in the Netherlands there was a heavily publicized case of a social assistance beneficiary who regularly received groceries from her mother and was sanctioned for not declaring this income. Regular gifts are indeed in many countries considered as income source (MISSOC, 2017).

However, numerous countries have undertaken efforts to make their social assistance schemes more employment-friendly (Eichhorst & Konle-Seidl, 2008). A 100% taper rate self-evidently poses a giant threshold to the take-up of small jobs (Immervoll & Scarpetta, 2012; Coady et al., 2021; Rat, 2022), whereas combining benefit receipt with some labour market attachment is expected to boost the long-term labour market prospects of claimants (Boschman et al., 2021). Therefore, over the past decades, countries have taken various initiatives. Whereas back-to-work bonuses, continued benefit receipt in the first months of employment, and (mandatory) active labour market participation are highly visible, other initiatives have focused on making the means-tests more friendly to employment income (Coady et al., 2021).

Many countries now include an earnings disregard of some sort (European Commission and Social Protection Committee, 2022). This may take the form of only taking a certain percentage of employment income into account as income. France implemented for instance a 64% earnings disregard when it introduced the 'revenu de solidarité active' (RSA) in 2009. The Czech Republic only takes 70% of employment income into account (Marchal & Van Mechelen, 2014, 2017; MISSOC, 2022). In contrast, Belgium only has a temporary earnings disregard, allowing the combination of employment income and social assistance receipt up to 253.8 euro of employment income, for a maximum period of three years (in a six-year period). In addition, a general disregard applies for all forms of income. This allows income from small haphazard income sources, but also allows those with small social insurance benefits to be somewhat better off. The Czech Republic also disregards a small percentage of social insurance benefits (MISSOC, 2020). In Chapter 4, Sections 4.3.1 and 4.3.6, we discuss these aspects at length.

Means-tests may also exclude some more specific benefits, depending on the purpose of the minimum income benefit. For instance, if the minimum income benefit is intended to cover living expenses, but is not expected to cover housing costs, housing allowances will not be considered in the means-test. The same goes for child benefits. Some countries have higher benefit rates for families with children, effectively increasing the benefit for each child and hence functionally replacing child benefits (e.g., Germany). Other countries, such as Belgium, fully intend the social assistance benefit as an income base that should be topped up by child benefits. Self-evidently, intermediary systems are possible, in which part of the child benefit is included in the means-test (European Commission and Social Protection Committee, 2022).

The income concept is in most countries defined at the household level. In Belgium for instance, the income of living-in adult children with a student job will be included in the means-test (this is however not the case for the income secured through student jobs of minor children) (POD Maatschappelijke Integratie, 2018).

Importantly, means-tests do not solely focus on incomes, but focus on all means of existence. These may include regular gifts, as the Dutch example showed. But all EU Member States also include savings and other assets into this concept (European Commission and Social Protection Committee, 2022). Marchal et al. (2021) provided an overview of the asset tests included in the European minimum income schemes' means-tests. Whereas some countries include all assets and leave it to the discretionary assessment of a social worker whether these have to be realized before receiving a benefit, most countries have rules that exempt the family home

*continued*

**Box 2.3** *continued*

and small amounts of savings. A number of countries, specifically, Belgium, Ireland, Luxembourg, the UK, Malta, and Portugal, take this further, and apply a taper rate on savings, gradually reducing the benefit if there are assets present in the household.

## 2.5.2 Housing Allowances

Minimum income levels can be set at a level considered appropriate to cover housing costs, for instance in countries where no housing allowances exist, or where housing allowances are included in the means-test. In the latter case, the minimum income benefit will serve as a top-up to the housing allowance. If one is not eligible for the housing allowance (or fails to take up the housing allowance), the full minimum income benefit will be paid. In other countries, housing allowances are paid on top of the minimum income benefit, or a specific housing cost-related component is part of the minimum income benefit. Clearly, we should look at the minimum income benefit and housing (and heating) allowances in combination.

Housing allowances partially depend on the actual housing costs. Although the variation in precise formulas to calculate the exact housing allowance amount is immense, often a percentage of housing costs is reimbursed. Too high actual housing costs can exclude a family from housing allowance eligibility, or the part above the threshold is not considered in the calculation. Other eligibility criteria that are designed to not subsidize 'luxurious' housing are maximum surface thresholds, a maximum number of bedrooms or requirements that only modest housing can be supported (Marchal, Siöland, & Goedemé, 2018). Figure 2.1 includes the housing allowances applicable for out-of-work families with housing costs equal to the median rent in each country (see also Box 2.1). We assume that additional eligibility criteria relating to the size of the dwelling are met. In some countries, higher housing costs are allowed in specific regions, such as capital regions where housing costs are typically more elevated than in the rest of the country (Marchal & Cantillon, 2022).

Minimum income beneficiaries may also benefit from contributions to the expenses related to heating one's home. Such support is in most countries not guaranteed by a general scheme but is scattered over various support systems depending on the ways used for heating one's home (e.g., wood, propane gas, oil), is in-kind or only applies after difficulties in paying heating bills have manifested. The dashed bars in Figure 2.1 include the value of heating allowances to the extent it is an easily accessible, general scheme, paid out to the households themselves. Note that, especially in large countries with different climatological conditions, such as Finland, heating allowances (included in the dashed bars) may differ between regions. Overall, and in contrast to the impact of housing allowances, the impact of these separate heating schemes on net disposable incomes is limited.

### 2.5.3 Child Benefits

Child benefits are common in the European Member States, yet they come in different guises. This is in line with the different policy purposes for which policy makers have designed, implemented, or reshaped child benefits. Traditionally, child benefits are favoured to boost fertility and to support the traditional breadwinner model, while they are currently also intended to support child wellbeing and gender equity (Penne et al., 2020). Adema (2012) for instance discusses the duality in terms of child benefits between a dual earner support dimension, in which child benefits and parental leave systems are beneficial to dual earnership and a traditional breadwinner dimension, that favours childcare leave benefits. In line with the social investment agenda, child poverty and life chances during childhood have come front and centre on the social policy agenda (Vandenbroucke & Vleminckx, 2011). This has led to new policy instruments, including a fiscalization of child support (Ferrarini, Nelson, & Höög, 2012) and a focus on child services, including childcare.

Recently, policy makers and scholars have become more and more interested in child benefits (and functionally equivalent policies, such as child tax credits) from the perspective of combatting child poverty (Van Mechelen & Bradshaw, 2013). To this end, some scholars have looked into the effectiveness of different forms of child support. Van Lancker and Van Mechelen (2015) for instance, assessed the effectiveness of respectively universal and targeted child benefit systems in terms of poverty outcomes. They found that a combination of universal and targeted support (targeting within universalism) was preferable. In a recent paper, Aerts, Marx, and Parolin (2022) find indications that child support packages tend to be higher in more universal countries, although exceptions exist.

In Figure 2.1, panel B, we distinguish between universal child benefits (the light grey bars) and means-tested child benefits (white bars). Clearly, child benefits have a key role in guaranteeing minimum incomes. The total of universal and means-tested child benefits generally accounts for over 10–20% of the guaranteed minimum income protection package (and in some countries its importance even increases to over 50%). There are only two exceptions: the United States and Greece have no child benefits whatsoever. This does however not mean that support for children is not provided in a different fashion, e.g., through tax credits, other benefits, or higher minimum income protection levels (see also Aerts, Marx, & Parolin, 2022). Spain excludes minimum income protection beneficiary families from the national child benefit scheme (Navas Román & Villazán Pellejero, 2021).

All but eight countries (Italy, Greece, Malta, Portugal, Croatia, the Czech Republic, Spain, and Cyprus) provide universal child benefits, accessible to all households with children. Benefit levels usually vary by age and degree of disability. For a lone parent with two children aged seven and 14, the universal child benefit ranges from only 5% of the at-risk-of-poverty threshold in Latvia and Bulgaria, to around 20% in Luxembourg and Romania. Poland is an outlier with a universal child benefit nearing 30% of the at-risk-of-poverty threshold.

In half of the countries, means-tested child benefits exist. These income-tested social supplements usually represent an important additional income source. It amounts to at least 30% of the total child support, and even over 50% in the Netherlands, and Bulgaria. In Cyprus, Portugal, Malta, Croatia, the Czech Republic, and Greece, the entire child benefit package is means-tested.

Note that additional conditions may apply for child support receipt. We assume that the children in the hypothetical household regularly attend school. Failing this condition could lead to lower child benefits in a number of countries. In Portugal, it is additionally required that children attain good school results. Child benefits are tied to the regular school year in yet another way: many countries, including Poland, Belgium, and Luxembourg, pay an additional child benefit at the start of the school year. In some countries, specific lone parent child support benefits exist.

### 2.5.4 Other Income Components

Figure 2.1 finally shows a number of other income components that are relevant for the guaranteed minimum incomes. In some of the Scandinavian countries, the Netherlands and Luxembourg, social assistance benefits are included in the tax system. Both taxes and social insurance contributions are due. Self-evidently, the gross amounts are adapted to this reality. In other countries, social assistance benefits are non-taxable income, but this does not preclude social assistance beneficiaries from receiving tax credits in Austria, Belgium, and Luxembourg. Similarly, in a number of other countries, child tax credits are awarded to social assistance beneficiaries. However, as they are paid out as a monthly benefit, they are included in Figure 2.1 as child benefits. This is the case in Austria, the Czech Republic, and Slovakia.

Finally, Figure 2.1 includes the category 'other benefits' that represents country-specific benefits and supplements that are not easily classified. For the Netherlands this includes a health insurance subsidy, specific to the Dutch context, where one is obliged to subscribe to private health insurance, but in lieu, specific benefits to contribute to meeting the cost of private health insurance are available. For Malta, we use this category to classify monetary bonuses that are paid to beneficiaries of specific means-tested benefits (see also Vella, Said, & Apap, 2021). For the United States, the category other benefits represent the benefits provided under the TANF scheme (Temporary Assistance for Needy Families), as opposed to the support provided by the federal Supplemental Nutritional Aid Program (SNAP). TANF is only accessible to families with children, although for both types of programmes, behavioural conditions apply (Parolin & Luigjes, 2019).

**Box 2.4 Minimum income support during COVID-19**

The non-working population was in many countries not immediately recognized as a target group in need of additional non-discretionary support during the first COVID-19 lockdowns. Immediate efforts were concentrated on employees at risk of dismissal for lack of work and the self-employed who had to halt their activities (Cantó et al., 2022; Eichhorst et al., 2023). To offer protection to the latter group, some countries relaxed access conditions to their means-tested minimum income schemes (Eichhorst et al., 2023).

We did see a swift rise in discretionary support throughout Europe (Marchal & Cantillon, 2022). In Belgium for instance, local welfare agencies received additional funds to support those affected by COVID-19. It was indeed clear that those in poverty could not rely on traditional survival strategies: non-official employment was not an option as the economy came to an abrupt standstill, charities had trouble finding volunteers, and coupon-hunting was no longer an option as logistic chains hampered. Shoestring budgets did not allow for the price rises and empty shelves observed during the first lockdown (Cantillon et al., 2020). Ad hoc surveys showed that food banks

*continued*

**Box 2.4** *continued*

all over Europe saw additional demand (De Wilde, Hermans, & Cantillon, 2020; FEBA, 2021; Greiss et al., 2022).

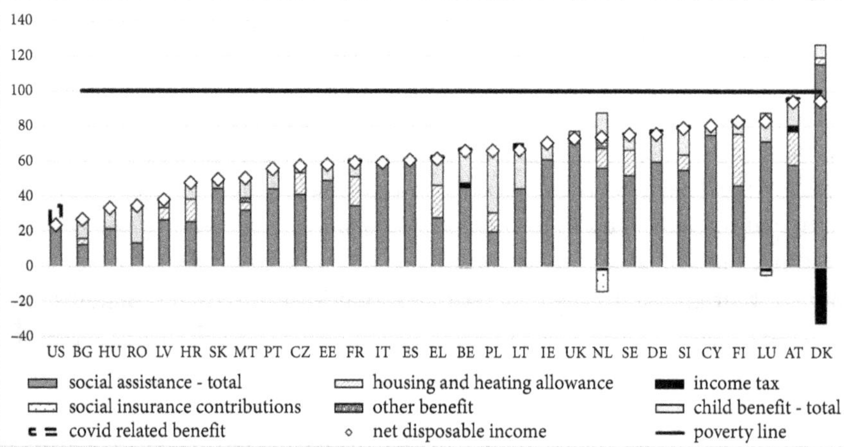


**Figure 2.2** Minimum income protection packages for a non-working active age couple with two children, including non-discretionary COVID support in 2020–2021.
*Source*: MIPI-HHoT, based on the COVID-19 policies included in the 2020 EUROMOD programming. Data for the US include the measures that were temporarily implemented under the Biden plan and refer to 2021 (see Aerts et al. 2022). Data for the European Member States focus on the situation in 2020.

Against this background, it is surprising that additional non-discretionary support for the non-working population was usually only implemented with a certain lag. Still, by summer 2020, a number of rights-based income support measures also including the non-working population got implemented.

The most structural change was the introduction of the means-tested national minimum income scheme in Spain (see Section 2.2). Elsewhere, the changes were more piecemeal and explicitly temporary. In Figure 2.2 we show the average annual value of the COVID-19 measures introduced throughout 2020 in the overall minimum income package of those out-of-work, as they are available in EUROMOD. In general, the values appear to be relatively limited. This is due to the rather modest value of the top-ups available to minimum income beneficiaries. Usually, the benefits were limited to one-off bonuses (e.g., a 200–360 euro child bonus in Lithuania, Germany, and Austria), or repeated but limited supplements to the minimum income benefits for a number of months (e.g., a 75 euro supplement in Finland, from September to December 2020, or a 50 euro supplement for the last six months of 2020 in Belgium). The impact on the annualized income therefore remains limited. The United States forms a notable exception. Here the Recovery Act foresaw a sizeable refundable child tax credit (Aerts, Marx, & Parolin, 2022). This is in line with earlier observations in the literature, i.e., that countries without sufficient safety nets tend to provide ad hoc support in times of sudden and unexpected downfall (Dolls, Fuest, & Peichl, 2012).

## 2.6 Guaranteed Minimum Incomes as a Poverty Reducing Device

How do these minimum income protection packages perform in reducing or mitigating poverty?

The overall effectiveness of minimum income protection as an anti-poverty policy is hard to disentangle. Overall national poverty rates are not only a consequence of the effectiveness of minimum income protection benefits, but also of (among other things) the economic situation in a country, its labour market situation, and the effectiveness of its social insurance schemes.

Studies on the impact of social assistance on overall poverty rates suggest rather limited effects, although there are big variations across countries. The Commission Staff Working Document accompanying the proposal for a recommendation on minimum income protection reports the results of a pre-post analysis of the impact of minimum income protection benefits on the at-risk-of-poverty rate performed on the EU-SILC, the workhorse survey to track changes in income and living conditions in the European countries. According to these results, the impact of minimum income benefits on poverty tends to vary a lot across the Union but is overall fairly limited. Significant impacts are only measured in Ireland, Cyprus, France, and Slovenia. The Staff Working Document considers the modest impact unsurprising, considering the low benefit levels (see also Figure 2.1 in this chapter). The impact becomes indeed more outspoken when focusing on alternative hardship measures, such as the 40% at-risk-of-poverty rate, or the at-risk-of-poverty gap. Still, even against these alternative measures, reductions remain marginal in a number of Member States, including Hungary, Bulgaria, Latvia, Estonia, and Poland (European Commission, 2022a).

Avram (2016) focused on the effectiveness and efficiency of minimum income protection in eight Eastern European countries. She estimates the reduction to overall poverty rates in these countries thanks to minimum income protection to vary between around 5% and 20%. The reduction of poverty specifically among those who actually receive a minimum income protection benefit is higher, but still below 40% in each of the countries considered. The reduction is higher when not looking at the impact on poverty rates but focusing on the poverty gap. She attributes these relatively disappointing results to low benefit levels, and small programme expenditure. In addition, the considered social assistance programmes fail to reach the poor. Tasseva (2016) calculated the impact of means-tested benefits on poverty in Bulgaria. She found that the benefits did not substantially contribute to lower poverty outcomes. Poverty incidence decreased by a mere 4%, while the poverty gap decreased by 13%. In line with Avram, she attributes these results to the low level of the benefits and the low coverage of the poor.[4] For Slovakia, Gerbery and Miklošovič (2018) point at the very low benefit levels, that do not correctly account for increased needs due to the presence of children in the household. They find that an increase of the benefit level to 75% of the at-risk-of-poverty threshold would lead to a 9% drop in poverty rate. Ayala et al. (2021) thoroughly investigate the impact on poverty of a broad range of regional and national benefits in Spain, including the regional minimum income benefits. They find that overall, contributory benefits have a larger poverty reducing impact than means-tested benefits. Regional means-tested minimum income benefits have however an important impact on the situation of families below the poverty threshold (as they reduce around 70% of the poverty gap) and substantially contribute to limiting the poverty risk of families with children. Also here, the authors conclude that the low coverage of means-tested minimum income benefits in terms of the number of households receiving a minimum income benefit and the large variation in protection offered—both across regions and between household types—is problematic in terms of its poverty-reducing capacity. Some of these shortcomings should be addressed by the newly introduced national minimum vital income (Badenes Plá & Gambau-Suelves, 2020). Note that in general, the studies cited above focus on the means-tested minimum income benefits guaranteed by the minimum income scheme, rather than on the full minimum income protection packages that we consider in this chapter.

Taking a different approach, Vandenbroucke et al. (2013) did assess the correlation between the adequacy of minimum income protection *packages* (expressed as a percentage of the 60% at-risk-of-poverty line) and at-risk-of-poverty rates over all the EU Member States and found this to be relatively weak. The correlation grew stronger when focusing on the poverty gap, and on poverty rates at the 40% threshold. Importantly, the correlation was most convincing for people living in households with low work intensity. They concluded that social assistance benefit generosity correlates only weakly with overall national poverty levels. This result was attributed to the fact that poverty outcomes are related to the functioning of the broader welfare state edifice. Yet they do derive from the relatively strong correlation for people on a larger distance from the labour market, that social assistance does have a significant role to play in protecting more marginalized groups, with less self-evident access to contributory benefits.

In a more recent study, we did a similar exercise, focusing on the benefit generosity and social outcomes for the specific group of lone parents (see Cantillon, Marchal, & Luigjes, 2019). We did not solely focus on the adequacy of minimum income protection for those out of work, but also included policy indicators of in-work income protection, the minimum wage, financial incentives, and the additional income support targeted to working lone parent families, and assessed their correlation with the poverty head count using the 40% poverty threshold among lone parent families. We found that the generosity of net social assistance for lone parent households tended to co-exist with lower poverty rates among persons living in working age lone parent households. Also the generosity of net minimum wages for full-time working lone parent households correlated with lower poverty rates, while there were no consistent correlations between the generosity of lone parent's minimum income protection packages and their employment rates.

In Figure 2.3, we report the results of a similar exercise. Figure 2.3 shows the correlation between the general at-risk-of-poverty rate in each EU Member State, and the adequacy of its minimum income protection packages, operationalized as the average over four hypothetical households. Some reservations apply: the correlations are based on a small group of cases that in no way can be considered a representative sample of all countries. Moreover, we do not control for other country characteristics. Hence these correlations can only serve to illustrate potential and tentative relations and can in no way be interpreted as causal mechanisms. Overall, our results are in line with those reported previously: we find a negative correlation between at-risk-of-poverty rates and the adequacy of minimum income protection packages. As in previous research, we find stronger correlations when we zoom in on severe poverty (it is at the 40% at-risk-of-poverty threshold). As minimum income protection packages are themselves usually below the 60% at-risk-of-poverty threshold, this is to be expected.

The correlations that we find are in line with those reported in European Commission and Social Protection Committee (2022). Focusing on the adequacy of minimum income protection packages for a single adult household, they find rather strong and negative correlations with the 2019 at-risk-of-poverty rate among households with a very low work intensity

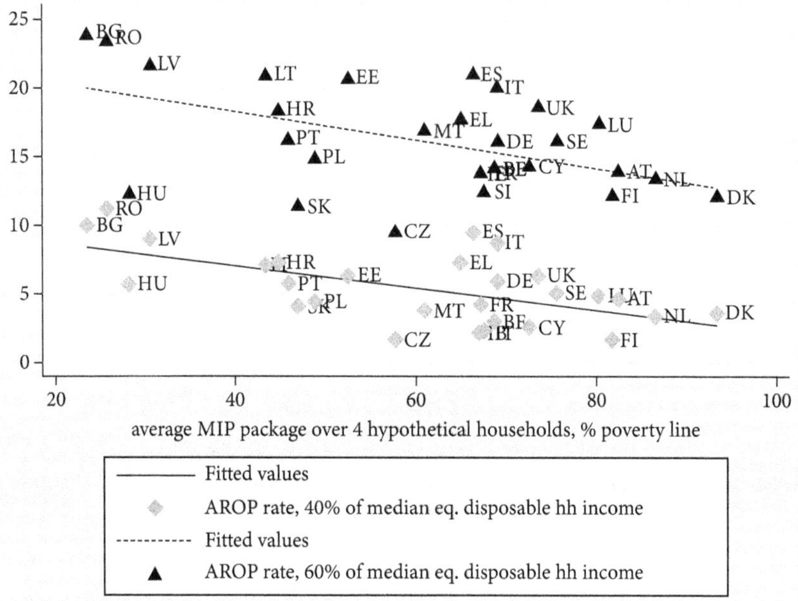


**Figure 2.3** Relation between MIP income package adequacy (average over four hypothetical households) and general at-risk-of-poverty rate, 2019.

*Note*: correlations are −0.59 for AROP40, −0.50 for AROP60. Both MIP packages as poverty rates refer to the situation in 2019. 2019 incomes (based on EU SILC 2020) were the most recent available for every country at the time of writing. Data for the UK refer to the situation in 2017.
*Source*: MIPI-HHoT, Eurostat, own calculations.

(−0.47), the poverty gap among these households (−0.72), and their severe material deprivation rate (−0.64).

In a more advanced analysis, Nelson (2012) disentangles the relation between minimum income protection adequacy and material deprivation. Controlling for contextual variables, such as the amount of non-means-tested social spending, he finds that minimum income protection levels do significantly reduce the extent of material deprivation in a country. This appears to be in line with our own observations and the observation of Vandenbroucke et al. (2013) that minimum income protection generosity might be able to reduce poverty among disadvantaged groups.

In general, from the literature review above, we can conclude that social assistance has a limited but discernible impact on overall poverty figures. For families suffering from serious destitution adequate social assistance schemes are clearly important. In addition, Figure 2.3 illustrates that a sound social floor correlates to some extent with lower overall at-risk-of-poverty rates, and especially severe poverty. In the remainder of this chapter, we present a number of explanations for the limited poverty reducing effectiveness of minimum income protection at the population level, as indicated by the summarized pre-post analyses, and as to be derived from the correlations presented above. We first discuss the inadequate benefit levels. Next, we discuss the limited coverage of minimum income protection.

## 2.7 Mismatch between Minimum Income Protection and Poverty Measures

In a way, the limited poverty reducing effectiveness of minimum income protection packages for those out-of-work is not surprising, as they are so much lower than the poverty threshold we use as the main reference throughout this book. Why is that the case? Wouldn't it make sense to align the benefit levels of a scheme that has as aim to prevent poverty, with the income that is deemed necessary to escape poverty?

A first reason has to do with the legitimacy and the reasoning behind the 60% at-risk-of-poverty threshold, issues that were discussed in Chapter 1. Whereas this indicator has clear merits on comparative and methodological grounds, it may not always concur with what is societally seen as 'being poor'. The approach found in the Scandinavian countries, in which social assistance benefit levels bear remembrance to the value of underlying goods and services that one should be able to afford, shows a different, more absolute, conception of poverty one wants to fight (see Section 2.5.1). Implicitly, this may also be the reasoning behind low benefit levels in other countries, where the national conception of poverty (or severe poverty) that one wants to fight might not reflect the international consensus. In the Netherlands for instance, the official poverty indicator reflects the real value of the means-tested minimum income benefit level as it stood at its highest level in 1979 (Centraal Bureau voor de Statistiek, 2023), effectively illustrating the relevance of this inverse reasoning. In a recent paper, Aprea, Gallo, and Raitano (2022) note that the misalignment between the official Italian poverty measure, and the eligibility criteria included in the Italian means-tested minimum income scheme that focus on wealth measures and take account of prior residence, leads to a less performant minimum income scheme when assessed in terms of poverty reduction against the official yardstick. One can also interpret the finding that international studies do indeed find a more outspoken link between severe poverty or material deprivation and minimum income protection levels (Nelson, 2012, see also Figure 2.3 above) in this regard: at this level, the national poverty concept used in the design of the minimum income protection package, and the yardstick used to assess its effectiveness, may be more likely to overlap.

We find this discrepancy between minimum income protection package levels and the 60% at-risk-of-poverty threshold not only in the absolute income level that is guaranteed, but also in relation to how different needs by household sizes are taken into account. Minimum income protection benefit levels are in general differentiated by household size (Frazer & Marlier, 2016). This comes as no surprise since the main premise of minimum income protection is to protect households against poverty. Clearly, the benefit levels necessary to obtain this goal increase as there are more persons present in the household. Benefits generally do not increase one on one with additional household members. This is in line with common views in social policy and poverty research: household members are expected to benefit from economies of scale that stem from the fact that accommodation and appliances are shared (Ayala, Martinez, & Ruiz-Huerta, 2003).

The precise extent to which economies of scale benefit different household types and sizes is subject to a large empirical literature. Economists have developed various methods to estimate the benefits stemming from living in certain households relative to living alone (Bradbury, 2014). In this regard, it is common to speak of 'equivalence scales', measures that reflect how much higher the income of a certain household type vis-à-vis a reference household should be in order to achieve an equal standard of living or welfare, taking account both of additional needs and of economies of scales (EU China Social protection reform project, 2015). The 60% at-risk-of-poverty threshold is built on the modified OECD equivalence scale, in which the first adult counts for one, additional household members older than 14 count for 0.5, and children younger than 14 count for 0.3. In Table 2.1, we compare the equivalence scales implicit in the minimum incomes with this modified OECD equivalence sale. The MIP-implicit equivalence scales are calculated by taking the ratio of the simulated minimum income levels for different family types to the guaranteed minimum income level for a single person household. For instance, if the ratio of the guaranteed minimum income for a couple vs for a single is 1.8, this means that a couple is entitled to a minimum income that is 80% higher than the benefit of a single. A similar approach to calculate implicit equivalence scales in tax benefit schemes can be found in van de Ven et al. (2017), who calculate implicit equivalence scales for minimally guaranteed incomes in 12 European countries in 2012 based on model family simulations.[5]

Clearly, there is a mismatch between the modified OECD equivalence scale, and the equivalence scales that are actually implemented in minimum income protection packages. The modified OECD scale was proposed for use in the (then) European Community, where the European Commission favoured a common equivalence scale for comparisons of its Member States[6] (de Vos & Zaidi, 1997). According to this scale, there are non-negligible economies of scale for larger households, and the needs of children require less additional income than the needs of adults.[7]

Whereas compensation for the additional adult in case of couple households (and for additional household members in the case of couples with two children in the old EU MSs) is on average in line with the modified OECD scale, cross-country variation is large. Minimum income protection levels for adults are very nearly individualized in Denmark, whereas there is nearly no compensation for a second adult in Malta. The variation in implicit equivalence scales may reflect that in the specific national institutional and socio-economic context additional household members do require far more or less additional income to reach an equal living standard than a single household. Yet the extent of the variation in implicit equivalence scales points to the relevance of additional explanations.

Van de Ven, Hérault, and Azpitarte (2017, p. 267) suggest that the variation in implicit equivalence scales reflects differences in wider policy considerations 'than a limited response to consumer needs'. Whereas van de Ven, Hérault, and Azpitarte (2017) do not offer further explanations, the implicit equivalence scales presented in Table 2.1 can provide some insight. The widespread favourable treatment of family types (and especially lone parents) with children evident from Table 2.1 may reflect common deservingness notions (van Oorschot, 2000; Lepianka, Gelissen, & Van Oorschot, 2010) in a resource-constrained context (Arlotti & Sabatinelli, 2017), rather than an assessment of actual needs. Whereas able-bodied single adults or couples are often considered to be responsible for their own situation, this reasoning is far less clear-cut when there are children present in the household. If deservingness notions are more outspoken in some countries than in others, they could lead to further variation in benefit levels. Such considerations could be at work in the Central and Eastern European countries.[8] The United States offers an extreme case of this reasoning. The benefit levels for single person households and couples are based solely on food stamps (SNAP), leading to exceptionally low benefits. The higher TANF-complemented benefits for families with children lead to implicit equivalence scales unseen in a European context, not even in Lithuania, Poland, or Romania, the European countries in which families with children are ostensibly supported the most relative to single adults.

**Table 2.1** Implicit equivalence scales in guaranteed minimum incomes, 2021

| Country | Single | Couple | Lone parent with 2 children | Couple with 2 children |
|---|---|---|---|---|
| AT | 1.00 | 1.42 | 2.03 | 2.40 |
| BE | 1.00 | 1.33 | 1.98 | 1.98 |
| BG | 1.00 | 1.46 | 2.63 | 2.94 |
| CY | 1.00 | 1.35 | 1.81 | 2.15 |
| CZ | 1.00 | 1.49 | 1.79 | 2.04 |
| DE | 1.00 | 1.56 | 2.16 | 2.49 |
| DK | 1.00 | 1.94 | n.a. | 2.67 |
| EE | 1.00 | 1.38 | 2.19 | 2.53 |
| EL | 1.00 | 1.50 | 1.94 | 2.13 |
| ES | 1.00 | 1.50 | 1.68 | 1.85 |
| FI | 1.00 | 1.58 | 1.93 | 2.40 |
| FR | 1.00 | 1.35 | 1.75 | 1.97 |
| HR | 1.00 | 1.20 | 2.67 | 2.50 |
| HU | 1.00 | 1.90 | 2.70 | 3.35 |
| IE | 1.00 | 1.67 | 1.71 | 2.40 |
| IT | 1.00 | 1.26 | 1.26 | 1.51 |
| LT | 1.00 | 1.90 | 4.18 | 4.88 |
| LU | 1.00 | 1.48 | 1.87 | 2.18 |
| LV | 1.00 | 1.56 | 2.53 | 2.74 |
| MT | 1.00 | 1.08 | 1.37 | 1.40 |
| NL | 1.00 | 1.38 | 1.59 | 1.71 |
| PL | 1.00 | 1.47 | 4.44 | 4.63 |
| PT | 1.00 | 1.70 | 3.03 | 3.46 |
| RO | 1.00 | 1.80 | 5.55 | 5.80 |
| SE | 1.00 | 1.43 | 1.92 | 2.26 |
| SI | 1.00 | 1.55 | n.a. | 2.74 |
| SK | 1.00 | 1.79 | 1.95 | 2.54 |
| UK* | 1.00 | 1.22 | 1.92 | 2.03 |
| US* | 1.00 | 1.84 | 14.96 | 17.28 |
| Average—Europe | 1.00 | 1.49 | 2.33 | 2.63 |
| Average—all | 1.00 | 1.51 | 2.80 | 3.14 |
| Modified OECD scale | 1 | 1.5 | 1.8 | 2.3 |

*Source:* own calculations based on MIPI-HHoT. Data for the UK refer to 2020. Data for the US are based on Aerts, Marx, and Parolin (2022).

A second reason there may be a mismatch between minimum income protection packages and internationally comparable poverty measures, is that policy makers also struggle with more practical concerns when establishing benefit levels and equivalence scales. Budgetary concerns may not allow for an across the board increase in benefit levels. This issue may be amplified by a desire to keep a wedge between out-of-work minimum income protection, and income from work. Cantillon, Marchal, and Luigjes (2019) have for instance argued that the erosion of social assistance benefits is tied to the erosion of the minimum wages one can earn at the labour market. The decline of minimum wages has made the need for in-work benefits for low-wage earners more pressing but has also made it more costly to increase social assistance benefits and to maintain a reasonable wedge between out-of-work and in-work minimum incomes. If minimum incomes fully take account of additional needs, the possibility exists that large households will have larger out-of-work than in-work incomes. For this reason, a number of European countries have introduced benefit caps (Navicke, Avram, & Demmou, 2016). This may mean that from a certain number of household members, a certain benefit will no longer increase. In Croatia, for instance, the total amount of social assistance cannot exceed the level of the minimum wage, regardless of the number of household members (MISSOC, 2022). This concern may also be behind the expression of individual minimum income benefit levels as a percentage of the minimum wage, or other social benefits (see also Section 2.5.1). Alternatively, the total amount of benefits one family can receive, from different sources, may be capped at a certain level.[9] These approaches stand of course in stark contrast to results from reference budget-based, or other empirically estimated equivalence scales, that usually indicate non-linear increases for additional children, with hikes for especially large families, as cars and housing become more expensive (Gray & Stanton, 2010; Goedemé et al., 2015). Policy makers may also need to take account of incentives regarding household formation (Genettian & Millar, 2004; Pingle, 2005). For Belgium for instance, a report by Steenssens et al. (2016) highlighted the consequences of the rather low equivalence scales for couples without children, and the complete lack of differentiation between a lone parent with two children or a couple with two children, despite an additional (adult) mouth to feed (see Table 2.1). They find that such regulations can lead to forms of undeclared cohabitation or—more worryingly—postponement of new relations, keeping persons in more vulnerable household constellations. An individualization of benefits, as seems to be the case in Denmark, will not have these negative effects, but will of course be more expensive. At the same time, a recent study by Brink and Bouwmeester (2022) on the household dimension in Dutch social assistance legislation illustrates the difficulties posed by a generally accepted household-level concept of needs, and a societal movement towards ever more complex and partially individualized household formations. Clearly, policy makers juggle here with different objectives.

## 2.8 Not All the Poor Get Minimum Income Protection

### 2.8.1 There Are Far Less Minimum Income Beneficiaries than People in Poverty

In Table 2.2 below, we list the number of poor working age individuals in each country, at the 40% and at the 60% poverty threshold, as well as the number of minimum income protection beneficiaries according to the OECD Social Recipients (OECD SOCR) database. This dataset provides recipient numbers for old age, disability, unemployment, and social assistance schemes, as well as to other, more supplementary benefits. Depending on the specific national context, we find the schemes that are relevant to our target group (the non-working of active age) under the unemployment or the social assistance heading. Table 2.2 shows for each country the total number of recipient units of benefits relevant for the non-working of active age. For instance, for Germany, we show the total number of recipients in the (more unemployment focused) Arbeitlosengeld II, and in the general social assistance scheme Sozialhilfe. For the United States, we show the combined number of SNAP and TANF recipients. Also for other countries, we include the recipient number of categorical schemes for (lone) parents. For most countries however, the non-working of active age will fully fall under the general social assistance scheme. We exclude schemes that have very specific target groups (such as the disabled or newly arrived migrants), or do not serve to provide a minimum income.

It should be noted that recipiency numbers are notoriously hard to compare. Administrations keep track of beneficiaries according to their own definitions. In addition, minimum income protection benefits are needs-based, and are generally designed in order to cover the needs of households. Hence, the benefit may be a household benefit, but may also be split between the adults present in a household, or will only be split under specific conditions. Elsewhere, the administration may keep track of the number of beneficiaries, looking at the number of individuals living in each beneficiary household. Furthermore, recipient numbers may refer to the total number of households or recipients covered throughout the year, or refer to the stock at a particular moment in time. The OECD does an admirable job in streamlining the numbers provided by the administration. Still, quite some variation exists, as can be expected from different national legislation and practices. In Table 2.2 we provide the absolute number of recipient units, and, as a (not fully comparable) reference series, the number of people living in (severe) poverty.

**Table 2.2** Minimum income protection beneficiaries and number of working-age people living in poverty, 2018

| Country | Recipient units | Number of working age people living in a household with income < 40% median | Number of working age people living in a household with income < 60% of median |
|---|---|---|---|
| AT | 172,447 | 239,000 | 731,000 |
| BE | 159,512 | 256,000 | 1,043,000 |
| BG* | 102,744 | 381,000 | 795,000 |
| CY* | 43,664 | 13,000 | 76,000 |
| CZ | 69,040 | 117,000 | 495,000 |
| DE | 3,462,699 | 2,663,000 | 8,022,000 |
| DK | 108,472 | 210,000 | 499,000 |
| EE | 6,317 | 59,000 | 131,000 |
| EL | 871,491 | 603,000 | 1,275,000 |
| FI | 342,033 | 92,000 | 381,000 |
| FR | 1,907,228 | 1,072,000 | 4,779,000 |
| HR | 72,759 | 190,000 | 418,000 |
| HU | 106,052 | 330,000 | 818,000 |
| IE | 210,667 | 87,000 | 391,000 |
| IT | 243,027 | 3,838,000 | 7,544,000 |
| LT | 40,440 | 159,000 | 314,000 |
| LU | 10,316 | 25,000 | 64,000 |
| LV | 13,659 | 106,000 | 209,000 |
| MT | 8,542 | 10,000 | 40,000 |
| NL | 497,206 | 459,000 | 1,467,000 |
| PL | 317,560 | 1,431,000 | 3,602,000 |
| PT | 101,551 | 397,000 | 1,055,000 |
| RO | 202,976 | 1,497,000 | 2,611,000 |
| SE | 206,000 | 301,000 | 947,000 |
| SI | 52,862 | 44,000 | 156,000 |
| SK | 72,024 | 118,000 | 397,000 |
| CH | 172,693 | 181,000 | 591,000 |
| NO | 75,668 | 196,000 | 464,000 |
| UK | 2,063,531 | 2,461,000 | 6,465,000 |
| US* | 20,738,969 | *32,862,136* | |

*Note:* Data refer to 2018, at the time of writing the most recent year for which data were available in the OECD SOCR database. Number of poor are downloaded from Eurostat, with the exception of the US, for which we use the OECD SOCR-provided reference series. This reference series uses the OECD definition, i.e., it is based on a 50% threshold. The most recent recipient data available for BG and CY refer to 2016.
*Source:* https://www.oecd.org/social/recipients.htm, Eurostat.

The number of recipient units (often individuals) is usually substantially below the number of people at-risk-of-poverty at the 60% poverty threshold. Immervoll et al. (2022) report pseudo-coverage rates among the households below a 50% at-risk-of-poverty threshold, based on the SOCR dataset and referring to the situation in 2016. They find the number of income-poor household to be close to the number of recipient households in France, and around 75% in the Netherlands, Germany, and the Slovak Republic. In most other countries, recipient number are substantially lower. As minimum income protection packages are often well below 60% at-risk-of-poverty threshold, this comes as no surprise. Clearly, with benefit levels that are that inadequate, minimum income protection will have a hard time in lifting beneficiaries above the poverty threshold. Yet in most countries, this is also the case, though less outspokenly so, when we zoom in on severe poverty. In all but eight countries, the data listed in Table 2.2 show a (far) larger number of severely working age poor, than the number of recipient units. Moreover, mistargeting might mean that some of the recipient units are actually to be found above the poverty threshold. Clearly, minimum income protection schemes do not cover everyone with incomes below the guaranteed benefit level. Why is that the case?

## 2.8.2 Residualism in Action

Eligibility criteria define access to minimum income protection. These access criteria do not one on one overlap with 'being poor'. As minimum income protection is a residual scheme, first rights to other benefits need to be exercised. National poverty outcomes are indeed also influenced by the coverage and generosity of all relevant benefits in combination, of which specific minimum income benefits are only a small part. The European Commission and Social Protection Committee (2022) defines coverage as the share of population living at-risk-of-poverty or in quasi-jobless households that receives any benefit. Note that this indicator counts any benefit receipt (with the exception of old age benefits) as relevant in its definition of coverage. Partially, this is for pragmatic reasons: it is hard to identify specific benefits in the underlying survey data used to calculate coverage. At the same time, this operationalization highlights the residual nature of minimum income protection: it aims to fill the gaps left by other benefits. When those other benefits reach a substantial part of those in need, the task that means-tested minimum income protection benefits is up against, becomes less daunting. On average, 78.5% of the population that is either at-risk-of-poverty, or living in a quasi-jobless household (or both) is covered by some benefit in the EU in 2020 (up from 73.2% in 2015). As always, this average hides large country differences: less than 60% of this target population is covered in Romania and

Croatia, while Ireland, Finland, France, and Denmark reach coverage rates of over 95%. The report finds indications that a higher (overall) benefit coverage correlates with substantially lower poverty gaps among the quasi-jobless population (−0.62). Correlations between overall benefit coverage and poverty and material deprivation rates among the work poor are more limited (−0.3). Also the correlation between overall benefit coverage and the adequacy of means-tested minimum income protection benefits is rather weak at 0.4.

Also Eichhorst et al. (2023) stress the importance of the combination of provisions: they assess the adequacy of income protection for the unemployed. They highlight that an adequate protection requires both minimum income support as a benefit of last resort, but also—what they call—upstream benefits. Upstream benefits are the social insurance benefits that come first into play upon an unemployment spell. Even when taking account of both minimum income and upstream unemployment insurance benefits, they find large variation in the share of the unemployed covered, from as little as 10% in Poland, to nearly 90% in Belgium. They find higher coverage rates in the Scandinavian and continental European countries, relative to the Eastern European and Southern European countries. Ireland and the United Kingdom find themselves somewhere in between. Overall, they note that bar a few exceptions, the rankings according to overall coverage rates, and to the coverage rates of minimum income support separately, are similar. Only the Anglo-Saxon countries have a disproportionately large role for means-tested minimum income support in covering the unemployed (and vice versa for Belgium). They relate the overall coverage rates of the unemployed with the national at-risk-of-poverty rates, and highlight that the strong negative correlation between both 'forcefully illustrate that higher coverage rates coincide with improved social resilience' (p. 84).

Overall, these (social insurance) benefits are not necessarily much higher than the minimum income benefit. In the United Kingdom for instance, contributory-based jobseeker's allowance was before the introduction of the universal credit equal to the means-tested minimum income scheme for the non-working able-bodied of active age (i.e., the income-based jobseekers' allowance). Elsewhere, benefits may be somewhat higher, but generally not enough to escape the risk of poverty (Swedish Institute for Social Research, 2016; Van Limberghen et al., 2020). Part of the poor population will therefore be catered for by other inadequate benefits, such as unemployment or disability benefits. Only if no other scheme can step in, minimum income protection will step in for those who satisfy the eligibility criteria. Even then, these eligibility criteria can exclude specific groups of poor people.

### 2.8.3 On Eligibility: Access Conditions

Clasen and Clegg (2007) distinguished three types of eligibility criteria: conditions of category, of circumstance, and of conduct.

*Conditions of category* generally refer to the general target group that is considered in terms of broad, demographic characteristics such as age, nationality, and residence. There is quite some variation between countries: most countries in principle allow all active age, adult persons to file a claim. There are however some exceptions, such as Spain (at age 23), France and Luxembourg (at age 25), Cyprus (28), and Denmark (30) (European Commission and Social Protection Committee, 2022; MISSOC, 2022). The underlying principle is often that before that age, parents are still responsible to help their children make a start in life (Frazer & Marlier, 2016). Exceptions only apply if one already has a child of his or her own. Alternatively, categorical schemes may exist that cater specifically to younger citizens. In Denmark, young adults can for instance rely on the *Education allowance*, which has different conditions of conduct than the regular minimum income scheme. Also for countries who do allow access to the general scheme from age 18 onwards, some differentiation may apply: it can be the case that one can already be eligible for support from age 18 onwards, but that stricter conditions of (rarely) circumstance or (more often) conduct apply (European Commission and Social Protection Committee, 2022).

Within the EU Member States, it is generally required to be an EU citizen, but allowances are made for different types of migrants (either by extending eligibility to certain categories of recognized refugees or asylum seekers, or by separate assistance schemes) (Sainsbury, 2006; MISSOC, 2022). Importantly, residence requirements are common. This is in line with the purpose of minimum income protection as a tool to decrease or mitigate national poverty. Minimum income protection is not earned by prior contributions, hence, one is not entitled to a replacement income to do with as one sees fit. It is generally not allowed to structurally stay abroad while claiming minimum income protection benefits (Van Mechelen et al., 2011). Some countries take this requirement further: they expect there to be a longer-term connection between the home country and the claimant. This is especially relevant for non-EU citizens (European Commission and Social Protection Committee, 2022). The Italian Reddito di Cittadinanza for instance requires an overall residence of 10 years, of which at least two consecutive years immediately prior to the claim (https://www.redditodicittadinanza.gov.it/). Other countries apply less severe residence requirement (commonly three months, in line with European requirements, although longer time periods are possible) (MISSOC, 2022).

*Conditions of circumstance* are vital to minimum income protection's eligibility criteria. Minimum income protection is needs-based: it tops up available incomes to a minimum threshold in order to mitigate or combat poverty. Hence the assessment of available incomes is a crucial element of the means-test. As a general rule, all incomes are included, and the part between own incomes and the minimum income threshold is paid out as benefit. However, limited earnings from work may be exempt, or only taken into account for a certain percentage, in order not to remove all incentives to work (so-called earnings-disregards). Also, countries differ to the extent minimum income benefits can be combined with other benefits (see Box 2.2).

In addition, Eardley et al. (1996) and Marchal et al. (2021) have looked at the prevalence of asset requirements in the means-test. Assets are indeed important contributors to well-being which should be accounted for when making assessments of who is worse off (Christelis et al., 2009; Kuypers & Marx, 2019). Eardley et al. (1996) observed that along the axes of liquid capital disregards and the exemption of the family home, it was especially the Scandinavian countries, Austria, and Switzerland that had stringent asset tests. Marchal et al. (2021) distinguished between two main types of means-tests, rather than assessing stringency across an axis: (i) the disqualification type, that sets a threshold above which the possession of assets disqualifies for MIP, and (ii) the fictional rate of return type, in which assets are taken into account at a fictional rate of return, above what can realistically be expected, so that over time, assets will need to be realized in practice. Three countries have more atypical assessment of assets: France and Poland only assess assets if there is a large discrepancy between declared income and shown living standards, whereas Estonia fully depends on a discretionary assessment by the municipality of all assets and income in combination.

A final dimension of variation in the conditions of circumstance, both for income and for assets, relates to the extent the broader family members are held accountable to help in a situation of need. Usually, means are assessed at the household or family level (see also Box 2.2), although there is variation in terms of the exact relation to the household member. Frericks, Och, and Höppner (2019) found in their analysis of 10 countries that income of cohabiting partners is generally included when charting the need (and hence eligibility) of a prospective claimant. Some differences apply with regard to the existence and size of a disregard that is applied to a partner's income. In five out of 10 countries, this disregard decreased over time, increasing the household dimension of the means-test, whereas it increased (but often from a lower level) in three countries. The inclusion of the incomes of inhabiting children is generally less strict, and this is even more so when looking at incomes from more distant family members, especially when they are not cohabiting in the household.

Finally, *conditions of conduct* usually refer to the requirement that active-age non-working beneficiaries should aim to improve upon their situation by looking for work, the so-called 'willingness to work' criterion (Marchal & Van Mechelen, 2017; De Wilde & Marchal, 2019). Indeed, minimum income schemes in principle require all work-able recipients of working age to actively seek work (European Commission and Social Protection Committee, 2022). In a substantial share of countries, this willingness to work criterion is defined relatively vaguely. Claimants should be ready to accept a job offer, and take steps to look for work. However, legislation usually allows for good reasons to relax this willingness to work criterion, and related, more concrete, activation requirements: the Belgian legislation refers for instance to health and fairness reasons. The result is that the actual implementation of this requirement is often unclear and ultimately depends upon the discretion of social workers (see De Wilde & Marchal, 2019). Elsewhere, this requirement can be defined more stringently in the eligibility criteria: usually, it refers to the obligation to subscribe to the public employment agency prior to benefit receipt. Some countries also apply work-conditional benefit supplements (e.g., the Slovakian activation allowance) or make the entire benefit conditional upon a certain number of hours of community service (this was the case in Romania). Often, it is required to accept a job if one is offered, or to participate in active labour market programmes or training if these are offered (European Commission and Social Protection Committee, 2022).

Again, it is hard to assess how such requirements, which ultimately also depend on the availability of suited labour market programmes and jobs, play out on the ground (see also Marchal & Van Mechelen, 2017). In general, even when there is no direct tie between the benefit and participation in public works, participation in community service programmes will be expected when offered, at the risk of losing one's benefit. Such arrangements exist for instance in Croatia, Czechia, Hungary, and Latvia (European Commission and Social Protection Committee, 2022). Also other European countries report that public employment programmes are the activation programmes that are most commonly offered to minimum income beneficiaries (European Commission and Social Protection Committee, 2022). This is disconcerting, since meta-analyses have identified this form of active labour market programme to be the least effective (Card, Kluve, & Weber, 2010).

Policy evaluations of the effectiveness of either conditions of conduct, or more specifically active labour market programme participation of minimum income beneficiaries are hard to come by. The European Commission and Social Protection Committee (2022) report mentions that only few data are available, that are in addition hardly comparable. Still, it appears that levels of labour market activation for the target group of means-tested minimum income beneficiaries are relatively low, with often less than 10% of minimum income beneficiaries participating in an active labour market measure per year. Generally, this measure will not be specifically tailored to the needs of minimum income beneficiaries. Minimum income beneficiaries that transition towards the labour market after participating in active labour market policies vary widely between countries, ranging from 6% to around 50%, based on the administrative data summarized in the report. At the same time, the report stresses that around one third of minimum income beneficiaries have some (weak) form of labour market attachment, as observed from EU SILC analyses. Actual transitions from minimum income receipt towards labour market attachment observed in the EU SILC range from 5% to 30% between the different EU countries.

Specific groups, such as lone parents with young children, can be exempt from certain activation requirements, either because they face less stringent eligibility conditions (such as in Malta), or because they are covered by a separate means-tested income support scheme altogether. Such specific schemes for lone parents are usually less stringent on work search requirements (even going as far as to completely exempt lone parents with a young child) and in some countries also somewhat more generous in terms of disregarded incomes or benefit levels. However, whether or not a lone parent has access to such a scheme depends on the age of their (youngest) child. In Figure 2.1, our hypothetical lone parent household is covered by such a functionally equivalent benefit scheme specifically for lone parents caring at home for their children only in Ireland. The age threshold is currently being lowered, and will ultimately render the family type considered in Figure 2.1 ineligible. Even now, they are no longer covered by the one parent family payment, but are covered by the transitional jobseeker's allowance. Whereas a few years ago, lone parents with children aged 14 were still eligible for the separate one parent family benefit, in 2021 the youngest child should be younger than seven. This process makes more and more lone parent families subject to stringent job search requirements (Millar & Crosse, 2018). Before the implementation of the Universal Credit, also the United Kingdom had separate lone parent support, although the age requirement for the youngest child was more stringent than in Ireland. Also here, the children's age requirement was gradually tightened. In most other countries, lone parents are catered for under the general scheme for the able-bodied of active age, although the specific job search requirements this group faces may be relaxed. Marchal and Van Mechelen (2013) summarize for instance the job search requirements applicable in the EU Member States' minimum income schemes in 2012, and find that a lone parent with a young child will usually face less stringent job search conditions than a single person without dependents. Most countries rely for this assessment on the discretionary judgement of the social worker following up the beneficiary, but in some countries, for instance the Netherlands, such relaxations were at the time made explicit in legislation. In a more recent survey performed by Immervoll and Knotz (2018) various OECD countries indicate that the unavailability of child care for young children may be considered a valid reason to refuse a job offer. Still, explicit rules on this are rare.

### 2.8.4 As a Result: Relatively Low Eligibility Rates

Figari, Matsaganis, and Sutherland (2013) calculated the overlap between those eligible for minimum income protection based on legal criteria, and those considered poor for a number of European countries using the EU-SILC microdata. They programmed the non-discretionary eligibility conditions of category and conditions of circumstance to minimum income protection into the microsimulation model EUROMOD to identify which respondents were eligible for minimum income support, and compared their eligibility with their poverty status. (Note that the eligibility that they calculated in this way is a different concept from the recipient numbers mentioned above. Eligibility indicates whether someone would be entitled to a benefit, not whether they actually receive it.) They calculated theoretical coverage rates of minimum income protection among the poor population by dividing those who are both eligible to minimum income protection and poor, with the total number of working-age poor. They found that such theoretical coverage rates of minimum income protection among the poor population ranged from 17% in Austria to 73% in Poland, with coverage rates in most countries ranging from 25% to 50%. Zooming in on the population with incomes below 40% of the median equivalized household income, the coverage rate markedly increases to on average 70% over the 14 included countries. This leaves a large number of the poor still outside the realm of minimum income protection. They are not covered by minimum income protection *by design*, as they do not fulfil the conditions of category or conditions of circumstance other than income (such as assets) that are necessary for access to minimum income protection.

In a more recent analysis, also Immervoll et al. (2022) unsurprisingly found eligibility criteria to impact on the profile of minimum income beneficiaries. They estimated the likelihood of receiving a minimum income benefit relative to a number of socio-demographic characteristics, for a number of OECD countries. In countries that operate less stringent asset tests, homeowners and tenants were found to have similar probabilities of receiving minimum income benefits, while this was not the case in more stringent countries. Also Tervola, Mesiäislehto, and Ollonqvist (2023) find strong evidence for the importance of eligibility criteria in limiting benefit receipt. In their policy swap exercise on Finland and Sweden, they simulate the impact eligibility and generosity regulations have on the number of beneficiaries. They find that coverage rates are far higher in Finland because of typical design features, including less stringent means-tests that allow for some combination with income from work, higher norm levels and looser asset tests.

## 2.8.5 And Non-Take-Up to Boot

Low eligibility rates are even more problematic as we know from ample research that there is a large difference between those eligible to means-tested minimum income protection (the concept used by Figari, Matsaganis, and Sutherland (2013) for their analysis) and those actually receiving minimum income benefits. This discrepancy between those entitled and those actually taking up the benefit is characterized as non-take-up. Non-take-up rates can amount to over 60% for some benefits (Hernanz, Malherbet, & Pellizzari, 2004; Fuchs, 2009; Bouckaert & Schokkaert, 2011; Bargain, Immervoll, & Viitamäki, 2012). Specifically for means-tested benefits of last resort the estimates range from 49–62% in Austria, 57–76% in Belgium, 41.1–68.1% in Bulgaria, 72% in the Czech Republic, 55% in Finland, 50–64% in France, 43–45% in Hungary, 59–71% in Luxembourg, 72% in Portugal, 79% in Slovakia, and 39–45% in the UK (see Eurofound, 2015; Ko & Moffitt, 2022 for an overview of the estimates found in the literature). Note that these estimates are based on national, non-comparable studies. However, even though these estimates may not be directly comparable, it is clear that a large part of the target population is not being reached. This clearly impedes the potential of minimum income protection as an effective poverty-fighting policy tool.

Research into the causes of non-take-up usually focuses on the trade-off between the costs and benefits a potential claimant faces when claiming (social) assistance. Costs relate to the time and effort it takes to gather information on a benefit, realize one's eligibility, and take all necessary steps to start and finalize a claim, whereas benefits refer to the expected benefit level and duration of benefit receipt (Fuchs et al., 2020). Others have extended this framework with insights from behavioural economics (Baicker, Congdon, & Mullainathan, 2012). Scholars also stressed the importance of prohibitive access thresholds, and of feelings of stigma (Baumberg, 2016). Some see non-take-up as an additional targeting instrument that will make policies more efficient, as potential claimants will only self-select in support schemes when their need justifies the costs that one faces in applying for a benefit (Kleven & Kopczuk, 2011). Whereas this element is certainly at play, it does not unequivocally mean that we should not be concerned about non-take-up. This argument supposes that all potential claimants have the same competences to make this trade-off, whereas it has been demonstrated that this is not the case, especially not for those confronted with the highest need (Mani et al., 2013).

In addition, one should not neglect the role of the policy and of the implementation level. Non-take-up is generally higher for smaller benefits, as potential beneficiaries weigh the claiming costs harder than the expected benefits (Van Mechelen & Janssens, 2017; Janssens & Van Mechelen, 2022).[10] The organization of the claiming process, the user-friendliness of the system, the existence of automatic awarding or of broad information campaigns all contribute to lowering the risk of non-take-up (van Oorschot, 1994; Fuchs, 2009).

Means-tested minimum income protection benefits may perform less well on these domains than more well-known and bigger contributory benefit schemes. More so than other welfare state schemes, they are administered (and often also partially financed) at the local level (Sabatinelli, 2010), with substantial local variation as a consequence (Minas & Øverbye, 2010; Minas, Wright, & Van Berkel, 2011; Bonoli, Minas, & Trein, 2015; De Wilde & Marchal, 2019). The needs-based requirement is very strong in some countries: eligibility criteria may include discretionary assessments of assets and incomes (see Marchal et al., 2021). Some countries also only provide assistance after family members are contacted, or expect support to be paid back later under some conditions (MISSOC, 2017; Frericks, Och, & Höppner,

2019). Often, behavioural conditions apply that necessitate an assessment by social workers, which re-introduces less predictable variability in eligibility (De Wilde & Marchal, 2019). Some therefore say that minimum income protection is not always an effective guarantee (Panican & Ulmestig, 2016). Others argue that the possibility to appeal decisions, the clear regulations and an extensive administration that aims to deliver minimum income guarantees does represent an obvious breach from charity relief (International Labour Organization, 2016; Panican & Ulmestig, 2016), although high conditionality may make the actual exercising of this right less self-evident (Moreira, 2008).

## 2.9 What Do the Best Performing Countries Have in Common?

In sum, minimum income protection guarantees are a highly relevant part of the welfare state. They are designed as an ultimate safety net, showing a society's commitment to a social floor. As such, they represent a society's view on what a minimal social floor should look like. The research summarized in this chapter shows that this view does not necessarily equal internationally agreed at-risk-of-poverty concepts and definitions, that are commonly used to assess the effectiveness of social policies.

In addition, the data presented in this chapter show large variation in the level and composition of minimum income protection packages, ranging from less than 20% of the at-risk-of-poverty threshold in 2021, to just under 60% of the median equivalized household income.

Overall, and as already shown in Section 2.6, countries with higher minimum income protection packages generally tend to perform better with regard to at-risk-of-poverty rates. Figure 2.3 showed that *top performers in term of adequate benefits are also among the better performing countries in terms of at-risk-of-poverty rates, both at the 40% and the 60% threshold, with poverty rates well below the EU averages of 5.4% and 16.2%*. In line with the literature discussed above, this is not necessarily or always due to a direct link between both. Figure 2.3 also showed a number of exceptions to this general trend: both the Czech Republic and Slovakia have rather mediocre minimum income protection packages, but succeed in maintaining relatively low at-risk-of-poverty rates, especially at the 60% threshold (respectively 9.5% and 11.4%). This is also true for Hungary, one of the European countries with the lowest minimum income protection package.

In addition, minimum income protection retains an important signal function, as its level is usually the lowest protection level deemed acceptable by a society. Even when other income replacement schemes are responsible for the brunt of income protection and poverty reduction, the benefits these schemes provide are likely somewhat higher or equal to the guaranteed minimum income protection package.

This makes the question what matters for adequate minimum income packages highly salient.

This question was addressed recently by Aerts, Marx, and Parolin (2022), zooming in on the situation of (both working and non-working) lone parent households. They stress the importance of the generosity of the total child benefit package. Minimum income protection packages appear to be more adequate in countries that have generous child support packages. Generous child support packages are often made up of different layers, including means-tested and universal child benefits, as well as preferential treatment of children in the tax system and in other benefits. They also note that child support generosity tends to be higher when countries combine a universal layer with more targeted support. Building on Cantillon et al. (2020), they furthermore highlight the ceiling effect of low and minimum wages on minimum income protection packages for the non-working.

Figures 2.1 and 2.3 allow us to identify the top performers among the European countries in terms of adequate minimum income protection packages for those of working age. While there are clearly countries that provide relatively high benefits to specific family types, the number of countries that consistently are among the better performing for both families with and without children, as well as single person households versus couples, remains relatively limited. We find Denmark, Austria, the Netherlands, Finland, and Luxembourg in this group. With the exception of Luxembourg, these countries also rank among the better performing countries in terms of poverty outcomes.

Do we observe—apart from the level of their overall net minimum income protection packages—commonalities in the design of the minimum income provisions implemented in these countries?

A first—and obvious—observation is that *all four countries have a solid basis of means-tested minimum income protection benefits.* All four countries have a relatively comprehensive general scheme of last resort, that is in the case of Finland in addition to a more categorical scheme for the workable of working age. Main features and design elements of the minimum income scheme are generally decided at the national level (be it with substantial leeway to the regional level in the case of Austria), whereas the actual delivery of the benefits is executed at lower governance levels. Importantly, discretionary elements pertaining to benefit levels and eligibility criteria are relatively limited in all four countries (Frazer & Marlier, 2016). These features point towards fairly comprehensive and rights-based social floors. Whereas the actual basis on which the minimum income benefit level is determined differs (in line with actual living standards in Finland, the minimum wage in the Netherlands, or more ad hoc in Austria and Denmark), all four countries apply regular and fixed benefit uprating (Frazer & Marlier, 2016).

A second observation is that *all four countries explicitly aim to cover housing costs* through either a separate housing allowance scheme, or through a specific housing cost related part of social assistance[11] (de Vos, 2021; Greve & Azhar Hussain, 2021; Premrov & Fuchs, 2021; Räsanen & Simanainen, 2021). Evidently, means-tested minimum income protection levels do take account of this additional compensation offered to some extent, as minimum income protection levels are somewhat lower than they are in other countries where social assistance levels are in general supposed to cover housing costs. Still, there clearly is attention for this large expense category, in a way that is generally explicitly tied to the actual costs faced, rather than to a more fictional budget post, that may be rendered obsolete or defined in a more arbitrary way (see Section 2.5). Note that such a practice may also have drawbacks. In our conceptualization of the total net minimum income package (and hence also in our assessment of their relative generosity) we assume that all benefits to which a certain family is entitled, are also actually claimed and received. It goes without saying that the more fragmented the income support package is, the higher the risk that some components fail to get claimed (Buysse et al., 2017; Van Mechelen & Janssens, 2017).[12] However, this may also work in the other direction. To the extent that housing allowances are less stigmatizing and more generally available than means-tested minimum income support, they may offer a form of income protection to vulnerable households when they have not (yet) filed a claim for social assistance support. Such a mechanism may well be at play in three of our 'well-performing' countries, with recipiency numbers of the housing allowances schemes generally largely surpassing those of the means-tested social assistance schemes, in the Netherlands even with a factor of up to three (OECD, 2023b).

Third, we note, specifically for the minimum income protection packages offered to families with children, *relatively sizeable child benefit packages.*[13] These are largely, if not exclusively, universal in Finland and Austria (as well as in Luxembourg). The Netherlands provides a more limited universal child benefit, topped up by a means-tested benefit, that is very sizeable for single-parent families. Non-take-up is usually far less problematic for universal benefits. Finally, Denmark only provides a non-means-tested benefit to single-parent households. In addition, a means-tested child benefit exists, which increases the net disposable income of a hypothetical non-working couple with two children with 7% of the at-risk-of-poverty threshold. With an (annual) income threshold of around 110,000 euro before a withdrawal rate kicks in, the means-test appears to focus on excluding the wealthy, rather than targeting the poorest (Greve & Azhar Hussain, 2021).

Evidently, there are still differences in the subsequent treatment of these (quasi-) universal child benefits in the interplay with means-tested benefits that together make up the total minimum income protection package, but it is clear that they have the potential to provide a secure socle. Neither are these the sole provisions available to families with children. In Austria, family allowances and the child tax credit are disregarded in the minimum income protection means-test. On top of that, higher rates are applied within the minimum income protection scheme for families with children. Likewise, the level of the Finnish labour market subsidy includes child supplements, while at the same time disregarding child benefits in the means-test[14] (Räsanen & Simanainen, 2021). This is also the case in Denmark (Greve & Azhar Hussain, 2021). Also in the Netherlands, child benefits and child tax credits are excluded from the means-test, as are housing allowances which are higher for larger families. Social assistance benefit base rates generally do not differ for families with and without children, unless household heads are relatively young (de Vos, 2021). Overall, the practices to support low-income families with children in these four well-performing countries, appear to be in line with the findings from Aerts, Marx, and Parolin (2022) that *countries combining targeted and universal child support, succeed in guaranteeing more generous child support packages.* We return to the political economy arguments that underlie this issue in Chapter 5.

*The presence of more universal or easily accessible 'socle benefits' is especially relevant as we cannot—not even in the best performing countries—assume that all the poor have access to the residual minimum income scheme.* These benefits are explicitly conceived as last resort benefits, meaning that generally all means as well as one's own efforts to improve one's situation will be taken into account to establish eligibility. In all of the four well-performing countries, relatively stringent asset tests limit access to the means-tested scheme (Marchal et al., 2021).[15] With the exception of Finland, the coverage among the working age population is not exceptionally high. At 3% of the working age population, it is around the European average in Denmark and Austria, and somewhat higher in the Netherlands (at 5%). Finland has recipiency rates of around 10%, which is the highest in Europe, but not out of line with other countries that have specific categorical schemes for those able to work, such as Germany and Ireland. Partially, this high recipiency rate is also due to the functioning of the labour market subsidy as a top-up to low other benefits (OECD, 2023b). In Table 2.2, we already showed the discrepancy between minimum income protection recipient numbers, and the numbers of those below the at-risk-of-poverty threshold. In none of the four well-performing countries do these numbers align (nor do they overlap fully in other countries included in Table 2.2, at least not with the 60% at risk of poverty rate). *To the extent that other benefits—that may even be more easily accessible or less stigmatizing—fill up this gap, this is not necessarily problematic.* The extent to which relatively generous benefit schemes of last resort operate in well-functioning welfare states is therefore highly relevant (Natili, 2020; Eichhorst et al., 2023). The rather favourable poverty outcomes in our four examples of adequate minimum income protection package countries suggest that this is actually the case.

Finally, we consider the activation strategies targeted at minimum income protection beneficiaries in Austria, the Netherlands, Denmark, and Finland. Indeed, an important element regulating (continued) access to a benefit of last resort, is to demonstrate one's efforts and willingness to improve one's situation (Immervoll & Knotz, 2018). Actively looking for work—unless such a target is deemed to be impossible for health or fairness reasons (such as care responsibilities)—is a common eligibility condition in minimum income schemes (Immervoll & Scarpetta, 2012; Marchal & Van Mechelen, 2017). Also in the four well-performing countries we consider here, the requirement to actively participate to society (and preferably the labour market), is mentioned as an explicit eligibility condition, and further stressed in the name of the benefit in the Netherlands (the participation act in the Netherlands). Denmark even applies a specific benefit ceiling to claimants who fail to reach a specific number of hours worked prior to and during their social assistance benefit receipt (Greve & Azhar Hussain, 2021). Finland employed a similar reduction to the labour market subsidy benefit from 2018 to 2020 for those who failed to meet work requirements (Räsanen & Simanainen, 2021).

An in-depth comparison of more specific activation policies is hard, if not altogether impossible, given the individualized and discretionary approach taken in most minimum income schemes, that may moreover differ between localities (Kazepov & Barberis, 2013; Knotz, 2018; De Wilde & Marchal, 2019).

Immervoll and Knotz (2018) report on the results from a 2017 standardized survey among the OECD Employment, Labour and Social Affairs Committee delegates, and the Indicators Subgroup of the European Union

Social Protection Committee members. This survey asked after the legal behavioural requirements imposed on both unemployment insurance and social assistance beneficiaries. Their analysis summarizes the received answers in an overall strictness indicator, an indicator focusing on the strictness of availability requirements, job-search and reporting requirements, and benefit sanction provisions. No clear image appears from these strictness scores. Out of 26 OECD countries for which it was possible to calculate an overall strictness score, Denmark, Finland, and Austria find themselves among the less strict half, whereas the Netherlands are found just above the median. Scores on the subdomains vary however greatly. Finland is relatively lenient with regard to the definition of a reasonable job and precise job search monitoring, but relatively more strict with regard to the severity of sanctions that are possible in case of job or active labour market programme participation refusal, whereas Denmark shows the precise opposite. Also, it is hard to assess to what extent these legal differences also exist on the ground. Often, these requirements relate to the possibilities case managers have, but a discretionary assessment remains necessary. In addition, it is hard to gauge the practical implementation of these job and ALMP offers, nor does the survey inquire after the quality of the ALMP accessible to minimum income beneficiaries.

In Marchal and Van Mechelen (2017), the results are summarized from a custom-designed survey among national academic experts, probing into the treatment of specific cases of minimum income beneficiaries in a large city in each country. This exercise hence explicitly aimed to overcome the issues related to the localized and discretionary implementation of minimum income protection. Still, the comparison could not fully overcome these challenges. As a result, Denmark could not be included in the analysis. In addition, the focus very much was on requirements that could be expressed in local or national guidelines, as is also the case in Immervoll and Knotz (2018). Respondents were however encouraged to consider the specific characteristics of two hypothetical minimum income beneficiaries. In addition, the survey also inquired after the most likely type of ALMP available to minimum income beneficiaries, and the range of different types of ALMP—including training—to minimum income beneficiaries. The findings showed that the Netherlands, Finland, and Austria, together with Slovenia, Belgium, and Luxembourg, were relatively close to an active inclusion ideal type of activation strategies. This ideal type can be best described as combining adequate minimum income protection support with a broader range of ALMP types and protective labour market policies, while at the same time safeguarding incentives and targeting a range of additional services to minimum income beneficiaries. Different from other EU Member States, the incentives were generally in the form of job search requirements and monitoring, coupled to sanctions, rather than installing a gap between out-of-work and in-work incomes. Evidently, the extent to which the different countries focused on services, vis-à-vis enabling ALMPs and incentives differed. In this regard, it is worth noting that the recent report by the European Commission and Social Protection Committee (2022) mentions that Denmark performs exceptionally well relative to other Member States in providing education and relevant labour market training to minimum income beneficiaries. Both Denmark and Austria reward ALMP participation by minimum income protection beneficiaries financially. A recent paper by Bothfeld, Eydoux, and Leibetseder (2022) however highlights that after several years of continuous efforts to include Austrian minimum income beneficiaries in the target group for vocational training by the public employment service, these efforts have recently been scaled back for the hard-to-place target group. This makes the quality of training and ALMP offered once again more conditional upon the regional and local importance addressed to it. *Still, there are indications that the provision of adequate income support in the well-performing countries is generally coupled to both relatively stringent, but also high-quality activation policies.*

# 3

# Minimum Income Protection for Workers

## Guaranteed Incomes at the Minimum Wage

### 3.1 Introduction

This chapter looks at minimum income protection for workers—or, more exactly, people mainly reliant on earned income.

Over the last decades, the activation turn has put employment, as a tool to combat poverty, front and centre in policy debates. Still, efforts to guide out-of-work benefit recipients to work through a combination of policies, including sanctions and increased conditionality, next to training and work experience programmes, are only credible if employment actually provides people without work a real step forward. It is thus essential 'to make work pay', to use a much-used slogan. Stubbornly stable (or even increasing) in-work poverty rates show however that this is easier said than done.

In this chapter we look at what makes for adequate minimum income protection for workers. It is, however, far from straightforward to define what actually constitutes minimum income protection for workers, as it is not solely determined by legally guaranteed benefits, but also—or even mainly—by the incomes earned on the labour market.

A large part of this chapter looks at income protection guaranteed to workers who are full-time employed at the minimum wage, as an ideal typical benchmark case. The situation of minimum wage earners is a useful indicator to gauge the protection guaranteed to workers in general, as this situation should in principle be 'the least favourable'. It is supposed to capture the guaranteed incomes for legally employed workers, through a legal instrument (an enforced minimum wage) and its tax and benefit treatment.

Proponents of a minimum wage indeed often highlight the inherent value of adequate minimum wages, in providing fair remuneration and decent incomes for workers (International Labour Organization, 2008; Bray, 2013). Still, on top of these normative arguments, scholars have also highlighted the

*Zero Poverty Society.* Sarah Marchal and Ive Marx, Oxford University Press. © Sarah Marchal and Ive Marx (2024).
DOI: 10.1093/9780191967771.003.0003

beneficial function of a minimum wage in the broader economy. In the situation of a monopsony, the setting of a minimum wage may have beneficial effects, both on wages and on employment (Card & Krueger, 1994; Manning, 2021). In addition, spill-over effects can have a positive impact on the labour force at large, and not only on the affected workers (Cengiz et al., 2019). Minimum wages are considered useful to protect workers with low bargaining power (and will indirectly also address the gender pay gap). In addition, they can help make work pay and support domestic demand, hence adding to the resilience of the economy.

A recent study by Cantillon and colleagues (2020) highlights a functional argument in favour of sufficiently high minimum wages that stands slightly apart from this more economic focus. As the key determinant of the income that can be minimally gained from work, minimum wages co-determine the scope for increasing out-of-work benefits, as policy makers may want to safeguard financial incentives to access the labour market for the unemployed. Their study shows empirically that increases in out-of-work income protection predominantly took place in countries where in-work protection increased, either through raising the minimum wage or through increasing in-work benefits.

Both these normative and functional arguments in favour of the minimum wage have gained traction in times of increasing in-work poverty: One in six workers in the EU earns a low wage, while in-work poverty in the euro area increased from 7.5% in 2005 to 13% in 2021 (European Commission, 2020b). Series for the EU as a whole are more limited in time, but still record an increase from 9.7% in 2007 to 12.2% in 2018 (Eurostat, 2023).

In this chapter, we therefore focus on the role of the minimum wage in defining the minimum income protection guaranteed to workers. To this end, we sketch the history of the minimum wage (Section 3.2), its determinants (Section 3.3) and employment effects (Section 3.4). We then discuss the variation in the level and relevance of minimum wages in the overall wage distribution (Section 3.5). In Sections 3.6 and 3.7 we discuss in depth the adequacy and design of the different policy instruments that together define the adequacy of the minimally guaranteed net disposable income for a full-time minimum wage worker and his or her family. At the same time, it is clear that there are problems with the selection of a hypothetical full-time minimum wage worker as an ideal typical representative of the in-work income floor. Full-time employment is by no means evident for vulnerable workers. In addition, increasingly, atypical work forms limit the applicability of the minimum wage as an actual in-work income floor in many countries. We address these issues at length in Section 3.8. Finally, we assess the link between in-work income floors and poverty, and list which policy instruments appear to be most relevant in guaranteeing adequate minimum income protection packages for the working population (Sections 3.9 and 3.10).

## 3.2 A Short History of the Minimum Wage

Originally, minimum wages were usually developed at the company and sectoral level, at the instigation of the early trade unions (Dingeldey et al., 2021). Later, national minimum wages got introduced. Over the course of the twentieth century, most EU Member States and other Western nations introduced minimum wages (see Table 3.1). The United States acted very early, installing a minimum wage in 1938, in order to prevent exploitation of workers and to guarantee survival (living) wages. Also the Australian minimum wage goes far back, again with the focus on ensuring wages on which minimum wage households can live, in the absence of a strong welfare state (Bray, 2013). Belgium, France, the Netherlands, and Southern European countries installed a nation-wide minimum wage at the latest by the end of the 1970s. According to the Federal Ministry of Labour and Social Affairs (1999) the Belgian minimum wage was introduced to guarantee an acceptable social minimum to workers. Also in other countries that introduced minimum wages at that time, the main concern appears to have been inspired by the need for adequate living standards for workers (see e.g., Centre for Parliamentary History, 2014 for the Netherlands). The implementation of the minimum wage in Portugal was inspired by the Constitution, that effectively mandates the state to 'establish and update the national minimum wage, taking into account the needs of workers, the increase in the cost of living, the level of development of the forces of production, the requirements of economic and financial stability and the cumulative effect of these factors on development, amongst other factors' (as cited in Niscimento, 1997). The Eastern European countries all installed minimum wages after the collapse of the Soviet Union.

The UK was relatively late to introduce a national minimum wage. After a long foray with sectoral minimum wages, set by sectoral wage councils since the early 1900s that were eventually abolished in 1993 by a Conservative government, the incoming Labour government implemented a national minimum wage in April 1999. The level and form of this new national minimum wage were researched in the Low Pay Commission (LPC) prior to its implementation. The arguments in favour of the new national minimum wage were to eradicate the worst cases of exploitation (as stated by the chair of the LPC at the presentation of its report), but also to create a more committed, productive, and competitive workforce (Gilman, 1998; Edwards, 1999). Slightly different arguments were headed in Ireland that introduced a national minimum wage at around the same time (see Table 3.1), with trade unions arguing that the wealth generated by the—then—economic boom should also trickle down to low-wage workers, and that it would impede competition based on cheap labour. An important argument—that resurfaced in the UK during the Living Wage Movement of 2010 (cf. infra)—was that tax payers were effectively subsidizing low paying employers by funding means-tested welfare benefits that complemented low earnings. Employers on the other hand argued against the minimum wage, fearing it would lead to job losses in low paid sectors and increase the overall wage bill through spillover effects (Sheehan & Geary, 1998; Dobbins, 1999).

Germany followed suit in 2015, under a coalition of the Christian democrats and the social democrats. The late introduction was due to the fact that most leading parties were long time in favour of industry level minimum wages. Some of the earlier proposals were foremost preoccupied with making collective bargaining mandatory at the industry level, with a wage floor applicable to sectors of the economy that did not already have a minimum wage, for fear of too much interference with the labour market. Under impetus of the social democratic SPD party, the notion of a humane minimum wage gained traction, on grounds of human dignity and social justice. Also here, the argument was used that without a minimum wage, the government was subsidizing low-wage employment through welfare. Voices against stressed the risk of job losses in the regular labour market. The minimum wage was introduced in a context of high low-wage employment that had increased in the wake of the 2003–2005 Hartz labour market and social policy reforms, against a background of declining trade union strength and in a prosperous economic climate. At the same time, the *Arbeitlosengeld II*, the social welfare benefit for the non-working of active age, which set an implicit reservation minimum wage, became less generous (James, 2007; Schuseil, 2013).

Cyprus has implemented a national minimum wage on 1 January 2023. It is set at 940 euros per month, around 60% of the median wage, after six months of employment. This requirement will likely exclude seasonal workers from this higher amount. In the six-month probation period, a minimum wage of 885 euro applies. Certain groups are excluded, in particular domestic workers, trainees, and those working in the shipping, farming, and livestock handling sectors. Reductions of up to 25% to this base rate are possible if the employer provides food and accommodation, as well as reductions for minor seasonal workers (Theodoulou, 2022). The Cypriot government announced in 2019 that it would investigate the introduction of a minimum

**Table 3.1** Year of introduction of national minimum wages

| Country | Introduction | Source |
|---|---|---|
| AUS | 1923/1964/1977/1997 | years refer to broad reforms, Bray (2013) |
| BE | 1975 | OECD (2017) |
| BG | 1990 | Loukanova and Tzanov (2011) |
| CZ | 1991 | OECD (2017) |
| DE | 2015 | OECD (2017) |
| EE | 1991 | Vaughan-Whitehead (2010) |
| EL | 1955: national minimum wage set in national-level bipartite bargaining<br>2012: statutory minimum wage without any inputs from collective bargaining | Karamessini and Grimshaw (2017) |
| ES | 1963 | OECD (2017) |
| FR | 1970 (SMIC: salaire minimum interprofessionnel de croissance, successor of the SMIG—salaire minimum interprofessionnel garanti) | Concialdi (1999) |
| HR | 1998: national minimum wage by extension of the lowest bargained wage<br>2008: statutory minimum wage linked to the average wage | Vaughan-Whitehead (2010) |
| HU | 1989 | Vaughan-Whitehead (2010) |
| IE | 2000 | OECD (2017) |
| LT | 1991 | Vaughan-Whitehead (2010) |
| LU | 1945: general minimum wages<br>1957: minimum wages with regular adjustment | Starr (1981) |
| LV | 1991 | Vaughan-Whitehead (2010) |
| MT | 1974 | Vaughan-Whitehead (2010) |
| NL | 1968 (coverage later extended from 25+ to 23+) | Centre for Parliamentary History (2014) |
| PL | 1989 | OECD (2017) |
| PT | 1974–1978: national minimum wage (lower rate for agriculture, forestry and domestic workers)<br>1991: general national minimum wage (except lower rate for domestic workers) | Nascimento (1997) |
| RO | 1990 | Vaughan-Whitehead (2010) |
| SK | 1991 | OECD (2017) |
| SI | 1995 | OECD (2017) |
| UK | 1999 | Edwards (1999) |
| US | 1938 | James (2007) |

*Note:* we thank Henri Haapanala for his support in revising this table.

wage, to replace the outdated statutory sectoral minimum wages, if the unemployment rate decreased under 5%. A thorough investigation of the issue of a Cypriot minimum wage, aided by the European Commission and the ILO, was commissioned (Eurofound, 2019a, 2020a). Social partner involvement was encouraged throughout the negotiation process, with the trade unions advocating for a statutory minimum wage, on the grounds of preventing the exploitation of (mainly unskilled) workers. Employers stressed the dangers of harmful employment prospects, especially during crises, and argued for the exclusion of certain groups of workers, such as domestic servants and farm workers, who usually receive food and board as part of their remuneration package (Financial Mirror, 2021). While the plans were temporarily put on hold due to the COVID-19 crisis (ILO, 2021), by 2022 the introduction for a statutory minimum wage was firmly back on tracks.

The same type of arguments of job loss versus wage inequality, fairness, and—more recently—the desired interaction with in-work benefits in ensuring decent incomes (e.g., Wilson, 2017), emerge time and again when an implementation of minimum wages is considered. Similarly, when policy makers ponder substantial increases to the minimum wage, for instance after a welfare erosion of the value of the minimum wages, these arguments resurface. In Sections 3.3 and 3.4, we further touch upon the employment effects and determinants of minimum wage levels respectively.

For now, a number of EU Member States are still without a national minimum wage. This is the case in the Scandinavian countries, Austria, and Italy. Especially since the introduction of the German minimum wage in 2015, political agents in these countries have pondered the introduction of a national minimum wage, but so far these ideas have not gained much traction in the Scandinavian countries. In Denmark, one of the trade unions defended a national minimum wage as a prerequisite to fight social dumping; however, the other trade unions remain in favour of sectoral agreements (Jørgensen, 2015). In Finland, one of the employers' organizations advocated for the introduction of a statutory minimum wage, coupled with a reform of the collective bargaining system. Also this proposal was not pursued further (Eurofound, 2019a).

In contrast, social partners in Austria are slowly taking steps towards more national level coordination of minimum wages. In 2009, employers represented in the Chamber of Commerce and trade unions agreed on a minimum wage of 1000 euro per month, covering nearly all of the workforce (European Commission, 2010). Later, under threat of the introduction of a minimum wage by the government, the social partners developed a roadmap for introducing a minimum wage of 1500 euro by 2019 (Eurofound,

2019a). Again, this is not a statutory minimum wage. In fact, the new minimum wage was implemented through sectoral collective agreements along sector-specific timelines (Eurofound, 2017a). In Italy, the issue of the minimum wage has been readdressed in the last couple of years, with the Cinque Stelle movement advocating for binding sectoral minimum wage agreements between the employers' and workers' organizations that are most representative at national level, and in any case not below 9 euro per hour. Other parties made slightly different proposals, that mainly differ on the definition of the last resort level (for instance to be established by an independent board, or to be based on the average wages within a sector). These—and other—proposals were investigated and further considered (Eurofound, 2019a, 2019b, 2020a). Subsequent government changes have however derailed this former point of attention (Eurofound, 2022).

As already evident from the European Pillar of Social Rights, which explicitly mentions adequate minimum wages as one of its 20 main principles (European Commission, 2017), the European Commission has embraced a more positive stance regarding more protective labour market institutions (Müller & Schulten, 2022). This has resulted in a legislative trajectory towards a binding directive on adequate minimum wages, which was voted in the European Parliament in September 2022 (European Parliament, 2022b; Pape, 2022) and by the Council of the EU on 4 October 2020 (Council of the EU, 2022). The minimum wage directive will set EU Member States on a path to high level collective bargaining coverage or statutory minimum wages defined in line with a reference value such as 60% of the median wage. In Box 3.1, we discuss more fully the trajectory towards, and the contents of, this Directive.

## 3.3 Determinants of the Wage Floor

Arguments in favour of the introduction of minimum wages often centre on issues of fairness and the containment of wage inequality (see Section 3.2). It is important to keep well in mind that there are other institutions affecting wage inequality and effective wage floors, often even more so than legal minimum wages. Trade union strength is particularly important, as are collective bargaining institutions and regimes. There exists in fact a remarkably strong and consistent relationship at the country level between collective bargaining coverage and measures of wage compression and low pay.[1] This happens because trade unions generally pursue 'equal pay for equal work' agendas resulting in larger wage gains for workers in lower-paid occupations compared to workers in higher-paid occupations. This compresses earnings differentials, especially at the lower end (OECD, 2004; Grimshaw, Bosch, & Rubery, 2014; Salverda & Checchi, 2014; Alsos, Nergaard, & Van Den Heuvel, 2019; Vlandas, 2019; Fortuna & Neto, 2021; Garnero, 2021; Howell, 2021; Benassi & Vlandas, 2022; Bhuller et al., 2022; Howell & Kalleberg, 2022; Zwysen, 2022; De Becker et al., 2023; Haapanala, Marx, & Parolin, 2023).

Union membership and collective bargaining have generally declined in Europe and elsewhere in the rich world. It remains particularly strong in the Nordic countries (and more broadly the so-called Ghent countries, including for example Belgium) but even there union strength appears to be under pressure. Moreover, the changing composition of union membership may have brought a decline in solidaristic wage bargaining (Haapanala, Marx, & Parolin, 2023). With the decline in blue-collar manufacturing, the main groups of unionized workers in advanced democracies are white-collar professionals, public sector administrators, and other groups of middle-income workers (Becher & Pontusson, 2011). This may have brought a shift away from solidaristic wage bargaining as union members prioritize gains for their own reference group over broader equality in the wage distribution (Vlandas, 2019; Cronert & Forsén, 2023).

What is certain is that declining union membership and collective bargaining have coincided with an increase in the incidence of low paid work in at least a number of countries, Germany being a prominent case (Bosch, 2018). Having long resisted a legally set minimum wage, the German trade unions have in effect been forced towards an acceptance of a nation-wide statutory minimum wage.

Also other interest groups have started focusing on the minimum wage as a useful tool for a fair(er) labour market. Noteworthy in this regard is the living wage movement. This movement stands particularly strong in the Anglo-Saxon countries. It encourages individual employers and companies towards committing themselves to providing 'living' wages to their employees. The level of such living wages is determined based on what employees (and their families) need to have for a decent life, effectively bringing a reference budget logic in the determination of fair wages (Living Wage Foundation, 2016; Eurofound, 2018; D'Arcy & Finch, 2019). The proposed minimum wages may therefore show quite some variation, depending on the place where the company is located (and hence the housing and other costs that the living wage should be able to cover). In a national policy context, a living wage-centred minimum wage explicitly refers to the standard of living that should be attained by a minimum wage worker. In Ireland, the Low Pay Commission has received a mandate to prepare a report on the potential for a living wage in the Irish context, to be understood as the minimum income necessary for a single adult worker in fulltime employment, with no dependents, to meet his or her basic needs and afford a minimum acceptable standard of living (Eurofound, 2022). Experiences in Malta (where a preparatory research report was not published) and Romania (where the living wage failed to get implemented) highlight, however, the difficulties related to the definition of such a reference based budget living wage (Eurofound, 2022).

Recently, also the European Commission has taken an interest in promoting adequate minimum wages (European Commission, 2020a). In the context of the single market of the EU, additional considerations are at play in the promotion and coordination of adequate national minimum wages. Arguments in favour centre around combating externalities created by the single market, such as social dumping, and the need for transparent wage-setting mechanisms in order to foster economic growth (Watt, 2019; Andor, 2020). As can be inferred from the discussion in Section 3.2, not all national Member States' trade unions are in favour of a binding EU legislative initiative regarding minimum wages. Especially in the Scandinavian countries, where trade unions stand strong, there is no immediate demand for EU initiatives in this field. In the EU's consultation round prior to its proposal for a new EU Minimum wage Directive, the European Trade Union Confederation (ETUC) instead proposed that EU regulations should be modified to allow government contracting only for companies that participate in collective bargaining, or follow the agreements, or at the very least to no longer prohibit national governments from including such requirements in open tenders (ETUC, 2020). In Box 3.1, we discuss the resulting EU Minimum Wage Directive in more detail.

### Box 3.1 The EU minimum wage directive

Whereas the European Commission in the austerity crisis following the 2008 financial and economic crisis still advocated looser collective bargaining regulations and lower minimum wages, the latest couple of years have shown a profound commitment towards making Europe more social (Müller & Schulten, 2022). The proclamation of the (non-binding) European Pillar of Social Rights in 2017, by the European Parliament, Council, and Commission, was an important step in this regard. The commitments put forward in the EPSR have since been re-affirmed in the Porto Declaration (European Commission, 2021), and have given rise to various legislative initiatives by the current Von Der Leyen Commission.

European Commissioner for Jobs and Social Rights Nicolas Schmitt developed a proposal for a legal instrument to ensure workers in the EU have fair minimum wages, following up on principle 6 of the EPSR (European Commission, 2020c). Building on elaborate consultation rounds with various stakeholders (European Commission, 2020a; Marchal, 2020; Pape, 2022), this proposal ultimately gave rise to a provisional agreement between the Council and the European Parliament on new EU law on 7 June 2022. In September 2022, the European Parliament voted (with a large majority) in favour of this agreement (European Council, 2022; European Parliament, 2022b). Ultimately, the directive was adopted by the Council of the EU on 4 October 2022, after which the EU Member States have two years to translate the directive into national law (Council of the EU, 2022).

The directive hinges on two key points. First, it aims to ensure that adequate minimum wages protect EU workers, allowing for a decent living. Second, the directive aims to strengthen collective bargaining as the main instrument to ensure fair wages and working conditions (The European Parliament and the Council of the European Union, 2022).

In principle, the EU competences to interfere in national pay rates are limited. The legal basis of the directive is Article 153 of the Treaty of the Functioning of the European Union, which covers working conditions, but excludes interventions relating to pay (Official Journal of the European Union, 2016). In consequence, the directive does not prescribe specific minimum wage rates (nor, in fact, the introduction of a statutory minimum wage in those countries that rely solely on collective bargaining). Rather, the directive supports upward social convergence of minimum wages, pointing to the likely beneficial effects on the EU economy of fair and transparent wage-setting mechanisms and the favourable social impact (European Commission, 2020c; Pape, 2022). The directive hence focuses more on creating a binding framework that would ensure such upward social convergence of fair and transparent working conditions (Pape, 2022).

Consecutive consultation rounds and negotiations between the Member States, the Council, the Parliament, and the Commission ultimately led to the following key elements of the framework, that will apply to all EU workers who have an employment contract or an employment relationship. Those countries that have statutory minimum wages are required to assess whether these ensure a decent standard of living, taking account of socio-economic conditions, purchasing power, and long-term national productivity levels and developments. Clear guidelines are given to ensure that this adequacy assessment is done in a serious and transparent manner. Members may establish a basket of goods and services at real prices, or alternatively, compare minimum wage levels with reference values such as 60% of the gross median wage or 50% of the gross average wage. The European Union hence explicitly puts forward precise reference values. At the same time, the deal reached on the

*continued*

**Box 3.1** *continued*

Directive highlights the importance of collective bargaining and puts forward binding coverage targets. Sectoral and cross-industry collective bargaining is recognized as an essential factor for protecting workers. Member States with collective bargaining coverage below 80% of the workforce are required to create a public action plan to increase this coverage, involving the social partners (European Parliament, 2022a). This target is higher than the one originally proposed in 2020. Member States have two years to implement these changes (Pape, 2022). While the deal does not mention how collective bargaining should be organized, Müller and Schulten (2022) highlight that the 80% threshold is currently only reached by countries with sector level collective bargaining systems.

Eurofound (2022) traces a number of ongoing developments in statutory minimum wage rates back to the reference values proposed in the latest version of the EU Minimum Directive. A recent increase of the hourly minimum wage in Germany is expected to bring the minimum wage level in line with the 60% of median reference value proposed in the directive. Likewise, changes to wage-setting mechanisms and collective bargaining coverage in line with the proposal are being considered. Announced increases in Spain made explicit reference to the directive proposal. Also Croatia introduced a hike of its minimum wage up to the 60% threshold. In other countries, including the Netherlands and Greece, the reference values from the proposal have strengthened the trade unions' position in their demand for further increases to the minimum wage. Elsewhere, it is not clear whether the directive proposal has had an impact. Critics fear that as the collective bargaining coverage goal is effectively reached in Italy, further developments may be rather unlikely. In Portugal, current levels are above the reference values in the directive proposal, leading some to fear that they can be interpreted as thresholds. References to the proposal directive were rife in Cyprus and Lithuania, but in the context of minimum wage reform preparations that predated the proposal.

The Minimum Wage Directive contains two ambitious objectives. First, it aims to elevate minimum wages, preferably to 60% of the gross median wage or 50% of the gross average wage in each member state. Second, it requests member states to increase collective bargaining coverage to 80% of workers.

Research we did with Henri Haapanala and Zach Parolin (Haapanala, Marx, & Parolin, 2023) shows that these targets make sense if the aim is to lift wage floors. Our findings suggest that statutory minimum wages and collective bargaining both have distinct and complementary roles in establishing wage floors and reducing the share of low-paid workers. Statutory minimum wages help to lift wage floors and higher collective bargaining coverage is associated with a lower share of workers earning low pay. Improving the conditions for collective bargaining and union representation are thus important for reaching the objective of 'fair wages that provide a decent standard of living' expressed in the European Pillar of Social Rights, which the Minimum Wage Directive seeks to implement.

## 3.4 Employment Effects of the Minimum Wage

A classic argument against raising or introducing a minimum wage, is that it costs jobs. A wealth of empirical evidence has accumulated on this issue. Some studies, like the seminal Card and Krueger study from 1994, rank among the most heatedly debated in the profession. It seems fair to state that the measured effects of minimum wages have sometimes been positive, sometimes negative, sometimes neutral, but rarely very large (Machin & Manning, 1997; Kenworthy, 2008, 2011, 2022; Grimshaw et al., 2014; Belman et al., 2015; Salverda, 2018; Manning, 2021; Card & Cardoso, 2022). The fact that the measured effects have never been very large may be in part due to the fact that policy makers tend to err on the side of caution when actually introducing the raising of minimum wages. Martin and Immervoll (2007) have summarized it as follows: 'On balance, the evidence shows that an appropriately-set minimum wage need not have large negative effects on job prospects, especially if wage floors are properly differentiated (e.g., lower rates for young workers) and non-wage labour costs are kept in check.' The OECD now even recommends minimum wage increases in some cases, as for example in the 2020 Economic Survey of Poland or the 2022 Economic Survey of Estonia.

Arguably the most relevant and politically impactful recent test case is Germany. The introduction of a minimum wage with a real bite[2] has brought an abundance of new research on the issue, largely confirming that a minimum wage need not be harmful to employment if set at a level that the labour market can take (Caliendo et al., 2018; Bruttel, 2019). While the employment impact appears to have been limited in the German case, some evidence does point towards reductions in working hours and some other unforeseen effects. Schmitz (2019) found evidence that the minimum wage mostly increased incomes for those with marginal employment, leading to fewer welfare recipients.

That is not to suggest, of course, that there are no limits to raising wage floors. Obviously from some level on a minimum wage will start to impact on the demand for workers. At which level this will occur probably depends on many factors, such as the business cycle, the skills profile of the work force,[3] or the structure of the economy (e.g., the sectoral set-up or the extent of monopsony power). From a comprehensive review of the international (although mainly US-based) literature, Dube (2019) concludes that prior minimum wage increases up to 60% of the median wage generally had limited or no significant employment effects. That is not to say that this conclusion is universally applicable. As with most policy choices, wider context and circumstances are of the essence.

## 3.5 The Bite of the Minimum Wage

The extent to which a minimum wage can be considered a viable tool to protect workers and to ensure fairer wages self-evidently depends on the level it is set at and the number of people covered by it.

There is a large variation between national minimum wages in that regard: Table 3.2 shows that nominal minimum wages in 2022 ranged from 332 euro in Bulgaria to 2257 euro in Luxembourg. Other sources find similar variation (Schulten & Luebker, 2019; Eurofound, 2020a; Eurostat, 2020). The variation in purchasing power terms is smaller, but still substantial.

Most research focusing on the bite of the minimum wage, however, compares the value of the minimum wage vis-à-vis the median or average wage, the so-called Kaitz index (Ryckx & Kampelmann, 2012). Cross-nationally comparable data on the wage distribution in each country are hard to come by. The OECD has average wage series based on national accounts data. Most often used in the EU Member States are, however, the average and median wages derived from the Structure of Earnings Survey. This survey is conducted once every four years and provides, inter alia, information on the level of monthly and annual remuneration, annual paid leave, and working hours for employees working in enterprises consisting of 10 employees or more.

The four rightmost columns of Table 3.2 show national minimum wages relative to different operationalizations of median and average wages for 2018, the most recent year for which the Structure of Earnings survey is available. In 2018, most monthly national minimum wages were around 47–57% of the median wage, and 40–45% of the monthly average wage. Still, large variation exists, both between nations, as well as between different

**Table 3.2** Nominal and relative minimum wage levels

| Country | Monthly, euro (2022) | Monthly, PPS (2022) | Monthly, % median full-time wage (2018) | Monthly, % average full-time wage (2018) | Annual, % full-time median wage (2018) | Annual, % full-time average wage (2018) |
|---|---|---|---|---|---|---|
| BE | 1658 | 1462 | 47 | 44 | 45 | 42 |
| BG | 332 | 598 | 58 | 42 | 51 | 38 |
| CZ | 652 | 793 | 48 | 38 | 39 | 34 |
| DE | 1638 | 1517 | 47 | 41 | 39 | 33 |
| EE | 654 | 755 | 42 | 36 | 41 | 35 |
| EL | 774 | 885 | 47 | 45 | 46 | 36 |
| ES | 1126 | 1160 | 41 | 40 | 41 | 34 |
| FR | 1603 | 1424 | 65 | 51 | 57 | 46 |
| HR | 624 | 875 | 49 | 39 | 45 | 38 |
| HU | 542 | 832 | 57 | 41 | 46 | 37 |
| IE | 1775 | 1267 | 51 | 40 | 50 | 40 |
| LT | 730 | 1015 | 50 | 41 | 48 | 40 |
| LU | 2257 | 1705 | 57 | 43 | 50 | 37 |
| LV | 500 | 630 | 47 | 38 | 46 | 37 |
| MT | 792 | 894 | 42 | 35 | 39 | 33 |
| NL | 1725 | 1489 | 51 | 43 | 47 | 39 |
| PL | 655 | 1104 | 56 | 43 | 51 | 42 |
| PT | 823 | 920 | 64 | 52 | 63 | 45 |
| RO | 515 | 934 | 61 | 43 | 56 | 41 |
| SI | 1074 | 1218 | 61 | 49 | 48 | 41 |
| SK | 646 | 720 | 51 | 41 | 46 | 38 |
| UK | 1499[a] | 1265[a] | n.a. | 42 | n.a. | n.a. |
| US | 1110 | 908 | n.a. | n.a. | n.a. | 44[b] |

*Notes:* a Number refers to situation in 2020. [b] Percentage refers to situation in 2021, based on Aerts, Marx, and Parolin (2022), and therefore has a different methodology to calculate the underlying gross average wage.
*Source:* Monthly minimum wages are based on Eurostat (2022b). Monthly minimum wages relative to median earnings are based on Eurostat (2022a). Annual shares are based on simulated minimum wages, that include holiday payments, or 13th and 14th months, wherever relevant, from MIPI-HHoT Marchal, Siöland, and Goedemé (2018). Annual gross average and median wages are based on Eurostat (2022d). Eurostat calculates average and median earnings based on the Structure of Earnings Survey, most recent wave refers to 2018 (Eurostat, 2022c).

operationalizations of the average and the median wage (i.e., including or excluding holiday payments). This is no trivial matter, as minimum wage legislation in different countries may have different provisions as to which parts of holiday payments count towards attaining the minimum wage level. This is all the more relevant in light of the EU directive according to which countries should assess the adequacy of their minimum wages in line with a transparent and substantive benchmarking framework (see also

Box 3.1). The EU minimum wage directive proposes 60% of the median wage, or 50% of the gross average wage, as appropriate benchmarking values.

It is interesting that already a small number of countries have reached this benchmark. Depending on whether we compare monthly minimum wages to monthly median or average (full-time) wages, or also include holiday payments in annual wage concepts,[4] one to four countries reach the proposed benchmark, among which France and Portugal most consistently so. This 60% threshold is to some extent symbolic (it resonates the 60% of median equivalent household income threshold that is used as poverty line across the EU), but also reflects a wage floor lower than the low pay threshold that is commonly used in international comparisons (set at two-thirds of median earnings (OECD, 2020)). In addition, and depending on the national contexts, some researchers expect no large employment effects from minimum wages as long as they stay below this 60% of median wages mark (Dube, 2019). Clearly, some countries are nearer towards the provision of adequate wages than others.

The bite of the minimum wage cannot solely be derived from its level relative to the overall wage distribution. It is also important to know how many people are actually working at the minimum wage (and, how many are working at lower wage levels, in countries where enforcement issues may be more common).

Comparable administrative records on the share of the workforce that is paid at the minimum wage are lacking. Older estimates of the number of minimum wage earners are therefore based on national sources, that may build on survey data or tax data (for instance the number of tax earners that receive a tax treatment specifically for minimum wage earners, if such exists) (Marx et al., 2013; Eurofound, 2017b). More recently, Eurostat (2020) and Eurofound (2020a) have turned to calculating the share of minimum wage earners based on comparable surveys.

Eurostat (2022a) bases its proportion of minimum wage earners estimates on the structure of earnings survey and reports the share of employees earning less than 105% of the minimum wage. In Figure 3.1, we compare these estimates of the share of the workforce working around the minimum wage with the minimum wage level applicable in 2018 expressed as a percentage of the median wage. Overall, there appears to be a positive relation between both: if the relative minimum wage is higher, more people tend to work at (or below) minimum wage level. Still, there are some important digressions from this trend. Belgium for instance shows far fewer minimum wage employees than would be expected based on their relatively high minimum wage level. Belgium has indeed an entire structure of higher sectoral minimum wages on top of the statutory national minimum wage (Ryckx & Kampelmann, 2012). Also Portugal has a very low share of minimum wage earners relative to its minimum wage level. At the other end of the spectrum, we find Bulgaria, Romania and Slovenia. These countries have relatively high minimum wage levels. Still, they really stand out in terms of the share of the workforce working at a minimum wage. Eurostat reports that over 15% of the workforce works at or below the minimum wage. As the Eurostat figures report the proportion of employees working below 105% of the minimum wage, it cannot be excluded that this share also includes employees not covered by the minimum wage. Given that the Structure of Earnings Survey is based on enterprises consisting of at least 10 employees, this risk may however be small.

Eurofound (2019a) looks at different intervals around the minimum wage, distinguishing between the share of employees paid below 90% of the minimum wage, between 90% and 100% of the minimum wage, and between 100% and 110% of the minimum wage, calculated on the EU Statistics on Income and Living Conditions (SILC) survey. This survey is based on a representative sample of the population (rather than of companies with 10

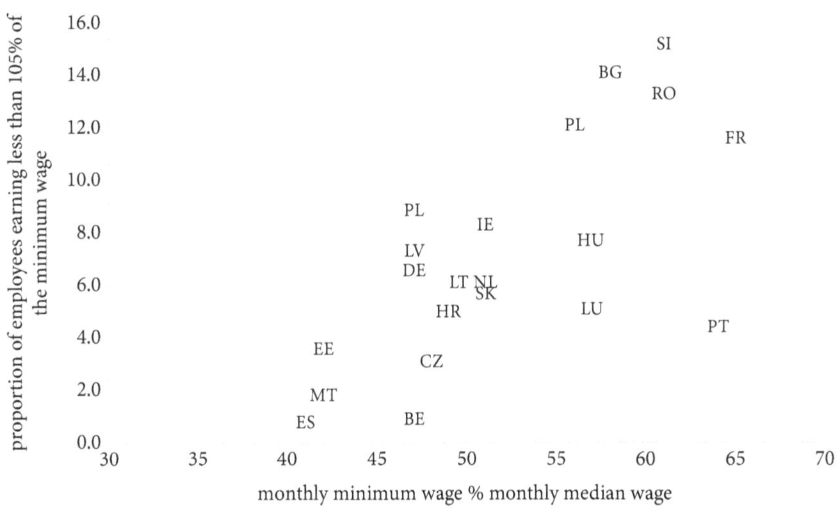


**Figure 3.1** Proportion of minimum wage earners versus the relative minimum wage level/Kaitz index, 2018

*Note:* proportion of minimum wage earners calculated as the proportion of the workforce earnings less than 105% of the minimum wage, based on the Structure of earnings survey. The x axis shows the monthly minimum wage expressed as a % of the monthly median wage. Correlation is 0.69.

*Source:* (Eurostat, 2022a).

employees or more), and hence is more likely to capture also non-standard employees. However, whereas the SES is explicitly designed to capture earnings information, the SILC focuses more on (annual) income in general. This leads to more uncertainty around estimates of monthly or hourly wages, which are the relevant wage concepts to compare to the minimum wage (Salverda & Rook, 2023). Looking at the correlation between the share of employees paid between 90% and 110% of the minimum wage, they do report a similar positive (be it smaller) relation between the minimum wage level and the share of employees paid around the minimum wage. At the same time, they report substantial variation in the share of employees paid below 90% of the minimum wage,[5] ranging from 1.3% in the Czech Republic to 8.7% in the UK. Such figures can be caused by noise in the data, with surveyed individuals misreporting wages or total hours worked. Also, some countries have lower minimum wage rates applying to parts of the population, for instance younger workers. Still, we cannot exclude the possibility that minimum wages are not always strictly enforced, for instance by employers under recording working hours in the grey economy or by a 'creative' definition of the employment relation in the absence of sound checks. The UK trade union congress estimates that around 250,000 workers in the UK may be affected by these types of practices (Hall, 2015; Trade Union Congress, 2015).

Finally, analyses on the Structure of Earnings Survey and on the EU SILC, as well as on national data, also allow to look into the characteristics of minimum wage earners. Unsurprisingly, the profile of minimum wage earners is quite similar to the profile of other low-wage earners. Overall, women, young persons, those with low educational attainment and part-time workers are overrepresented among minimum wage earners (Eurofound, 2022). Minimum wage workers are more often found in sectors with limited productivity, such as the food and accommodation services, elementary occupations, or the agricultural sector (Luzar, 2015; Perista et al., 2015; Eurofound, 2022). Still, exceptions exist. For instance, in Slovenia, the highest proportion of minimum wage earners is found in the manufacturing sectors (Luzar, 2015). To the extent that minimum wage earners are not the main earner of their household, low minimum wages may not immediately put household incomes under duress (although issues on fair remuneration and wage inequality still stand). In contrast, minimum wage increases would then mainly affect households higher up in the income distribution (Marx et al., 2012).

But even when minimum wage earners are main earners, the usefulness of the minimum wage as an income protection measure may be limited. It may be the case that only part-time work is a possibility for certain employees: think for instance of lone parent households that need to combine care duties and employment (Aerts et al., 2022). In such a case, minimum wage increases would need to be very substantial to provide adequate incomes for employees with nonstandard working times. Alternatively, minimum wage employment is concentrated in sectors and occupations in which a full-time roister may be rare (Eurofound, 2022). This may lead to a concentration of less than full-time jobs among vacant minimum wage jobs. Whereas the French SMIC was considered successful in bringing down wage disparities and providing adequate incomes in the first decade after its introduction, from the mid 1980s onwards this achievement was eroded by the increase in part-time employment, leading to new concerns on in-work poverty (Concialdi, 1999). This ultimately led to the adoption of new policy instruments, such as in-work benefits. But also more broadly, other policy measures, such as child benefits or housing allowances, have increased in importance since the genesis of minimum wages. A clear example is Australia, where initially jurisdiction pointed to the need of the minimum wage to be a veritable living wage, sufficient to cover the needs of a worker and his family. Only when other policy instruments, such as child benefits, were developed, a different role of the minimum wage was considered, in which the provision of a living income became a shared responsibility between employer and the state (Bray, 2013). A similar consideration is evident from the proposed translation of a living wage in Irish national policy. A living wage is there expressly defined as the wage level that would allow a single person *without dependents* a decent standard of living (Eurofound, 2022). The implicit underlying assumption is that the needs of dependents should not be met by employers, but by additional earners in the family or by the welfare state. Clearly, when we want to consider the adequacy of income protection for workers in contemporary, fully grown welfare states, we should expand our focus beyond merely assessing the level of the minimum wage.

In what follows, we zoom in on the other income components minimum wage earners are entitled to.

## 3.6 The Make-up of Minimum Income Protection for Employees

Nowadays, policy makers do not solely—or even mainly—rely on the minimum wage to guarantee adequate incomes to low-wage workers and their families. In Figure 3.2, we show the different income components of households where the main earner works for the minimum wage, expressed as a percentage of the national at-risk-of-poverty threshold. As in Chapter 2, this figure is based on a hypothetical household simulation (see Box 2.1). We defined the characteristics of a hypothetical person, and calculated how the tax benefit system would treat this person and would impact on its net disposable income. In this case, we assume the hypothetical person works full-time at the statutory minimum wage. We take the annualized income, taking account of the annual personal income tax and tax credits, as well as of statutorily guaranteed holiday payments. Income taxes and social insurance contributions are based on this gross income. Other benefits are awarded when the household is eligible for them.[6] In this section, we discuss the net disposable income and income components at the minimum wage excluding temporary COVID-19 related benefits. Box 3.2 shortly describes the impact of the COVID-19 measures relevant to the net incomes of minimum wage earners.

Figure 3.2, panel A shows that in most EU member states (16 out of 22 EU Member States with a minimum wage) full-time employment at the minimum wage suffices to provide a single person with a net disposable income above the 60% at-risk-of-poverty threshold, referring to the situation in 2021. The only exceptions are Estonia, Latvia, Malta, Hungary, Bulgaria, and surprisingly Germany. The latter country has since substantially increased its minimum wage (see Box 3.1). It is noteworthy that the federal minimum wage in the United States lags far behind the European countries in its potential to guarantee a net disposable income at 60% of the national median equivalent household income to a single person. Even when taking all potential additional income components into account, in this case SNAP food stamps and the earned income tax credit (see also Section 3.6.2 and 3.6.5), the net disposable income falls short of 70% of the at-risk-of-poverty threshold, as compared to 87% in laggard EU country Estonia.

The picture turns bleaker when we assess the situation of a hypothetical lone parent with two children. Also here, we assume full-time minimum wage employment. Net disposable income at a single minimum wage is in all but six of the countries included in Figure 3.2, panel B too low to cover the additional needs of a family of three, as reflected by the poverty line.

Lone parents are a particularly interesting case to look at when assessing the adequacy of in-work minimum income protection, as this group is by definition barred from mitigation strategies that are available to multi-adult households. Whereas couples with children have some potential to increase earnings beyond a single employment income, this option is far less evident for lone parents (Aerts et al., 2022). In fact, the full-time low-wage employment assumption may even be overly ambitious for this target group. Given the preponderance of minimum wage employment in service sector jobs and occupations with less evident roisters, and because of the challenges related to combining care and work responsibilities, one could wonder whether full-time minimum wage employment is a feasible option for lone parent households in the different countries considered in Figure 3.2. Figure 3.2 panel B should hence be interpreted as a 'most generous' case of minimum income protection for lone parents with a substantial labour market attachment.

### 3.6.1 Gross Minimum Wages Relative to the At-Risk-of-Poverty Threshold

The dark grey bars in Figure 3.2 show the gross minimum wage expressed as a percentage of the at-risk-of-poverty threshold, i.e., 60% of the median equivalized disposable household income. This threshold is increased for multiple person families in line with the modified OECD scale. This equivalence scale increases the poverty threshold for a single person household with a factor 0.5 for each additional household member older or equal to 14, whereas the needs of younger household members lead to an increase with a factor of 0.3. These equivalence scales are commonly used in cross-national comparative research, and are an integral part of the calculation of the EU at-risk-of-poverty indicators. These scales are assumed to capture the balance between cost-sharing in a household (for instance housing and heating costs can be shared), as well as the additional needs of an additional household member (such as clothes and food expenses, or the need for an additional room in the house).

As mentioned above, traditionally, wages were supposed to cover the costs of a household head and his dependents. We find traces of this in historical Australian jurisdiction (cf. Bray, 2013, see above), but also in the traditional involvement of employers in the organization of child benefits in continental welfare states (e.g., in Belgium, see Cantillon & Buysse, 2016), or the abolished marital wage premium of the Greek minimum wage (Kakoulidou, Konstantinou, & Moutos, 2020).

Over time, as welfare states became more comprehensive, (and double earnership became more common), this perspective shifted. This is very clear from the information provided in Figure 3.2. In panel A, where net disposable income and income components at the minimum wage are expressed as a percentage of the poverty threshold for a single person household, the

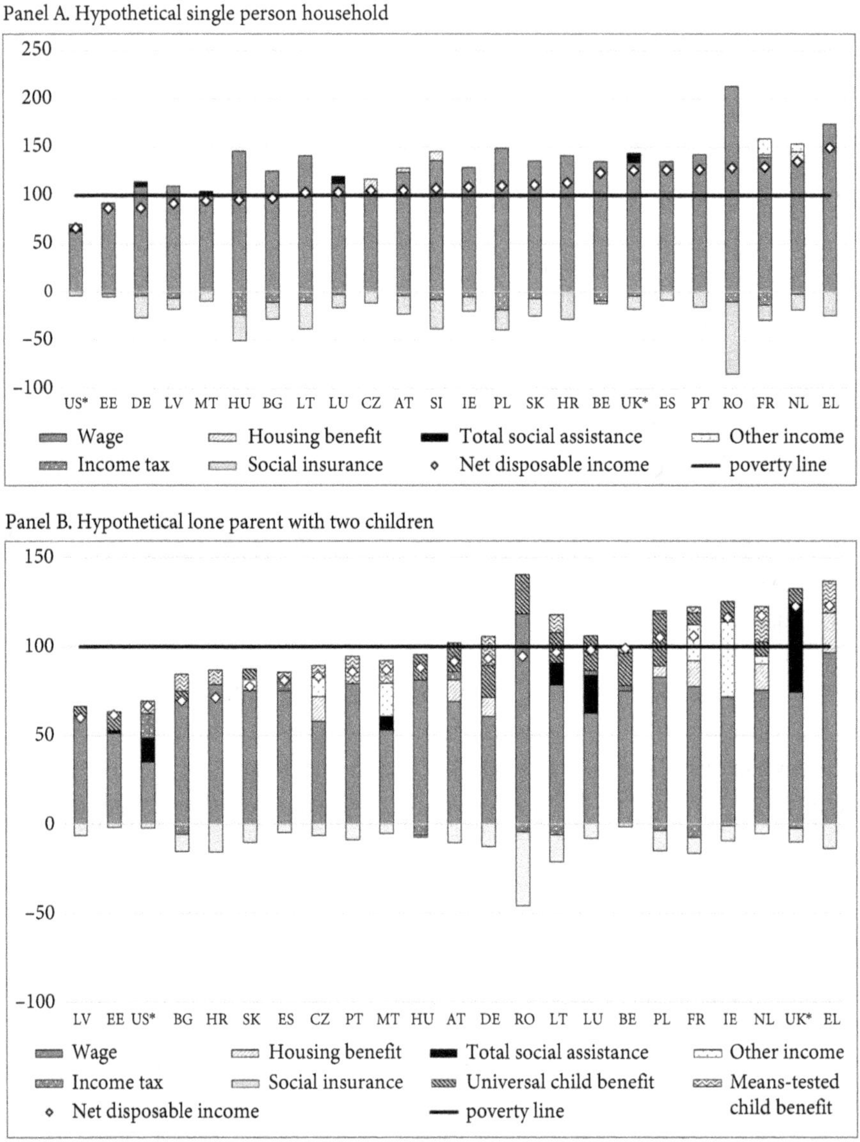


**Figure 3.2** Net disposable income and income components at full-time minimum wage employment, 2021

*Source:* MIPI-HHoT, see Marchal, Siöland, and Goedemé (2018). We thank Elise Aerts for valuable assistance in updating this dataset. Data for the UK refer to the situation in 2020. Data for the US are based on the calculations presented in Aerts, Marx, and Parolin (2022).

dark grey bars, that reflect the minimum wage level, are in nearly all countries above the poverty line. The only exceptions are the United States, and Estonia and Malta. Even in these latter two countries, the shortfall is fairly limited.

In those countries in which the net disposable income of single minimum wage earners fall below the at-risk-of-poverty threshold, it is usually taxes and social insurance contributions that bring down the minimum wage level.

Panel B on the other hand shows a completely different picture. With the exception of Romania, the dark grey bars that represent the minimum wage level are below the at-risk-of-poverty threshold everywhere. This is because the nominal wage levels are the same, regardless of one's household status. Yet, for a lone parent with two children, this labour market income must cover far more needs than for a single person.

## 3.6.2 The Tax Treatment of Minimum Wage Earners

Figure 3.2, panel A shows only a limited impact of personal income taxes in the net disposable incomes of single minimum wage earners. They are fully absent in Malta, the Czech Republic, Croatia, Spain, Portugal, and Greece, while they appear to be negligible in most other countries. They only reach or surpass 5% of wage income in Eastern European countries Latvia, Lithuania, Bulgaria, Poland (at 12.6%), and Hungary (at 16%). In this group, we also find the two continental countries France and Belgium. In the United States, a single minimum wage earner receives a small supplement through the earned income tax credit.

Panel B shows that tax rates are even lower for lone parent minimum wage earners. Tax rates are zero or negligible in all countries except for France, Bulgaria, Lithuania, and Hungary. Even then, they never surpass 10% of wage income. Rebates and allowances for children, and for lone parent households, bring taxable income close to zero in most countries. In some countries, lone parent households even enjoy refundable child tax credits. This is the case in Belgium, Luxembourg, Austria, Spain, and—very outspokenly so—in the United States.

Overall, the progressive tax structure in most European countries, as well as specific tax allowances and credits for low-wage earners, children, and lone parent households, substantially improve the net disposable income of minimum wage earners.

The impact of social insurance contributions on the other hand is far more negative. In contrast to personal income taxes, social insurance contributions are generally proportional rather than progressive. Romania, Slovenia, Germany, and Croatia for instance all levy relatively sizeable social insurance rates, of over 20% of wage income. Relatively few countries use reductions in social insurance contributions as a strategy to make work pay (Marx et al.,

2013). The most notable example is Belgium, where the regular contribution rate for employees of 13.07% of wage income is reduced for low-wage earners to around 2% of the minimum wage (Vandelannoote & Verbist, 2019).

### 3.6.3 Child Support for Those in Work

Section 3.6.2 already mentioned the large impact of favourable treatment of children and lone parent households within the personal income tax system. Families with children are however also supported in a more visible way, through universal and means-tested child benefits. With the exception of the United States, all countries included in Figure 3.2, Panel B have child benefits for families with children.[7] The overall child benefit package ranges from 4% (in Spain) to over 30% (in Germany) of the at-risk-of-poverty threshold for a lone parent household with two children. On average, the child benefit package ranges around 15%. In all but six (European) countries, at least part of this child benefit package is provided through a universal child benefit. The child benefit package is fully universal in Latvia, Estonia, Slovakia, Austria, Hungary, Romania, Luxembourg, Ireland, and the United Kingdom, and sizably so in Poland, Belgium, Lithuania, Germany, and France. In other countries, means-tested child benefits constitute a large part of the child benefit package. This is for instance the case in the Netherlands and Bulgaria.

Aerts et al. (2022) highlight the benefits of child support constituting of a universal socle topped up by a means-tested benefit. Overall, countries that pursue this strategy succeed better in providing generous child benefit packages, and, related, more generous minimum income protection provisions. The high child benefit packages in the Netherlands and Germany, that both combine sizeable universal child benefits with generous means-tested top-ups, appear to underscore their observation.

### 3.6.4 Other Means-Tested Benefits and Earnings Disregards

In some countries, minimum wage earners can supplement their net disposable income with a housing benefit. This is the case in Slovenia, Austria, the Netherlands, France, and the Czech Republic for single minimum wage earners, and in Austria, the Czech Republic, Germany, Poland, France, the Netherlands, and Greece for a lone parent household with children. Usually, such a housing allowance is conditional upon a low or modest rent or certain characteristics of the dwelling, as well as having low household income (see Marchal, Siöland, & Goedemé, 2018).

In addition, single minimum wage earners receive social assistance top-ups in Germany, Luxembourg, the United Kingdom (through the universal credit), Malta, and the United States (in the form of food vouchers). A lone parent with two children will additionally receive a social assistance top-up in Estonia, Lithuania, and more sizeable top-ups in the United States, Malta, Luxembourg, and the United Kingdom.

Yet social assistance benefits are generally lower than minimum wages (Cantillon, Marchal, & Luigjes, 2019). The fact that low-wage earners can receive a social assistance top-up in some countries is thanks to relatively generous earnings disregards in the means-test of social assistance benefits (European Commission and Social Protection Committee, 2022). Most social assistance means-tests do indeed disregard a small portion of labour market earnings (see also Section 4.3.7). In some countries this disregard only suffices to combine a sporadic or piecemeal labour market attachment with social assistance benefit receipt. In Belgium, the disregard is for instance limited to around 290 euros per month, and moreover, limited in time, rendering the hypothetical households included in Figure 3.2 clearly ineligible for a social assistance top-up. Elsewhere, the disregards may be more structural, for instance a continued disregards of 30% of all labour market income, but can—in combination with other incomes sources, and low social assistance thresholds, still render the combination of a full-time minimum wage and a social assistance top-up impossible (Marchal & Van Mechelen, 2013; European Commission and Social Protection Committee, 2022). In other countries, most notably the United Kingdom with its universal credit reform, the entire minimum income protection system is organized in such a way as to enable shifts from out-of-work to in-work minimum income protection. The relatively sizeable social assistance top-ups for singles and lone parents in the UK are testament to this aim.

It should be noted that on top of an earnings disregard, a number of countries also foresee back to work bonuses in their social assistance scheme. This means that when a former social assistance beneficiary takes up employment, he or she will continue to receive part of the social assistance benefit for a limited period in time (see also Section 4.3.6). These bonuses are not included in Figure 3.2, since we would then have to assume that the minimum wage earners just left social assistance, whereas the aim of this chapter is to discuss the minimum income protection packages that are available to all workers, not solely those who just left benefits. We refer the reader to European Commission and Social Protection Committee (2022) for an illustration and discussion of the impact of such back to work bonuses.

### 3.6.5 In-work Benefits

Finally, we would like to make some observations on in-work benefits. From the above, it must be clear that in-work benefits, i.e. benefits or policies that aim to further support the net disposable income of low-wage earners are rife in the countries included in Figure 3.2. It is, however, difficult to fully identify these benefits as a separate category, due to their interference with the tax system (in the case of tax allowances or credits for low-wage earners), the social insurance contribution scheme (in the case of reductions in social insurance contributions for low-wage earners), child support, or even social assistance.

In a number of countries, in-work benefits are implemented and distributed under a separate benefit scheme. We have included these benefits under the moniker 'other income' in Figure 3.2, together with other benefits that are hard to classify.

Most notably, other income refers to a specific in-work benefit in France, Ireland, and Malta. France introduced in 2016 its *prime d'activité*, to succeed the previous *RSA activité*, that was more expressly linked to the minimum income scheme, and the more generally accessible *prime pour l'emploi*. The new benefit was supposed to support all low-wage workers more firmly. The earnings ceilings to qualify for this in-work benefit make explicit reference to the minimum wage, with single persons being eligible if their income is below 1.5 times the minimum wage. This threshold is further increased to 1.7 for a lone parent with one child. (Note that the ceilings were raised in 2019, prior to this a single person would only qualify as long as his or her income was below 1.3 times the minimum wage.) The actual amount depends on the family work income (of which part is disregarded) and the housing benefit package (Bouvard, 2021).

The in-work benefit in Malta is exclusively reserved to working claimants with children (Vella et al., 2021). Also in Ireland, the in-work benefit, with the name Working Family Payment, is targeted at employees with children (Doorley & McTague, 2021).

In the other countries for which Figure 3.2 reports other income, the value rather refers to less easily classifiable benefits, such as the health benefit in the Netherlands, certain tax refunds in the Czech Republic and Slovakia, and additional supplements to means-tested benefits or specific lone parent benefits (combined with in-work benefits) in Ireland and Malta (de Vos, 2021; Kalíšková, Münich, & Pavel, 2021; Mikloš, 2021; Vella, Said, & Apap, 2021).

### 3.6.6 It's Crowded around the Minimum Wage

Most of the income components discussed in Sections 3.6.2–3.6.5 take, in some way or another, account of the actual incomes of wage earners. It is hence clear that increases in the minimum wage operate in a very crowded field of (means-tested) benefits and preferential tax treatments, especially when there are children present in the household. The OECD has calculated the impact of a limited 5% increase in the gross minimum wage on the net disposable income of a lone parent family (OECD, 2015). In around a third of OECD countries, less than half of such an increase would trickle down to the net disposable income. In one country, the net disposable income would even decrease.

Marchal (2020) reported on a similar exercise, in which we calculated the net disposable income for a single person household and a lone parent household in three different minimum wage scenarios: at the actual minimum wage, at 60% of the full-time equivalent monthly median wage, and at 60% of the full-time annual average wage. These increases are for most countries far more substantial than the 5% increase that the OECD assumed for its exercise. An increase to an EU-wide minimum wage target of 60% of the national monthly median full-time equivalent wage, would lift net disposable income for a single minimum wage earner over the at-risk-of-poverty threshold in more than half of the countries where this was previously not the case. An increase to 60% of the average annual full-time wage would lift the net disposable income of a single person above the poverty threshold in all EU MSs, although it would entail quite significant minimum wage increases. This was, however, not the case for lone parents with two children. Even at the highest increase considered in this exercise, accompanying measures would remain necessary. As many of the current supportive measures are concentrated around very low incomes, an increase in the minimum wage under current tax benefit regulations often means an increase in the relative tax burden, and a decrease in benefits, that sometimes only barely compensates for envisaged increases in gross minimum wages.

## Box 3.2 Minimum income protection for workers during COVID-19

Most of the efforts taken during the COVID-19 crisis centred on those at risk of losing their job. Short time work schemes were made more generous. Many welfare states recognized that those in non-standard employment forms were at risk of falling without support. As a result, specific measures for self-employed were extended or introduced, and the accessibility of social insurance schemes was in many cases widened to also include those on temporary contracts (Cantó et al., 2022). Other novelties were the introduction or easier accessibility of certain care benefits, to allow parents to take care of their children when schools were closed, or when children were quarantined (European Commission and Social Protection Committee, 2022).

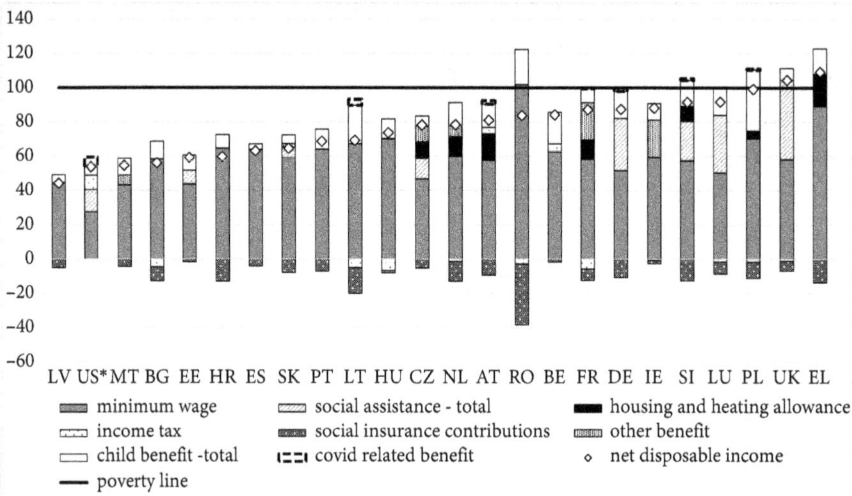


**Figure 3.3** Net disposable income for a couple with two children in 2020, including COVID related benefits

*Source:* MIPI-HHoT. Data for the US are based on Aerts, Marx, and Parolin (2022) and refer to 2021.

Specific measures to boost the incomes of those in-work, and not at risk of losing their job, were far more rare. Italy introduced a risk premium for workers in critical sectors, not able to work from home (Figari & Fiorio, 2020), but substantial increases to the minimum income protection packages of the working population were lacking. If their incomes were boosted at all, it was often by more general measures that aimed to support low-income families with children. In Figure 3.3, we present the net disposable income of a couple with two children, with one adult working full-time, in COVID-19 year 2020. We highlight the potential impact of the COVID related benefits that were included in the 2020 EUROMOD version, on the net disposable income of this family type.

Modest increases are apparent in Austria, Germany, France, Lithuania, Poland, and Slovenia. In Germany and Lithuania, this family type benefited from a one-off child bonus. Austria decreased the tax rate in the lowest tax band, and at the same time increased the commuter's tax refund. France and Slovenia introduced a small lump sum allowance for vulnerable groups. Finally, in Poland, the social insurance contributions for employees in small companies were reduced. The largest increase in net minimum income package can be observed in the United States, with the COVID-19 related increase in the child tax credit.

## 3.7 Trends

In the previous section, we showed that the net disposable income of minimum wage earners is affected by far more income components than solely the minimum wage earned on the labour market. In Marchal and Marx (2018) we looked at the trends in these different income components, and found that throughout the first decade of the 2000s, many countries saw a more favourable development of net disposable incomes than they did for gross minimum wages (see also Figure 3.4), in a period in which minimum wages often decreased or stagnated in relative terms. Whereas this is partially a mechanical effect due to the mitigating impact of progressive taxes when gross incomes decrease, in many instances this could be traced back to conscious efforts to lower taxes for low-wage earners or higher targeted benefits, especially in the case of a lone parent with two children.

While income tax liabilities were already low to begin with, thanks to the combined effect of child tax allowances and tax credits, further decreases were common. By 2009, average tax rates in most countries approached zero for our hypothetical lone parent household. Developments in taxes in Figure 3.4 also include changes in social insurance contributions. Social insurance contributions are usually proportional; they are defined as a percentage of individual earned wages. As such, they are generally the same for both hypothetical family types. Yet some countries, including Belgium, circumvented this logic by introducing substantial social insurance rebates for low-wage workers. Elsewhere, social insurance contributions increased for low-wage workers: a number of Eastern European countries added insurance categories.

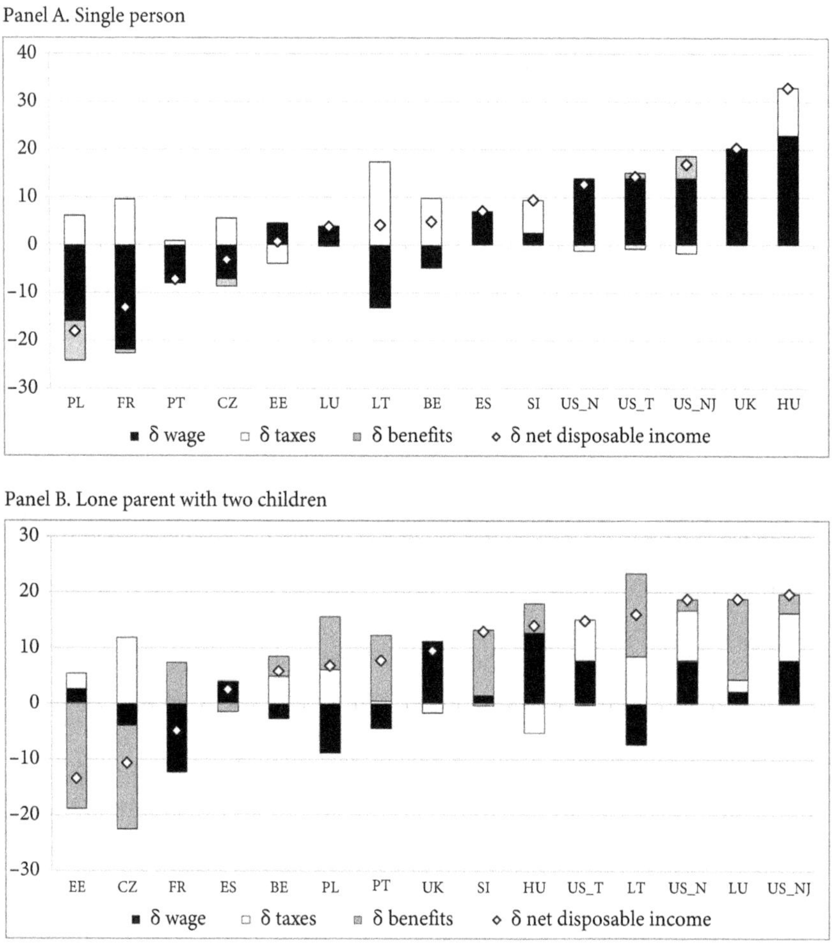


**Figure 3.4** Trends in net income package and its components of a one-earner family, employed at minimum wage, 2001–2009 (ppt change, relative to the 60% of median equivalent household income)
*Source:* CSB -MIPI.

Overall, child benefits remained fairly stable or decreased in the 2001–2009 period, although we did observe contrasting trends in Lithuania, Belgium, and Poland. Trends in social assistance top-ups are difficult to interpret as social assistance is a residual benefit. Its means-test in principle takes all possible income sources into account (in some countries, child benefits or housing allowances may be disregarded; see also Chapter 2). Changes in the impact of social assistance top-ups on net disposable income therefore do not necessarily reflect policy changes with regard to the social assistance benefit per se, but can just reflect changes to the other income components. Yet, it is clear that some countries sought to promote social assistance top-ups to low-income working families in the 2001–2009 period. That was for instance precisely the point of the 2009 French social assistance reform.

In this chapter, we extend this exercise to cover the 2009–2021 time span. The pattern in which net disposable income developed more favourably than gross minimum wages is no longer dominant in this period. Whereas from 2001 to 2009 we observed such a pattern for a lone parent with two children in two thirds of the included countries, from 2009 to 2021 the net disposable income increased more (or decreased less) than the gross minimum wage in less than half of the countries. Minimum wage increases were far more prevalent and also quite substantial in a significant number of countries. Evidently, progressive taxes mitigated the impact on net disposable incomes, as they dampened the effect of minimum wage decreases in the previous period. Still, in a number of countries, these minimum wage increases were explicitly pursued in order to rebalance the responsibility for adequate incomes between employers and the government.[8] Indeed, higher income from wages will, in a crowded means-tested income support field, automatically lead to lower government expenses. This point was made very clear in the UK's rebranding of the minimum wage to a national living wage: the minimum wage increase was accompanied by substantial cuts in child tax credits (included as benefits in Figure 3.5). Also the introduction of the German minimum wage stemmed partially from a concern that the government was effectively subsidizing the income of low-wage workers through social assistance top-ups.[9] In Hungary, the substantial minimum wage increase was enacted in order to mitigate negative consequences from the flat tax reform, which increased income tax liabilities for low-wage earners.

Elsewhere, benefit increases still amplified the effect of minimum wage increases or mitigated or counteracted the impact of decreasing minimum wages. In Lithuania for instance, both minimum wages and benefits increased for the lone parent household, due to an expansion of the child benefit scheme.

## 3.8 A True Income Floor for Working People?

So far, we have focused in this chapter on the minimum income protection package guaranteed to households with one full-time earner, employed at the minimum wage.

This choice is made for a number of reasons: in the case of single-person households and lone parents, this is the minimum that can be guaranteed

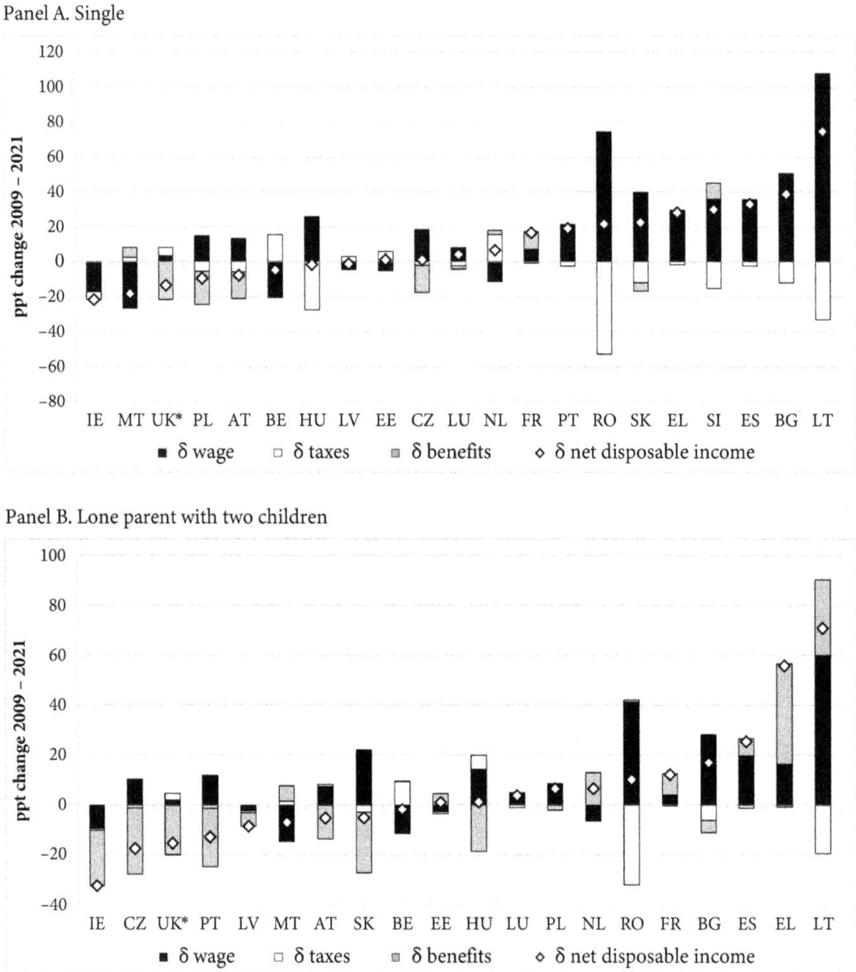


**Figure 3.5** Trends in net income package and its components of a one-earner family, employed at minimum wage, 2009–2021 (ppt change, relative to the 60% of median equivalent household income)

*Note:* Data for the UK refer to 2009–2018.
*Source:* MIPI-HHoT.

when the potential working time in the household is fully realized. Also, minimum wages have important signal functions, both in the set-up and design of the welfare state (Cantillon, Marchal, & Luigjes, 2019; Cantillon, Parolin, & Collado, 2020), and in terms of the perceived fairness of the wage distribution (Müller & Schulten, 2020).

However, while they are certainly not without merit, it is hard to make the case that the minimum income protection packages discussed in this chapter constitute a true income floor for working people, at least not in the same vein as our assumption that the minimum income protection packages discussed in Chapter 2 represent a true income floor for those unable to find work. In this section, we discuss more in-depth the issues related to interpreting minimum wage based minimum income protection packages. Some of these issues echo problems that are also relevant for social assistance schemes, such as the extent to which people are actually covered or have access to these protection measures. Others are related to the very specific situation of the labour market, and the kind of work that is increasingly becoming available to low-wage workers, which posits its own challenges in terms of securing adequate in-work (minimum) incomes.

We discuss in turn the challenges and issues related to (i) minimum wage enforcement and non-compliance; (ii) the difficulties related to the assumption of being full-time employed; and how this is amplified by the increasing prevalence of new types of atypical work forms. Finally, (iii) we discuss how the latter two issues challenge policy makers when securing adequate in-work incomes, and how these make the case for certain forms of in-work benefits (as discussed in Section 3.6) even more stringent.

### 3.8.1 Minimum Wage Non-compliance

Using wage information derived from the income data reported in the EU-SILC, Eurofound (2022) estimated the share of employees paid below the minimum wage to range from 1.3% in the Czech Republic, to 8.7% in the UK. As already discussed in Section 3.5, we should note that the EU-SILC is not designed to derive precise information on hourly or even monthly wages, that can easily be compared to statutory wage levels. Rather, the EU-SILC focuses on deriving comprehensive annual income concepts, that allow to assess individual's and household's at-risk-of-poverty status, and broader living standards.

Still, also more precise national calculations, that build on data that allow to track in more detail the number of hours worked, and hence to more closely delineate the wage concept to the definition of the statutory wage, indicate that certain employees may not be paid at the prevalent statutory minimum wage. Burauel et al. (2017) estimated that after the 2015 minimum wage implementation in Germany, 1.8 million employees were still paid lower wage rates in 2016, to further decrease in the subsequent year. The UK Low Pay Commission (2020) used an administrative data set to find that 23% of employees were paid below the relevant minimum wage, while the

US Bureau of Labor Statistics reports that 1.58% of all hourly paid employees earn wage rates below the federal minimum wage.

Why do empirical studies find wages below minimum wage level? Employees can be (partially) employed in the grey economy, and employers can make (conscious or unconscious) mistakes in applying the minimum wage including misreporting working hours or confusing the wage concepts actually included in the minimum, such as holiday payments or certain in-kind benefits. Importantly, countries often also allow exceptions to the general minimum wage legislation for specific groups of employees, in order not to harm the employment prospects of less productive workers. Many countries know lower minimum wage rates for younger workers (Eurofound, 2022). In some countries, entire sectors may be exempt from minimum wage regulations. The minimum wage introduced in Cyprus offers a prime example. Elsewhere, lower minimum wages may apply in specific sectors. The US know for instance lower wage rates for workers who commonly receive tips, assuming that the tips will raise their incomes above minimum wage level. Upon the introduction of the minimum wage in Germany, employers were not required to pay long term unemployed who re-entered the labour market the minimum wage. Finally, minimum wage rates usually do not apply in the context of activation trajectories, apprenticeships, or vocational training programmes (Eurofound, 2019b). All these exemptions may further hollow out minimum wage legislation and provide a viable explanation for the observation of workers who earn below the minimum wage.[10]

### 3.8.2 Atypical Work Forms

This chapter so far centred on the minimum income protection package guaranteed at one full-time minimum wage. This is however (and increasingly) a far from evident point of departure.

17.2% of all EU employment is currently part-time, 18% of which is involuntary part-time employment (Eurostat, 2022c). Overall, women, young persons, those with low educational attainment and part-time workers are overrepresented among minimum wage earners (Eurofound, 2022). In addition, minimum wage and low-wage employment is more common in service sectors such as restaurant and accommodation services, where full-time work schedules may be rare, or will be split across mornings, evenings and nights, rather than coming in eight-hour blocks. This makes involuntary part-time employment a far from negligible problem at the lower end of the wage distribution (Horemans, 2016). In addition, and especially for single persons who also have care duties, more flexible and full-time employment can be hard to hold (Aerts et al., 2022). Childcare services usually keep (somewhat extended) office hours, or at the very least require a certain predictability in the timing and amount of required hours. Even when such care services would be available, the combination of at home care and full-time employment can easily become overly taxing. US research has in the past found this challenge to be one of the main reasons behind the disappointing re-entry trends among benefit dependent lone parents (Scott et al., 2004) (see also Millar and Crosse (2018) for a similar point regarding lone parent activation in Ireland).

Such observations are especially worrisome as various sources find atypical employment forms, in particular part-time and fixed term employment, to be on the increase in a substantial number of countries (Nautet & Piton, 2019; OECD, 2019). In addition, empirical studies show own-account self-employment to be on the rise (Horemans & Marx, 2017; Conen & Schippers, 2019). Growth in the number of self-employed is to a non-trivial extent due to employees combining their employment with a self-employed activity (Ghuesquière, 2020). At the same time, new forms of work are being introduced that further increase the allowed flexibility in terms of work hours, schedules, and payment rates. Many of these new work forms show characteristics that were previously limited to self-employment, such as on-call work, while a substantial number of the new self-employed perform their activities through online platforms that put concerns about bogus self-employment front and centre (De Stefano, 2016). The share of employees currently active in platform work has risen to 4.3% of the European labour force, with 1.1% of the labour force having platform work as main activity (Piasna et al., 2022). Workers active in non-standard work forms generally face less favourable working and remuneration conditions (e.g., Booth, Francesconi, & Frank, 2002; Lohmann & Marx, 2018; Conen & Schippers, 2019; Bekckmannshagen & Schröder, 2020). They share for instance a higher unpredictability of earnings, and more insecurity in general, relative to standard employees (Seo, 2021).

Overall, these trends have given rise to concerns about the formation of a precariat class, that consists of workers faced with increasing work and financial insecurity, a decreasing autonomy and limited access to social rights stemming from a growing mismatch between income protection and changing employment patterns (Standing, 2011, 2014; Palier, 2019). At the same time, it should be noted that not all those working in these new work forms do so involuntarily. Those in new work forms, such as platform work, often indicate that they appreciate the added flexibility (Pesole et al., 2018;

Murgia & Pulignano, 2021), while the self-employed generally report higher satisfaction levels than employees (Nautet & Piton, 2019).

Still, it cannot be denied that these atypical work forms thoroughly question the assumption that an actual minimum income floor for those in work is constituted by full-time minimum wage employment, as both the full-time schedule and the minimum wage protection are undermined by the preponderance of these new, more flexible work forms. Zero hours contracts, as well as day, or week contracts, leave serious uncertainty around the number of hours worked in a week or month, as do bogus self-employment, and platform work. Whereas zero hours contracts still fall under the minimum wage legislation, be it with large uncertainty on the hours worked, this is not the case for bogus self-employment and platform work. As self-employed, workers are 'free' to negotiate their own wages. This negotiation power may be heavily skewed in favour of a monopsonist employer (such as a platform). Some countries have tried to act against these trends by forcing platforms to pay minimum wages, or even sectoral minimum wages. Elsewhere, platform workers have tried to unite for better working and wage conditions. The success of these efforts has so far remained limited (Kilhoffer et al., 2019).

Piasna et al. (2022) are among the first to provide a comprehensive assessment of the profile and earnings of platform workers in Europe, building on the second wave of the representative European Trade Union Institute's Internet and Platform work survey, conducted in 14 European countries. They find that most internet and platform workers combine their platform activity with other forms of non-standard work, most commonly as freelancer or self-employed without employee. Still, a substantial share of them is not free to set their own pay rates. Among those self-employed active as platform worker in the transport sector, 42% cannot set their own prices. The large majority of platform workers reports that their platform activity provides an income lower than 20% of full-time median earnings, with only 8% reporting income higher than the median. As a result, it is not surprising that the ILO (2021) finds that many platform workers work more hours than regular workers in order to earn a similar income.

### 3.8.3 Challenges for the Design of In-Work Benefits

The increasing relevance of less than full-time work arrangements, and atypical work forms that do not necessarily guarantee a minimum wage, make it harder to assess what minimum income protection is still relevant for the working population (if such still exists at all). It also poses new challenges to policy makers.

First, these trends challenge the value of the minimum wage as a policy benchmark. It becomes harder to assess what the actual wage floor is when atypical work forms and irregular work schedules make it increasingly difficult to predict the actual wages earned at the bottom of the labour market. As the minimum wage is not solely a tool to guarantee fair wages, but also acts as a reference value in the welfare state set-up, this is no trivial issue (Cantillon, Parolin, & Collado, 2020).

Second, more variation in earnings types, and unpredictability of earnings, put severe challenges on the design of in-work benefits and income support measures for workers. Issues related to the reference period over which incomes are assessed in order to determine eligibility to earnings top-ups, the types of incomes (wages or also other earnings, or more occasional incomes from internet activity) that are included, ... appear to be technical, but can have very real impacts on people's livelihood (Hills, 2015). The more detail income-tests aspire to, the greater the challenges put to the administration level as well as the individual claimants (Hardy, 2017). In combination with harsh sanctions in terms of faulty claims, this may well exacerbate financial problems rather than mitigate them (Whiteford, Mendelson, & Millar, 2003; Millar & Whiteford, 2020).

Third, on a more practical level, means-tested income top-ups are commonly faced with large non-take-up rates. This is no surprise, as they combine a number of risk factors that have been identified in the literature as main causes of non-take-up. Benefits that serve to supplement incomes will often be lower than income replacement benefits, meaning that the expected return on a claim will be smaller (Janssens & Van Mechelen, 2022). In addition, and especially if they are combined with volatile earnings, it is hard for potential claimants to predict or even understand how high their benefit will be, how to file a claim, and how to demonstrate their regular earnings. The fraught introduction of the Universal Credit, that aimed to overcome many of these issues by implementing a more or less automated IT system that tracked changes in earnings, perfectly illustrated the challenges that arise in keeping track and regularly reporting highly changeable earnings (see Chapter 4 for an in-depth discussion). These issues may be even more at play when the top-up to in-work incomes is solely accessible through a claim with the means-tested social assistance scheme. Impediments that may be relatively specific towards the scheme of last resort, such as the stigma related to it, or the even more intrusive means-tests, that generally also includes an assessment of assets (Marchal et al., 2021), may further discourage potential claimants.

Fourth, how should policy makers regulate access to income support measures when there is no longer such a thing as 'regular' low-wage employment? As discussed in Chapter 2, social assistance benefits, that may act as a top-up to the incomes of (very) low-wage earners, are generally conditional on job search efforts, and on the obligation to take up reasonable employment if such is offered. Marchal and Van Mechelen (2017) report that the definition of a reasonable job in some countries takes account of work schedules (in the sense that work hours should come in blocks of at least four hours), or of overall working time (for instance, a job at less than 30% of full-time employment is not considered reasonable). However, the countries that make such minimal job requirements explicit are very rare. More often, the interpretation of what is a reasonable job offer depends on the assessment of the local case manager, who is supposed to take both job availability as well as private circumstances of the claimant into account. The newly introduced universal credit in the United Kingdom alternatively pushes claimants to demonstratively keep looking for full-time employment, through constant job search, and to combine various small jobs. In a context of irregular work schedules, this is by no means an easy feat. Wright and Dwyer (2022) highlight and criticize the extensive strain that this requirement puts on working universal credit claimants, and contrast it with the previously existing scheme that provided in-work benefits and top-ups without additional job search requirements as soon as individuals worked at least 18 hours per week. Alternatively, or additionally, in-work benefits or means-tested income top-ups will be designed in such a way that their value increases with number of hours worked. Such a design aids in encouraging stronger labour market attachment, but may be less helpful in safeguarding sufficiently high income floors (Vandelannoote & Verbist, 2019).

Finally, as even a full-time minimum wage generally does not suffice to safeguard an adequate income floor for minimum wage earners with dependents (see Section 3.6), in spite of substantial additional supportive measures, the question remains as to the income levels that are actually guaranteed when labour market attachment is even more spotty.

By means of illustration, Figure 3.6 shows the net disposable income that is guaranteed for earners who have only a limited attachment to the labour market, as employee, and as self-employed. In both cases, we assume their earnings to be at 20% of the median wage.[11] For the employee, we assume these earnings to be in line with minimum wage regulations, i.e. we assume that their working hours are such that this wage level is in line with the hourly minimum wage. The necessary working time to (legally) earn 20% of median earnings at the minimum wage, for an employee, ranged

Panel A. Net disposable income and income components at 20% of median wage relative to the at-risk-of-poverty threshold, single employee, 2018

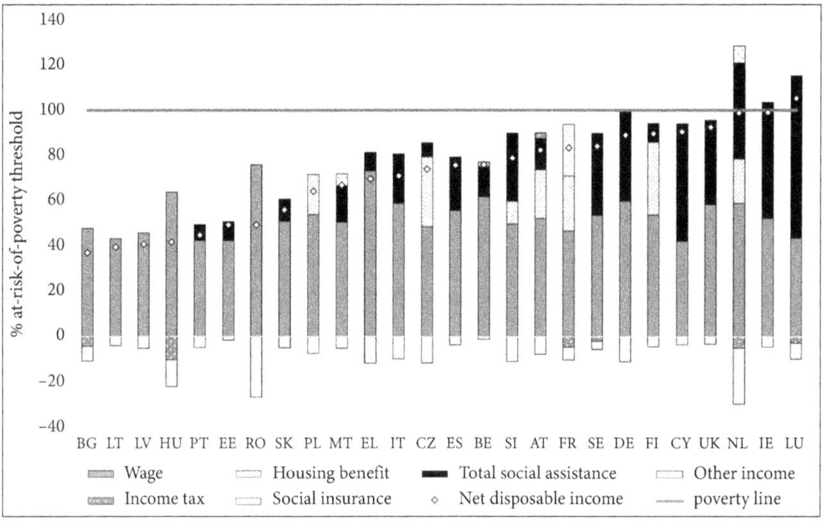


Panel B. Net disposable income at 20% of median wage and at 100% of minimum wage, single employee and single self-employed, 2018

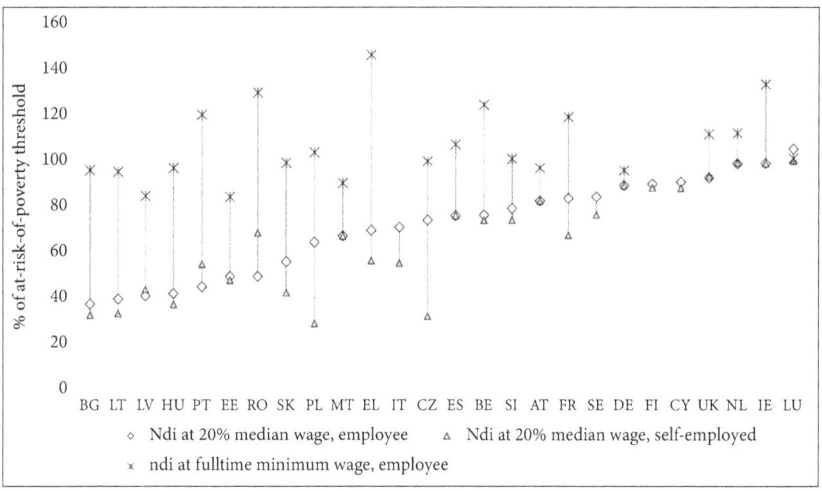


**Figure 3.6** Net disposable income and income components at limited labour market attachment, single person household, 2018

*Note:* Self-employed earnings are notoriously hard to measure and as a consequence also to assess in a means-test. Readers should therefore note that the simulations regarding the net disposable income of a self-employed include several additional country-related assumptions, and should be approached with great caution. We thank Elise Aerts for invaluable assistance in providing these simulations. Data refer to 2018 in order to be able to use cross-national comparative estimates of the median wage.

*Source:* HHoT module of EUROMOD, median wages from the Structure of Earnings Survey.

in 2018 from 12 hours in France, to 23 hours in Austria, with an average of 17 hours.[12] For the self-employed case, such an assumption is not necessary. We show whether these earners have (in principle) access to a social assistance top-ups, other means-tested (in-work) benefits or preferential tax treatment. Importantly, we compare their final net disposable income to the relevant at-risk-of-poverty threshold.

Figure 3.6 illustrates that as soon as the assumption of full-time minimum wage employment is relaxed, working single person households in most countries fail to have a net disposable income higher than the at-risk-of-poverty threshold. In most cases, their incomes are still supported by housing benefits, by in-work benefits, or by a top-up from social assistance. Recall that we noted previously that especially the latter may be hard to access for workers, as additional conditions can apply, such as asset tests, or because the means-test may be hard to understand and lead to non-take-up. The United Kingdom, with very near adequate in-work protection even in the case of spotty labour market attachment, has been criticized for the stringent behavioural conditionality and job search regime tied to the universal credit top-up, that may lead to sanctions barring workers from the full benefit (Wright & Dwyer, 2022). Still, these additional support measures appear to be indispensable in protecting the incomes of households with only partial labour market attachment, substantially improving the income situation of the typical case shown in Panel A of Figure 3.6 in over half of the countries.

In contrast, it is also clear that a number of countries that scored relatively well in terms of minimum income protection adequacy for full-time minimum wage earners through an exclusive or primordial focus on high minimum wages, do far worse with regard to the protection of persons whose earnings are limited to 20% of the median wage. Both Romania and Greece fall substantially back in the country ranking, as additional support measures appear to be inaccessible.

Panel B of Figure 3.6 furthermore compares the net disposable income at 20% median wage for an employee with that of a self-employed person, in line with concerns that non-standard work forms may further worsen access to social protection. Please note that the simulations for a self-employed are particularly tentative. Self-employed earnings are notoriously hard to measure. Hence, social assistance means-tests (and even social insurance contributions or taxes) may be based on notional self-employed earnings, rather than actual earnings. The simulations show in these cases the results of the legal reality, without taking account of discretionary assessments that may supersede apparently unrealistic notional values in a more personalized social assistance intake investigation. On a more technical note, some favourable tax treatments for low income self-employed are not included in the EUROMOD model (whereas they generally are for employees) and may—depending on the working of the social assistance means-test—lead to slightly higher or lower net minimum income packages for the self-employed. This is for instance the case in France and Sweden. Elsewhere, a notional social insurance contribution base or very high social insurance contributions lead to very low or negative earnings for the self-employed, and lead to differences in the simulated income packages (e.g., in Slovakia and Poland). In the Czech Republic, the notional value applied to self-employed earnings in the social assistance means-test renders the hypothetical household ineligible for the social assistance top-up, and substantially reduces the housing benefit. Overall, the net minimum income package guaranteed to an employee with limited labour market attachment, and the net income of a low-income self-employed appear to be in the same range in most countries. The correlation between both is around 0.82.

Finally, Panel B also shows the net disposable income at a full-time minimum wage as a reference value. It is immediately clear that the minimum income protection package at a full-time minimum wage may differ substantially from the net incomes in case of limited labour market attachment. The correlation between both is limited to 0.30. In fact, and not surprisingly in light of the results shown in panel A, the adequacy of income packages in case of limited labour market attachment appears to be far more strongly connected to the adequacy of out-of-work minimum income protection packages. The correlation between the net income packages depicted in panel A, and the out-of-work minimum income protection package for a single person household in 2018 amounts to 0.84. Interestingly, out-of-work income protection packages remain generally lower, because of overall income disregards, or specific disregards for earnings. We treat these issues more in-depth in Chapter 4.

## 3.9 In-Work Minimum Income Protection and Poverty

In contrast to out-of-work minimum income protection, in-work income protection as we have operationalized it in this chapter does not have as its main raison-d'être to protect vulnerable workers from severe poverty. Rather, the different elements that together make up minimum income protection for those in full-time employment, combine different goals. Minimum wages can be also (or even foremost) thought of as a tool to guarantee a fairer wage distribution, while in-work benefits may aim to make work pay rather than to guarantee adequate in-work incomes. Also child benefits may not first and foremost serve to protect against poverty, but rather to aid in the costs related to raising children, or even to encourage educational attainment. Social assistance top-ups will on the other hand likely aim to provide an income floor also to households with some labour market attachment, but as we have discussed before, these are not very common for full-time minimum wage earners. A relationship between in-work minimum income protection and poverty may therefore be less clearcut than policy makers might hope.

There exists extensive research tracking the relationship between minimum wages (rather than full in-work minimum income protection packages) and poverty. Microsimulation exercises that assess the first-order effects of a minimum wage increase, disregarding behavioural changes by employers and employees, find no or only a very limited effect. To the extent that minimum wage earners mainly constitute secondary earners in households, an across the board minimum wage increase (while perhaps warranted from a fairness perspective, or from an interest in making work pay) may ultimately mainly benefit those households that already find themselves higher up in the distribution (Marx, Vanhille, & Verbist, 2012; Atkinson et al., 2017).

More sophisticated econometric analyses that assess the longer-term impact of minimum wage hikes do aim to take account of second order effects of minimum wage increases. Mainly, this research strand focuses on the employment effects of the minimum wage (see the discussion in Section 3.4), finding that overall, effects appear to be relatively limited (Card & Krueger, 1994; Cengiz et al., 2019). There is also some evidence for spillover effects that may cause overall limited income increases and modest additional economic growth (Overstreet, 2019).

In Figure 3.7 we focus not on the minimum wage as such, but explore the relationship between different poverty measures and average in-work net minimum income protection packages, focusing on those families who rely on one single full-time minimum wage. Overall, the correlation between the adequacy of average in-work minimum income protection packages and the 60% and 40% at-risk-of-poverty rates is relatively limited. Rather than pointing towards a direct instrumental relevance of in-work minimum income protection as an anti-poverty device, these limited correlations might perhaps indicate the importance of the overall generosity of welfare state support in at the same time combatting poverty and in securing adequate in-work minimum income protection. This appears to be supported by the more detailed explorations reported in Cantillon, Marchal, and Luigjes (2019), that zoomed in specifically on income protection and poverty rates among

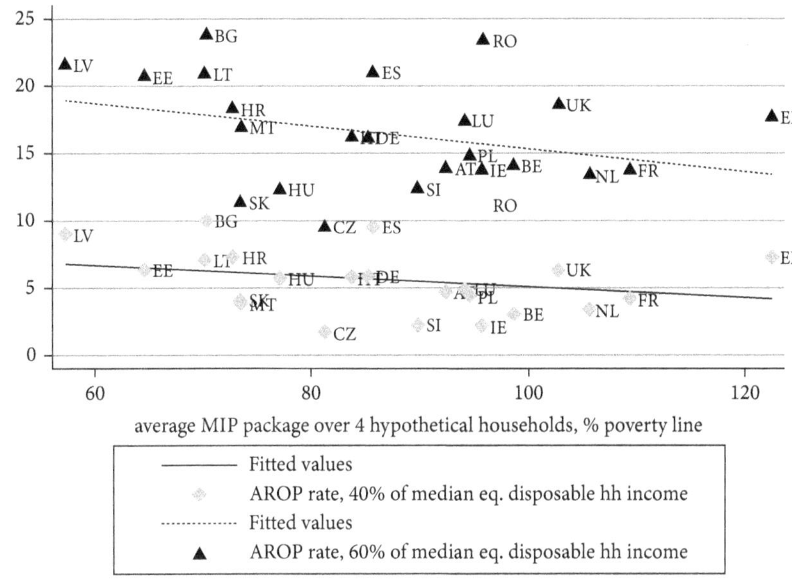


**Figure 3.7** Average in-work MIP package over four hypothetical households, relative to 60 and 40% at-risk-of-poverty rate, 2019

*Note:* Correlation average in-work minimum income protection package and 60% at-risk-of-poverty rate is -0.29. Correlation average in-work minimum income protection package and 40% at-risk-of-poverty rate is -0.25. Data for the UK refer to 2017.
*Source:* Eurostat and MIPI-HHoT.

lone parent households, and found for this specific target group a far more pronounced association. Clearly, it is impossible to draw stark conclusions from these correlations, but at least they do not negate that adequate in-work minimum income protection packages, apart from their relevance and beneficial effects for individual households, may be associated with positive poverty outcomes.

Such an intuition cannot be gathered from Figure 3.8. Here we zoom in on the association between in-work minimum income protection (again at full-time minimum wage employment), and in-work poverty rates. Figure 3.8 shows no indication for a (positive or negative) association whatsoever. It is a well-researched finding that individual work conditions do not necessarily—or even predominantly—lead to in-work poverty, as household dynamics and welfare state intervention are important buffers (Crettaz, 2013; Horemans, 2016). As in-work poverty is to large extent determined by household composition, and the extent of labour market attachment (Horemans, 2016; Hick & Marx, 2022), the issues highlighted under Section 3.8 regarding the

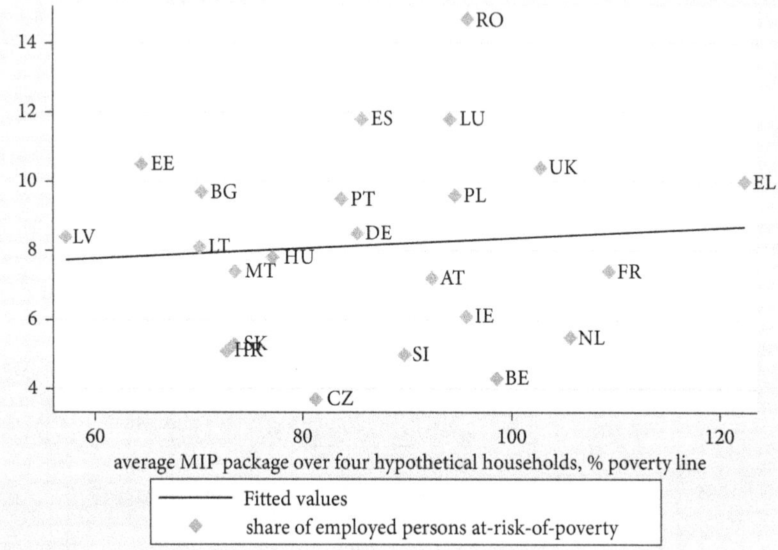


**Figure 3.8** Average in-work MIP package over four hypothetical households, relative to in-work poverty rate, 2019

*Note:* Correlation average in-work minimum income protection package and share of employed persons living in a household with income below the 60% at-risk-of-poverty threshold is 0.08. Data for the UK refer to 2017.
*Source:* Eurostat and MIPI-HHoT.

relevance of full-time minimum wage employment as benchmark for in-work minimum income protection, come to the forefront.

## 3.10 How to Guarantee Adequate Minimum Income Protection Packages for Those in Work?

This chapter discussed the different instruments that are relevant in guaranteeing minimum income protection to working people. It highlighted the different functions of the minimum wage and the considerations that underlie its level. Importantly, it showed how the minimum wage is combined with additional income support measures in order to secure a minimum income floor for those who work full-time. An important caveat in this regard is that the relevance of full-time minimum wage work can no (longer) be simply assumed as a true minimal employment case. More flexible work forms, that are not necessarily full-time, nor necessarily paid at the minimum wage, abound. This puts additional challenges to policy makers aiming to design supportive measures that can guarantee adequate in-work incomes, as to researchers when aiming to assess the adequacy of wage floors (see Section 3.8). Overall, the link between the adequacy of in-work minimum income protection packages measured at full-time minimum wage employment, and both general as work-specific poverty rates is rather tenuous (see Section 3.9).

Nonetheless, we argue that in an era of activation and in light of the attention to making work pay, continued attention for the minimal incomes guaranteed at full-time employment remains relevant. In which countries does employment at one full-time minimum wage suffice to protect individual households against poverty? And what are the policy mixes used to guarantee such an adequate in-work income floor?

Figure 3.2 in Section 3.6 taught us that adequate net disposable incomes are quite common for single person households working full-time at the minimum wage. With the exception of Malta and Estonia, minimum wages in European countries are sufficiently high to surpass 60% of equivalent median disposable household income for a single person. It is mainly limited personal incomes taxes and, more importantly, social insurance contributions that bring net disposable incomes below the at-risk-of-poverty threshold in Germany, Latvia, Hungary, and Bulgaria. The highest net income guarantees for full-time single minimum wage earners are found in Greece, the Netherlands, France, Romania, Portugal, Spain, the United Kingdom, and Belgium, which all guarantee net minimum income packages of at least 120% of the at-risk-of-poverty threshold (in contrast to the 113% in the middle group of countries). Of these countries, Romania and Greece (and to a lesser extent also Spain and Portugal) simply guarantee sizeable minimum wages or, in the case of Romania, that are not overly taxed. Social insurance contributions remain substantial. There are no additional support measures, at least not for single person households.[13] France, the Netherlands, and the United Kingdom legislate minimum wages that are comparatively generous: both in terms of the Kaitz-index as relative to the at-risk-of-poverty thresholds, these countries' minimum wages find themselves around average or higher. Taxes and social insurance contributions are relatively modest. In addition, all three countries provide additional means-tested benefits to working single persons. These additional means-tested benefits also ensure relatively high net disposable incomes for workers with more limited labour market attachment, as shown in Section 3.8.3. Finally, also the Belgian minimum wage finds itself in the upper half of the countries included in Figure 3.2, relative to the at-risk-of-poverty threshold, but also relative to average and median wages. The combined impact of taxes and social insurance contributions is even lower than it is in France, the Netherlands, and the UK, mainly as a specific reduction for working low-wage earners is implemented through the social insurance contribution calculation. On the other hand, a Belgian in-work single person household does not qualify for additional means-tested benefits.

An important observation from Figure 3.2 was that—as soon as more people depend on one single minimum wage—the wage no longer suffices to cover the additional needs. For the lone parent with two children depicted in Figure 3.2, the pre-tax and pre-social insurance contribution minimum wage level would only suffice in Romania (but see note 13). Net disposable incomes that suffice to protect against a poverty risk are only guaranteed in Poland, France, Ireland, the Netherlands, the United Kingdom, and Greece (and, should we round upwards, in Belgium). We also calculated the adequacy of in-work minimum income protection at one single minimum wage for a breadwinner couple and a breadwinner couple with two children. A breadwinner couple was only protected against the poverty risk in France and Greece (with Luxembourg, the Netherlands, the United Kingdom, and Belgium following relatively closely). A couple with two children only has a net disposable income above the at-risk-of-poverty threshold in Greece. While the inadequacy is near-general, the better performing countries remain familiar, with the United Kingdom, France, and, to a lesser extent, also Luxembourg, Poland, Ireland, Slovenia, Austria, Belgium, and Germany.

In Figures 3.7 and 3.8, we combined the results obtained for these four model families in an averaged adequacy indicator. We found the United Kingdom, the Netherlands, France, and Greece to provide most consistently adequate minimal in-work income protection, with the average net disposable income for these four model families above the poverty threshold. Belgium (at 99% of the poverty threshold), Ireland and Romania (both at 96%) follow relatively closely. Austria, Poland, and Luxembourg report average adequacy indicators above 90% of the at-risk-of-poverty threshold.

Which of these countries can we now identify as best cases? We focus on those countries that are consistently among the best performers in terms of guaranteeing adequate in-work income protection to full-time minimum wage earners: the United Kingdom, the Netherlands, France, Greece, Belgium, Ireland, and Romania. However, Figures 3.7 and 3.8 additionally indicate which countries also report above average values in terms of social outcomes in the fields of poverty and in-work poverty. While the link between social outcomes and adequate in-work income protection is far from evident (see the discussion in Section 3.9), high adequacy indicators in combination with high in-work poverty or poverty rates might indicate that the adequacy indicators are capturing a 'paper reality' rather than actual protection levels. This might be the case in Romania, the United Kingdom, and Greece. For the United Kingdom, multiple sources highlight that relatively large shares of employees earn less than the minimum wage (Trade Union Congress, 2015; Eurofound, 2019a) (see also the numbers cited in Section 3.8.1), while Greece and Romania are often identified in the literature as countries with large shadow economies (Ruge, 2010; Herwartz, Tafenau, & Schneider, 2015). Davidescu and Schneider (2017) find indications that large minimum wage increases in Romania might in the long term even contribute to increases in the shadow economy. Both Romania and Greece also foresee sizeable legal exemptions to minimum wage regulation (Eurofound, 2019a; Rat, 2022). This is a reservation that we should keep in mind when discussing the different options through which countries provide adequate in-work income protection.

Which policy mixes do we observe in countries providing (relatively) adequate in-work minimum income protection?

A first observation is that most of these countries have implemented *relatively generous statutory minimum wages*. Minimum wages relative to the at-risk-of-poverty threshold generally find themselves in the upper half of the countries depicted in Figure 3.2. Only in Ireland is the statutory minimum wage slightly below average.

A second observation is that—with the exception of Romania—the bite that *social insurance contributions and income taxes take out of gross pay at the minimum wage level remains relatively modest.* A relatively generous minimum wage, in terms of the prevailing levels, combined with low taxes and social security contributions suffices to safeguard full-time working single persons from financial poverty. However, this is no longer the case when more people depend on that income, whether adults without income or dependent children. For one, the social insurance contribution rate remains the same in all but two countries. Tax rates tend to be slightly lower when more people depend on one income, but as they are—due to the progressive tax schemes in most European countries—already low to begin with, not by enough to bring net disposable income above the at-risk-of-poverty threshold. Once more people are dependent on a single income, not even generous minimum wages and the lightest of tax burdens suffice to guarantee an adequate minimum income.

*The countries that do succeed in providing (at least on paper) adequate income packages to breadwinner households, whether consisting of one or two adults, do so through providing an additional or even multiple layers of direct income support. These often consist of (quasi-) universal benefits, such as child benefits, in combination with means-tested benefits.* These means-tested supplements can be specifically related to child benefits but can also refer to specific in-work benefits (either or not tied to the presence of children in the household, as is the case in Ireland), housing benefits, or social assistance top-ups. As always with means-tested top-ups, the disclaimer applies that take-up may be problematic (see also Section 3.8.3). Still, such top-ups have the potential to also improve the adequacy of protection packages of households with more limited labour market attachment. Chapters 4 and 5 explore the issues related to targeting in more depth.

# 4

# Design Considerations

## On Optimal Targeting, Control, and Support

### 4.1 To Target or Not to Target, That Remains the Question

The next two chapters are essentially about the eternal key issue in the design of income support. To what extent should we target any income support towards those in need and only those in need? If adequate minimum income protection is our priority then it would appear obvious that we direct redistribution primarily and efficiently to those in most need.

Targeting remains among the most contentious issues in social policy. Literally diametrically opposed reasoned opinions exist on this issue. On the one side there are those who believe that a welfare state can only fight poverty effectively and efficiently if and when benefits are targeted to those most in need. As Goodin et al. (1987, p. 215) put it more than 30 years ago in *Not Only the Poor*: 'the beneficial involvement of the non-poor in the welfare state is not merely wasteful—it is actually counterproductive. The more the non-poor benefit, the less redistributive the impact of the welfare state will be.' This view is still strongly held by some. International organizations like the World Bank have long promoted strongly targeted minimum income schemes, although they have shifted towards a more nuanced stance.

But not everybody is so keen on the idea that we should target social benefits and services primarily if not exclusively towards the more needy.[1] The grounds of opposition are diverse. Targeting by need is said to be administratively complex and costly. It requires a level of intrusion into private lives (household finances, assets, living arrangements, and even daily habits) that can feel demeaning and stigmatizing. A potential consequence of this is that people become reluctant to take up the rights they are entitled to and that we want them to have to be able to live a life in minimum dignity. Strongly targeted benefits are also said to distort work and family formation incentives, even sometimes to such an extent that they are effectively exacerbating underlying problems. One further and strongly debated counter-argument is

*Zero Poverty Society*. Sarah Marchal and Ive Marx, Oxford University Press. © Sarah Marchal and Ive Marx (2024).
DOI: 10.1093/9780191967771.003.0004

that proponents of selectivity pursue a 'mechanical' argument that ignores the political processes determining how much is actually available for redistribution. An often heard claim is that 'benefits for the poor become poor benefits'. Walter Korpi and Joakim Palme (1998) have famously and influentially claimed that, paradoxically, strong pro-poor targeting does not yield more poverty reduction but exactly the reverse. Better outcomes are achieved, they have claimed, by systems that have spillovers to the benefit of the politically powerful non-poor.

In this chapter and the next one we revisit the issue of targeting and the arguments pro and contra. We will also look at other key design issues related to targeting design, such as the broader (behavioural) conditionality of benefits. Do we need to impose conditions on minimum income recipients? Do we need to monitor and sanction people who do not abide by those conditions?

## 4.2 The Many Costs of Complexity

### 4.2.1 Targeting Means Complexity

The better one tries to target minimum income protection on those in financial need and only on those in need, from exactly the moment that situation of need arises until it ends, the more complex a policy execution challenge it becomes.

Need for income support obviously depends on a host of factors. Most important of course is the household's income situation but it also matters how many people share that income and depend on it. Particular circumstances such as bad health may exacerbate financial need.

Effective and timely income support requires that one can assess the need situation quickly and correctly. But this is often more easily said than done.

We tend to think about minimum income provisions using stylized representations of what is often a far more messy and complex reality. When assessing minimum income protection adequacy, as we did in Chapters 2 and 3, we tend to assume that the population can be neatly divided up in a limited range of relatively static and clear-cut household and income situations. A person is either single or partnered, has children or does not have children. That household has an income that is either too low or adequate.

In reality people live far more complex lives. They may have partners or children that do not reside in the household, or only part of the time. They may cohabit, at least part of the time, with partners or stepchildren but still maintain separate finances.

The 'typical' situations that we use to think about policy either assume that people have work or do not have work, and if they do we too easily assume that it is a full-time job paying a steady salary. That, again, is rarely the case. People on low incomes can have very fluctuating, complex labour market trajectories, moving in and out temporary and/or part-time jobs, taking on gig work at irregular times and so on (Hills, 2015). Such unstable income patterns have far reaching consequences for the appropriate design of minimum income schemes (Trlifajová & Hurrle, 2019).

In what follows we consider the complications such complexity brings when thinking about optimal ways to provide adequate minimum income protection. We first consider why complexity is such an important issue, especially when it comes to ensuring that people secure access to protection provisions under what often are challenging and stressful circumstances. We explain how rule and procedural complexity lead to non-take-up of social rights, not only because of information deficits and cognitive limitations but also because of stigma. In this context we also look at the role of case workers and particularly the issue of case worker discretion. We then ask whether (partial) automation of eligibility detection and determination is the way forward.

### 4.2.2 The Cost of Finding, Understanding and Processing Information

The more targeted and conditional income support provisions are, obviously the more complex they become.

One memorable demonstration of this happened at a gathering of experts at a meeting organized by the European Commission to foster 'mutual learning' across EU Member States on ways to organize minimum income protection. Delegates were asked to explain to each other the provisions in place in their respective countries. Many struggled to do this in any detail, even people with very senior managerial roles in those very systems. When prompted with detailed questions on qualification criteria, applicable incomes, and assets in means-tests or taper schemes, many had to resort to their documentation, which they sometimes failed to retrieve. One could hardly have wished for a better illustration of how opaque minimum income provisions tend to get.

Usually provisions start out relatively straightforward only to become more complex as they mature. People lead complex lives (Hills, 2015). They may draw on many different sources for their incomes. Incomes from work may not be regarded in the same way as for example alimony payments (Trlifajová & Hurrle, 2019). People may have complex or unusual living arrangements, especially when they are newly re-partnered or when there are other adults living in the household, for example dependent elderly people. Cohousing arrangements also sit very uneasily with rules written for more conventional households (Bakker & Mulder, 2013; Steenssens et al., 2016). All these complex and sometimes exceptional situations require rules to determine eligibility and to ensure fairness vis-à-vis those in comparable situations. Just by way of example: one household in Belgium became embroiled in a lengthy fight with a welfare agency because that agency refused to consider the migrant refugee that the family had offered temporary shelter in a spare room as a separate household. The family argued that there was no income sharing and limited consumption sharing. The welfare agency thought otherwise, prompting a dispute.

Rule complexity obviously increases the effort required on the part of applicants to find out what they are entitled to and how that may change if something changes to their circumstances (Janssens & Van Mechelen, 2022). Then there is the issue whether people have the time and capacity to process the complex rules determining eligibility. People who need minimum income support are rarely highly educated. Students and school leavers applying for income support may be an exception, insofar that they are not covered by separate schemes of income support and loans. But the vast majority of people who have to resort to minimum income support provisions for their very survival are not highly educated people, let alone sophisticated would-be bureaucrats. Significant numbers of minimum income applicants are recent migrants with limited language skills.

Financial need is often triggered by an event that in itself may be very stressful, hampering people's ability 'to think clearly', let alone to deal with complex information and tedious bureaucratic procedures. That event can be a divorce, an accident, or job loss. For people living on a modest income, a worsened financial situation can quickly spiral out of control. It may even cause them to take on loans offered by 'helpful' loan sharks, eventually exacerbating their plight. All this can cause intense stress, feelings of shame, and even result in social exclusion. What is worse, it can make finding a solution even more difficult, as they fall victim to a sense of hopelessness. There is growing literature showing that this will hamper people's ability to get out of their highly problematic situation. Psychologists studying people's behaviour under such circumstances argue that this becomes especially problematic when it results in 'tunnelling', hampering the cognitive power needed to solve problems, reason, or retain information. It may also limit executive control and reduce people's ability to plan ahead. Their focus becomes immediate: putting food on the table, paying rent and other bills (Mullainathan & Shafir, 2013).

### 4.2.3 Behavioural Insights

Let us look more closely at what research by scholars working in the intersection of psychology, sociology, and economics teaches us about how people in poverty or facing the risk of poverty actually think and act. This burgeoning field of behavioural science has certainly added much sophistication and insight.

Economics in particular has moved significantly away from the working assumption that people hold coherent, well-informed beliefs and that they pursue their goals rationally and in their own best interest. That notion, while mostly motivated by methodological convenience, has of course always been pretty absurd but it has in effect shaped much of the empirical economics literature on poverty and what policy can do about it, especially through money transfers. There is a vast difference between how people are supposed to behave in the neoclassical universe of thinking and how they actually behave. We will come back to this at various points in this chapter. Overall the body of sophisticated research we have today has clearly demonstrated that people's actual behaviour is often far removed from what the standard models would predict (see e.g. Bertrand et al., 2004, 2006; Beaulier & Caplan, 2007; Mani et al., 2013; Mullainathan & Shafir, 2013; Schilbach, Schofield, & Mullainathan, 2016).

Some scholars have veered towards somewhat extreme views (see for example Beaulier & Caplan, 2007). There are those who view the poor as having various psychological and attitudinal shortcomings causing their views to be often misguided, their behaviours lacking and their choices fallible. Such thoughts are usually expressed in veiled or coded ways, especially in the academic literature, but Richard Herrnstein and Charles Murray's *The Bell Curve* (2010) is a prime example of a book that ascribes poverty in major part to a lack of cognitive ability. Books like these may thoroughly lack in scientific rigour but they are influential nevertheless, especially in the political sphere.[2]

Prominent behavioural scientists seem to be of the position today that the behavioural patterns of the poor are neither perfectly calculating nor especially deviant. In their book *Scarcity*, Sendhil Mullainathan and Eldar Shafir (2013) report convincingly on their combined research that demonstrates that people living in poverty have the same weaknesses and biases as other people have. But these may manifest themselves in more pronounced ways and can lead to worse outcomes, especially since poor people have narrow margins for error (see Bertrand et al., 2004).

Low-income people are said to be susceptible to many of the same idiosyncrasies as those who live in comfort, but 'whereas better-off people typically find themselves, either by default or through minimal effort, in the midst of a system composed of attractive "no-fee" options, automatic deposits, reminders, and so forth, that is built to shelter them from grave or repeated error, less-well off people often find themselves without such "aids" and instead are confronted by obstacles—institutional, social, and psychological—that render their economic conduct all the more overwhelming and fallible' (Bertrand et al., 2006, p. 8).

A couple of mechanisms stand out, all relevant to the way we should think about policies to prevent poverty.[3]

First, as we already mentioned: eligibility rules and procedures of existing minimum protection programmes tend to be complex. Of course, a critical requirement for the success of any social programme is that people know it and understand it. In reality there is rampant ignorance of programme rules, benefits, and opportunities. Randomized experiments have shown the huge impact of outreach activities, such as informing potential beneficiaries of the programmes they might be eligible to (Van Gestel et al., 2022). Even highly educated and 'sophisticated' people often do not understand programmes or offerings aimed at them, as we will illustrate in this chapter when we discuss the American EITC.

A second factor that contributes to low take-up are the 'hassle costs'. To a classical economist these will appear as too minor to be taken seriously but research finds that hassle can in fact be detrimental for take-up. Application forms can be far too long and far too hard to understand, often because they are full of bureaucratic jargon, acronyms, and legalese. Quasi-experiments that benefit from variations in claiming procedures between groups over time find that take-up rates are higher among those groups that were faced with lower claiming costs (Kopczuk & Pop-Eleches, 2007). Using innovative purpose-collected cross-sectional survey data for Belgium, Julie Janssens finds in her PhD thesis, in a collaboration with Tim Goedemé and Manon Bolland (Janssens, 2023), that both information costs, and costs related to the administrative process of claiming a benefit, are among the more important drivers of non-take-up.

Third, people procrastinate by nature. Hassle factors may worsen this. Even if people go to a welfare office, the chance that they achieve what they set out to do may be frustratingly low. There may be long lines and delays, forms may be so complicated that additional information or help is often needed and some required document is bound to be forgotten. Procrastination may be further enhanced by present bias.

### 4.2.4 Shame, Pride, and Stigma

Lack of information and lack of ability, energy or mental focus to process that information may be a first hurdle to taking up benefits and regaining self-reliance later. There may be other hurdles on the way.

Societal norms for one. In most advanced economies people at working age who are capable for work are expected to earn their own living and be self-reliant. Not only is there a positive view of self-reliant people, economic success tends to be celebrated and revered.

In such a context, benefit receipt may well be perceived as a deviation from the work norm and as a sign of failure. An individual may thus fear a loss of social status or disapproval from others—family, friends, and neighbours. To the extent that a norm is internalized, an individual may also experience 'personal costs', or 'mental dissonance' from violating it. If that is the case, the constraint on action is internal. A person may avoid violating the norm even when no one will ever find out about them claiming or receiving benefits.

There is quite a bit of research that there is stigma attached to social assistance receipt and that this has real consequences on people's lives, including their ability to regain the self-reliance policy makers and politicians often deem so important. Lone mothers on benefits in the UK for example have reported being seen primarily as failed workers and citizens, rather than as struggling mothers trying to support their children in difficult circumstances (Jun, 2022). This stigma is internalized as feelings of shame and damages their social identity.[4]

The extent of stigmatization may well depend on the policy context, the dominant policy discourse and the prevailing economic conditions, notably the level of unemployment and the number of vacancies. Clearly, in some countries what are sometimes labelled 'neoliberal' interpretations of unemployment and poverty have become more dominant. Even 'progressive' parties have (at times) become more sympathetic to neoliberal narratives.

In such narratives, outcomes are framed as resulting from individual failures to make the right decisions, to try enough, to put in enough effort or simply to have enough self-discipline and diligence. Policy makers have in some cases used stigmatizing discourses to portray the unemployed as undeserving of social assistance benefits. This has gone hand in hand with increasingly punitive welfare conditionality and benefit sanctions in at least some cases (Marchal et al., 2014; Immervoll & Knotz, 2018). Public attitudes have in some cases also shifted towards an anti-welfare stance with people on benefits being distinguished as different. A 'them and us' mentality has become apparent in political and media discourses in some countries, as the late John Hills (2015) vividly documented for the UK.

From that perspective it seems like a good idea to have integrated benefits for people out of work and people in work, partially or completely. Some countries have made significant steps towards integrated income-support systems for people out of work and (at least partially) in work. The United Kingdom's Universal Credit or the (now reformed) French RSA scheme (Revenu de Solidarité Active) are examples of means-tested benefit scheme offering income support to the non-employed and to low-paid workers alike.

However, the stigma associated with means-tested benefits may still hamper take-up, especially in combination with the factors already enumerated under Section 4.2.3. One telling anecdote in this context was recounted by a German official at a European peer learning event who told the story of his hairdresser, a relatively low-paid single mother. In Germany, the so-called Arbeitslosengeld II (Unemployment Benefit II, UB II) (now replaced by the Burgergeld scheme), colloquially known as 'Hartz IV', was not only an unemployment compensation scheme. It was also used to top-up wages that were below the household-specific level of UB II. The number of individuals who, despite being employed, are eligible to supplementary UB II, known as 'Aufstocker' (Topupper), amounted to about one million in 2020, most of them working in part-time or Minijobs. While the hairdresser was likely to be entitled to the top-up, she was reluctant to apply because it meant that she would have to stand in line with applicants for unemployment benefits. That she experienced as demeaning precisely because she was working as a single mother and providing for her child on earnings alone, a fact she took pride in. That non-take-up was a significant problem within the German scheme, most likely for a variety of reasons, was confirmed by a study by Harnisch (2019). Using micro-simulation modelling, she estimates non-take-up of *Arbeitslosengeld II* at a very significant and stable 56% of the eligible population during the period she looks at, 2005–2014. That percentage was even higher among those employed (in the range of 73–78% during the period under analysis) and as high as 83–90% among the self-employed. Non-take-up rates were much lower among the economically non-active, at around 18–25% in the period covered. So while it makes perfectly good sense to have integrated income support arrangements for non-workers and workers alike from the perspective of work incentives and administrative efficiency, other considerations may plead against this.

### Box 4.1 Targeting without stigma? Lessons from Australia

Australia has a welfare system where means-testing is comprehensively used to determine eligibility. The Australian case is particularly interesting in that benefits are not only means-tested but also targeted at large portions of the population. Several Australian means-tested benefits are not primarily targeted at the very poor but have been designed to exclude those with relatively high incomes. Incomes at which benefits are phased out tend to lie close to, and for some benefits clearly over, median incomes. Because a large portion of the population receives such means-tested benefits, it may be seen as less degrading to receive them than elsewhere.

Carina Mood (2010) has studied the take-up of benefits in Australia, where virtually all cash benefits are means-tested. She estimated the general take-up rate of benefits among people with low assets and incomes and carried out a detailed analysis of take-up of one particular benefit, Parenting Payment. She finds take-up rates to be high, suggesting that comprehensive means-testing can work. The explanation she puts forward is that stigma of means-tested benefits in Australia is low because they target a relatively large proportion of the population.

Means-testing in Australia seems to work relatively well because it is comprehensively used throughout the system. There is administrative capacity since means-testing has been ubiquitous for a long time. This has allowed for administrative optimization of the process of means-testing. Work disincentives are far less severe than in other means-tested systems because the Australian system is in effect rich-tested rather than poor-tested. Usually social assistance schemes have very high withdrawal rates, sometimes moderated by earnings disregards up to a level of earned income (see also Section 4.3.7). Yet in Australia benefits are reduced at a much lower rate, first by 50% and then by 60% as additional income is earned. For lone parents, the withdrawal rate is even lower at 40%. Additional payments for children are separately income-tested, with a withdrawal rate of only 20–30% (Millar & Whiteford, 2020).

The Australian case seems to show that comprehensive means-testing is possible. After decades of experience with means-testing and continuing readjusting and

*continued*

**Box 4.1** *continued*

refining, the tax-benefit system seems to have become a relatively well-integrated system. Comparative cross-country analysis shows Australia to have one of the most targeted and 'cost-efficient' transfer systems in the rich world. This is illustrated in Box 5.1.

Yet there are problems. The Australian system seeks to be highly responsive to changing needs. Income support payment periods are generally fortnightly and the usual assessment period is also 14 days. This cycle aligns with most wage and salary earners in Australia, who also have fortnightly pay, although not necessarily according to the same schedule as the assessment period.

Millar and Whiteford (2020) show that responsiveness can be particularly challenging when changes in income and circumstances are frequent and unpredictable. That can result in payments getting out of step with circumstances resulting in underpayments or overpayments, and hence debts to be repaid (referred to as 'robo-debt'), which can lead to individual hardship and political controversy for governments.

The Australian approach mostly works correctly if individuals receive exactly the same income each fortnight. Yet people who move between different jobs frequently, or who have short interruptions to work, are potentially exposed to debts. A significant proportion of Australian workers have variable earnings. According to Millar and Whiteford (2020), in 2018, 24% of all employees reported earnings varying from one period to the next (excluding overtime payments). One in five Australian workers often worked a different number of hours each week, and an equal share had no guaranteed minimum number of hours each week.

That inevitably results in frequent miscalculations of entitlements, especially because of Australia's 'pay now, reconcile later' approach. It also results in tens of thousands of Australians ending up in debt when they are unable to settle overpayments from the income and savings they have. The costs are high, Millar and Whiteford (2020) point out, not just financially but also in relation to the perceived legitimacy of the system.

Some are even more critical of the Australian welfare state. In 'Half a Citizen: Life on welfare in Australia', John Murphy, Suellen Murray, Jenny Chalmers, Sonia Martin, and Greg Marston castigate the Australian welfare state for being inadequate, unsupportive, and stigmatizing. Drawing on 150 interviews, the authors paint a picture of people, often working people, struggling to make ends meet financially while also fighting to maintain their dignity in a welfare system that treats them as half citizens.

The authors point out that Australia's combination of funding from general taxation and comprehensive means testing has made the moral character of the welfare state transaction different from countries where entitlements are 'earned rights' through social contributions or where entitlements are citizen rights without income tests.

'The Australian model of means tests has meant that welfare support has always been efficiently targeted to those most in need, and that this accounts for the low level of expenditure on welfare in Australia. But it may also mean it has consequently had lower popular legitimacy, because a means-tested welfare system is only ever about others. It can be too easily seen as a system in which taxpayers pay for other people [...]' (Martin et al., 2020, p. 8).

While comprehensive means-testing seems to work relatively well in Australia, the system is clearly not without its problems nor without its critics.

### 4.2.5 The Reality Is: Non-Take-Up Is a Fundamentally Serious Issue

Summing up so far, minimum income schemes naturally work by rules and procedures, usually complex rules and procedures. Applicants often struggle to find out what the rules and procedures exactly are, what they mean and how they can navigate them. Additionally, the life events that cause people to require minimum income support can be quite stressful, hampering their ability to apply for the protections they need easy access to. They may of course also provide a trigger to do exactly that. Yet feelings of shame may be a hampering factor. The combined result of all of this may well be that many people do not access the support that is available to them, fully and in time.

There is no denying that a vast discrepancy exists between the economic subsistence rights people are entitled to by law in many countries nowadays and the often harsh realities of accessing those paper rights, including cumbersome application processes and of case managers prodding deeply into applicant's private lives, their incomes, their possessions, their living arrangements, and even their consumption and daily life habits. Instead of being treated as claimers of legitimate rights, minimum income applicants are not seldomly treated as potential frauds and shirkers.[5] Demeaning, stigmatizing application processes inevitably bring non-take-up, which is a far from trivial problem when it comes to provisions offering the final safety net against misery and loss of dignity.

A study for the Netherlands, building on interviews with low-income households, shows that such issues actually matter. Several participants mentioned that 'the government wants to know everything about you', which they experienced as humiliating (Simonse et al., 2023).

Non-take-up of rights is a fundamental public policy challenge. It is especially problematic when it comes to 'last resort' support. The empirical evidence on non-take-up is fragmented but it still adds up to a worrying picture. Ko and Moffitt (2022) provide a comprehensive overview of previous studies on take up (see also Chapter 2, Section 2.8.5, Eurofound, 2015; Fuchs et al., 2020). Estimates from these various studies indicate that in many Western European countries perhaps more than half of those eligible for social assistance at active age may not receive it, at least not in full and in time. Some studies have arrived at even higher estimates. The new Spanish minimum income scheme for example reaches only 40% of the target population, using 56% of the expected budget (Eichhorst et al., 2023). Now, it must be added right away that these estimates differ a lot because they pertain to very different programmes across a wide range of countries.

That is not to say that high non-take-up has to be accepted as a fact of life. Finland is an interesting case in this context because a fundamental shift occurred in the way eligibility for social assistance benefits is determined (Mesiäislehto, Moisio, & Ilmakunnas, 2022; Tervola, Mesiäislehto, & Ollonqvist, 2023). Before 2017 local discretion applied. Since the 2017 reform, eligibility for basic social assistance (there are still discretionary supplements in the form of supplementary and preventive social assistance) is assessed by a centralized system where decisions are essentially automated, based on the same criteria. Basic social assistance can be applied for online and receiving the benefit does not require a meeting with a social worker. However, a 'red flag' algorithm identifies long-term social assistance beneficiaries, who in principle receive attention from a social worker. In a comparative analysis of Finland and Sweden, Tervola et al. (2023) find that there is more widespread use of social assistance in Finland, a fact which they attribute in part to the automation of the eligibility determination there. The Swedish system still requires a personal meeting with a social worker and eligibility is individually assessed, also taking into account willingness to work. The Swedish systems also allows for harsher sanctions, which may act as an additional deterrent increasing non-take-up.

While the Finnish approach seems to yield better results in terms of take-up there also seem to be downsides. On the basis of interviews, Laatu et al. (2020) find that the people in the most vulnerable positions—people who have the most complex cases and who are perhaps facing challenges such as drug dependence or mental health issues—are the least satisfied with on-line claiming. Often, these people also need to interact with their municipal social workers for either supplementary or preventive social assistance or for non-financial support. So perhaps they are in some way 'losers' from the centralization, in the sense that the municipal social workers knowing these people's specific cases could have applied their discretion in a more humane way.

A study by Fuchs et al. (2020) for Austria is also revealing because it shows that well-intentioned (and well-designed) procedural reform can help boost take-up rates significantly. The study analyses the impact of a reform of the Austrian minimum income scheme that took place around 2010. The reform had a number of objectives but one of the principal aims was to make the application procedure more transparent and efficient. The aim was also to reduce non-take-up because of shame, essentially by giving claimants the option to bypass their less anonymous local municipal offices and making a more remote and anonymous claim with another agency. At the same time, insecurity regarding the prospective benefit level was reduced through binding minimum standards, a less stringent accounting of assets, and more limited maintenance obligations. Benefit receipt also entitled to health insurance, increasing their expected value. The analysis suggests that the estimated non-take-up of social assistance dropped from some 53% to around 30%. That is quite a sizeable impact, demonstrating the point that procedural simplicity and anonymity can help to boost take-up quite significantly. The authors note that part of this decrease may be related to an increased knowledge of the scheme among the prospective claimants, as the benefit reform was extensively covered in the media and the public debate.

A study by the Inspectorate of the Dutch Social Affairs and Work Ministry (2021) reveals persistently high rates of non-take-up, even within the much audited and frequently reorganized Dutch social assistance administration, where non-take-up has long been an issue of attention. The study by the Inspectorate is particularly interesting because it has both a quantitative and a qualitative component. The quantitative component, drawing on rich administrative data, reveals some interesting patterns.

The overall picture is one of a relatively high rate of take-up of Dutch social assistance, which is among the more generous provisions in Europe (cf. Chapter 2). Take-up is estimated at around 65%, which is higher than for many similar provisions elsewhere (see Fuchs et al., 2020; Ko & Moffitt, 2022). Interestingly, of all the characteristics studied, the level of income has the strongest correlation with the likelihood of non-take-up. Non-take-up is highest among those who are entitled to the lowest amounts, which is consistent with standard economic theory. Perhaps more surprisingly, age is also a strong predictor of non-use. Younger adults in particular are less prone to applying for social assistance. That also applies to people who are self-employed.

But the qualitative part of the study is particularly revealing. The administrators interviewed indicate that they have little or no insight into the extent of the non-use of social assistance within their municipality. Municipalities restrict their actions to providing information, largely by putting it on their website. Citizens are not actively approached in the municipalities interviewed for the study. In fact, municipalities say they are more focused on getting people out of welfare. In some municipalities actions are taken to trace (potential) non-users, for instance by cooperating with other welfare agencies, housing corporations or energy suppliers. Municipalities mention stricter privacy procedures as an obstacle to enhanced outreach to non-users. The welfare legislation itself (the Participation Act) is perceived as complicated, making it difficult to provide information and to cooperate in an integrated way with professionals in related fields.

In sum, the study shows that even in a setting with an already comparatively high level of take up of benefits, improvements remain possible and achievable. There may be real trade-offs here with other legitimate concerns such as privacy and due legal process. But other factors, such as the fact that welfare agencies are more strongly incentivized, politically and budget-wise, to reduce caseloads than to increase them are firmly within the realm of political choice. If there is a political will, then there remains room for improvement. If the political pressure is to reduce caseloads and cut welfare spending then this will almost inevitably translate into actions (or non-actions) conducive to high non-take-up. This is a choice, not an inevitability.

### 4.2.6 Case Worker Discretion Cuts Both Ways

Social assistance case workers usually have considerable discretion to judge a person deserving of support or not. To that end they have considerable powers of investigation into how applicants live, what their income is, what their assets are, with whom they live and even what their life style is. House visits are a common element of social assistance claim assessments in European countries, although in some countries these should also be understood as a way to identify other needs, rather than as a controlling mechanism (Marchal & De Wilde, 2019). Furthermore, the receipt of benefits is generally conditional upon the willingness to work (Immervoll & Knotz, 2018). That requirement is usually not very strictly defined nor is it easy to define as it requires a personalized assessment of each client's situation

(De Wilde & Marchal, 2019). This again is commonly done by individual case workers with considerable powers of discretion.

The task of assessing the willingness to work (or alternatively, specific individual needs) clearly leaves ample discretion to case managers in its implementation. It is of vital importance to take personal situations into account when attempting to support and activate people with vulnerable profiles. It is obviously impossible to capture every specific case in legislation, or even in local guidelines (Minas et al., 2014). Kazepov and Barberis (2013) use the term *interpretative discretion* to refer to discretion arising from multi-layered responsibilities and a lack of concrete (or consistent) rules. Alternatively, *discretion within a standard rule* presumes the interpretation and assessment of clear legislation or guidelines. Finally, Kazepov and Barberis (2013) highlight the possibility (and sometimes even need) for *contrasting discretion*, it is when case managers break existing regulation or do more than they are expected to do, when the individual client's situation calls for it.

All that discretionary power can cut both ways. It can empower case workers to help people who would otherwise have trouble navigating official procedures and meeting predefined requirements (as is usually the case with social insurance provisions). It can make sure that specific needs and individual challenges are identified and remedied. As in the earlier discussed Finnish case, automated eligibility determination has its advantages but it can also deprive less procedure-savvy people from benevolent discretion.

But that same power of discretion, which can be used as a force for the good, also awards a level of power to the case worker that can have a darker side, as it can lead to a variation in treatment between beneficiaries that is hard to defend from a social rights perspective.

How do case workers actually use their discretionary room? Marjolijn De Wilde looked into the workings of caseload worker discretion in some depth, in quantitative case studies for Belgium.

This is what she did. She conducted a so-called factorial survey among 584 case managers deciding on eligibility for social assistance in 89 Belgian municipalities. In a factorial survey experiment, each respondent gets to read stories (vignettes) about individuals, and then rates them. In her study, she asked the respondents to assign experimental ratings to a variety of vignettes concerning hypothetical social assistance clients with regard to the likelihood that they would lose their social assistance benefits if they were to refuse a job offer. In an alternative scenario, she asked the likelihood of a prospective claimant to be awarded a social assistance benefit, with characteristics that represented different levels of need and motivation to work or study. Each respondent rated nine vignettes with variations across 14 client characteristics which were selected based on the existing literature, as well as on interviews with case managers, team leaders, and academics. The characteristics that were kept constant in all vignettes were age (22 years), marital status (single), income and debts (none), contact with parents (none), not cohabiting with antecedents or adult descendants, and physical health (healthy). The 14 client characteristics that were varied had to do with socio-demographic characteristics, as well as characteristics that are considered as being likely to affect the ways in which case managers assess individual situations, such as indicators of willingness to work. Over 14,000 experimentally varied client cases were assessed in this way.

This approach yielded some remarkable findings.

*First*, most of the variation in the treatment of individual cases was related to the client level: the individual client characteristics explained to large extent the variation in decisions related to (continued) access to social assistance benefits. Generally, the impact of client characteristics was in line with common deservingness notions (de Wilde & Marchal, 2016).

*Second*, she found little variation at the municipal level in the assessment of the vignettes. Belgian social assistance is strongly decentralized, owing in part to its historical roots in local charitable poverty relief initiatives. That high degree of local autonomy allows in principle for the establishment of municipal social policy practices in tune with local circumstances and needs. Although sensible arguments can and have been made for decentralization of social policies (e.g., it creates scope for policy experimentation, and to align assessments of work willingness with the local labour market situation) it is not the case that local autonomy automatically yields large (consistent) local policy variation, at least not in the assessment of work willingness and the administration of sanctions. The local variation that was found, could be explained by the political constellation of the political board responsible for the administration of the social assistance benefits, and by the organization of the overall team involvement in sanction decisions (De Wilde & Marchal, 2019).

The most surprising finding was, however, the very substantial variation found at the case-manager level, at least in the assessment of the likelihood of initiating a sanction upon (repeated) job refusals. Variation in the assessment of initial eligibility turned out to be fairly limited. In fact, motivation to work or study did not substantially impact initial eligibility assessments, social workers appeared to favour a stabilization of the individual situation, before further following up on work willingness (De Wilde, 2016). In contrast, the established magnitude of variation was quite large in the assessment of job refusals while already receiving a benefit. Some case workers were very prone to sanctioning welfare applicants for not being sufficiently work-oriented while other case workers were much more relaxed about this and did not consider lack of work-willingness as a ground for sanctioning. While the individual client characteristics still accounted for most of the variation in treatment, variation in case managers' assessment was a close second (De Wilde & Marchal, 2019). Variation at the case manager level could partially be explained by the age of the case manager, where older case managers were more likely to be mild, and by the attitudes and ideological proclivities of case managers regarding the necessity of sanctioning and the proclivity of welfare state overuse (De Wilde, 2018; De Wilde & Marchal, 2019). A substantial part of the variation in case managers' assessments remained unexplained.

The fact that case workers have discretion and use that discretion puts applicants at jeopardy of being treated in a rather arbitrary way against which they may have little recourse. There is no easy solution for this. It is obviously impossible to capture every specific case in legislation, or even in guidelines for supervising authorities and managers. Appeals procedures can provide a safeguard but we know that these can be unnerving and lengthy. Interpretative discretion is the only workable way for a final safety net that can handle any imaginable situation. Perhaps the best compromise is to be relatively lenient and generous at first—as was also found to be a common practice among Belgian case workers—so as to stabilize what may well be a severely disrupted life. By the time some people apply for social assistance for a first time they may well be in a quite challenging if not desperate situation. In a later phase there is perhaps more scope for case workers to use their discretionary powers in function of other objectives, such as stimulating steps towards self-reliance. But such discretionary powers have a darker side and we need to be well aware of it. Automation is for sure not a superior alternative, as we will discuss next.

### 4.2.7 The Illusion of Real-Time Targeting

In a 2019 report on ways to modernize social protection, the OECD has suggested that: 'policy makers should consider [...] making means tests more responsive to people's needs by shortening the reference periods for needs assessments and by putting appropriate weight on recent or current incomes of all family members' (OECD, 2019, p. 325).

Systematic, high-frequency means-testing appeals to some politicians because it allows them to sell the illusion that adequate poverty prevention can be done in a very cost-efficient way. This is, as we will argue now, far more easily said than done. Getting income support finely attuned to the established needs of people in a correct and timely way is unfortunately a far more daunting policy execution challenge than many politicians seem to realize or care to admit.

The experience in Australia, the country with the most comprehensively means-tested welfare system, vividly demonstrates this point (see Box 4.1). It appears to work relatively well there but the Australian experience also shows that responsiveness can be particularly challenging when changes in income and circumstances are frequent and unpredictable. It often causes payments to get out of step with circumstances resulting in underpayments or overpayments. Overpayments can lead to debts, sometimes problematic levels of indebtedness. Apart from the individual hardship this brings to many people it also has damaging political fallouts. While the political motive behind 'real-time' means-testing is to increase public support for welfare payments (by making the system more 'cost-effective' by only giving money to those in 'real need'), the actual result is often controversy and eroded legitimacy.

Perhaps the most sobering tale in this context is provided by the less than smooth roll-out of Universal Credit in the United Kingdom. The Universal Credit was to become a flagship reform of the UK's historically strongly means-tested benefits system under the Conservative government of David Cameron, rolling together six so-called 'legacy' benefits into one benefit paid monthly to claimants. The aim, for which there was at the time support across the political divide, was to simplify the benefit system, make it more efficient and increase the incentives for people to work rather than stay on benefits.

On paper it all made a lot of sense. The fact that there were multiple means-tested benefits in place meant administrative multiplication. Multiple applications, multiple forms, multiple decisions. The interactions between the various benefits were often so complex that claimants had no idea of what their next income would be.

The entirely sensible claim was that Universal Credit would replace multiple calculations with a single simpler sum. Beyond easing the transition into work, an entirely plausible claim was that having one benefit rather than six would help boost take-up and that it would ensure that people received all the money to which they were entitled.

What made Universal Credit so ambitious was the objective to deliver benefits in close to 'real time'. The idea was that UC would be re-calculated every month, taking into account changing incomes and family circumstances, and some forms of expenditure such as housing and childcare costs.

Legislated in 2011, the plan was to roll it out across the UK by 2017. But a series of management failures and IT glitches—abundantly documented in countless official and media reports—rapidly caused it to fall way behind schedule (Millar & Bennett, 2017; NAO, 2018). In part, it has to be said, those problems had been expected. The government had opted for a gradual learning-by-doing roll out instead of a sudden country-wide launch with all systems in place and tested.

One study, commissioned by Gateshead Council on the impact of the roll out of Universal Credit (UC) in two localities in north-east England conducted by researchers at Teesside and Newcastle Universities in late 2018 (five years after the first roll-out of Universal Credit), found that claiming the benefit was experienced as complicated, difficult and demeaning. Participants described a labyrinthine, dysfunctional UC system prone to administrative errors, experienced as impersonal, hostile, punitive, and difficult to navigate (Cheetham et al., 2019).

The requirement to initiate and manage a UC claim online was strikingly problematic for many participants. Digital literacy, lack of computer access, bank account and/or email address, and problems verifying identification online added to the difficulties. Consequences of waiting for payment[6] of between five and 12 weeks pushed many into debt, rent arrears, and serious hardship, which included going without food and utilities. Another report, published in 2018 by the UK's Department for Work and Pensions (Foster et al., 2018), found that one in six claimants reported that they did not have internet access at home. They had to rely on computers in libraries, cafes, or jobcentres to apply for, or update their claim for, the primarily online benefit.

For all its theoretical benefits, universal credit has been immensely problematic in practice. A massive gap emerged between how the system was meant to work and how it actually operated, putting claimants at heightened risk of hunger, debt and rent arrears, ill-health, and homelessness. Food banks, for example, reported significant increases in their work load when universal credit was introduced into the local area.

The greatest disillusionment followed from a naïve faith in the power of ICT to deliver real-time delivery of benefits. Lord Freud, the responsible minister at the time of the roll-out, sounded convinced that Universal Credit would be responsive to people's real needs every month (Sainsbury, 2014, p. 40).

But people's lives turned out to be far more complicated than the politicians advocating the scheme were able to fathom. As John Hills and colleagues (Hills, Smithies, & McKnight, 2006) found when investigating changes in incomes, these were multiple and often related to other sources in addition to pay. Low-income families also tend to experience frequent changes in other circumstances, such as housing costs and number of people in the household.

Jane Millar and Fran Bennett (2017) cite Baroness Hollis, another former minister, as responsible: 'It is fair to say that when we introduced the Tax Credits Bill we did not predict that 50 per cent of lone parents would undergo more than a dozen changes in circumstance a year.'

Millar and Bennett also point out that people often did not report changes in circumstances immediately, in part because many changes were inherently short term or unstable. For example, children in separated families living with one parent and then moving to live with the other.

In a book on low-income families with children in Northern Ireland, Daly and Kelly (2015, p. 176) talk of 'not a gap but a chasm' between policy assumptions and the actual lives of low-income people. They state that 'the assumptions underpinning the design of Universal Credit are divorced from what we know from research on life in low-waged and often insecure employment (or living on a low income out of work)'.

Universal Credit is a sobering demonstration of what a major disconnect between wishful thinking on the part of politicians and the real world can lead to. In the words of Jane Millar and Fran Bennett: 'Universal Credit could be seen as an example of a "cultural disconnect", in which policy-makers assume that people live as they themselves do and, in the case of social security, do not readily understand the realities of life for people without employment and income stability and with few cushions against adversity' (Millar & Bennett, 2017, p. 174).

But more fundamentally, the pile of excellent research on what went wrong with the UK's Universal Credit illustrates the dilemma facing those in search of income support policies that are highly responsive to changes in need and circumstance. Families' incomes and circumstances can vary frequently and significantly, putting them at risk of having to make refunds of money that they no longer have. On the other hand, more 'real-time' responsive payment systems appear far more complex to put into practice than one would think. The data and data processing capacity is simply not there (yet).

As Jane Millar and Peter Whiteford conclude from the UK and Australian case studies, benefit systems that respond very quickly to changes in earnings and other circumstances create problems of overpayments and debt by design. 'Many citizens have been directly, often adversely, affected by these policy choices, advertently or inadvertently. These issues are far from resolved in these countries, with ongoing legal challenges in both the UK and Australia, as well as political and popular debate about the future purpose and design of income-tested benefits for working-age people. Timing issues are increasingly visible, as income-testing and in-work benefits are expanding. There will always be trade-offs in designing such benefits but there is much that can be learnt from these UK and Australian policy examples' (Millar & Whiteford, 2020, p. 16).

### 4.2.8 Information Technology and Artificial Intelligence to the Rescue?

The UK's Universal Credit and its promise of 'real-time' benefit adjustment has been a very public failure for much of its existence. A ray of optimism is offered, perhaps, by the enormous advances that are taking place in information technology. These may well make accurate, timely, and cost-effective eligibility detection and determination soon more achievable than what has proved possible so far. After all, governments nowadays have ever richer and far more up to date information about their citizens. At the same time, 'big data' and artificial intelligence are among the most vibrant fields of applied science.

Automated forms of decision-making (ADM) are becoming more important in the administration of minimum income benefits. In many ways these systems work faster, more accurately and far cheaper than human beings. Technology optimists also argue that they know no prejudice, ensure equal treatment and are better equipped to identify potential beneficiaries.

As we have seen, because rules and laws can never take due account of every specific circumstance or situation, case workers tend to enjoy considerable levels of discretion that allow them to make a subjective judgement case by case whenever necessary. A case worker may have to judge whether a client is searching hard enough for work. This can lead to unwarranted differences in the treatment of similar individuals, as we discussed earlier. If individuals are treated differently on the basis of differences that are not relevant for the decision, this poses problems in terms of fairness and equal treatment. This is far from illusory. Even the best intentioned officials can have very subtle and unconscious prejudices. While this may lead to a different treatment of similar cases (cf. above), it does allow for taking account of factors that are hard to programme.

The effectiveness of any minimum income protection system critically depends on people getting what they are entitled to in a timely way. Means-tested minimum income provisions can have very high levels of non-take-up, as we have seen. The causes of non-take-up are manifold, but lack of knowledge, human error, and prejudice are an important part of the story (see

Sections 4.2.1–4.2.5). ADM systems hold the potential for making decision processes less biased and more consistent. Yet there are also fears that ADM systems can also compound the effect of simple errors and that existing prejudices, however subtle, can become incorporated into algorithms.

Minimum income provision is of course a high-stakes process. 'Computer says no' is annoying in many situations but in the case of decisions about minimum income support it amounts to an existential decision.

Reliance on ADM can also negatively affect the accuracy of decision-making. The underlying data on which decisions are based can be biased or plainly wrong. As we have noted, many people often have complex lives in terms of their living arrangements and employment patterns. Automated systems, even if they are top notch, may not always be able to cope with these complexities, even if all the necessary data is provided in an accurate and timely way, which is a big if, as the experience with the UK's Universal Credit has demonstrated.

An important inherent limitation on the accuracy of automated decision making is that applicants are often required to self-report changes in household composition, incomes, and living arrangements. People do not always report such changes in a timely way. That may be because they are not aware that they have to report these or because they do not know how to do so. Lack of access to internet, other hardware problems, (technological) illiteracy, and stress of a daily existence on very low means are further complicating factors.

Also, many of the existing databases rely for another part on input by social professionals, who may make mistakes when registering client information. It also happens that social professionals deliberately 'game' the system by circumventing or resisting electronic registration systems (Veale et al., 2018).

The experience with Universal Credit in United Kingdom has provided a vivid demonstration how inapt systems can be in dealing with fluctuations in earnings and living arrangements.

The Australian experience, where benefits are almost comprehensively means-tested and the administration highly automized, also provides vivid illustrations how error-prone highly automated benefit systems can be (Millar & Whiteford, 2020). Particularly worrying is the scale at which Australian families have ended up in problematic debt because of overpayments. Not surprisingly, this affects already vulnerable families with irregular incomes disproportionally. Particularly problematic here is the scale and speed at which automated benefit systems can accumulate errors and cause hardship. Social professionals can be prejudiced leading to problematic and unfair unequal treatment of clients. But automized decision-making systems, by their very nature can create havoc at a very different scale and pace, affecting thousands of beneficiaries in no time.

There are even more sinister pitfalls. While automated systems may appear more neutral at first sight the reality is that existing patterns of prejudice can get incorporated into algorithms, effectively reproducing them with perhaps greater consistency than humans. Automation may thus reinforce existing forms of exclusion of, e.g., low-income families, minorities, or other persons at risk of exclusion.

In the Netherlands the 'Toeslagenaffaire' ('supplements affaire') thrusted this issue to the front pages of the newspapers when it came to light that households holding double nationality and characteristics indicating that they belonged to an ethnic minority were being withheld child care supplements by the Dutch tax authorities. Apparently, the tax authority was running algorithms to that effect, illegally denying people benefits to which they were eligible. The affaire brought accusations of institutionalized racism, prompted parliamentary enquiries and eventually caused the collective resignation of the Rutte government, in addition to a number of senior civil servants.

Clearly then there is a danger that administrations become too reliant on automated processes (Parasuraman & Manzey, 2010). The more it is used, the less apt social professionals may become in detecting and correcting mistakes. Instead of overseeing the whole process from beginning to end for each client and taking 'ownership' of it, in a highly automated setting the professional's job may become restricted to handling one particular task in the process for many clients at once. This may well change their responsiveness to the needs of clients and hamper their ability to build a relationship of trust with them, hampering the 'benevolent' side of discretion.

In conclusion, we do see a growing role for information technology, especially in view of the spectacular advances we are seeing at this time. The earlier cited Finnish example shows that simple online applications and automated eligibility determinations can boost (timely) take up and awarding of benefits in a very significant way. However, cautionary tales from encompassing rollouts of more automated decision-making systems highlight the need for important precautions. A 'red flag' algorithm identifying people in actual need of attention from a social worker may help to concentrate human effort on those most in need of it. Importantly, in light of the target group of minimum income protection, the possibility for real-life applications remain necessary, as well as more personalized needs assessment of individual households struggling with various problems at the same time. It would appear, in short, that technology has a lot of potential in supporting human intervention, not in replacing it.

## 4.3 Does Targeted Income Support Worsen the Underlying Problem? On Work and Other Incentives

In 1984, American conservative commentator and author Charles Murray published a book about US social policy entitled *Losing Ground*. It would turn out to be one of the most controversial and also consequential books ever written about American social policy. Its basic thesis was that policies to help the poor eventually become self-defeating. The better one protects people against poverty the more likely they are to become and remain dependent on that support. They reward short-sighted behaviour not conducive to escaping poverty in the longer term. Most controversial was Murray's thesis that welfare as it existed then had brought the breakdown of the traditional family and had led to more children born out of wedlock.

The book ignited a storm of criticism from US policy scholars but the fact that it resonated in the public sphere said a lot about the perceptions and concerns that apparently lingered in the minds of many. Few books on social policy received as much attention in the mainstream media. The topic of the book became an important issue in the 1992 US Presidential campaign, when Bill Clinton ran on a slogan 'To End Welfare as We Know It', essentially acknowledging and echoing Murray's critique.[7]

The controversy surrounding Murray's book was epic but similar debates have existed elsewhere, albeit often in more veiled terms. There is perhaps more reticence in Europe to talk about incentive issues, be it in relation to work effort or family formation, but one has to wonder why benefit levels remain so inadequate in many countries, even in countries where the fight against poverty is a loudly proclaimed policy priority. It is totally reasonable to suspect that concerns about dependency traps play an important role here, even when they are not as vociferously articulated.

Let us for the purpose of the remainder of the discussion assume that taxpayers (or at least a critical mass of the electorate) support adequate minimum support provisions only in so far that these minimize structural dependence and foster economic self-reliance. Also, they will want to keep the overall cost and hence their tax liability within reasonable limits.

These requirements form something of a policy trilemma for the simple reason that generous benefit levels are only compatible with strong work incentives if benefits are withdrawn slowly against additional income from work (see also Collado et al., 2019). But generosity combined with slow tapering has a significant fiscal cost, especially in countries where earnings are comparatively compressed. It is simply impossible to have at the same time high levels of out-of-work support, strong work incentives, and low tax requirements (unless of course there is some magical source of money that can be redistributed at will and without any negative economic consequences). The issue of benefit tapering is thus of crucial importance. Alternatively, you could imagine that policy makers square this dilemma by focusing on non-monetary work incentives, through a strong behavioural conditionality, rather than through providing strong financial incentives. However, stringent monitoring, activating, and sanctioning administration is expensive in its own right.

### 4.3.1 Work Incentives in Minimum Income Schemes Are Not Good (at All)

Minimum income protection for people not in work mainly comes in the form of social assistance in most countries. In a textbook social assistance scheme, any additional earned income reduces the state transfer at a euro for euro rate until that amount exceeds the level of the benefit. Table 4.1 shows that most of the Western means-tested minimum income schemes for able-bodied people of working age—at least in principle—apply such a stringent taper to earned income, although there are exceptions.

The recipient is often effectively facing a 100% marginal 'tax rate' until he or she has an earned or alternative income exceeding the full benefit level. In standard neoclassical economic theory, such a high effective marginal tax rate naturally stands in the way of the benefit recipient transitioning towards self-reliance (see Figure 4.1). It simply makes no economic sense to take up a small amount of work, think for example a part-time job, because there is zero gain in disposable income.

Moreover, social assistance programmes are means tested at the level of the 'core family'. A spouse's or cohabiting partner's income and the couple's assets are taken into account for determining eligibility, be it usually beyond a certain minimum threshold. That means that all adults in the households face a disincentive to work until the earned income exceeds the total benefit level by some margin. Add to that the fact that taking up work usually also comes with extra costs, for example transport and other work related expenditures like work clothes.

Now, in reality social assistance schemes allow for exceptions in the form of earnings disregards that allow beneficiaries to earn some additional money for some time before their benefit is affected (more on that below, see Section 4.3.7).

**Table 4.1** Rates at which earned income is included in the means-test of the main out-of-work minimum income scheme for work-able adults, 2020

| Country | % of earned income |
|---|---|
| AT | 100% |
| BE | 100% |
| BG | 100% |
| CY | 100% |
| CZ | 70% |
| DE | 100% |
| DK | 100% |
| EE | 100% |
| EL | 80% |
| ES | 100% |
| FI | 100% |
| FR | 100% |
| HU | 100% |
| IE | 60% |
| IT | 100% |
| LT | 65–85% (depending on family composition) |
| LU | 75% |
| LV | 100% |
| MT | 100% |
| NL | 100% |
| NO | 100% |
| PL | 100% |
| PT | 80% |
| RO | 100% |
| SE | 100% |
| SI | 100% |
| SK | 75% |
| UK | 63% |
| USA | 80% |
| CH | 100% |

*Note:* For Finland, information refers to the Labour Market Subsidy. For Ireland to the Jobseeker's Allowance. For the USA, we provide information for the Supplemental Nutritional Assistance Program. Rules for the Temporary Assistance to Needy Families vary by state.
*Source:* OECD Benefits and Wages Country descriptions; EUROMOD country reports

Such an earnings disregard changes the picture in two important ways. First, the recipient is no longer 'punished' at a rate of 100% for any work effort. In fact, the marginal effective tax rate for the first hours of work can

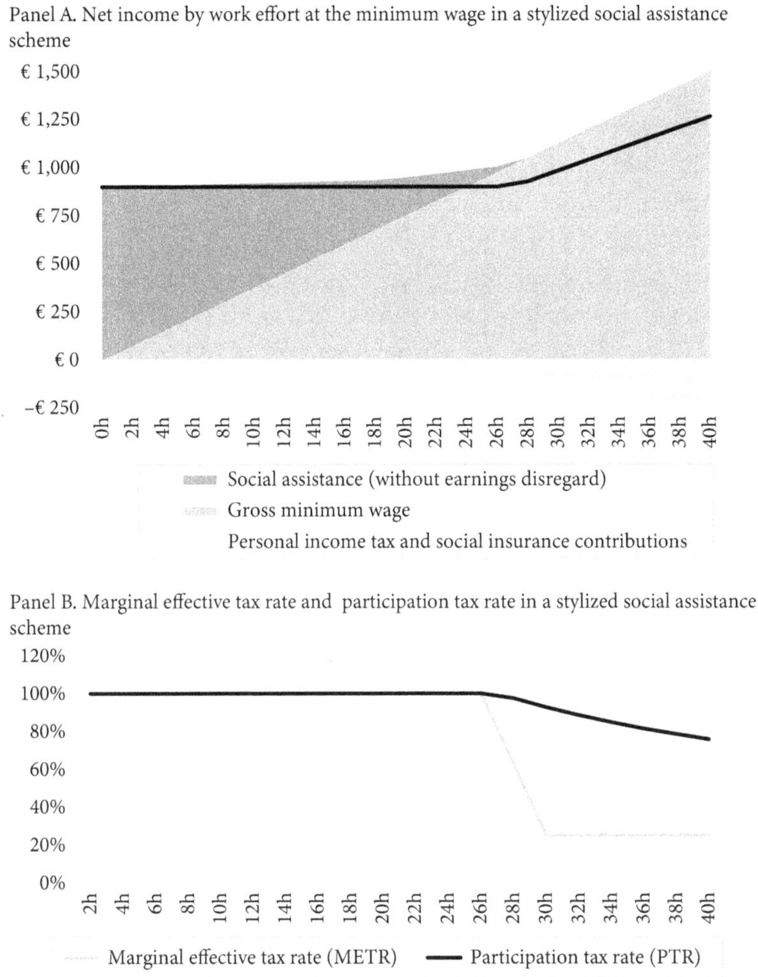


**Figure 4.1** Work incentives in a stylized social assistance scheme, without earnings disregard

*Note:* Hypothetical income and work incentives for a single person in a stylized social assistance scheme, by number of hours of work effort (h). We thank Elise Aerts for creating these graphs.

be as low as zero. That may help to 'draw' people on social assistance into the world of work, potentially improving their prospects of upward mobility. Second, it provides an immediate income boost that can potentially even lift people out of poverty. Yet as with a regular social assistance scheme, the work incentive becomes very weak when the earned income exceeds the amount that is disregarded in the means-test. The 100% effective marginal tax rate kicks in again (see panel A and C of Figure 4.2).

In reality, the situation is more complicated and often also less dramatic, at least if work incentives are the principal concern. That is because minimum income recipients may also receive benefits that are not means-tested or tapered less severely than social assistance. Universal child benefits, for example, are not tapered so there is no disincentive to taking up work (although there may be an income effect)—at least when they are not included in the social assistance means-test (see Box 2.2 in Chapter 2). Low-income targeted child benefit supplements, where these exist, tend to be tapered at a much more gradual rate so as to include the low-paid (Chapter 3). The same may apply to other benefits such as housing, heating, or child care allowances. Also, in-work benefits may make a transition to work financially attractive. Such in work benefits have become far more prevalent over recent decades, as we documented in Chapter 3. So in reality the work incentives facing social assistance recipients may be less dismal than when only their social assistance benefit is considered. This is illustrated in Figure 4.2, panels B and D.

On the other hand, minimum income beneficiaries are in many European countries entitled to non-discretionary in-kind benefits or services, or they will receive more discretionary support (see also Box 2.4 in Chapter 2) that is often organized at the local level. When these additional support measures are directly tied to minimum income receipt, with minimum income benefits acting as a so-called 'passport benefit', or very tightly targeted, transitioning from out-of-work minimum income support to employment income can go hand in hand with the loss of this support. The actual value of such in-kind benefits and services to individuals and households is hard to gauge. It depends on the need they have for that specific expense, how often they use it, whether it is actually available in their municipality. Studies that look into the impact of more local, in-kind or discretionary support on financial incentives, find that although such support measures do impact somewhat on financial incentives, the extent to which they do depends on the actual constellation of the beneficiary family (Anne & L'Horty, 2012; Penne, Cornelis, & Storms, 2020). (See also Box 2.4 for estimates on the impact of local and discretionary support on the adequacy of out-of-work benefits.)

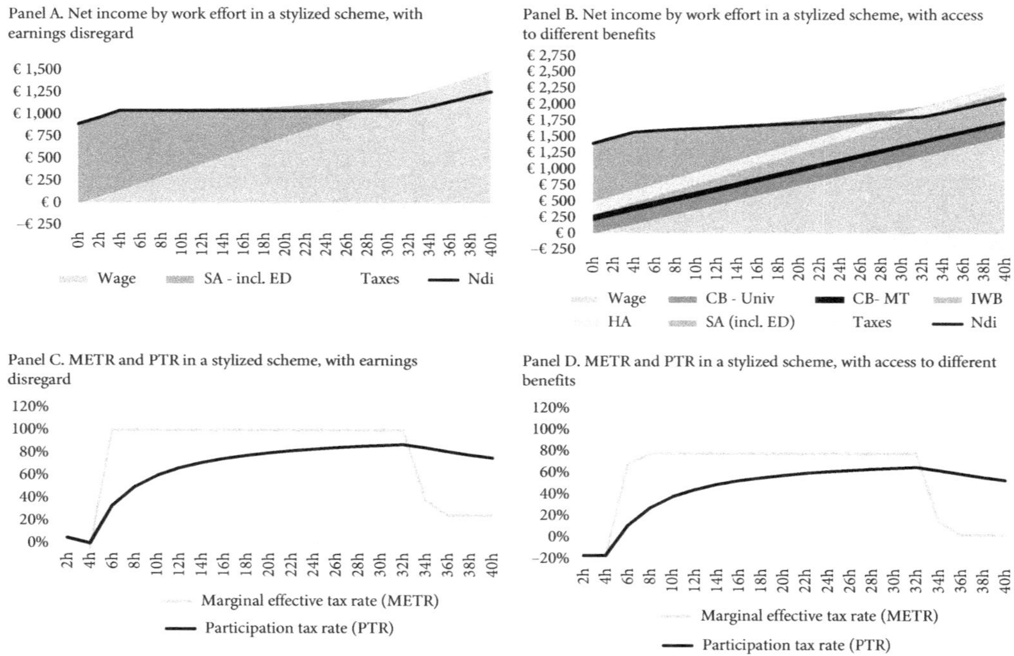


**Figure 4.2** Work incentives in a stylized social assistance scheme, with earnings disregard and access to other benefits

*Note:* SA—incl. ED: social assistance, including earnings disregard. Ndi: net disposable income. CB: child benefit. Univ: universal. MT: means-tested. IWB: in-work benefit. HA: housing allowance.

### 4.3.2 Where Are Minimum Incomes Now Relative to the Glass Ceiling?

It is widely taken as a matter of principle and common-sense economics that, in general, work needs to pay more than not being in work, at least if it comes to able-bodied people at working age. That people with work-hampering disabilities may require levels of income support that exceed the net incomes of the lowest paid workers is generally accepted, especially in the light of the higher expenses they are often faced with. Also, it is accepted that relatively high earning people with long unemployment insurance contribution histories receive unemployment benefits (well) in excess of minimum pay levels for a limited period of time. But generally speaking it is not deemed acceptable that people who are fully capable for work can be better off on benefits than people working, at least in jobs that are deemed to be minimally acceptable. Jobs paying the minimum wage can be thought of as determining the level of what is acceptable. It is for this reason that minimum wages matter so much in policy thinking and discourse, even if few people actually work in minimum wage jobs. The minimum wage has been called 'the glass ceiling' of minimum income protection for those not in work (Cantillon, Parolin, & Collado, 2020). In some countries this is not just an unwritten principle. In Germany, for example, it was for a while a principle enshrined in law (the so-called 'Lohnabstandsgebot').

So what is the situation? Figure 4.3 benchmarks two key minimum income measures against the relative poverty level in 2021 in a set of countries: the net income of social assistance recipients and that of minimum wage workers, taking account of taxes and social security contributions, but also child benefits and other potential income supplements. This is shown for a single person and for a lone parent with two children. It is important to stress here that we compare total net income in both situations and not the gross amount of the minimum wage or the social assistance benefit (which is taxed in some countries). We refer to Box 2.1 in Chapter 2 for more information on how these minimum income protection packages are calculated.

As we discussed in detail in Chapter 2, the guaranteed minimum incomes for people not in work generally fall well short of what would be needed to lift them out of relative poverty. However, net incomes of minimum wage workers do exceed the poverty threshold in a substantial number of countries, as we demonstrated in more detail in Chapter 3. In the case of lone parents putting in full-time work effort (hard as that may be) net incomes (taking into account not only taxes and social security contributions paid, but also transfers such as child benefits) rarely exceed the amount needed to

Panel A. Single person

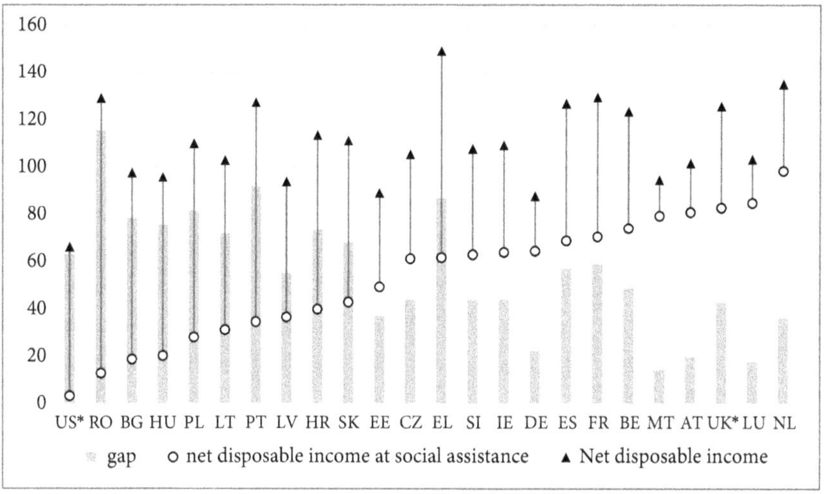


Panel B. Lone parent with two children

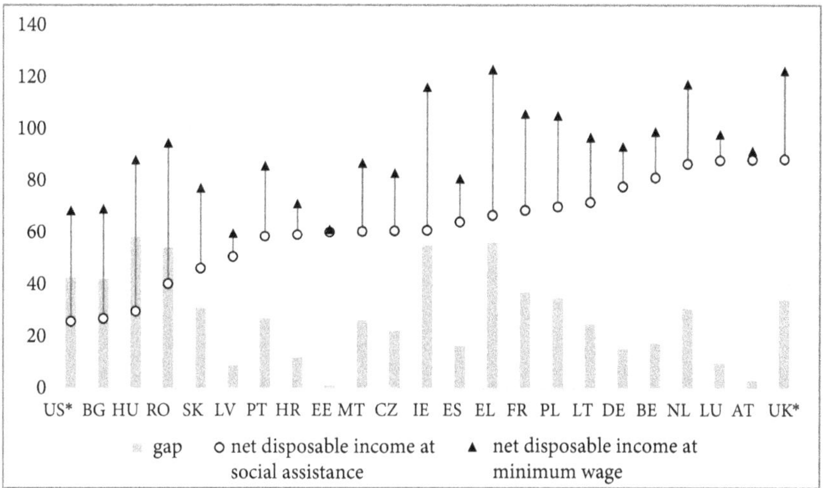


**Figure 4.3** Net disposable income at social assistance and at full-time minimum wage employment, relative to 60% poverty threshold, 2021

*Note:* see Box 2.1 for more information on the method used. Data for the US are based on the figures reported in Aerts, Marx, and Parolin (2022). Data for the UK represent the situation in 2020. We exclude temporary measures specifically linked to the COVID crisis.
*Source:* MIPI-HHoT (see Marchal, Siöland, & Goedemé, 2018). We thank Elise Aerts for valuable assistance in updating this dataset.

stay out of poverty, and where they do they only do so marginally (see again our discussion in Chapter 3).

The ranking of the countries here is by the adequacy of minimum income protection for those not in work. It can be seen that in the more generous countries, relatively speaking, the gap between the net income in a full-time minimum wage job and the net income when fully on social assistance level is generally much smaller than in the less generous countries. In fact, hypothetically increasing net guaranteed minimum incomes for those out of work to the level of the poverty threshold would in many countries eliminate any financial incentive to work in a minimum wage job or thereabouts. In other words, raising minimum incomes of those not in work cannot be done without simultaneously raising the wage floor, if one would seek to maintain some significant work incentive. Of course, net incomes of the lowest paid workers could also be lifted by providing more generous in-work or universal benefits, such as child benefits. That, however, tends to be costly because of the sheer numbers involved.

Recall that, as we documented in Chapter 3, there may be a substantial difference between the official 'headline' minimum wage and the de facto wage floor that actually prevails. In countries with comprehensive collective bargaining, effective wage floors tend to sit at significantly higher levels than the minimum wage used in these graphs. However, it is important to stress that in policy discussions the headline minimum wage does tend to play a large role, if only because it is a most often used benchmark in calculations of work incentives. How pervasive potentially reduced work incentives from higher social assistance or social insurance benefits are in reality depends of course on how many people actually work or can work for the headline minimum wage. Yet the wage floor is only one of several potential ceilings, as we will discuss in the next section.

### 4.3.3 Is It Becoming Harder to Push Up the Social Floor?

Policy makers may well be faced with increasingly tougher structural constraints towards improving minimum income protection adequacy. This hypothesis, which we will elaborate and partially test in this section, follows from the notion that incomes from various sources tend to sit in a certain hierarchy in advanced welfare states. The argument here essentially builds on the thesis developed and demonstrated by Cantillon, Parolin, and Collado (2020) that minimum income protection is subject to a 'glass ceiling', as set by the effective wage floor. In fact one could argue that there is a layer of glass ceilings constraining any lifting of the minimum floor. The argument runs as follows.

At the bottom of the income hierarchy sits the minimum income floor as it is provided in most rich countries (and elsewhere) through social assistance (Figure 4.4). This is in principle the minimum income below which nobody

**Figure 4.4** The income hierarchy

can fall. It is in most cases ensured by law at the national level. Where no nationally regulated safety net exists it is sometimes provided at regional or local level (see Chapter 2).

Above the minimum income floor provided by social assistance sit the minimum benefits provided within various social insurance schemes. These entitlements are acquired through contributions and work histories. The logic in most systems seems to be that rights acquired through past contributions sit somewhat higher in the incomes hierarchy than benefits that are provided because of sheer need, and on the basis of compassion or other notions of decency and social justice. We make a broad generalization here. Such a strict hierarchy need not always apply: in some cases social insurance benefits replacing earnings will be equal to or lower than social assistance, yet access can still be considered to be somewhat easier if contributory conditions are met, since no full-scale means-test applies. Those whose contributory benefits fall below the social assistance threshold, may still be eligible for a social assistance top-up.

Next we have the lowest wages. It is a widely accepted principle that work needs to pay more than living on a benefit, certainly as far as people at working age are concerned. This may not apply to those who are incapacitated for work, for example because of illness or injury, but a situation in which work capable people are able to live on benefits that are higher than what work pays for extended periods of time is generally not seen as very desirable or sustainable.

The wage floor is usually demarcated by the minimum wage. Note that what actually matters here is the net income level around the wage floor. For the clarity of the discussion we will simply focus on the minimum wage itself because that is the main determinant of what work minimally pays. Note also that there may be a substantial difference between the official 'headline' minimum wage and the effective wage floor. In some countries the minimum wage serves more of a benchmark purpose than anything else: it constitutes the absolute bottom line of the wage structure. 'Real' minimum wages (i.e., pay scales for the youngest, least qualified, and least experienced workers) may well be higher than the nationwide minimum wage. As we saw in Chapter 3 there is in reality only a fuzzy relationship between the level of the minimum wage as captured by institutional indicators and the actual share of workers around the minimum wages.

However, it is important to point out that in policy discussions the minimum wage does tend to play a large role, if only because it is a most often used benchmark in calculations of work incentives. How pervasive potentially reduced work incentives from higher social assistance or social insurance benefits are in reality depends of course on how many people actually work or can work for the headline minimum wage, and in this respect there are considerable country differences. But work incentives around the level of the minimum wage tend to loom large in policy thinking and political debates.

Then there is the rest of the wage building that lies above the wage floor. It is, again, a widely accepted principle that there needs to be some spread in wage levels by such characteristics as acquired level of education, experience, and, where measurable, performance in order to have a properly functioning labour market. How large such wage premia actually need to be in order to have a properly working ('clearing') labour market in which people are optimally allocated to jobs is an issue of endless debate among economists. Suffice it to say that everybody agrees that there needs to be a certain level of wage inequality in order for an economy to function properly. Paying everybody (almost) the same has clearly never worked. But that is not to say that there is no scope for some compression in countries where wage differentials are large. Countries like for example Denmark or the Netherlands show after all that comparatively compressed wage structures can be perfectly compatible with maintaining dynamic economies generating high employment rates and low unemployment rates. How much pay compression is workable may however depend on the wider institutional context (notably education regimes), as varieties of capitalism authors have stressed (see for example Iversen & Soskice, 2009).

If we accept the incomes hierarchy applies then the clear implication is that lifting the minimum income floor—notably raising social assistance benefits—will have reverberations throughout the whole income distribution. Raising social assistance will put pressure on minimum benefits in social insurance provisions and that may in turn put pressure on minimum wages, with possible ripple effects further up the wage distribution.

Everything depends on what the actual distances between the different income layers are and how the layers are situated relative to the poverty threshold. If there is a very considerable distance between the minimum income floor provided to those not in work on the one hand and the minimum wage on the other then there may be ample scope for some lifting while maintaining work incentives. Similarly, if minimum benefits in contributory schemes are substantially above the wage floor then it may be possible to raise the floor without causing ripple effects to above minimum income benefits. But if the distances are already small, any lifting of the minimum income floor will have reverberations up the incomes building.

As Chapters 2 and 3 show, in actual fact the wage floor sits only marginally above the poverty line in many countries and in a number of countries below it. Minimum benefits for people out of work are way below the poverty line just about everywhere. It is clear that significantly lifting the minimum income floor would have far reaching repercussions. It would in effect require lifting a large part of the income building, including wage floors, or at least net incomes at that level. Collado et al. (2019) calculated the costs related to raising out-of-work minimum incomes to the poverty threshold in a scenario that disregards the income hierarchy, and in a scenario that takes the income hierarchy seriously in three Western European countries. That study clearly demonstrates that a scenario that seeks to maintain pre-existing work incentives when increasing minimum income protection is twice as expensive. We return to this issue in the next section.

But what is even worse: it may well be the case that this is becoming even more of an uphill struggle. How can this be possible? Does the poverty line not move up in step with wages and other income components? Not necessarily. Remember, the relative poverty threshold is calculated on the basis of equivalent disposable household income (cf. Chapter 1). Disposable household income is the sum of the incomes—labour and non-labour—of all household members. If wages, including wage floors, remain stagnant but the number of earners per household increases, for example because of rising female labour participation, living standards, and thus relative poverty threshold will go up.

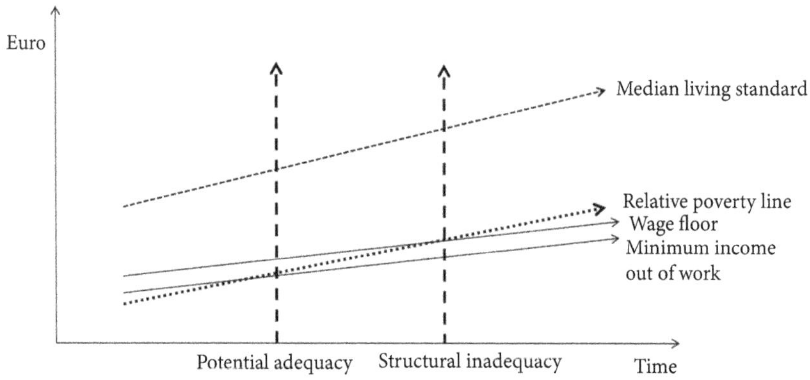


**Figure 4.5** Why adequacy is harder to maintain when living standards outpace wages

And in effect, this has happened in some cases (Thewissen et al., 2015; Nolan, 2018b). In the Netherlands, for example, sustained wage moderation was at the core of a concerted strategy by governments and social partners to boost employment. Being highly successful in this respect, living standards outpaced wages considerably in the years when wage moderation went accompanied with rising female labour participation (Marx, 2007).

In this context it is easy to see how a divergence of real wage growth and living standards growth may bring a situation in which minimum income adequacy becomes increasingly harder to bring about, as depicted in Figure 4.5. Minimum income levels and minimum wage levels are after all constrained by wage growth, especially at the lower end. If low wages in particular are structurally lagging, for example because of skill-biased demand shifts due to globalization and skill-biased technological change, the challenge gets even worse. That is not to say that minimum income adequacy becomes impossible to achieve but it will require that multiple income layers are lifted at the same time.

What has actually happened? Are wages, and the lowest wages in particular lagging behind living standards? Figure 4.6 shows trends in low wages (P10) relative to the poverty line for a set of countries, drawing on Structure or Earnings data for wages and EU-SILC data for relative poverty thresholds (60% of median equivalent income). A first noticeable thing is that we observe vast variation in P10 wage levels relative to the relative poverty threshold for a single person. In a country like Belgium, the P10 gross wage is almost twice as high as the relative poverty threshold for a single person. In Estonia that is closer to 22%. A second important observation is that we do not observe a

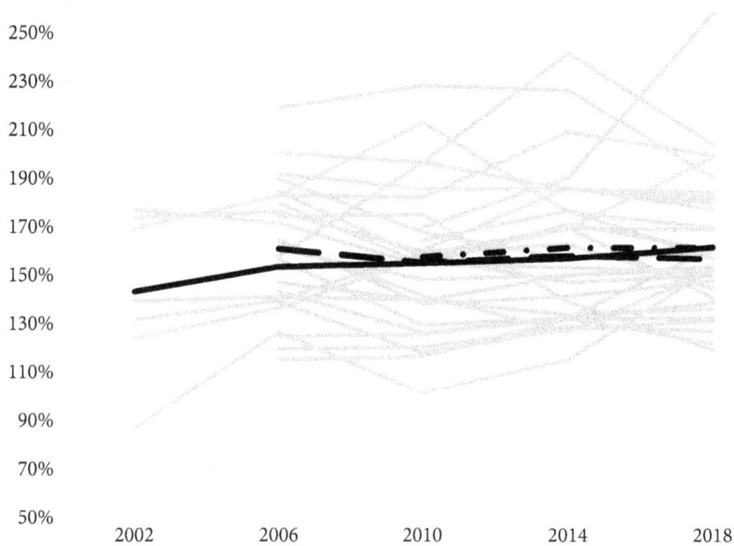


**Figure 4.6** Low wages (P10) relative to the poverty line in EU countries, SES data

*Note:* based on full time equivalent wages (including full-time and part-time earners). Black lines refer to the average over countries that are available in 2002 and respectively 2006 and 2010.

general erosion of low wages relative to relative poverty thresholds. The picture is quite mixed though. For some countries, mainly the Western European nations, the picture is indeed that of the lowest wages in what appears to be an uphill struggle relative to poverty thresholds. But that is not everywhere the case. In Germany, for example, we see a substantial decline until 2010 and then a stabilization followed by a more articulate increase by 2018.

All in all, there are no uniform patterns when we compare countries. Cross-country comparisons of trends, whether they concern wages, individual incomes or indeed household living standards, rarely yield patterns that neatly fit grand narratives, for example on the impact of intensified global economic competition or skill-biased technological change. While there is a tendency to see uniform, structural trends across the rich countries the empirics rarely fully support such (naturally appealing) perceptions. In fact, if there is one thing that comparative research has taught us then it is that country variation remains remarkably persistent (see for example Nolan et al., 2014; Atkinson, 2015; Nolan, 2018a).

### 4.3.4 The True Cost of Poverty Reduction

Several studies have calculated how much it would cost to lift all household incomes to the 60% at-risk-of-poverty threshold. That number is surprisingly small. In many countries, the expenditure needed to bring every single citizen to the relative poverty line would not even be in excess of two or three percentage points of GDP (see for example Vandenbroucke et al., 2013; Collado et al., 2019).

Unfortunately, such a mechanical calculation ignores how people would behave the day after minimum income floors were lifted to the poverty lines. Working people might switch from low-paid, menial jobs to social transfers. People already dependent on transfers might well move off income support at a slower pace or not at all. In light of the incomes hierarchy thesis described in the previous section, also other reactions are conceivable. People currently living on contributory benefits above the minimum might well demand increases since they paid contributions. Workers might demand higher wages. The real cost of such an operation is almost certainly higher than the mechanical first-round effect. The calculation may thus be seen as indicating not more than a lower boundary for the distributive effort that is required.

Because of the shape of the income distribution, the problem does not just worsen proportionately, as is illustrated in Figure 4.7. The share of households with very low incomes—think around the prevailing social assistance levels—is typically small. But that share goes up sharply once you move up the income ladder. We use the individual gross earnings distribution here to illustrate this point (the illustrative figure is based on the case of Belgium). Of course, in reality the situation is more complicated because what really matters are *net* incomes in work, which differ by household circumstance. Clearly, social assistance benefits (or minimum income packages) around the level of the poverty threshold would confront a very sizeable share of the working age population with worrisome work incentives, unless wage floors are much higher up, which they rarely are. The key point here is that the share of the population potentially affected by first and second round 'ripple' effects in benefit increases does not just increase gradually. It goes up sharply once increases in out-of-work benefit levels reach levels where the bulk of the working population already resides.

With such effects in mind it becomes clear that poverty reduction will come at a much larger cost than simply bringing the lowest incomes to the poverty line. In a sophisticated micro-simulation analysis for Belgium, Denmark, and the UK, aptly titled 'The end of cheap talk about poverty

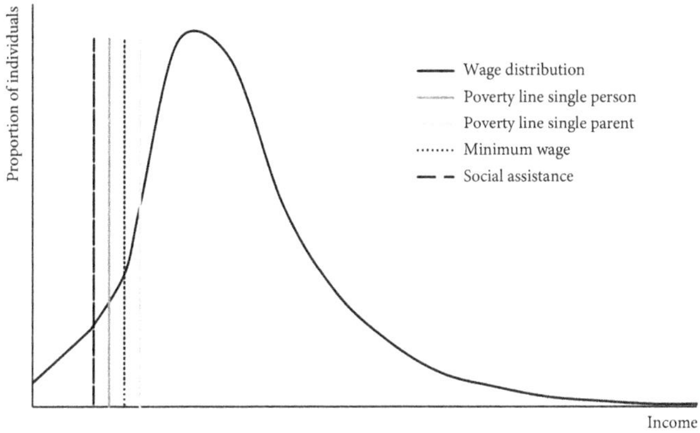


**Figure 4.7** The cost of more adequate minimum income can rise fast from a certain point onwards

reduction', Collado et al. (2019) find that the cost of closing the poverty gap while maintaining existing average labour-market participation incentives at the bottom of the income distribution would be substantially higher than the 2% or 3% of GDP a back-of-the-envelope calculation yields. When work incentives are maintained at their existing levels, the cost would double to 5% or 6% of GDP. That is still perhaps not outside of the realm of the politically feasible but it cannot be denied that it is a significantly higher number.

### 4.3.5 What Do We Actually Know about Social Assistance Dynamics?

Work incentives loom large in debates about minimum income protection and never more so than when it comes to recipients of social assistance and related forms of minimum income protection.

In part this is a matter of principle. For people to support adequate safety nets they generally demand that 'work pays'. But then there is the far more tricky empirical question: how do people actually react to financial incentives or disincentives?

An enormous literature has accumulated on the issue, yielding very mixed results, and that is putting it mildly.[8] Nobel Prize Winners Esther Duflo and Abhijit Banerjee have said in a 2019 *New York Times* opinion piece that 'economists have somehow managed to hide in plain sight an enormously consequential finding from their research: Financial incentives are nowhere near as powerful as they are usually assumed to be.'

That may be because so many other factors come into play. Job availability and job quality will matter, as well as its likely stability and duration. Calculations of financial incentives rarely take the full financial consequences of a transition into account. Non-cash benefits are usually not included. In some cases people on social assistance get non-cash benefits such as special rates for water, heating, electricity, telecommunications, transport, or even cultural events. They may get rent reductions in social housing. They may also get health care at reduced rates or at higher rates of compensation. If such benefits are categorically tied to their status as social assistance recipient, the additional disincentive to move into work may well be important.

Then there is another cost that typically does not feature in such calculations. As we discussed earlier, applying for benefits, be it in cash or in kind can take substantial time and effort. Filling out multiple forms, accessing sometimes complex websites, suffering waiting cues, etc. This implies pure time and sometimes transports costs, but there are also psychological costs. By means of example: A survey probing into the implementation of social assistance in Belgian local welfare agencies, asked whether the social investigation that is part of the claiming process was simplified in case a former recipient refiled a claim after four months of minimum wage employment. 72% of the participating local welfare agencies indicated that the social investigation would be repeated in full, including the more intrusive elements of a house visit, assessment of savings, and work willingness. Almost 94% of municipalities indicated that it would take at least two to four weeks (and in rare cases even over one month), before this claimant would have certainty about the renewal of his or her benefit, and this after only a four-month break (unpublished data, description of the survey is available in Janssens & Marchal, 2022). That may make people reluctant to give up a benefit even if they are offered a job paying well above that benefit, especially if that job is temporary or insecure.

Research has paid much more attention to these factors. Financial incentives as we show here and in similar studies are usually the result of complex calculations that require a lot of information. Moreover, the end outcome of such calculations—the net gain from making the transition to work—is often a result of very complex interactions between different entitlements. Steven Anderson (2002) interviewed 60 American welfare recipients about the way they perceived and felt about work incentives. He found that people often did not understand the incentives provided. They lacked knowledge and were often confused about eligibility rules and benefit calculations. That was not due to a lack of interest in working. The core problem was the sheer complexity of the regulations and procedures.

This said, other studies do in fact find sizeable effects of financial incentives. In a study of social assistance recipients in Quebec, Thomas Lemieux and Kevin Milligan (2008) found 'strong evidence that more generous social assistance benefits reduce employment'. Similarly, Michalopoulos et al. (2005) looked at a social experiment that provided a financial incentive in the form of a negative income tax for welfare recipients to leave welfare and work full-time. It was found to increase full-time employment, earnings, and income.

So what do we actually know about the dynamics of people who have to fall back on social assistance?

One of the things we know for sure is that long durations of dependence on social assistance benefits are actually rare. This is of crucial importance given widespread concerns and perceptions. Critics of (adequate) minimum income protection schemes portray benefits recipients often as being 'trapped' in dependence, eroding their capacity and possibly appetite for self-reliance.

Thanks to the increased availability of data from administrative records, research on dependence dynamics has flourished. The picture is rather mixed across countries. It is hard to make exact comparisons because studies are sometimes quite dated, use different methods or focus on certain subpopulations like young people or migrants only.

A major comparative study pertaining to the late 2000s/early 2010s for Canada, Germany, Latvia, Luxembourg, the Netherlands, Norway, Sweden, and the United Kingdom—the selection was mainly guided by data availability—found annual rates of social assistance receipt around 4–6% of the working-age population (Immervoll et al., 2015). In any given month, about 2–4% of working-age individuals were found to receive SA benefits. They did find, however, that exit rates did differ a lot between countries.

For five countries they had high-quality longitudinal data allowing individuals to be tracked month by month over a longer period of time. They were found to fall into two groups with distinct patterns of benefit receipt dynamics. In Latvia, Norway, and Sweden, the duration of benefit spells was typically very short. Median spell durations amounted to only two to three months! But most benefit recipients did have multiple spells during the observation period. In the Netherlands and Luxembourg, by contrast, median spell durations tended to be much longer (nine and 15 months, respectively) but benefit leavers were less likely to return to benefits. A study of a cohort of first-time recipients in Belgium found a median duration spell of around seven months (Carpentier et al., 2017).

In a further look at Luxembourg, the Netherlands, Norway, and Sweden, using the same data as the Immervoll et al. study, Sebastian Königs (2018) confirms that benefit dynamics varied considerably across countries. In the two Nordic countries, long-term benefit receipt was found to be a rare exception although many recipients were found to have multiple spells. In Luxembourg and the Netherlands, long-term benefit receipt was more frequent, but benefit leavers were much less likely to return to benefit receipt after exit. The total duration of benefit receipt per individual across spells was found to be two to three times as high in the Netherlands and Luxembourg as in Norway and Sweden.

This suggest that social assistance systems fulfil different functions across countries. In the Nordic countries it appears to play the intended role of providing short-term emergency assistance for individuals in need. In other countries, however, social assistance does provide longer-term income support, with seemingly lower rates of progression to self-sufficiency.

Not all the evidence is consistent however with the picture emerging from comparative studies. One study for the Dutch city of Rotterdam by Snel et al. (2013) found substantial long-term benefit receipt. About two-thirds of spells that started in the late 1990s and early 2000s lasted longer than 12 months. One in four recipients remained on benefits for five years or longer (over a seven-year period) once repeated spells were taken into account.

What the available studies do not shed much light on is on what exactly drives the different patterns observed across countries. Immervoll et al. (2015) express surprise at the fact that year-on-year exit rates from benefits remained remarkably stable during the time period they looked at, even though this period was marked by the increased deployment of policies focused on moving benefit recipients on a path towards self-sufficiency. Similarly, the Königs (2018) study, informative as it is, does not really pinpoint what accounts for the fact that some countries are better at avoiding long-term or repeated dependency than others.

Importantly, if a person is observed as leaving social assistance benefit receipt that does not necessarily mean that this person becomes self-sufficient with adequate means of existence, let alone a job. The studies we have on social assistance dynamics rarely tell us what happens to people after they exit from social assistance, let alone that we know whether they find a durable trajectory out of poverty.

Fortunately there are exceptions. A fascinating study for Norway looks at the life-course over 20 years of young recipients of social assistance in

Norway around the mid-1990s (Lorentzen & Dahl, 2021). The exceptionally rich longitudinal linked administrative data that is available for a country like Norway allows for an unusually broad perspective on the trajectories of one-time social assistance recipients. The study looks at spells of social security receipt, schooling, work, and earnings.

The study brings to light the enormous diversity of social assistance dynamics, reflecting the fact that people who end up in a final safety net provision like social assistance early in their lives do so because a variety of reasons. The 'typical' social assistance recipient hardly exists.

For many, a spell on social assistance is a short life episode. But the generally limited duration of social assistance dependence masks some worrying longer term dynamics. Few find a path towards economic self-reliance and even fewer a path to economic success. An important exception are students who for some reason make use of social assistance for a while. Many of them have what could be called 'successful' life courses in terms of achieved education and work. Yet some have prolonged interrupted educational trajectories leading to less well-paid work.

A very striking finding from this study for Norway is the big role of health problems, temporary or permanent, in the trajectories of people who had to resort to social assistance at a young age. Close to half of the young Norwegians tracked in this study followed trajectories in which health-related benefits were of significant importance.

The fact that most eventually obtain access to disability benefits says a lot about the capacity of the Norwegian welfare state to provide for its citizens with health problems. If instead the observation had been that many stayed in social assistance or relapsed, that would have probably told us more about the capacity of the broader Norwegian social protection system to care for people with health issues then about Norway's success on the 'activation' front.

This finding holds an important general lesson. In interpreting social assistance dependence spells we should be very careful not to reduce these to reflections of 'work effort' on the part of clients or to failures to 'activate' on the part of welfare agencies. Social assistance receipt may well be indicative that a person is in need of help in other areas of life than finding a job and becoming self-reliant.

Another study for Norway confirms this picture (Heggebø et al., 2020). This study also draws on exceptionally rich data, particularly a survey among long-term recipients of social assistance in Norway taken in 2005. This survey collected data on childhood disadvantages, health, psychological resources, and social ties, in addition to basic sociodemographic characteristics. This survey data was then linked to tax register data for

2005–2013. That provides an exceptionally rich picture of the characteristics of long-term social assistance recipients who prove unable to reach financial self-sufficiency. Surprisingly few of the characteristics for which data was available were associated with long-term social assistance receipt, with two important exceptions: people with drug problems and immigrants were both observed to have a much higher probability of long-term social assistance receipt.

The researchers express surprise at the level of apparent randomness involved in social assistance dynamics. They found it very challenging to 'predict' statistically long-term or repeated social assistance spells. Merely three out of 28 explanatory variables were associated with social assistance in a consistent and substantial manner.

The researchers speculate about the role of 'luck'. Some social assistance recipients are perhaps fortunate while being assigned a particularly caring, supportive and competent caseworker. Similarly, getting a 'lucky break' from a supportive and compassionate employer could 'kick-start' a work career.

As we said, there is no typical social assistance recipient.[9] People end up in social assistance for a variety of reasons. A group that has grown in importance in many countries are newly arrived immigrants, especially refugees. There was an influx of refugees in many European countries after the breakup of Yugoslavia in the beginning of the 1990s. Continued flows resulted from the period of conflicts in Kosovo and Chechnya, followed around the early 2010s by asylum seekers from Afghanistan, Iraq, and Russia. Around 2015 and thereafter the wars in Syria, Iraq, and Afghanistan brought new waves. The war in Ukraine has brought millions of refugees to the European Union. Because they gained access to the EU under the Temporary Protection Directive, they gained direct access to social assistance in some countries, bringing significant increases in caseloads.

These people, often traumatized and separated from their families and networks, face particular challenges when they receive refugee status or some equivalent status. They need to settle in a totally new society about which they usually know very little. They do not know the local language, the customs, they lack formally recognized skills and diploma's, they lack the weak social ties that are so important for access to housing and jobs. That makes them particularly prone to recourse to social assistance after access becomes available. That allows them to settle, to become accustomed, to learn the language, to develop social ties, to acquire qualifications or have theirs recognized and to look for work.

In research for Belgium—a country that has seen very significant influxes of refugees—we found that this can take years (Lens, Marx, & Vujić, 2019).

We also found that refugees run a disproportional risk of exiting the labour market again and re-entering social assistance or, more likely, social insurance after they appear to be successfully integrated. Hence, refugees face a double jeopardy. It is not clear why exactly this happens. One possibility is that refugees become discouraged in the types of jobs that they are able to get access to. Formal credentials count for much in advanced, knowledge-driven economies, especially in better paid jobs. Refugees usually do not have these. Even if they acquired advanced levels of education in their home countries, their diplomas and credentials rarely get recognized (in part because people fleeing war and persecution rarely have the time and opportunity to take the required documentation with them). The jobs they are able to acquire tend to be insecure and unattractive. The better educated tend to work in jobs far below their qualifications.

This goes to illustrate that patterns of dependence, especially the higher propensity of new migrants to spend longer spells on social assistance, have as much to do with structural economic, sociological, and institutional exclusion factors as with the personal characteristics and attitudes of the recipients.

### 4.3.6 Earnings Disregards and Their Effects

As we said at the start of the preceding section, work incentives of social assistance recipients are a major concern in policy debates. In theory a social assistance benefit is reduced by the full amount of the income from work, resulting in limited financial incentives to take up employment or extend working hours (see Section 4.3.1). Or to be more precise: in theory there is no direct incentive for beneficiaries of social assistance to take up work that does not pay significantly more than the benefit. Of course, beneficiaries may consider the longer-term benefits of work, value the non-pecuniary benefits of a job, or they may fear sanctions.

Countries have introduced earnings disregards to tackle this problem. Under such arrangements people do not lose their benefit entirely or immediately on a euro-for-euro basis for any additional income earned. The size and duration of these earnings disregards differs (Table 4.2 provides an overview). If used to the fullest, an earnings disregard may provide a significant income boost. In some countries full take up will even bring social assistance beneficiaries above the poverty threshold.

Does this help social assistance recipients to find work? There is research for the Netherlands suggesting that social assistance recipients are in effect more likely to become self-sufficient when they can be active in low-income

**Table 4.2** Additional earnings disregards and back to work bonuses in the main out-of-work minimum income scheme for work-able adults, 2020

| | Type | Amount/Rate | Duration |
|---|---|---|---|
| BE | Disregards | General income (all sources) disregard of €155-310 annually<br>Socio-professional earnings (SPI) disregards of €291.63/month[a] | SPI: 3 years (spread over 6 years) |
| DE | Disregards | €100 of earned income per month; 20% of earned income from €101–1000; 10% of earned income between €1001–1200 (€1500 for families with children) | Not limited in time |
| DK | Disregards | DKK 28.04 per hour worked, max. 160 hours per month | Not limited |
| EE | Disregards<br>subject on 2 months of benefit receipt and return to work | 100% of earnings for the first 2 months; 50% in next 4 months | Once per 24 months |
| EL | Back to work bonus | The amount of income support is fixed for a 6 month reference period: taking up employment does not affect the amount of the benefit until reassessment. | N.A. |
| ES | Disregards<br>subject on prior benefit receipt and return to work | Part of the salary is temporarily exempt to calculate the amount of the GMI benefit. | N.A. |
| FI<br>LMS | Disregards | For a single/family: €311/1044, and 25/50% of additional income<br>Also, upon re-entry into part-time employment: earned income disregard of €300, and 50% of earned income above that threshold | N.A.<br>Not limited |
| HR | Back to work bonus<br>Subject on 1 year uninterrupted prior benefit receipt | Full GMI benefit in first month, 75% in second and 50% of GMI benefit in third month | 3 months |
| HU | Back to work bonus<br>Subject on taking up employment while taking part in public work program | 2* employment substituting benefit (HUF 22,800) | Planned duration of the public work programme |
| IE | Disregards | €20 per day, max. 3 days per week | Not limited |
| IT | Disregard<br>subject to taking up employment upon prior benefit receipt<br>Social insurance contribution exemption subject to taking up permanent FT employment | 20% of the new employment income<br>Exemption is limited to €780 per month, impact on both net take home pay and wage cost for the employer | Remainder of the fiscal year plus 12 months<br>18 months minus number of months of benefit receipt |

| | Type | Amount/Rate | Duration |
|---|---|---|---|
| LT | Back to work bonus subject to conditions regarding duration prior registration employment service, duration of prior benefit receipt, and filing a claim | first 3 months: 100% of the average benefit amount in the 6 months prior to employment next 3 months: 80%, final 6 months: 50% | Max. 12 months |
| LV | Disregards Subject to re-entering employment | Net earnings from new job are disregarded up to the amount of the net monthly minimum wage | 3 months after start employment |
| MT | Back to work bonus subject to prior receipt of > 1 year, and earnings ≥ minimum wage, and application | Tapering of benefit scheme: 65% of max. SA benefit amount in first year (excl. bonus supplements), 45% the second, and 25% the third one. Preferential treatment for lone parents. | Max. 3 years |
| PT | Disregards subject to return to employment | Earnings disregards of 50% (instead of 20%—see Table 4.1) | 12 months (consecutive or not) after return to employment |
| RO | Disregards<br>Back to work bonus[b] subject to re-entry in 24 month employment | Income and benefit thresholds are increased by 15% for households with a working member<br>Continued benefit payment | No time limit.<br>6 months |
| SE | Disregards[b] subject to 6 months of benefit receipt | 25% is disregarded | Up to 2 years after entering work |
| SK | Back to work bonus subject on earned income < 2*minimum wage | Specific benefit for unemployed recipients starting a new job; €126.14/month months 1–12; €63.07/month months 13–18 | 18 months |
| UK | Additional disregards subject to having children or limited capability for work | Maximal disregarded amount depends on receipt of housing support: £292 (with support) and £512 (without) | Not limited in time |
| USA SNAP | Disregards | $30 per quarter from irregular income; standard deduction of $178–240 per year | Not limited in time. |

[a]Amount refers to 2022.
[b]From September 2021 onwards.
*Note:* France no longer employs an earnings disregards within its rSa scheme, but has introduced a separate in-work benefit, the prime d'activité. Slovakia provides an activation allowance within the minimum income scheme, for household members who take part in an activation programme, or who earn at least the minimum wage. Disregards upon re-entry to work exist in Austria and the US TANF scheme, but details vary by Länder/state. Poland and the Netherlands allow municipalities to disregard earnings in line with their own discretion, within a certain limit (see text).
*Source:* EUROMOD country reports, OECD country policy descriptions and MISSOC tables.

work. Municipalities in the Netherlands are allowed to deviate from the 100% taper rate, albeit within specific nationally legislated ranges. Earnings disregards are limited to six months (30 months for single parents) and 25% of the additional income. They may not exceed about 250 euros a month. (Because of the local variation, the Dutch disregards is not included in Table 4.2.)

Boschman et al. (2021) find evidence that Dutch social assistance recipients are more likely to become self-sufficient when they also have earnings. This applies in particular to benefit recipients with limited work experience. Temporary employment agencies are found to be a particularly effective stepping stone towards self-sufficiency in the Netherlands.

So what are the channels through which this works?

First, being able to do some work in addition to a social assistance benefit can help to enhance a welfare recipient's earning capacity and employability. Through work, people acquire additional skills, while persistent joblessness usually leads to a deterioration of human capital and therefore earning capacity.

Secondly, it can bring social and cultural capital. It can bring knowledge and it can help foster social ties, including to potential employers.

Thirdly, employers have limited information about skills, productivity, or work ethic of potential employees. They thus depend on signals in their decision whom to hire. Employers are sometimes reluctant to hire welfare recipients because they perceive benefit receipt as a sign of lack of work ethic. If welfare recipients manage to find and keep a job, this may signal to employers that they want to work and possess work skills. This makes them more attractive than welfare recipients without a job. Holding a job, even if it does not earn a living wage, can thus be an effective employability strategy. Employers may also use low-wage, low-quality jobs as a way to screen new workers. If they prove themselves, they can be promoted to better jobs (Gruen et al., 2011).

Other studies are less clear, even for the Netherlands. An evaluation of the Dutch social assistance experiments (see below) found that a more generous earnings disregard had no effect on the outflow to full-time work (Verlaat & Zulkarnain, 2022). But in some municipalities a positive effect on the outflow to part-time work was found. To be clear: participants were not allowed to earn more than 200 euros (net) per month in addition to their benefit. It is worth stressing that the experiments involved limited numbers of participants in multiple municipalities, making it difficult to establish statistically significant effects.

Similarly, a study for Finland failed to find much of an effect (Palviainen, 2023). In 2002, the Finnish government introduced an earnings disregard experiment the aim of which was to stimulate social assistance clients to take up temporary or part-time work. The study found no significant employment effects overall although there were some indications of a potentially significant effect on women. The same conclusion has been found by later studies on the earnings disregard as well as the Finnish basic income experiment (Hiilamo & Lehmus-Sun, 2020).

The evidence is thus not extremely clear-cut. That may be for various reasons.

*First*, administrative rules and execution. Belgium, for example, has applied earnings disregards in its social assistance schemes for many years now. People on social assistance can earn up to 250 euro each month without seeing their benefit reduced. That is a sizeable extra sum relative to the amount of the benefit itself, some 900 euro for a single person. But the provision is remarkably little used. That, case workers say, has to do with the administrative complexity of the provision and the amount of (virtual) paperwork that is required. For example, there are complex rules regarding the exact calculation of the disregard. That provides already overstretched case workers with little incentive to guide their clients towards the provision and to encourage them to make use of it. Similarly, in the study for Norway by Palviainen (2023) the suggestion is made that rule complexity accounts for the lack of a significant effect.

*Second*, the effectiveness of earnings disregards may depend on the types of jobs available. Part-time work and temporary agency work is plentiful in the Netherlands. In other countries social assistance beneficiaries may have a much harder time finding jobs consistent with the limited working time an earnings disregard typically allows for.

But overall, the results seem to suggest that an over-economic approach to activation has its limits. From an economic perspective earnings disregards make a lot of sense. It is not surprising that social assistance recipients do not take up low-paid, part-time jobs if they face 100% effective tax rates, even if such small jobs offer a stepping stone to better labour market positions. Human capital and signalling theory lead us to expect that low-wage work in combination with benefits will increase work experience and thus human capital and will function as a signal of reliability and willingness to work. This then should allow social assistance recipients to find better jobs: jobs with more (stable) work hours or a higher hourly wage thus becoming completely independent of social assistance. This happens but only to a limited extent. That is consistent with what we know from other research on social assistance dynamics, namely that many social assistance recipients face other barriers to self-sufficiency than purely work-related limitations. These may be related to personal characteristics, for example health issues, or behaviours, for example substance use. But equally important are structural exclusion mechanisms, especially in the case of migrants.

### 4.3.7 The Perils of Adequate Protection: How Real Are 'Dependency Cultures'?

The idea that welfare systems foster 'welfare cultures' or 'cultures of dependency' exists in the public mind as well as in political discourse, especially, but not exclusively in the Anglo-Saxon world. Publicists like Charles Murray in the US and Theodore Dalrymple in the UK have built lucrative careers out of lamenting the 'underclasses' nurtured by well-meaning but naïve governments. It is a contentious, charged issue. Even if totally fictitious, these ideas propagated by conservative critics of the welfare state have had very real consequences on welfare policies. Ignoring or dismissing them off hand is not smart if we are thinking about realistic ways to move income protection forward.

The idea is that welfare support itself changes the attitudes of welfare recipients and thus produces a 'culture of dependence' that results in welfare dependency being passed from one generation to the next. In particular, the concern is that growing up in families or in neighbourhoods heavily reliant on social assistance alters children's preferences by weakening their work ethic and reducing the stigma associated with welfare receipt.

This notion of a welfare culture goes back to theories of poverty cultures from the 1960s. These attributed welfare dependency to the values and attitudes that children learn from their parents and neighbours (Duncan et al., 1988; Corcoran & Adams, 1995; Bartholomae, Fox, & McKenry, 2004). As such, intergenerational welfare dependency represents a form of cultural transmission in which preferences, beliefs, and norms of behaviour develop through social interactions both across and within generations.

Contentious though this issue is, there actually is evidence of intergenerational transmission of welfare dependence as well as of neighbourhood and social network effects. There is a good deal of research for the US (Gottschalk, 1996; Lee, Singelmann, & Yom-Tov, 2008) but also for the Scandinavian countries, in large part because of the wealth of high quality administrative and survey data available there (Stenberg, 2000; Bratberg, Nilsen, & Vaage, 2014; Dahl, Kostøl, & Mogstad, 2014).

But does that mean that benefit receipt as such causes intergenerational poverty? Evidently, this statement cuts (more than just) a few corners short. Several mechanisms are thought to play a role in the intergenerational transmission of benefit receipt. To start with, parental benefit receipt may indeed affect beliefs and norms about welfare and work. Children may see it as a more legitimate and acceptable option, possibly of last resort (Bertrand, Mullainathan, & Shafir, 2006; Dahl, Kostøl, & Mogstad, 2014). Furthermore, if parents receive benefits, mental processing, and application costs may decline, as parents are able to provide their children with first-hand information on how the system works (Dahl, Kostøl, & Mogstad, 2014). Incidentally, very much like how middle-class parents can teach their children on how to navigate the world they are familiar with. Thirdly, the very causes of parental benefit receipt can have a negative impact on children's educational level, which in turn may increase the likelihood that they will resort to benefits.

Some research suggests that this last mechanism, is in fact the primary mechanism linking welfare receipt across generations. A study for Australia (Bubonya & Cobb-Clark, 2021) found that adolescents in welfare-reliant families experience more disruptions in their schooling (e.g., school changes and residential mobility, expulsions and suspensions) and receive less financial support from their families both of which impact on their chances of completing high school and avoiding the welfare roll. Young people's risk-taking behaviour (smoking, illicit drug use, delinquency, and pregnancy) was also found to be a key mechanism underpinning intergenerational welfare reliance. Physical and mental health, work-welfare attitudes, and academic achievement, in contrast, were found to have a more modest role in transmitting welfare receipt across generations. Evidence for similar dynamics were found in other studies, like one for the Netherlands by Boschman et al. (2019) who find parental benefit receipt lowers the child's educational attainment, subsequently resulting in more benefit receipt. They also see beliefs and norms playing a more direct role in intergenerational transmission.

The eternal issue in such studies is to separate out spurious effects from causal ones. In other words, the fact that there are statistically significant intergenerational correlations in benefit dependence may result from shared characteristics between parents and children. For example, parents and children are often exposed to the same local labour market conditions, share the same ethnic background, and are similar in characteristics such as ability and health.

But it may also be the case that structural drivers and endogenous mechanisms reinforce each other, as a study by Carina Mood (2010) for Sweden brings out. She argues that endogenous growth in benefit recipiency may start due to purely exogenous factors, e.g. a drop in demand for workers due to a recession. When more individuals receive social assistance, these may in turn exert an influence on non-recipients. Through social influence from recipients, people in social settings where welfare dependence is common may have a higher probability of applying for minimum income support than those affected only by 'exogenous' drivers like unemployment. Mood analyses the extent to which social influence processes of this kind played a role in the increases and decreases in the reliance on social assistance among young adults in Stockholm County during the period 1990–1999. Results indicate that the level of social assistance use in one year has a positive effect on the next year's inflow of new beneficiaries and a negative effect on the outflow when other relevant factors are controlled for, lending support to the hypothesis of a self-reinforcing process.

Mood makes a very interesting observation in the conclusion. While most people will find it obvious that people are influenced by others' behaviour, the potential effects of social influence are all too often ignored or forgotten by scholars when studying welfare or labour market outcomes. The analytical focus tends to be placed on the decision-making individual. That individual is in effect thought of as a well-informed, isolated individual making fairly rational decisions, weighting benefits against costs. That is not how scientists really think about people, of course, but it is all too often the way they actually analyse them.

Mood's study shows how a macro-level phenomenon (the aggregate social assistance recipiency) affects a micro-level phenomenon (the individual's beliefs and attitudes) which in turn affects another micro-level phenomenon (the individual decision whether or not to apply for minimum income support), and these decisions generate the observed macro-level phenomenon (aggregate recipiency rates, at the next point in time).

This interplay between macro- and micro-level phenomena also has policy relevance. For a decrease or increase in social assistance recipiency rates will stimulate a further change in the same direction.

The idea that benefit receipt has an intergenerational and cultural dimension is a politically sensitive one. It has often been (mis-)used as an argument for curbing benefit levels or restricting access in order to avoid 'cultures of dependence' to develop. While large part of intergenerational transmission of poverty and benefit dependency is presumably due to similarities in the risk factors faced by, and characteristics of, parents and children, the evidence shows that outright dependency fears, even if overblown, cannot just be dismissed. Yet the dynamics are quite complex. Carina Mood's thoughtful research shows that structural drivers and endogenous drivers may well reinforce each other. When more people receive social assistance, because of structural exclusion factors or exogenous shocks, these may in turn exert an influence on patterns of behaviour and perceptions of normality among non-recipients. Such dynamics can be countered, first and foremost, by addressing the structural factors that make people having to resort to support. At the same time, actions can be centred on dependent individuals themselves. This brings us to the role of so-called activation policies.

### 4.3.8 What Use Is 'Activation'?

There has been a widespread trend towards activation in income protection schemes (Marchal & Van Mechelen, 2013). Activation efforts usually employ carrots and sticks at the same time. Part of the carrot arsenal are financial and non-financial stimuli intended to make the transition to work more attractive. These may be accompanied with measures aimed at boosting human capital, such as education, vocational formation, and other services to promote employability. Sticks include strict availability, work search and training requirements, and the (threat) of sanctions and benefit terminations. There are a considerable number of studies looking at activation efforts of all sorts, which we cannot review here at length (see for example Diop-Christensen, 2015; Eleveld, 2016; Holcomb, Hetling, & Yeo, forthcoming). Let us look however in a bit more detail at the recent Dutch experience because it is quite instructive.

In 2015 the Dutch government introduced a new law on social assistance, the Participation Act. One of its main features was a stronger role to the local level in the administration of social assistance. It also introduced stricter entitlement conditions, including mandatory participation in job search and training. The Act also introduced a form of workfare. That is to say: claimants became obliged to perform social services so as to make them do something in return for the social assistance money they received. But perhaps the most exciting feature of the Participation Act was a provision (article 83) that opened the way for suspending the conditions stipulated in the act for the purposes of experimentation. That opportunity was not lost and several experiments ensued.

All this matters because Dutch social assistance benefit levels are among the most generous in Europe. Indeed, as we have seen in Chapter 2 the Netherlands is just about the only country in Europe providing at least parts of its population minimum income protection close to the relative poverty threshold. It is almost unique in that respect and in that sense a very relevant case. What makes the Dutch case even more striking is that the country has an extraordinarily dynamic labour market. Employment levels are among the highest in Europa and long-term unemployment is low.

Experiments were set up in six municipalities (Verlaat & Zulkarnain, 2022). The main aim was to study the effects of scrapping job-seeking requirements and mandatory training. Another objective was to gauge the effect of lowering the withdrawal rate of labour market earnings on top of the assistance grant. While the impact on work behaviour was a key focus, researchers also looked at the health and well-being of claimants as well as the job satisfaction of case workers.

Those experiments have delivered a wealth of information because they involved multiple municipalities and because they were closely monitored and analysed by several researchers. The exemption from labour and reintegration obligations was found not to have a statistically significant effect on the outflow to work. This was found for all municipalities. Conversely, more intensive job search assistance was also not found to have an effect on the outflow to full-time work, but sometimes it did have a positive effect on the outflow to part-time work.

However, researchers at the Dutch Central Planning Bureau point out that the estimates are rather unprecise. It is worth keeping in mind that in each municipality less than 1000 people participated, so that the different treatment groups were all of limited size. Researchers have also pointed out that in some municipalities the effects cannot be interpreted directly as the (sole) effect of the intervention. In some municipalities, considerable differences in the outcome variables between the treated groups and the control group emerged before the start of the experiment.

Yet the experiments have in many ways yielded striking results, given the trends towards 'activation' and 'social reintegration' that we have seen in many countries. Conditions, requirements, monitoring, and sanctioning has been intensified in many countries to achieve the goal of making people self-reliant again. It is significant and important, to say the least, that experiments such as the Dutch ones do not suggest such efforts, or their absence, to have much of an impact.

But apart from such methodological considerations we should think carefully about what such experiments actually teach us. Especially about what they learn about conditionality in other settings than the Dutch one. One important consideration is that the experiments were limited in time. People presumably knew that there would be a return to the stringent enforcement of work search and training requirements. They also happened in a country that culturally puts a high value on work. Getting people into work has been close to an obsession of Dutch governments since the 1990s. It is fair to assume that Dutch people have internalized the importance of work to a strong degree. It is moreover for the most part a Protestant country with very high levels of social control. Living on benefits while shirking work is not just administratively discouraged and sanctioned, it is also frowned upon.

### 4.3.9 What Do Sanctions Actually Do?

Social assistance benefits are needs-based and almost never time-limited, that is, needs will be re-assessed at regular statutorily decided intervals, but, bar a few exceptions—most significantly the lifetime limits in the US minimum income provisions—benefits generally remain available for as long as the needs persist. However, they are usually linked to certain compulsory measures for reintegration into the labour market, i.e., counselling, retraining programmes or accepting any reasonable job offer at hand.

There is, as we already noted, a very fundamental tension between the noble, well-articulated social rights now enshrined in law in many countries, even constitutional law in some cases, and the many restrictions and conditions, usually not so eloquently codified in law, that actually qualify access to those rights.

One of the many examples that could be provided is that of a woman who got sanctioned from the UK's Universal Credit. She got sanctioned because she had missed an appointment the day after she had had a miscarriage. In a letter received seven months after her miscarriage, she was told in stark language: 'You didn't come to a meeting with us. . . . Because of this, you'll lose some or all of your universal credit payment for a time. We call this being sanctioned.' The letter goes on to explain that she will lose £10.40 every day for 229 days, a total of £2,381.60. The letter sparked a downward spiral which the woman claims saw her falling back into drug use, attempting to take her own life and ending up in prison for shoplifting (WalesOnline, article published 19 August 2019).

Stick measures have become an important element of the activation arsenal in many places. There is quite a bit of research on benefit sanctions. This has produced mixed results. While some studies show increased transition to employment (Røed & Westlie, 2012; Boockmann, Thomsen, & Walter, 2014) other studies give far less reason for optimism (Smedsvik & Iacono, 2022). Some show that sanctions push people into jobs of questionable stability and earnings (Hillmann & Hohenleitner, 2012). Other studies suggest that sanctions sometimes throw vulnerable people into (deeper) destitution (Malmberg-Heimonen & Vuori, 2005; Watts & Fitzpatrick, 2018). A study by Løken, Lommerud, and Holm Reiso (2018) on a 1998 reform in Norway targeted at single parents provides rich insights into the longer-term effects of activation via sanctioning, including the educational performance of the children of the single mothers that were affected. The introduction of a time limit on a benefit paid specifically to lone parents (the vast majority of whom are women) did increase their working hours, as was the intention of the reform. It did, however, not have a positive effect on their disposable income as mothers traded off reductions in benefits with increases in earnings from work. Most remarkable was a significant but moderate drop in the school grades of the children indirectly affected. The authors see the reduced parental time at home as the main mechanism for the observed moderate drop in children's grades. The effect was larger for children of mothers with no informal network to help with child care.

This study is interesting because it shows that the longer-term effect of sanctions, as in this case the human capital formation of children, may be less positive than the immediate effects. Of course, Norway has an extensive set of welfare provisions, including child care facilities and high-quality public education, that one presumes limited the effects of the reform.

## 4.4 Lessons from a Paradigmatic Revolution: US Welfare Reform

No country has done activation of welfare recipients quite like the US. The assault on the US welfare system by the likes of Charles Murray, Lawrence Mead, and other conservative commentators, eagerly echoed and amplified by politicians from the American (centre-) right, had far-reaching consequences for actual policy, culminating in reforms aimed at cracking down on 'dependency' in a most merciless way. In 1996, the Roosevelt era Families with Dependent Children (AFDC) programme—the primary cash assistance programme for low-income families—was abolished and replaced by Temporary Assistance to Needy Families (TANF). The name of the programme reflected the main purpose of the reform: cash aid was to become time limited. Credible and enforceable work requirements were introduced, as were time limits on the receipt of benefits. The Personal Responsibility and Work Opportunity Reconciliation Act of 1996 (PRWORA) not only replaced AFDC with TANF but it also devolved more powers to the states. This law essentially removed almost all federal eligibility and payment rules, giving states much greater discretion in designing their own social assistance programmes. For that they received a so-called federal block grant of limited size (Blank, 2002).

Around the same time, however, there was an expansion of the Earned Income Tax Credit (see Box 4.1), a sizeable refundable tax credit for households with low earnings. The EITC was a provision within the US personal tax system designed to promote and reward work but also to offer income support, especially to working parents (Nichols & Rothstein, 2016).

What makes the US case so interesting and relevant in the context of this book is the fact that a truly complete policy shift occurred in the way income support was provided. Support for people out of work was curbed in a most radical way while support for working people on low incomes was almost equally radically expanded. There are few other examples to be found of an equally paradigmatic policy shift. Moreover, some of the most sophisticated and high quality research of the past decades has focused on the many reforms that were part of this shift, in parts or in combination.

That said, while there is much to be learned from the American experience it is also true that the American context remains a highly peculiar one. One has to be cautious and indeed wary about extrapolating findings. Another complicating factor is the large and widely varying role of the states in many aspects of social policy. The impact of the federal reforms can only be properly understood if the state and local policies, and possibly policy shifts, are properly accounted for. To give just one example: Although the Welfare Reform Act of 1996 imposed a time limit on cash assistance receipt, the states could exempt up to 20% of their caseload from this limit, could set shorter time limits if they chose, or could continue funding assistance to families entirely out of state funds after 60 months (Blank, 2002).

## Box 4.2 The Earned Income Tax Credit: a new paradigm for the rich world?

### The origins of EITC

The origins of the Earned Income Tax Credit, America's prime channel of redistribution for people at working age nowadays and a model to be emulated elsewhere in the rich world according to some (see for example Kenworthy, 2011), is associated with two surprising names: Chicago economist and free-market champion Milton Friedman and Republican President Richard Nixon.

The EITC grew out of the 1960s debates over the negative income tax (NIT), powerfully advocated by Milton Friedman, and the early 1970s debate over the Nixon administration's Family Assistance Plan (FAP).

Milton Friedman put forward his idea of a negative income tax in his book *Capitalism and Freedom*, published in 1962. He wanted to give poor people cash rather than an array of welfare provisions. People could then use the money as they saw fit. This, he argued would alleviate poverty and simplify the system since it would be administered centrally by the federal tax authority instead of many different welfare agencies.

Nixon's Family Assistance Plan was a negative income tax for families that would have replaced the welfare system, which primarily was Aid to Families with Dependent Children (AFDC). AFDC was a means tested benefit effectively targeted at lone parents that would later suffer under severe critiques from both politicians and academics. Charles Murray's Losing Ground and Lawrence Mead's Beyond Entitlement stand out as particularly influential. Both the NIT and FAP would have operated through the income tax system to provide an income floor.

The EITC was enacted during the Ford administration in 1975 as a temporary refundable tax credit for lower-income workers. It was meant to offset the Social Security payroll tax. The credit was made permanent by the Revenue Act of 1978. The EITC was considered both an anti-poverty programme and an alternative to welfare because it incentivized work (Ventry, 2000). The Tax Reform Act of 1986, signed by President Reagan, indexed the maximum earned income and phase-out income levels to inflation. President Reagan deemed it 'the best anti-poverty, the best pro-family, the best job creation measure to come out of Congress' (Snyder, 1996 cited in Hungerford & Thiess, 2013).

Around the early 1990s, welfare reform came to occupy centre stage in the political debate and Bill Clinton ran his first campaign in 1992 on a slogan to 'end welfare as we know it'. What ensued was a major shift in US social policy. The 1993 expansion in particular turned the scheme into the country's pre-eminent anti-poverty programme for families of active working age.

Thanks to surprisingly broad and robust political support (cf. Chapter 5) in America's polarized political landscape, spending has increased making it the US's preeminent anti-poverty programme. The Personal Responsibility and Work Opportunity Reconciliation Act of 1996 (PRWORA) imposed time limits on social assistance receipt and strengthened work requirements, further encouraging the take-up of work, if not making it essential for longer-term economic survival.

The generosity of EITC has increased almost steadily over its existence. Both Democratic and Republican dominated legislatures have increased amounts, usually with strong bipartisan support.

To claim the EITC, a tax return with proper documentation must be filed with the US Internal Revenue Service (IRS). The amount of the credit changes every year and is based on earnings, the number of qualifying children and marital status (National Conference of State Legislatures, 2023).

The maximum credit for a household with three children amounts to $6,935 a year in 2022 (Figure 4.8). Low-income workers with no children are also eligible for the EITC, but the maximum credit ($560 in 2022) is just a fraction of that for families with children.

More than 25 million eligible tax filers received almost $60 billion in federal EITC during the 2020 tax year. The average EITC amount received per tax filer was $2,411 during the 2020 tax year.

The EITC is designed to encourage and reward work. When earnings are zero the EITC is also zero. Then there is a phase-in zone, the slope of which depends on the number of children. For a household with children, the tax credit rises at a rate of 40%. So on top of every dollar earned, the household gets an additional 40 cents through the tax system. Once earnings hit a certain level, the EITC levels out. It remains the same over a fairly narrow income band and then declines. In the case of a two or three children household the phase-out out occurs at a rate of 21.06%. That is fairly flat phase-out (far flatter for example than in the case of Universal Credit in the UK). This implies that households with sizeable earned incomes still receive some EITC. For households with three kids the EITC stops completely at just over 51,000 dollars (for single or head of household filers), for a household with two kids that is almost 48,000 dollars (National Conference of State Legislatures, 2023).

*continued*

**Box 4.2** *continued*

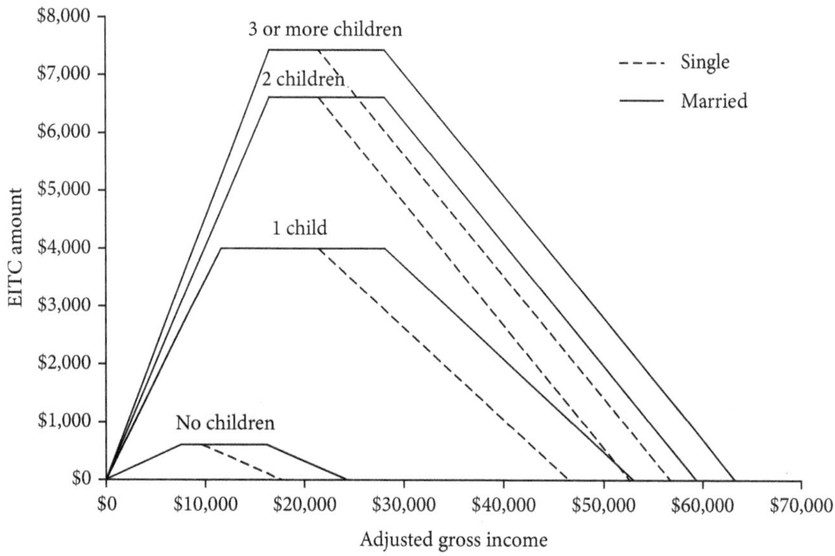


**Figure 4.8** US Earned Income Tax Credit benefit structure

Many states offer supplements to the EITC. At this time, 34 states, the District of Columbia, Guam, Puerto Rico and some municipalities have EITCs in addition to the federal EITC. That, together with differences in statutory minimum wage levels, leads to sizeable differences across states in minimum income protections for working lone parents, as Laird et al. (2018) demonstrate. State EITC policies are mostly modelled after the federal credit, but vary (somewhat) on eligibility, credit amounts, refundability, awareness, and outreach efforts.

State EITC eligibility requirements often match federal requirements. There are differences. Wisconsin's credit does not apply to childless workers, and California's credit focuses on a narrower segment of income levels than the federal credit. Most states—with notable exceptions including California, Minnesota, North Dakota, and Washington—calculate their EITCs as a percentage of the federal credit, ranging from 3% in Montana to 125% in South Carolina.

The momentous reforms of the 1990s in the United States went accompanied with equally momentous changes in outcomes. In an authoritative and much cited evaluation of US Welfare Reform, the late Rebecca Blank writes 'At the same time as major changes in programme structure occurred during the 1990s, there were also stunning changes in behaviour. Strong adjectives are appropriate to describe these behavioural changes. Nobody—of any political persuasion—predicted or would have believed possible the magnitude of change that occurred in the behaviour of low-income single-parent families over this decade' (Blank, 2002, p. 1115).

Most notably was a massive drop in welfare use and an almost equally strong increase in the employment rates of single parents, particularly single mothers. There was a remarkably rapid decline in AFDC/TANF caseloads between 1994 and 2000. These declined by a whopping 56.5%. At the same time there was a strong increase in employment among the same group. Between 1994 and 1999 the labour force participation of single mothers rose by an unprecedented 10 percentage points.

It remains a matter of debate to what extent this was due to the favourable economic context at the time and the almost simultaneous expansion of the EITC (Box 4.2). Early studies attributed the quite sizeable employment effects mostly to the expansion of the EITC. Eissa and Liebman (1996) found particularly strong increases in employment among single women with and without children. Meyer and Rosenbaum (2001) estimated that the EITC accounted for over 60% of the employment increase of single mothers between 1984 and 1996. Similarly, studies from Eissa and Hoynes (2006), Hotz and Scholz (2006), Bastian (2020), and Gelber and Mitchell (2012) found strong employment effects of the EITC. There are many other studies and outstanding overviews available, for example in Nichols and Rothstein (2016).

Yet an extensive re-assessment by Kleven (2019) has cast doubt on the impact of the EITC on labour market participation. Kleven argues that the employment increases in the mid-late nineties were very large, but they were influenced by the confounding effects of welfare reform and a booming economy. Based on different approaches that exploit variation in these confounders across household type, space, and time, the paper shows that the employment effects align closely with exposure to welfare reform and the business cycle. Single mothers who were unaffected by welfare reform (but eligible for the EITC) did not respond. Contrary to consensus, Kleven concludes that the evidence for sizeable employment effects of the EITC is fragile.

Why is this? Kleven argues the informational and psychological frictions specific to the EITC have reduced its impact. The complex schedule of the scheme accounts in part for these frictions as do the procedures for filing taxes and claiming the credit. And in effect, a number of studies have documented that most potential recipients are either unaware of the EITC or have a limited understanding of the schedule and eligibility requirements.

Most low-income families have heard about the EITC and know that working is associated with getting a tax refund check when they file their taxes. But very few recipients know whether working more would increase or reduce their EITC amount (Weisner et al., 2002).

A study by Chetty and Saez (2013) was especially illuminating. They conducted a randomized experiment with 43,000 EITC recipients. Tax preparers gave simple, personalized information about the EITC schedule to half of their clients. Chetty and Saez find no significant effects of information provision on earnings in the subsequent year in the full sample. They observed quite varied responses on both self-employment income and wage earnings across the tax preparers involved in the experiment. So just providing information about tax incentives does not systematically affect earnings on average. But they did find that tax preparers could influence their clients' earnings decisions by providing advice about how to respond to tax incentives.

Kleven concludes that 'EITC is not an a priori likely candidate for finding large labour supply impacts.'

But the issue appears far from settled. A paper by Whitmore Schanzenbach and Strain (2021) estimates the EITC-employment effect(s) by pooling all expansions together in one difference-in-difference model in an attempt to estimate the impact of the programme as a whole—apart from individual expansions—on labour supply. It uses variation over time and states in the size of the maximum EITC credit to estimate the employment response and claims to find robust evidence of an effect on labour participation. It finds that a $1,000 increase in the size of the maximum credit is associated with a 3.2 to 3.7 percentage point increase in employment among unmarried mothers with low levels of education. When examining both federal and state expansions together, it estimates a 2.9 to 3.3 percentage point increase in employment. The authors argue that their results are different from Kleven's striking finding that the EITC had little or no effect on employment because of the methodological choices made.[10]

In conclusion, it seems hard to pinpoint the exact impact of a measure as large as the EITC. If a measure of this size fails to produce robust and sizeable effects in a setting with plenty of low-paid jobs and a distinctly unattractive fallback position, one may legitimately wonder what difference the much smaller financial incentives in many other places make.

### 4.4.1 EITC Is Uncontested as a Successful Anti-poverty Programme

As far as the impact on poverty is concerned the studies are more unanimous. Judged as an anti-poverty programme, the EITC is generally deemed to be successful, at least if measured against the US's rather idiosyncratic poverty lines. It is clear that the EITC is by and large well-targeted at those who need it. Hoynes and Patel (2018) show that it is concentrated among families whose incomes (after other taxes and transfers) would otherwise be between 75% and 150% of the poverty line. In fact, the effect of the EITC peaks at around 100% of the American poverty line.

That stands in marked contrast to in-work benefits in many other countries. Very often, these are aimed at low-paid workers and not at low-earnings households. That makes an enormous difference. We know that most low-paid individuals are secondary or tertiary earners. For that reason they are more often to be found in the middle and even higher ranges of the household income distribution than at the lower end of that distribution. For that reason, benefits targeted at low-paid individuals tend to end up with households above the poverty line, usually far above it. By design, that is not the case with EITC.

Moreover, studies suggest that the EITC has important impacts on parent and child health, and on children's academic achievement. There is a growing empirical literature on this, from which Nichols and Rothstein conclude that 'there is robust evidence of quite large effects of the EITC on children's academic achievement and attainment, with potentially important consequences for later-life outcomes' (Nichols & Rothstein, 2016).

### 4.4.2 Does Supporting Low-Paid Workers Worsen the Underlying Problem of Low Pay?

An important and credible argument that critics of the EITC (and in-work benefits in general) make is that what is intended as a support for low-paid individuals or households effectively amounts to a subsidy to low-wage employers, who are able to attract workers at lower wages than they otherwise would have to pay. While some of these workers are partly compensated by the government via the EITC, if they apply and if they are eligible, the workers who do not qualify or do not apply (and that is by all available estimates a significant number) may end up with reduced wages.

Critics of the EITC suggest that the heavy reliance on the EITC is one major reason why the US leads the OECD in the share of jobs that pay relatively low wages. The EITC is even thought to be making things worse by exerting downward pressure on wages, especially of workers who are not covered. The EITC is after all very small for workers without children and non-existent for undocumented migrants. People eligible for substantial EITC refunds may become less inclined to bargain for higher wages if they are compensated by the government.

So while EITC is intended to encourage work, EITC-induced behavioural effects may drive wages down, shifting the intended transfer towards employers. Rothstein (2010) simulates the economic incidence of the EITC under a range of supply and demand elasticities and finds that in all scenarios a substantial portion of the intended transfer to low-income single mothers is in effect captured by employers through reduced wages. The transfer to employers is borne in part by low-skill workers who are not themselves eligible for the EITC. There is some empirical evidence that corroborates the potential wage erosion effect of EITC (Leigh, 2010; Chetty & Saez, 2013). Using variation in state EITC supplements, Leigh (2010) finds that a 10% increase in the generosity of the EITC is associated with a 5% fall in the wages of high school dropouts and a 2% fall in the wages of those with only a high school diploma, while having no effect on the wages of college graduates.

In their extensive review Nichols and Rothstein (2016, p. 140) conclude that: 'Although none of the evidence is airtight, it appears that employers of low-wage labor are able to capture a meaningful share of the credit through reduced wages. This comes to some extent at the expense of low-skill workers who are not eligible for the credit.'

### 4.4.3 Why EITC Type Schemes Will Not Proliferate

Despite its relative success in the US setting there remain quite serious issues with the EITC, especially as an effective system for income support. As a provision within the already complex personal tax system, is not sufficiently widely known and understood. That leads to take up rates far below the number of people entitled. Then there is the problem that even if people apply and qualify, the tax refund arrives only after a long delay, possibly much later than when people actually need the income support. It is after all a tax transfer calculated on earned income the previous year. There is a system of prepayments but that requires knowledge to navigate to avoid having to make refunds.

There are worries that the EITC discourages work effort in the phase-out zone of the benefit. After people receive the maximum they only have a limited financial pay-off to working longer hours or to seeking a promotion and higher earnings. And there are concerns that systems like the EITC may be exacerbating the actual underlying problem of inadequate pay. Those are some of the reasons why EITC is seen as a qualified success even in the US, where it is now the largest anti-poverty programme by far.

There are some additional reasons why an EITC type scheme is unlikely to take hold in much of Europe.

The US context differs in many crucial respects from the situation in Europe. The US has large contingents of low-paid workers while the gap between the lowest wages and the wages in the middle and higher up is quite considerable. Earnings inequality tends to be far smaller in most European countries. In order to be affordable within reasonable limits, an EITC type tax credit would have to be strongly targeted in much of Europe simply because otherwise too many households would qualify. However, strong targeting is bound to create prohibitive mobility traps. If support is withdrawn fast and at a hefty rate, people have no incentive to work longer hours since the net gain is too small. Likewise, they have little incentive to seek a promotion and higher earnings. Such problematic mobility traps can only be avoided if taper-off rates are made sufficiently flat. But that comes at a very considerable cost if the lower end of the (household) earnings distribution is densely populated, as is the case in many European countries. This cost can only be avoided by making the amount of the tax credit itself smaller, but in that case the anti-poverty effect is reduced.[11]

An EITC tax credit is not only hard to implement because the sociodemographic and socio-economic setting in Europe differs but also because the institutional context differs. Many European countries have moved away from joint taxation of couples towards more individualized taxation. Of course, in order to be effective as an anti-poverty measure it is absolutely crucial that refundable tax credits are targeted towards low earnings households and not low earnings individuals. The fact that there has been a move away from joint taxation in many countries makes this harder. A 2022 Report by the on taxation and gender equality finds that some 63% of 43 rich countries surveyed base taxation on an individual unit. Six countries (Belgium, France, Iceland, Indonesia, Switzerland, and the United States) use a household unit and nine countries allow taxpayers to choose between the individual and household unit. The countries with individual taxation surveyed by the

OECD indicated that this unit of taxation encourages female labour participation. Household-based income taxation naturally entails negative work incentives for second earners. Yet it is also true that many countries that tax personal income on an individual basis, apply tax credits or allowances on a household basis. Individualized taxation does not preclude household based (refundable) tax credits but the fact remains that the move in most countries is away from the household unit. This makes it less straightforward to use the personal tax system as a channel of income support. As an instrument for incentivizing work, tax credits make sense, be it that the evidence remains contested. As a channel of supplementary income support on top of other provisions that secure resources for basic needs they may also make some sense. But as principal income support provisions replacing direct social transfers, EITC type schemes have far too many limitations.

5

# What Kind of Minimum Income Protection Is Politically Viable?

## 5.1 Politics Matters

So far we have mainly dealt with what one might call the more 'technical' issues in the design of minimum income protection.

To stop there would not be exceptional. A lot of writing about minimum income protection makes abstraction of the political processes driving redistribution towards the poor and needy. That is the case, for example, for much of the economics literature on optimal targeting in income support schemes. That literature focuses on issues such as target efficiency (poverty reduction per euro spent), financial work incentives, and the potential responses to these. Yet a scheme that provides the biggest bang for the buck in terms of poverty reduction on paper may not necessarily appeal the most to politicians or voters.

The same applies to other strands of the literature dealing with issues of administrative implementation, bureaucracy, social worker discretion, and the resulting issues of non-take up and stigma. A minimum income scheme with a lot of conditions attached and with close monitoring and sanctioning of claimants may be hard to implement and not terribly cost-effective but it may also be the scheme preferred by voters and politicians.

Politics clearly matter when it comes to thinking about minimum income protection. This section addresses some of the political economy issues relating to minimum income protection. We will not review all of the extensive political science and political sociology literature but we will discuss what we think are some of the most interesting and relevant findings. These include such questions as: How do people think about deservingness? It is often said that 'benefits for the poor become poor benefits'. Is that really true? Is support for the working poor different? Are integrated minimum income support systems more politically robust?

*Zero Poverty Society*. Sarah Marchal and Ive Marx, Oxford University Press. © Sarah Marchal and Ive Marx (2024).
DOI: 10.1093/9780191967771.003.0005

## 5.2 Who Is Seen to Deserve Support?

There exists quite a lot of research on what is usually called 'deservingness' perceptions. Who is seen to be entitled to what, under which circumstances?

Distinctions between poor people deemed more deserving of support, in cash or kind, and those deemed less deserving or even undeserving have existed a long time.

Some scholars have even proposed that the way people think about deservingness is rooted in psychological categories that evolved over the course of human evolution to regulate small-scale exchanges of help. Michael Bang Petersen (2012) argues that such heuristics—'judgmental shortcuts' allowing people to form opinions in the absence of substantive knowledge—are rooted in human nature rather than representing the product of specific cultural, institutional, or ideological environments.

He argues that the propensity to categorize needy individuals on the basis of their effort is not learned but rather it is an evolved solution to problems relating to the provision of assistance in the small social groups of our Pleistocene ancestors (see also Petersen, 2012). In evidence he cites fossil records showing that our ancestors have cared for the crippled and injured as early as 1.77 million years ago. People have also hunted cooperatively and shared meat in groups for at least 400,000 years. In that context providing help was only adaptive to the extent it was reciprocal. That required the evolution of cognitive categories enabling the individuals to represent and discriminate between 'cheaters' and 'reciprocators'.

Much closer to the present day, it is well documented that the earliest poor laws made such distinctions. The 1834 English Poor Law famously distinguished between the 'deserving' and the 'undeserving poor'. Deserving were those who through no fault of their own—disability, age, sickness—could not provide for themselves. In the second category were the 'feckless and work-shy, a burden on their communities and undeserving of any but the harshest of treatment from good hardworking people and the instruments of the state' (Golightley & Holloway, 2016).

These distinctions seem to persist. A relatively large body of research on public deservingness perceptions finds that citizens across countries and social groups share a relatively common and consistent deservingness culture.

The 'CARIN' theory claims that five criteria influence the perceived welfare deservingness of a group (van Oorschot, 2000; van Oorschot et al., 2017). Seen as more deserving are those who are perceived as not being responsible for their situation (**C**ontrol), appearing grateful for the benefits they receive (**A**ttitude), have contributed or able and willing to contribute (**R**eciprocity), 'look and act like us' (**I**dentity), and seem in need of help (**N**eed).

The elderly people tend to be seen as most deserving, the unemployed as less deserving and immigrants as still less deserving (Van Oorschot, 2006).

There is a good deal of congruence between deservingness perceptions among the wider public with actual policies. Welfare states have tended to offer somewhat more generous and less conditional social protection to those groups that are deemed most deserving by the general public.

Tijs Laenen (2018, 2020) argues that this is not just a consequence of public opinion neatly finding its reflection in policy practice. He claims that this is better read as the product of a reciprocal relationship between popular deservingness opinions on the one hand and social welfare policies on the other. In other words, deservingness is not the static reflection of immutable 'underlying' beliefs and convictions. Welfare deservingness and welfare policy interact over time and possibly reinforce each other. Context and historical contingencies (potentially solidarity triggering 'events' such as disasters, major crises, or wars) also play a role here. The interaction of all these factors will thus produce somewhat different perceptions of deservingness across countries and across time.

You would think that the more sophisticated and deep-delving the deservingness research gets, the more profound the insights become that drive people's sentiments towards those claiming help. That is only partially true. People's opinions about deservingness tend to be fairly superficial and intuitive. A study focusing on single mothers in Hungary compared responses to direct questions about deservingness to the results of a vignette-based survey experiment in which the deservingness criteria were translated to characteristics of hypothetical mothers (Herke & Janky, 2021). The study finds that in the absence of explicit and specific deservingness cues, values (in this case adherence to traditional family values) play a strong role in determining attitudes. Yet when presented with more specific deservingness cues in the vignette experiment, people discounted the importance they attached to family values and stereotypes, and perceived need became the strongest predictor of single mothers' deservingness. These results support the importance of fairly simple, intuitive judgements in determining how the vast majority of people think about deservingness. It is those superficial opinions—call it prejudices—that consequently may weigh heavier on political preferences and responses to policies than the more sophisticated judgements that researchers are able to draw out in people they sample for research.

## 5.3 From Preferences to Politics

People's viewpoints, their political preferences—even the way they actually vote—do not translate into policies and practices in any straightforward way. The processes in between voter preference and actual policy outcomes are notoriously long and complex.

The influential power resources theory set out by Walter Korpi (2006) holds that redistributive policies, including minimum income policies, are essentially a function of 'left power'. That includes not only political parties on the left but also organized labour and associated organizations.

Yet research on the politics of minimum income benefits has not offered a very clear picture conforming to this or indeed any theoretical narrative. In his 2009 comparative study of social assistance, Kenneth Nelson found it impossible 'to distinguish any clear cross-national patterns or groups of countries that correspond neatly with previous attempts to cluster welfare states into certain institutional types' (Nelson, 2008, p. 114). Natascha Van Mechelen (2010) in her doctorate similarly struggles to establish clear country patterns consistent with any of the dominant typologies or theories.

Jinxian Wang and van Vliet (2016) find 'cautious' evidence for a positive relationship between left governments and benefit levels but their results are neither very robust across model specifications nor very strong (see also Wang et al. (2018). In a study that focuses specifically on minimum income benefits, Alain Noël (2019) finds some evidence that parties do not seem to matter much in the politics of minimum income benefits: 'If anything, the consequences of social-democratic cumulative power are marginally negative' (p. 18). A bit of an outlier is Swank (2020) who finds a significant and rather strong positive impact of left partisan government on minimum income protection. One of the most recent studies only adds to the already considerable confusion. Taschwer (2021) analyses 16 OECD countries over the period of 1990 to 2009 and again fails to find clearcut results for party politics. If anything, the study finds that right *and* left parties are associated with benefit cuts. In line with the power resources approach, trade unions show a consistently strong association with higher benefits, but they cannot constrain right nor left parties in cutting benefits.

The overall picture emerging from many scholarly attempts to 'explain' patterns of minimum income provision across countries is that the politics seem to escape any grand theory neatly explaining observed outcomes. It is even hard to identify necessary conditions, let alone sufficient conditions.

That the politics of minimum income protection are a muddled field is also clear from detailed country studies. Marcello Natili (2018, 2019) presents an elaborate, in-depth comparative analysis of the policy trajectories of minimum income schemes in Italy and Spain between the mid-1980s and 2015. That is quite interesting because Italy and Spain were among the last countries in the old EU to institutionalize minimum income schemes (see also Chapter 2). Before that general out-of-work minimum income protection for the active age only existed at the local or regional level and not even everywhere. Italy now has a national scheme, Spain recently supplemented its diverse set of regional minimum income schemes with a national scheme. While Spain's story is one of more or less gradual expansion at the regional level, Italy's trajectory is less linear and includes episodes of retrenchment.

Natili, also in a later article together with Matteo Jessoula (Jessoula & Natili, 2020) does his best to provide an overarching narrative for what has happened in both countries. He argues that the institutionalization of minimum income protection resulted 'from the interaction of socio-political demand with political supply'. The argument here essentially is that at one point political 'demand' in Italy reached enough critical mass to force a path breaking departure. This happened when a broad range of actors ranging from charities to NGOs, from trade unions to social movements coalesced to actively advocate the introduction of a national minimum income scheme.

Still, it remains a struggle to explain the different paths taken in Spain and Italy, especially Italy's rather erratic trajectory.[1] Minimum income politics clearly does not lend itself easily to grand, neat theories. Indeed, Natili pointedly observes that potential beneficiaries of minimum income protection can have very different characteristics, interests and identities. 'Single mothers with dependent children, young first time job-seekers, low-skilled workers trapped in irregular jobs and precarious contracts, long-term unemployed and migrants are social groups unlikely to recognize that they have a common interest'. (Natili, 2018, p. 117). Add to that the fact that the pool of potential beneficiaries is not stable over time at all. For most people the need for minimum income support through last safety net provisions is temporary, either because their situation of need ends or because they move on to another programme (see also our discussion in Chapter 4). That makes social assistance beneficiaries unlikely to organize themselves into an organization or lobby, let alone a party engaging in political action. Also, almost by definition minimum income beneficiaries lack the financial and other resources necessary to be politically effective.

An additional observation is in order here. In many countries social assistance schemes (and equivalent provisions) have seen a significant influx of immigrants (Conte & Mazza, 2019).

Such increases were in part driven by inflows of people seeking refuge and shelter from conflicts all around the world. Refugees usually have little option other than to resort to social assistance and related provisions for support once they have established some form of legal residency that opens up entitlements. That is especially the case in countries where contributory schemes are the main source of social protection. New immigrants are almost by definition excluded from such provisions since they have no prior labour market attachment and contribution records. Yet who is exactly entitled to what differs quite considerably across countries (Lafleur & Vintila, 2020).

Research points to the very crucial role social assistance plays in enabling new immigrants to build up an existence in their new country of residence (Lens et al., 2019). It provides them the means to establish themselves, to learn the language and local customs, to send their children to school, to get their own qualifications recognized, to acquire skills and training, to find housing and to integrate in the local community, among other things.

The fact is that in at least some countries immigrants now account for a very substantial share of the population claiming social assistance. In the Netherlands, for example, immigrants with a non-Western migration background are estimated to account for more than half of the non-elderly population on social assistance in any given month.

The overrepresentation of immigrants in social assistance looms large in political debates in many European countries. Anti-immigrant parties use it for political gain. Immigrant welfare 'tourism' or 'profiteering' features prominently in their campaigns. Suggestions that migrants are draining public resources at the expense of natives are made in subtle and sometimes not so subtle ways. Such intimations are moreover not the monopoly of the radical-right side. Sweden's social democratic foreign minister, Margot Wallström, said in 2015 (at the height of the asylum seekers influx from Syria) that 'we cannot maintain a system where perhaps 190,000 people will arrive every year—in the long run, our system will collapse' (as cited in Burgoon & Rooduijn, 2021).

Such perceptions put mainstream parties under pressure. Welfare is increasingly used as a tool to restrict migration, as the take-up of social protection is often a condition for exclusion upon renewing residence permits or requesting family reunification or citizenship (Lafleur & Vintila, 2020). Sometimes it goes further. The Belgian city of Antwerp, a city where an anti-immigrant party has made headway, at one point even started to hire private detectives to investigate whether immigrants applying for social assistance had properties outside of the country. They were not coy about that initiative.

Alesina et al. (2004) argued many years ago that support for welfare policies in Europe would decrease as European countries became more ethnically diverse. It is unclear whether migration actually undermines popular support for adequate social protection. While it may not necessarily reduce support for the welfare state in general, it can lead to more restrictive and dualistic, so-called 'welfare chauvinistic' tendencies where immigrants are less entitled to certain welfare programmes than natives or more heavily scrutinized and perhaps sanctioned.

Brian Burgoon and Matthijs Rooduijn (2021) argue that two competing mechanisms may be at work. On the one hand there may be an 'anti-solidarity effect', where anti-immigration feelings fuel worries that welfare resources will go to less deserving residents. On the other hand there may also be a 'compensation effect' if anti-immigration feelings fuel worries about one's own economic security, increasing support for welfare redistribution. They effectively find that both of these mechanisms are at play. The net-effect, so to say, depends on a country's context.

Such findings resonate with the impression one gets listening to debates across Europe. A momentous event in living European history like Brexit happened after all in the context of Britain seeking opt outs from benefit payments to immigrant workers, be it in-work (child) benefits in this particular case. Far right, nationalist and so-called populist parties are on the rise and exploit migrant welfare use with ruthless efficiency. It seems patently clear that immigration is a factor to be reckoned with when thinking about the politics of minimum income protection, especially non-contributory protection.

## 5.4 Is the Paradox of Redistribution Still Alive?

Korpi and Palme's (1998) article 'The Paradox of Redistribution and Strategies of Equality' has been of extraordinary importance for the way social policy scholars think about effective poverty relief. Not only because of the claims made in it but also because of the rich follow-up literature and debate it spawned.

In that article, Walter Korpi and Joakim Palme make a claim that is of key importance for the design of minimum income protection. They argue that stronger targeting of money and services towards the poor paradoxically does not yield more inequality reduction in any linear way. On the contrary, stronger targeting is said to be associated with a weaker redistributive impact. Universal benefits, by contrast, even if less redistributive towards the poor by design are said to bring more redistribution simply because universal programmes tend to be bigger programmes. Benefits targeted solely or almost solely at the poor, the argument goes, have a tendency to become poor benefits since they serve too narrow an electoral constituency. Universal benefits have much wider constituencies with an interest in their improvement.

One of Korpi and Palme's key pieces of empirical evidence was an analysis showing an inverse relationship at the country level between the extent of pro-poor targeting in benefits and inequality reduction. Some scholars were totally unconvinced by such evidence on methodological grounds (Bergh, 2005).[2] A number of studies have reinvestigated Korpi and Palme's seminal and highly influential finding. Lane Kenworthy (2011), using the same data, methodology, and the same set of countries, found that the relationship that held in the 1980s weakened over the 1990s and 2000s. Brady and Bostic (2015) have expanded the analysis to three dimensions of welfare transfers, the share of benefits in household incomes, the extent of low-income targeting, and the degree of universalism. They find mixed results. Consistent with Korpi and Palme, poverty reduction seems to be stronger in more universalist countries, defined as homogeneity across the population in benefits, coverage, and eligibility. But contrary to Korpi and Palme, low-income targeting does not weaken poverty reduction or benefit generosity as captured through the transfer share.

In Marx et al. (2016) (updated in Box 5.1), we show that the overall cross-country relationship between the extent of pro-poor targeting in the benefit system and income inequality reduction is in fact very weak and not at all robust against plausible alternative empirical approaches (Marx et al., 2016). But more interestingly and more importantly, a detailed disaggregated analysis reveals that the most redistributive benefit systems do contain subsystems that are strongly targeted to the poor by intent and by design. In fact, means-tested systems play a crucial role in bringing about a strong redistributive impact of the overall system, even if their relative size in terms of spending is small. Strong pro-targeting within such subsystems is in fact essential for real redistributive impact. It thus appears that benefits for the poor are not doomed to be or become poor benefits if and when they are embedded in benefit systems that satisfy wider redistributive needs and rationales. Theda Skocpol (1991) labelled such a strategy 'targeting within universalism'.

Overall, the strongest redistribution to the benefit of the poorest appears to occur in countries that employ this strategy. That is to say, strong redistributive impacts occur when strongly targeted subsystems are part of more comprehensive transfer systems, making their redistributive impact less distinguishable from the flows generated by other redistributive principles, like social insurance or cost compensation for children.

Olivier Jacques and Alain Noël (2021) point out that targeting is usually but wrongly seen as the opposite of universalism, a fact also stressed in Brady and Bostic (2015). They propose that we should consider targeting and universalism as two distinct dimensions of the welfare state, the opposite of universalism being more usefully understood as residualism, and not as pro-poor targeting. That makes total sense. It is essential to distinguish between institutional intentions and actual distributional outcomes, which in large part are driven by contextual factors. A child benefit may be universal by intent and design but if lower income households have more children it will appear to be a (mildly) targeted programme (see also Marchal & Van Lancker, 2019). If in fact child benefits are to some extent low-income targeted they will appear even more strongly targeted, even if there is a strong universal component present.

In that sense, Korpi and Palme's fundamental claim may still hold validity. While the Danish benefit system, for example, shows up as a quite strongly targeted one in the empirical analysis, it is still part of a comprehensive, universal welfare state catering to broad sections of the electorate. Perhaps it is precisely because of this that there is scope for effective redistribution towards the poor.

Yet clearly the picture today looks totally different from the one presented by Korpi and Palme, using data for the 1980s. Perhaps it is the case that the way targeting works in many advanced welfare states nowadays is substantially different from the way it worked decades ago, perhaps accounting for substantially different political dynamics and outcomes. One of the factors that made targeted benefits politically weak and prone to spending cuts in the 1980s was the fact that these systems were seen to foster 'dependency'. Activation efforts and discourse may have made social assistance more palatable to voters. Benefit systems have also been remodelled not only to be more work friendly, but even to encourage and reward work. As we demonstrated in Chapter 4, most social assistance schemes now operate earnings disregards and other activation measures. Some targeted provisions have even been remodelled to cater to the non-working and working alike, blurring the line between those dependent on benefits and those contributing. In that sense, the politics of targeting may be fundamentally different nowadays, as we elaborate further in the next sections.

### Box 5.1 The paradox of redistribution is no longer

Does the purposeful targeting of benefits towards the poor actually enhance or weaken their redistributive impact? Korpi and Palme's (1998) 'The paradox of redistribution and strategies of equality' has been of major influence to this debate. In that article they argue that, paradoxically, strong pro-poor targeting does not yield more income inequality reduction.

One of their key pieces of empirical evidence was an analysis showing an inverse relationship, at the country level, between the extent of pro-poor targeting in benefits and actual, observed inequality reduction. In a 2016 article we revisited that study and found that the paradox had ceased to exist, at least as conceptualized by Korpi and Palme. The next graphs provide a partial update, using LIS Wave X, of the analysis presented in Marx, Salanauskaite, and Verbist (2016). We restrict ourselves here to conveying the main message, for methodological details we refer to that article since we use the same concepts and methodology.

Figure 5.1 shows that, totally contrary to what Korpi and Palme demonstrated using data for the 1980s, that there exists in fact a strong association between the overall pro-poorness of a country's benefit system, as captured by the concentration coefficient of transfers, and the actual extent of redistribution that takes place, as captured by comparing the pre- versus post-transfer disposable income distribution. The role of means-tested benefits (for the most part consisting of social assistance benefits) in making systems redistributive towards the poor is much more important than one would expect given their usually limited share in overall social spending. There is no consistent relation across countries between the extent of means-testing and overall transfer generosity (Figure 5.2).

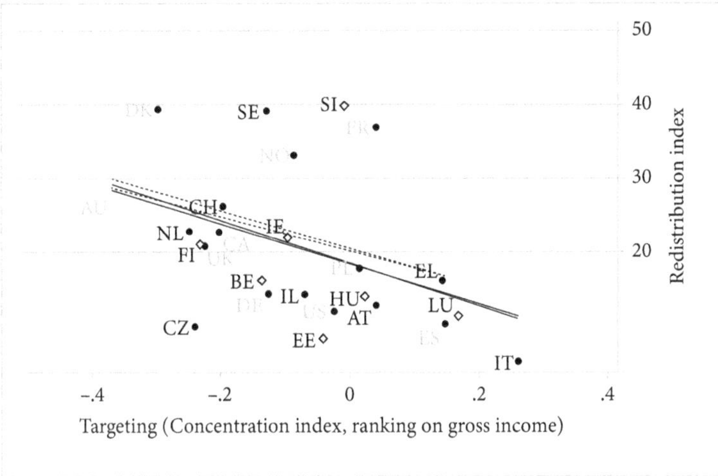


**Figure 5.1** The association between the overall level of targeting of social transfers and redistributive impact

*Source:* own calculations on LIS data.

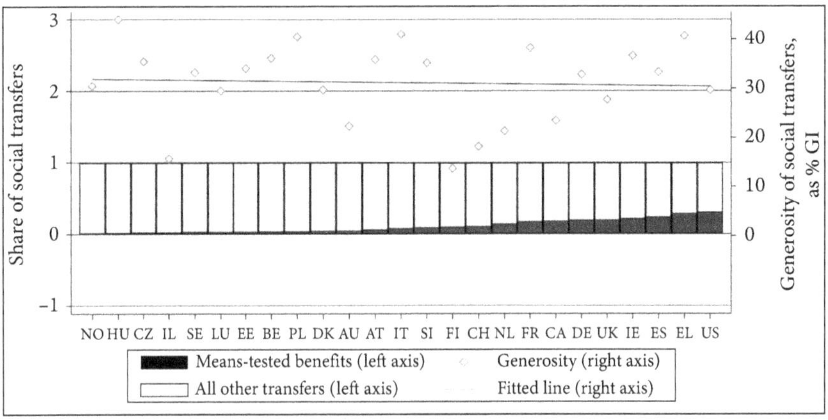


**Figure 5.2** The share of means-tested benefits and overall generosity of social benefits

*Source:* own calculations on LIS data.

The contributions of means-tested benefits to the overall redistributive impact of social transfers often goes well beyond their share in overall social transfer spending. That is shown in Figure 5.3. This figure shows the contribution of means-tested benefits to the concentration coefficient of benefits—a measure of redistributive impact. In a few countries, as in the UK, Ireland, and the US, the contribution of means-tested benefits to the overall redistributive impact of transfers even surpasses their relative size in a rather exceptional way.

*continued*

**Box 5.1** *continued*

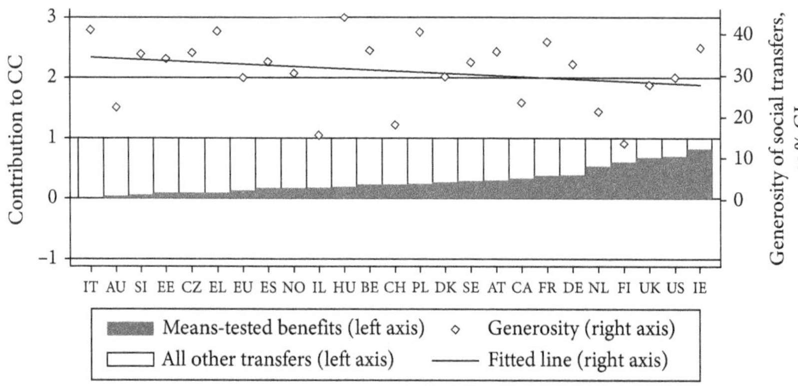


**Figure 5.3** The contribution of means-tested benefits to the redistributive impact of the overall transfer system (measured by their contribution to the overall concentration coefficient of transfers)
*Source:* own calculations on LIS data.

Overall, the most redistributive systems do contain means-tested and otherwise targeted benefit programmes that are strongly targeted to the poor by intent and by design. Even when relatively modest in terms of their share in overall social transfer spending, these benefits play a crucial role in bringing about redistribution.

## 5.5 What Explains the Apparent Withering of the Paradox?

The notion that 'benefits for the poor become poor benefits' is a catchy soundbite but it does not provide much useful guidance for actual policy design. There are 'successful' targeted programmes, especially within more comprehensive welfare systems.

Political support for low-income targeted benefits is clearly not simply the outcome of a rational cost-benefit calculus by the strictly self-interested (median) voter. This is a far too reductive approach. People's rational self interest in specific programmes (as estimated by their age, labour market opportunities or earnings potential, etc.) does not always or even typically predict their stated support. Notions of deservingness and fairness play a role. Perceptions regarding whether benefits end up with the 'right' people and whether they stimulate or undermine self-reliance also matter (Van Oorschot, 2006). Within the CARIN model we discussed earlier, attitude counts.

What may be particularly relevant here is that low-income targeted benefits in many countries look totally different today from the days when Korpi and Palme demonstrated 'the paradox of redistribution'. Recall that their analysis effectively pertained to the 1980s. That period and the decade that followed saw the ascent of neoliberal thinking and indeed of neoliberal politics, or at least politicians embracing neoliberal discourse. It was a time when protracted weak economic growth and persistent high unemployment became to be seen as ills brought about by the overgenerous welfare policies and excessive regulation.

In that context income protection provisions, especially last safety net provisions, became a prime target for political attacks from the right of the political spectrum. One of the factors that made social assistance so politically contentious in the neoliberal 1980s was the fact that they were castigated for having detrimental effects on claimant's behaviour. They were seen to foster 'cultures of dependency', a topic discussed in Chapter 4.

This shift is perhaps most vividly illustrated by what happened in the United States at the time. The main means-tested system, the Aid for Families with Dependent Children (AFDC) became the focus of bitter ideological and political debates, as we already noted earlier. The likes of Charles Murray (2008) and Lawrence Mead (1986) launched the brutal attacks of this final safety net provision as it was then in place. That system was vilified as the main culprit in creating an 'underclass' of chronically welfare dependent single mothers. Welfare reform came to occupy centre stage in the political debate and Bill Clinton ran his first campaign on a slogan to 'end welfare as we know it'.

What ensued was a major shift in US social policy, also discussed in Chapter 4, more specifically Section 4.4. Statutory time limits on social assistance benefit duration were introduced. This move was accompanied by the expansion of a targeted benefit of an altogether different nature: the Earned Income Tax Credit. Initially introduced as an exemption from employees' social security payments for poor working households with children, the 1993 expansion in particular turned the scheme into the country's pre-eminent anti-poverty programme for families of active working age.

The Earned Income Tax Credit is not a last safety net provision. But it is a very important income support programme and it is a strongly targeted one, albeit not as targeted as the AFDC was. Spending has increased massively and it has become the US's most important income support programme.

What is very interesting is that this provision enjoys broad and robust political support, despite the fact that it caters to a relatively small segment of the electorate.

In 2007, Page and Jacobs (2009) asked whether the EITC should be increased, decreased, or kept about the same. More than 90% wanted it increased or kept the same. Clearly, the system now caters to large sections of the electorate, including the (lower) middle class, and this also may account for that support. But an equally if not more important factor may be the fact that the system is perceived to encourage and reward work; it enjoys greater overall legitimacy and that may explain why spending on EITC has risen dramatically (Kenworthy, 2011).

It is particularly striking that the EITC in the US has enjoyed such robust support from Republic politicians. The EITC has been expanded under presidents George W. Bush and Trump. This stands in stark and striking contrast to the many cuts in other programmes for the poor.[3]

Cecile Murray and Elizabeth Kneebone of Brookings note that the EITC reaches across the demographic divides that characterize American elections, particularly those of race and education. They illustrate that point for the 2016 presidential election which saw Republican candidate Donald Trump elected and Democratic candidate Hillary Clinton defeated. Two-thirds of white voters without a college degree backed Donald Trump, versus 28% who voted for Hillary Clinton. Clinton, however, captured large margins among black and Hispanic voters.

Both segments of the electorate benefit from the EITC. According to Murray and Kneebone (2017), the vast majority (86%) of EITC-eligible taxpayers do not have a bachelor's degree, and just over half have no more than a high school diploma. About half are white. What they label the 'white working class' makes up 40% of all taxpayers eligible for the EITC. But at the same time, black and Latino working class, also account for some 40% of all taxpayers eligible for the credit. This includes people in traditional blue-collar jobs in transportation and construction, as well as people in service-sector jobs like retail, food service, and health care. What is also striking is that so many of the white working class potential EITC recipients live in small, economically struggling rural communities. That matters because these areas are heavily Republican.

In other words, the at first sight perhaps surprisingly strong and robust bipartisan support that EITC enjoys in America's increasingly polarized political landscape has a clear electoral logic to it. But then again, there are many non-existent redistributive programmes that would have a clear electoral logic.

One additional explanation perhaps is that the expansion has been to the benefit of powerful supporters of the Republican Party. It has been calculated that Walmart may be one of the biggest indirect beneficiaries of EITC in the US simply because so many of its employees receive it (Kenworthy & Marx, 2018). Walmart can be thought of as an indirect beneficiary because a programme like EITC allows it to pay lower wages than its employees would otherwise accept (cf. Chapter 4). The perception that big companies are the de facto beneficiaries of government subsidies paid out to their workers prompted Bernie Sanders to introduce in 2018 a Senate bill—the 'Stop BEZOS Act'—that would have required large employers such as Amazon and Walmart to pay the government for various forms of federal government assistance received by their workers. The bill's name is of course a dig at Amazon's Jeff Bezos and stands for 'Stop Bad Employers by Zeroing Out Subsidies Act'.

Again, EITC is not a final safety net provision but it is the United States' most important income support programme. It is also a strongly targeted programme. Our point here is that the degree of political support for the programme cannot be understood as a straightforward and simple function of its degree of targeting. Other factors, notably the fact that it is seen to encourage and reward work clearly also play a role.

Low-income targeted programmes have undergone similar metamorphoses elsewhere in the rich world. This happened as 'Third Way' and 'Active Welfare State' doctrines came to the fore in the 1990s, essentially as a progressive response—some might call it a capitulation—to the neoliberal critiques of the welfare state dominating political discourse in the 1980s. That translated into stronger efforts to 'reintegrate' and 'activate' people claiming social assistance and associated benefits.

Welfare scholars like Aust and Arriba (2005), Marchal and Van Mechelen (2014), and Immervoll and Knotz (2018) have documented the strongly increased focus on activation of social assistance recipients (and other 'passive' benefit recipients such as the long-term unemployed) right across Europe during the 1990s. Social assistance recipients in particular became a prime target group for activation efforts through a range of instruments; 'social insertion contracts', temporary earnings-disregards, enhanced monitoring and sanctioning, tighter job requirements, job and personal counselling, public employment programmes, etc.

When in 1989 the Revenu Minimum d'Insertion (RMI) was introduced in France, under impetus of socialist president François Mitterrand, the law established not only the legal right to a minimum income for all those in need above the age of 25 but also and at the same time the right to 'insertion' or (re-)integration (Palier, 2004a). The combination of the two was an innovation at the time (Vlandas, 2013). The idea was to fight both poverty and social exclusion simultaneously. While the guarantee of social integration was codified as a 'right' it in effect also established a moral obligation. The RMI law stipulated that rights and duties were to be written down in an integration contract and signed by both parties, the state and the recipient of social assistance. There was at the time no common understanding of what insertion meant. A range of activities were seen as qualifying, including activities not remotely similar to paid work. But, and perhaps not surprisingly, what started out as a right to integration broadly understood gradually morphed into an obligation while activities deemed to amount to integration became more narrowly defined (see below).

Other countries saw at least equally momentous welfare state change. After the victory in the elections 1997 and in tune with Blair's now iconic Third Way strategy, the Labour government engaged in major reforms of the British welfare state to transform it 'from a safety net in times of trouble to a springboard for economic opportunity'. The aim was to rebuild the welfare state around work.

Changes also took place in countries with longer established minimum income guarantees. In Finland, for example, the 2001 Act on Rehabilitative Work required municipalities to provide different kinds of activation measures and participation in rehabilitative work experience was made compulsory for those under 25 years in danger of social exclusion. In Sweden, the revised Social Services Act of 1998 explicitly stated that young adults under 25 could be required to participate in programmes to qualify for social assistance. The Netherlands saw perhaps the most radical shift towards pushing more people into work. The 1990s saw consecutive and substantial reforms in this direction, culminating in the Work and Social Assistance Act (Wet werk en bijstand, WWB) of 2004, which aimed to transform the classical safety net into a 'trampoline'. That law introduced sanctions on municipalities not doing enough to get people into work. That resulted at times in public outcries over what were seen as unduly hard sanctions (Knijn & Van Berkel, 2003; van Berkel, 2007).

The point is that means-tested minimum income support provisions, especially social assistance provisions, look totally different today from the systems in place in the 1980s, when at least some evidence pointed to more feeble support for poor-targeted provisions? Whereas the old systems were vulnerable to strongly stated critiques, especially from the political right, the new targeted systems seem to be far more palatable to middle-class voters. That is especially the case because there has been a concurrent trend, the recognition that income support does not legitimately end as soon as people find work.

## 5.6 Discovery of the Working Poor

Two concurrent trends have been very influential in shaping minimum income protection policies over the past two decades. One has been the trend towards activation, reintegration and 'making work pay'. A concurrent but not altogether congruent trend has been the growing awareness that work does not always pay enough to live a poverty free existence. Even people in full-time work, thus doing their utmost to be economically self-reliant, sometimes fail to make ends meet. Policy makers have become increasingly aware of that.

That was not always the case. Until 20 or so years ago the so-called 'working poor'—for lack of a better term—were in most European eyes as quintessentially American a phenomenon as baseball and Budweiser. These were the people toiling away in lousy, under protected and underpaid jobs in places like fast-food joints, supermarkets, hotels and bars. The working poor were seen as the prime victims of neo-liberalism and 'free markets' zealotry gone too far, a product of weak or muzzled unions, non-existent or ineffectual collective bargaining, and a state failing to impose and enforce decent minimum wages and other protections for workers (Lohmann and Marx, 2018; Marx, 2019). The consequence of that largely misguided perception was that in-work poverty was seen as a non-issue in countries with extensive labour protections, especially minimum wages at significant levels. In Europe only post-Thatcherite Britain came close to this stereotypical but also essentially erroneous perception of the nature of 'in-work poverty', as it is more commonly referred to in most of Europe.

The idea that 'the working poor' were and are only to be found in the so-called 'liberal' economies lacking organized labour and proper regulatory correction turned out to be completely wrong. The working poor are omnipresent in Europe and elsewhere in the rich world, as research has abundantly documented (Marx & Verbist, 1998; Lohmann & Marx, 2008; Lohmann, 2009; Crettaz, 2013; Marx & Nolan, 2014; Horemans, 2016). According to Eurostat close to one in 10 workers in the EU are at risk of financial poverty. In some countries this share is somewhat higher than one in 10, as in Romania, Spain, or Luxembourg. In other countries it is well below one in 20 workers, as in Belgium, Slovenia, Slovakia, Finland, or Ireland.

In Hick and Marx (2022), we present estimates drawn from the Luxembourg Income Study for a broader set of countries, including the United States. The proportion of workers living in poverty is found to range from under 5% in Finland to about 14% in the United States. In terms of the incidence of in-work poverty, the United Kingdom and Australia can be found among the more encompassing welfare states of Norway and the Netherlands.

The country variation in the incidence of in-work poverty thus defies any of the commonly used country clustering classifications in the comparative welfare state or industrial relations literature, or indeed the 'varieties of capitalism' literature (Lohmann & Marx, 2008). The working poor are certainly not confined to the so-called liberal welfare regime.

Why is this? Essentially because the phenomenon of in-work poverty is a complex one (Horemans, 2016; Lohmann, 2018). In part this has to do with the complicated way in-work poverty is usually defined. The most used approach builds for one part on the labour market status of the individual under focus and for another on the living standard of the household where that person resides. For example, Eurostat defines the working poor as those individuals who have been mainly working during the reference year (either in employment or self-employment) and whose household equivalized disposable income is below 60% of the median in the country in question. Employment status is gauged on the basis of monthly calendars completed by survey respondents, with 'in work' taken to mean that the status he/she declares to have occupied for at least seven months is employee or self-employed.

Conflating individual labour market status and household income, adjusted for household size, in one measure inherently complicates interpretation. Because of that definition, the whole household context matters. It makes for example a big difference whether the person under focus has a working partner or not, or whether that person or any other adult in the household has other sources of income. The number of dependent children, if there are any, also matters. A moderately paid job may provide a decent living standard to a single person but may be totally inadequate for a sole earner with dependent children. Furthermore, the fact that a full year is usually the reference period in the most commonly used statistics also complicates interpretation. Those working for part but not all of the year may be in poverty on an annual basis for that reason even if they were not poor while working. In fact, the most precarious workers, those with volatile and marginal labour market attachment during the income reference period, are not even included in the most commonly used in-work poverty statistics.

The statistics shaping policy debates are clearly problematic and prone to misinterpretation. But at least the 'working poor' have ceased to be a non-issue. Most European governments have come to acknowledge in-work poverty as a reality and policy challenge of some magnitude. That acknowledgement has finally emerged after decades of proclamations by countless politicians that 'a job is the best protection against poverty'.

The European Pillar of Social Rights, adopted by all EU governments in 2017, explicitly acknowledges the problem under Principle 6: 'Workers have the right to fair wages that provide for a decent standard of living. Adequate minimum wages shall be ensured, in a way that provide for the satisfaction of the needs of the worker and his / her family in the light of national economic and social conditions, whilst safeguarding access to employment and incentives to seek work. *In-work poverty shall be prevented*' (European Commission, 2017, our emphasis).

The way this principle is stated is perhaps the best illustration that profound misperceptions persist as to the nature of in-work poverty. Principle 6 is about wages and about wages only. In-work poverty is thus reduced to an issue of low or inadequate wages. If perhaps not completely wrong this idea is still profoundly misleading. Many people working for relatively low wages are not poor by any commonly used definition. While it is certainly true that many of the working poor work for relatively low pay, a sizeable share of the working poor have wages that are significantly higher than any of the widely used low pay thresholds. A sole provider with dependent children can easily be 'working poor' even with earnings way above any low-pay threshold.

Single earners with dependent children are at a particular disadvantage in societies where dual earner living standards set the norm. As Nieuwenhuis and Maldonado (2018a, 2018b) have argued, single parents face a triple bind of inadequate resources, employment, and policies. The lack of a partner deprives them of additional income as well as care support to maximize their own earnings potential. Women face additional challenges, including pay discrimination and fewer opportunities for promotion, especially sole mothers. Without available, affordable, and quality childcare it is particularly difficult for single parents to negotiate work and family responsibilities. Lone parents constitute the core of the working poor in many countries in the rich world (Horemans & Marx, 2018). The challenges they face go well beyond low pay, contrary to what Principle 6 of the social pillar seems to suggest.

While in-work poverty is certainly a reality in the rich world, it is not necessarily the case that the problem is growing. Recognition that in-work poverty is a reality also in Europe, welcome as it is, has sometimes veered towards exaggeration. Part of this stems from the fact that economies and labour markets are changing. The sprawling services sector, where atypical work and low pay is rampant, has been growing and continues to grow. The latest source of concern comes from the emergence of the so-called platform economy—think Uber or Deliveroo. Platform workers, often officially 'self-employed', tend to lack social and employment protections available to other workers (Horemans & Marx, 2017). Also, there is concern that pay levels are significantly lower than normal wages for similar jobs and even lower than national minimum wages. Hence, the fear that the platform economy is a new source of in-work poverty.

While plausible for a number of reasons, the idea that in-work poverty is on the rise is not unequivocally supported by the empirical evidence we have at present. While it is true that in-work poverty rates have been trending (slightly) upwards in a number of countries, there is not anywhere near a universal trend. There are even countries where there has been a decline.

However, it is important to remain well aware of the difference between risks and shares (Table 5.1). People who have a job remain far less likely to live in financial poverty than people without work. But then workers tend to be far more numerous than people at active age without work. The consequence is that among the total population of people living in poverty at working age, workers may still make up a larger share than people without work.

Yet keep in mind that, as we have already stressed, it would be wrong to maintain too strong of a distinction in our minds between workers and non-workers. People can have a multitude of labour market statuses over the course of a year ranging from full-time employment over various forms of part-time employment and gig work to non-employment.

## 5.7 The Emergence (and Disintegration) of Integrated Minimum Income Support Schemes

The trend towards activation and 'making work pay' has coincided with a growing awareness that work does not always pay enough to live free from poverty. As a consequence, some countries have taken steps towards expanding minimum income support provisions for people not in work to people in work. But interestingly enough such integrated systems of income support have not turned out to be equally politically robust. In some countries they appealed for a time only to be disintegrated later. It is interesting to consider the politics behind such initiatives.

**Table 5.1** Incidence of poverty among people in work and share of working population in population in poverty at working age, 2021 or most recent year

| Country | Percentage working poor | Share working poor in poor population at working age |
|---|---|---|
| Austria | 7,9% | 43,9% |
| Belgium | 3,9% | 24,4% |
| Bulgaria | 9,7% | 41,7% |
| Switzerland | 7,5% | 45,6% |
| Cyprus | 7,9% | 49,3% |
| Czechia | 3,6% | 39,7% |
| Germany | 8,3% | 45,4% |
| Denmark | 5,8% | 33,3% |
| Estonia | 10,5% | 51,5% |
| Greece | 11,2% | 32,4% |
| Spain | 13,1% | 41,6% |
| Finland | 2,9% | 19,8% |
| France | 6,7% | 34,8% |
| Croatia | 5,2% | 22,2% |
| Hungary | 7,7% | 47,6% |
| Ireland | 4,3% | 26,9% |
| Italy | 11,8% | 37,7% |
| Lithuania | 7,8% | 39,2% |
| Luxembourg | 13,7% | 59,7% |
| Latvia | 10,3% | 41,4% |
| Malta | 7,4% | 43,4% |
| Netherlands | 5,4% | 29,5% |
| Poland | 9,1% | 41,5% |
| Portugal | 11,3% | 50,3% |
| Romania | 15,1% | 52,9% |
| Serbia | 6,6% | 18,5% |
| Sweden | 6,7% | 33,3% |
| Slovenia | 4,9% | 34,3% |
| Iceland (2018) | 7,4% | 68,7% |
| Norway (2020) | 6,0% | 35,5% |
| Slovakia (2020) | 5,3% | 40,2% |
| United Kingdom (2018) | 10,4% | 50,9% |

*Note:* a person is considered 'in work' when he/she worked (whether as employee, self-employed, or both) at least six months during the reference year (2017 for Iceland and the United Kingdom; 2019 for Norway and Slovakia; 2020 for the other countries). Poverty is defined as having an income under the poverty threshold of 60% of the median equivalized disposable household income in the respective country.
*Source:* own calculations based on EU-SILC 2018 for Iceland and the United Kingdom, EU-SILC 2020 for Norway and Slovakia and EU-SILC 2021 for the other countries.

The French RSA scheme (Revenu de Solidarité Active), combining an out-of-work benefit (RSA socle) with an in-work component (RSA activité), was a prime example of a means-tested minimum income scheme that offered integrated support for the non-employed and (part-time) low paid workers alike. The RSA was introduced in France in 2008 with the specific aim of remodelling the incentive structure of people on social assistance, and particularly to make work more appealing and lucrative.

The RSA incorporated the previous 'Lone Parent Benefit' (Allocation de Parent Isolé—API) introduced in 1977 and the 'Minimum Integration Income' (Revenu Minimum d'Insertion—RMI) introduced in 1988. The RSA was in part a continuation of the RMI, notably the aim of ensuring a minimum standard of living. The 'right and duties' contractual approach was already present in the RMI but the RSA made the duties part more explicit and prominent. The RMI already allowed recipients to combine their benefit with income from work for a limited period of time but the RSA went further in this respect.

It in effect ended a clear-cut distinction between programmes aimed at people who cannot work and those that are in work. The benefits received from RSA activité while working were higher than in the RMI and unlimited in time. Another notable difference was that the RSA was available to people already in work. They did not first have to go through a period of non-employment. The taper rate was considered very generous from a cross-national perspective at the time (Marchal & Van Mechelen, 2014).

While the RMI was introduced by socialist president François Mitterrand, the RSA reform was introduced by a centre-right government under the Sarkozy presidency yet subsequently expanded again by centre-left governments under François Hollande. As Tim Vlandas (2013) points out, the RSA reform was introduced by Nicolas Sarkozy as part of an electoral strategy that had clear reminiscences of Bill Clinton campaign 'To end welfare as we know it' and Tony Blair's Third Way strategy more than a decade earlier. Sarkozy's campaign revolved around the promotion of the value of work and its opposition to 'welfare dependency'. Sarkozy further framed the reform as a showcase for his promise to realize a 'rupture' with the past.

Yet interestingly support was much broader. The RSA was even among the proposals of the socialist presidential candidate in 2007. The cross-party consensus that parliamentary debates displayed over the RSA reform was striking (Vlandas, 2013). That broad cross-party support for the RSA was driven by different motives. The RSA was seen to embody the right's preoccupation with improving work incentives and putting an end to 'dependency'. The left saw it as a way to fight social exclusion. Bruno Palier called the reform 'polysemic' (Palier, 2004b, p. 118) in that it allowed for multiple interpretations each serving different interests.

The RSA activité did not last. Studies showed very low levels of take-up, especially among those in work. Chareyron et al. (2018) estimated the non-take-up rate for the basic component to lie between 29% and 35%. Non-take-up of the supplemental income support component aimed at those in work was estimated at a staggering 68%. One perceived reason was that when in work people were reluctant to take up a 'welfare benefit' (as was the case of Arbeitlosengeld II in Germany, cf. Chapter 4).

In 2016 a new in-work benefit known as the Prime d'activité was introduced. This merged two previous employment bonus schemes ('RSA activité' and 'prime pour l'emploi') into a single scheme. This 'prime d'activité' had been part of RSA when it was introduced—under the moniker RSA activité—but it was extended to strengthen work incentives ('make work pay') and avoid stigmatization stemming from the integration of in-work benefits into poverty-preventing assistance RSA.

The Prime d'activité is a means-tested in-work benefit for employed people who work few hours or at low wages. It can be combined with RSA. Both are administered by a single entity, the 'Caisse des allocations familiales' or CAF. Compared to the 'prime pour l'emploi' (which was an annual tax credit) the 'prime d'activité' is both more generous and paid out on a monthly basis. It was further augmented after the 'Gilets Jaunes' protests.

President Emmanuel Macron has announced a further merger of benefits into what will or should become the Revenu Universel d'Activité (RUA). If effectively implemented, France would in effect move towards the UK's Universal Credit (UC)—a major reform which merged a host of previously existing means-tested benefits. But its implementation remains highly doubtful at this time.

Perhaps the experience with the UK's Universal Credit (UC) plays some role here. As we already discussed in Chapter 4, UC was meant to be a simplification of existing benefits, reducing bureaucratic cost, hassle and complexity. As with the RSA and the planned RUA, the UC credit aimed to integrate and align support for the working and the non-working (Clegg, 2015).

The UC followed a massive expansion of pre-existing tax credits for low-income working households by Tony Blair's New Labour government in an effort 'to fulfil our objectives of promoting work incentives, reducing poverty and welfare dependency, and strengthening community and family life' (Clegg, 2015, p. 494). Blair was of course New Labour's preeminent advocate of the Third Way doctrine, which would come to inspire political thinking far beyond the UK, especially on the political left. A core notion that social justice should not preclude an aspiration to encourage and celebrate self-reliance. The EITC (cf. Box 4.1) was seen as an example of how this could be achieved with political appeal, especially among the middle classes that New Labour was courting at the time.

'Labour seemingly believed that pro-poor redistribution would be inherently more popular and durable if directed to workers and organised through the tax system. While the existing structure of the UK tax and benefit system made it impossible to import EITC as a policy, they clearly hoped to import its politics' (Clegg, 2015, p. 495).

It is interesting that Labour's original expansion squarely focused on bestowing more largesse on those working. That was consistent with its rhetoric and political strategy but it did come at the expense of the jobless, a part of the electorate that basically only had Labour to look after its interests. 'Indeed, the permissiveness (and generosity) of working tax credits was used to legitimate the increasing severity of behavioural controls on the jobless; carrots for "doing the right thing" (that is, working) justified the beating of those who were not with bigger sticks' (Clegg, 2015, p. 497).

Remarkably, it was the Conservative party, after ousting Labour from power, and forming a coalition with the Liberal Democrats, which undertook to merge tax credits and a range of existing means-tested benefits for those out of work into a new integrated measure, Universal Credit. (So as in France, the integrated benefit was developed and initiated by a political party on the right of the spectrum.)

The principal rationale for the UC reform, as discussed in Chapter 4, was to ensure simplification and a reduction of bureaucracy. A single payment with a standard withdrawal rate over different earnings levels was also intended to make the rewards of increasing work intensity more transparent than under the then existing system of overlapping benefits and tax credits with differing rates of withdrawal. Plus, there was a naïve faith in the power of ICT to deliver correct and timely benefit almost in real-time. As we already mentioned in Chapter 4, Lord Freud, the responsible minister at the time, was convinced that Universal Credit would be responsive to people's needs (Sainsbury, 2014, p. 40; see also Millar & Bennett, 2017).

The Conservatives' Universal Credit was not a radical break with New Labour's tax credits. On the contrary, it pursued broadly the same aims of 'making work pay'. Like the tax credits, Universal Credit aimed to make support from government look more like a wage than a traditional social security benefit. With greater encouragement to take up small part-time jobs it was more of a shift in emphasis within the Make Work Pay consensus that had developed across a very large part of the political spectrum.

While the basic concept of the UC is relatively uncontroversial, the programme became mired in controversy of Homeric proportions, mainly because of the almost surreal failure of the initial rollout, generating countless news stories and endless political debate (cf. Chapter 4).

The UC provided ample fodder to the opposition, including the parties, like Labour, that essentially supported the system in principle. In addition, Universal Credit, a measure of considerable budgetary cost, became a prime target for spending cuts in the name of austerity. That too made the Universal Credit a prime political battlefield.

Even more fundamentally it is not sure that the UC will ever become a system that has robust broad universal support. As Daniel Clegg (2015) points out, a deep-seated ambivalence exists on the left to the principle of supplementing labour incomes because these effectively amount to taxpayer subsidies to companies that pay lower wages then they could probably afford. Such criticisms of the 'Byzantine tax credit economy' are becoming louder rather than fading away.

In conclusion, the shift towards 'activation' and more contractual/conditional relationships with beneficiaries of last resort minimum income benefits may have brought a 'new politics of minimum income protection' in the sense that such schemes may have become more palatable to middle-class electorates. But more radical shifts have not proved equally successful. The paradigmatic shift which happened in the United States proved politically robust. But the French and the British experience show that no uncontested 'new paradigm' enjoying robust political support has yet emerged. Reforms that once appealed to the political left there have brought major disappointments and even electoral decline if not near annihilation as in some cases. Of course, the reasons for the decline of social democracy remain hotly debated but the traditional left's embrace of Third Way ideas, as happened in the Netherlands, Germany, and France is often cited as a contributing factor. In this context it should perhaps not come as a surprise that there is some renewed appreciation of the traditional policy instruments and paradigms—minimum wages, social assistance, and social insurance schemes.

## 5.8 Emancipation vs Targeting

We come to a final political economy consideration relating to targeting and it is one that is not that often discussed. It is clear that any degree of targeting towards the more needy requires modulation of benefits by household income and by household composition, especially the presence of dependent children. Yet at the same time there has been a trend towards individualization of social and welfare rights out of emancipatory motives (Meulders & Jepsen, 2002; Frericks & Höppner, 2019; Alm, Nelson, & Nieuwenhuis, 2020). Advocates of gender equality in particular have pushed for social rights that are independent of marital status or household context. This has resulted in a decline of social security rights which distinguish by household status and thus indirectly discriminate against women, for example in the shape of higher benefits for sole breadwinners. Similarly, personal tax systems in many countries have moved away from joint taxation systems, which effectively tax dual earner household more, towards more individualized approaches (OECD, 2022).

There are very legitimate grounds for a trend in this direction but we need to be fully aware that there is a price in terms of (cost-)effectiveness of poverty relief. Alm, Nelson, and Nieuwenhuis (2020) provide a telling and in many ways sobering empirical illustration of what a consistent and radical individualization of rights can lead to. Poverty rates among lone parents in Sweden have surged as a consequence.

The principle that social entitlements, including monetary benefits, need to be awarded on an individual basis sits fundamentally uneasily with the empirical realities of household economics. There are clear cost sharing benefits to the joint usage of things like housing, heating, and many other things. Two adults living together need less joint income to achieve a similar living standard as an individual. One can debate the size of these joint consumption benefits endlessly, and indeed the debate remains ongoing, but that they are real is beyond dispute. The choice for purely individualized rights is legitimate but we need to be well aware that it comes at a price.

# 6

# Basic Income Advocates, Sober Up

## 6.1 A Basic Income Is a Basic Income

What if we would just make it simple and send every citizen a sizeable amount of cash every month, no questions asked, no conditions imposed? Lazy or thrifty, rich or poor, sick or healthy, everyone gets a guaranteed income from the state, every week or month. It is hard to imagine a more ironclad guarantee against poverty, at least if such a universal income grant was high enough to allow for a life in dignity.

Of course, we are referring here to basic income. But let us be clear from the beginning: many real-world debates about basic income are not in fact debates about basic income. Schemes such as negative income taxes, refundable income tax credits, and even social assistance schemes, are often taken to represent a basic income of sorts in debates. While some, like fully refundable tax credits, come close, most are in fact not a basic income. Social assistance, the most common embodiment of a basic economic right, does not even come close to a basic income. It is important for that reason that we restrict the discussion that follows to basic income proper since the rest of the book is of course about those other ways of ensuring minimum incomes.

The flight that basic income has taken is spectacular. While debates about minimum income protection tend to arouse only relatively small circles of academics and policy wonks, debates about basic income are sure to draw engaged interest from all corners of society. In a way this can be seen as encouraging. Apparently many people care about the issue of basic economic rights. But it is also true that people engage in basic income debates with different agendas, some far removed from the issue we are concerned with here. There is also a lack of terminological hygiene. When talking about basic income, people often mean very different things. And even when they talk about a basic income proper, amounts and criteria for eligibility often remain frustratingly vague (De Wispelaere & Stirton, 2004). Are we talking about a basic income for the whole population, elderly and children included? Is the

*Zero Poverty Society*. Sarah Marchal and Ive Marx, Oxford University Press. © Sarah Marchal and Ive Marx (2024).
DOI: 10.1093/9780191967771.003.0006

basic income restricted to citizens only or do (new) immigrants with non-citizen status also qualify? Are we talking about a small amount of money or about a sizeable chunk of GDP, such as the 25% of GDP some propose?

This is not the place to repeat in much detail the many philosophical and ethical arguments that have been put forward in defense of a basic income. Excellent summaries of such arguments exist, especially in Philippe Van Parijs' and Yannick Vanderborght's summing up, *Basic Income: A Radical Proposal for a Free Society and a Sane Economy.*

The question we address here is essentially this one: is a basic income a good idea if our goal is better minimum income protection and thus poverty relief? At first sight the answer seems to be obviously yes. But then again, a full basic income, defined as an unconditional monthly payment high enough to ensure a life in dignity on its own would represent an intervention of monumental proportions, with a budgetary cost to match. That is not to say that it would be infeasible but, as we will argue here, replacing existing income protection provisions with a basic income would not make much sense in most advanced welfare states, especially in countries where existing income protections perform comparatively well. We do not know with certainty what a world with a sizeable basic income would look like but we can make theoretically and empirically informed guesses about some of its likely outcomes. Those suggest that, even for all their flaws, gaps and shortcomings, it would be a foolish gamble to simply replace well-performing social protection with a basic income, at least if poverty prevention is the main concern.

The real discussion, we think, boils down to the role a partial basic income can play in providing one of several layers of minimum income support. A partial basic income would be a lower amount not replacing but complementing and at most only partially replacing existing social security, social assistance, and other transfer programmes (Atkinson, 2015). After all, many countries already have universal child benefits effectively granting a basic income of sorts to households with children. Extending such a right beyond households with children is not an unimaginable leap and may also make more sense than a full basic income.

## 6.2 Basic Income Claims

While this is not the place to review in great detail the many arguments made in defence of basic income, it is worth highlighting some striking aspects.

A first thing to note is that basic income advocates almost invariably entertain a rather dystopian view of the future. At the very least one can say they see a future of dishevelling change. Crucially, they envisage a world in which there will no longer be work for everybody, certainly not decent and interesting work. It is perhaps useful at this stage to quote at some length from Van Parijs and Vanderborght, two of the most prominent basic income proponents.

> We live in a new world, remade by many forces: the disruptive technological revolution brought about by the computer and the internet; the globalization of trade, migration, and communication; a fast-growing worldwide demand running up against the limits imposed by a shrinking pool of natural resources and the saturation of our atmosphere; the dislocation of traditional protective institutions, from the family to labour unions, state monopolies, and welfare states; and the explosive interactions of these various trends. (Van Parijs & Vanderborght, 2020, p. 4)

To deal with this vortex of upheaval, basic income is being advocated as a radically different and superior alternative to the dominant model of social assistance.

> Thus, the expectation that meaningful work will be lacking easily leads to the conviction that the growing jobless population must be provided with some means of livelihood. But there are two very different ways of fleshing out this conviction, and one of them is very unattractive. It consists of expanding the old model of public assistance first born in the sixteenth century and instantiated by today's guaranteed-minimum-income schemes of a conditional sort. (Van Parijs & Vanderborght, 2020, p. 7)

A basic income is put forward as the superior alternative.

> More than on any other front, action is needed to restructure radically the way in which economic security is pursued in our societies and in our world. In each of our societies and beyond, we need a sturdy floor on which we can stand as individuals and as communities. If we are to stem our anxieties and strengthen our hopes, we must dare to introduce what is now commonly called a basic income: a regular income paid in cash to every individual member of a society, irrespective of income from other sources and with no strings attached. (Van Parijs & Vanderborght, 2020, p. 4)

They then go on to list all the well-known advantages of a BI: its simplicity, predictability, lack of bureaucratic intrusiveness and complexity, and of course its supreme compatibility with free individual choice. A BI makes it easier to take a break between two jobs, reduce working time, make room for more training, take up self-employment, or take up volunteer or care work. Or do nothing at all.

If set at a sufficiently high level a basic income would almost by definition provide ironclad protection against financial poverty. But basic income advocates claim that the benefits go beyond the financial (Standing, 2017; Torry, 2019). A basic income could reduce stress caused by insecurity and thus improve health and well-being. Add to that claims that a basic income can help bring about a more sustainable way of life and it adds up to a potentially wonderful thing (Howard et al., 2019).

## 6.3 What We Know about the Impact of Basic Income on Poverty and Welfare State Performance

What do we know about the possible effects of a basic income on poverty? Several lines of empirical research provide some guidance. There is an increasing and fast-growing body of experimental and quasi-experimental research to draw on (Widerquist, 2018; Laín, 2022).[1] This research gives us an idea of how people or, in the best case, communities might react to a basic income or something approaching one. They tell us less about what the economy-wide impact would be.

Researchers have looked for example at lottery winners to see what happens if people suddenly receive free and unconditional money. Imbens et al. (2001) found that large lottery winnings had sizeable but not necessarily dismal effects on how much people work, a key point of contention in the debate. A boost in unearned income was found to reduce labour earnings at the rate of approximately 11%, with larger effects for older people.

Similar studies exist for other countries. A (relatively small-scale) study for Belgium is particularly insightful because it looks at lottery winners receiving an unconditional monthly grant of 1,000 euro for the rest of their lives (Marx & Peeters, 2008). That comes uncannily close to a sizeable basic income, at least for the lucky winners. About 80 winners were retraced and interviewed. Almost none of them had quit working, and less than a handful of winners had reduced their working time. The few that did quit employment cited reasons other than winning the lottery. And nobody switched from paid employment to self-employment, going against claims by some basic income advocates that people will become more entrepreneurial if they have a secure income. In short, receiving a sizeable, unconditional monthly income did very little to people's labour market behaviour. Interestingly, many respondents spontaneously stressed that the major effect of winning

Win-for-Life, as the lottery is called, was that they had become less stressed about the future. It provided them with a more relaxed way of living.

Such studies give an insight into how people react in isolation. That also applies to experiments such as the ones recently conducted in Finland and the Netherlands. In the much-publicized Finnish experiment, a sample of 2,000 unemployed people had their unemployment benefit or labour market subsidy replaced with a relatively small unconditional basic income (560 euro) for a period of 2 years (Kangas et al., 2021). In the Netherlands, municipalities experimented with relaxing the conditions imposed on social assistance recipients and rules regarding how much extra they could earn. These experiments suggest that people, or at least unemployed people, are relatively unreactive to measures that transform their conditional welfare benefits into an unconditional basic income (Verlaat & Zulkarnain, 2022). In the Finnish case, the effect on employment was small but people reported improved economic security and well-being. In the Netherlands the results suggested that relaxing conditions on social assistance recipients did not have a major effect on their likelihood to exit social assistance. But of course, the recipients of unemployment benefit or social assistance in both countries were well aware that their new situation was temporary. Participants in these basic income experiments would have had to be very naïve to think that the default regime of fairly strict conditionality, monitoring, and sanctioning in place would not resume at some point. Also, societal norms and thus social pressures related to benefit recipiency and work had presumably not changed in any substantial way because of the experiment. It may well take a much longer time and a changed policy discourse and climate for such (internalized) norms to change, thus also altering the way people behave when they receive a guaranteed, unconditional income.

There is also a smaller body of research looking at experiments in communities. David Calnitsky has written a couple of wonderful articles on the 1976 Manitoba Basic Annual Income Experiment, or Mincome (Calnitsky, 2016, 2020; Calnitsky & Latner, 2017). His research focuses on Mincome's 'saturation' site, the town of Dauphin, Manitoba, Canada where all residents were eligible for unconditional payments. This involved real money: Dauphin participants were offered guaranteed incomes equivalent to $19,500 for a four-person family, which was about 49% of median household income in 1976. But very important to add here: the payment took the form of a negative income tax. The payment diminished as earned income went up, be it at a slow rate. But to be clear: it was not a pure basic income.

Calnitsky's work confirms the picture we get from other research. He finds an 11.3 percentage point reduction in labour market participation among the people of Dauphin. Young and single-headed households withdrew from the labour market disproportionately. Participants cited as reasons care work, disability and illness, uneven employment opportunities, or educational investment.

Such findings are revealing but again they tell us little about longer-term effects and nothing about economic, let alone macro-economic effects. However, there are some hints. Calnitsky (2020) also looked at how firms reacted when the whole labour force in Dauphin had access to a guaranteed income. This matters because it is not clear what a basic income would mean for firms. One view argues that the guaranteed income is an employer subsidy, facilitating low wages and a 'low-road' industrial strategy. The second view suggests that in providing an alternative to work, the guaranteed income tightens labour markets and pulls wages up. Calnitsky finds more support for the second view.

All this is quite informative but still individual and local experiments essentially run on money falling from the sky. We know that in most countries, bar the unearthing of wells of additional revenue, a sizeable basic income would require additional taxes unless public spending on other items were to be slashed. A substantial basic income might well alter wages and thus the prices of goods and services. In short, (quasi-) experimental research, fascinating and informative as it is, does not really tell us much about the question of what a basic income at the scale of an entire economy could do for poverty and the living standards of the least advantaged.

Over the last couple of years a number of studies have sought to provide at least a partial answer to this question. These studies mostly use micro-simulation techniques. The purpose of microsimulation models is simply to generate some counterfactual situation which can be compared with the existing situation (Figari et al., 2015). A well-known limitation of most existing microsimulation models is that they only allow to create a hypothetical 'morning-after-the-reform' situations that makes abstraction of any behavioural responses. Of course, in the case of a radical reform like basic income, these would likely be quite substantial. People might reduce working hours, stop working altogether or demand higher wages. People on means-tested benefits, entrapped in situation where they have little to gain from earning a little extra money, might become more inclined to accept a job. Such changes might prompt further round effects on wages and prices altering the working of the economy and the labour market. Such changes in behaviour are not usually modelled or only partially. Still, microsimulation does offer great insights into the first-round mechanics of a basic income. And these are revealing.

Browne and Immervoll (2017) have explored the impact of a basic income on inequality and poverty in France, Italy, Finland, and the United Kingdom. In their study, a basic income is paid to people who have not reached the statutory retirement age in their respective countries. The reform is financed by abolishing the majority of the existing system of social support, including social benefits (such as unemployment benefits and social assistance) and fiscal benefits (for example work credits). Moreover, the basic income is made taxable. The Basic Income they simulate is set at the level of the 'Guaranteed Minimum Income' (GMI), which differs across the four countries. Rather unfortunately, this makes the comparability of the results harder.

The first striking and important finding: A basic income at the level of existing GMI's is at least on paper perfectly doable without extra government revenue. For France the cost of the BI is almost fully compensated by abolishing the existing social and fiscal benefits and making the BI taxable. In Finland and Italy the operation would also be close to budget neutral, be it for different reasons. Finland already has a strongly targeted benefit system while Italy had at the time of the study a comparatively low guaranteed minimum income. In the UK taxes would have to be raised considerably to give every working-aged adult a basic income at the level of the GMI.

Second striking finding: the introduction of this Basic Income reform would result in a diverse pattern of winners and losers across the four countries included in the study. But in no country except Italy would poverty actually go down as a first-round impact. That is because the current benefits in Italy are advantageous to those on higher incomes, effectively distributing money from the poor to the rich. But in the other countries poverty goes up after the introduction of basic income. This is notably the case in the UK, a country with substantial benefits targeted at the lowest incomes.

That means that a redistributive measure of massive proportions would result in more people living in poverty than is now the case in three countries. A comparable exercise for the Netherlands yields a similar result (see Box 6.1).

The impact of basic income on poverty levels in any country clearly depends on the system of income protection currently in place there. In countries with relatively generous benefits for unemployed and the sick or disabled, levelling down to the level of the GMI would naturally result in poverty going up. On the contrary, the winners of such a reform would be people currently not receiving any type of benefit, or those receiving only small amounts.

It is worth highlighting a couple of things a basic income does compared to existing systems:

1. If existing social and fiscal expenditures were used to finance the basic income, it would level down benefit entitlements for those receiving more than the GMI. That typically hurts people on social insurance benefits, for example unemployment, sickness, and disability benefits. These benefits are often, but not always, above the poverty line whereas GMI are not.
2. Basic income potentially removes or reduces the income taper for existing claimants of GMI benefits,[2] thus allowing them to earn extra money without losing transfer income as is currently the case. That is a potential positive effect and one usually not taken account of in simulations.
3. Basic income, by definition, expands the coverage of a non-means-tested benefit set at GMI level to all (legal) households. This matters because quite a substantial number of non-employed adults at working age do not receive benefits at all, for example unemployed people whose benefit has expired, school-leavers or homemakers who are still a substantial group in some countries. That may have a positive effect depending on where these people are in the income distribution. Homemakers, for example, can be relatively low but also very high up the income distribution if the partner has a well-paying job.
4. Basic income completely individualizes the benefit, creating an entitlement that is independent of family circumstance. This in effect hurts single adults and especially single parents, while large households are effective winners.

The 'levelling down' of any existing transfer payments to the GMI amount would result in losses for all income groups, which would be larger relative to income at lower income levels.[3] Further results show that average losses from levelling existing benefits would be more sizeable for families without children.

An in-depth study for Finland using micro-simulation is quite instructive about what basic income does and how it compares to an alternative approach of providing minimum income protection in the shape of a universal credit, similar to what exists in the UK (Pareliussen et al., 2018).

Finland already has a comparatively targeted approach to benefit provision be it that, as all targeted systems, the system suffers from well-documented complexity. The complex combination and interaction of working-age benefits, childcare costs, and income taxes in Finland reduces work incentives and holds people back from moving into work or working more.

The study by Pareliussen et al. (2018) compares Finland's benefit system with two benefit reform scenarios: a uniform benefit for all ('basic income') and a universal tapering rule ('universal credit'). It finds that replacing current benefits with a basic income would improve work incentives for many, but it would involve a drastic redistribution of income and an increase in poverty. Under a fiscally neutral BI, a fifth of Finns would see income losses of more than 10% and poverty would go from 11.5% to 14.3%.

Merging working-age benefits with similar aims and coordinating their tapering against earnings would on the other hand consistently improve work incentives and transparency, while preserving or improving social protection. This is what a UK-style Universal Credit aims to achieve. Under the UC scenario, the poverty rate would fall by 1.7 percentage points to 9.4%. The UC variant is perhaps less appealing in its simplicity, but it is a better compromise between the somewhat conflicting goals of keeping overall expenditure within limits while still providing adequate protection and maintaining acceptable work incentives. (Of course, as we have seen in the previous chapter, there are in fact many problems with UC as it actually works.)

This is also what a study for the UK, where Universal Credit has been gradually rolled out since 2013, suggests. Martinelli (2017a, 2017b, 2020) compares a range of BI schemes, from full to partial, to the baseline scenario of means-tested supports prior to the introduction of Universal Credit. The conclusion is again that Basic Income schemes lead to large household losses, including some disadvantaged groups falling deeper into poverty. A BI generous enough to avoid such losses would cost a lot. Partial schemes which retain the existing array of means-tested benefits largely avoid such losses but fail to achieve many of UBI's broader goals—including drastic reductions in bureaucratic complexity and the minimization of poverty and unemployment traps. Martinelli (2017a, 2017b) concludes that 'an affordable UBI would be inadequate, and an adequate UBI would be unaffordable'.

Now, a careful reader of microsimulation studies of basic income will notice that the outcomes do differ. This has naturally to do with context. As the Browne and Immervoll (2017) study shows, the effects of a basic income are entirely different if it replaces a generous and well-targeted social protection system, as in Finland, as opposed to when it takes the place of an underdeveloped and even to some extent pro-rich targeted system as in Italy.

But the reasons for divergence across studies go deeper. Outcomes depend on the exact specification of the basic income. Basic income advocates are often frustratingly vague about many of the choices that need to be made. In fact, on both sides of the debate, basic income is still presented in overly simplistic terms, while in reality it raises many complex policy issues. Crucial considerations are being swept aside, many of which apply to any basic income proposal.

A universal basic income is better understood as a myriad of potential schemes that can differ substantially along a range of policy dimensions rather than as one uniform, ready-made policy. Indeed, there are multiple design details at play when it comes to BI that need to be determined carefully. Key design dimensions include: coverage, adequacy, uniformity, financing, integration, and accumulation (De Wispelaere & Stirton, 2004). Choices have to be made; choices that go beyond the mere size of the benefit amount. Unless one is advocating the elimination of the entire existing tax-benefit system, it is especially crucial to consider which parts of the system remain, and how the basic income will then interact with the set of policies still in place.

Which parts of the existing tax/benefit system are maintained, and which parts are abolished, modified, or replaced? Is a basic income made taxable? Are amounts of other benefits affected by the basic income? Such issues hardly feature in many basic income debates but they matter in fact a great deal.

In Aerts, Marx, and Verbist (2023) we show that such choices matter. Although the level of the basic income is a crucial dimension of variation, even apparently 'minor' choices regarding the transformations to the tax/benefit system matter, sometimes a lot. Strikingly, we find that a higher basic income will not necessarily always have 'better' distributional consequences, especially if poverty reduction is the goal. That is because a lower or what we may call 'partial' basic income is potentially much more complementary, if not supportive, to existing (targeted) provisions than a full-fledged basic income replacing existing provisions. This shows that besides the amount of the basic income, there are many other design details that matter just as much, if not more. When a basic income would be implemented as a wholesale replacement of existing social protection arrangements, poverty would increase without exception. Alternatively, replacing tax allowances—which tend to benefit those with higher incomes—with a basic income would reduce poverty rates. (But then again, any rechannelling of tax benefits away from the middle and higher incomes towards the lower ones, even via existing benefits, would reduce poverty rates.) Whether or not a basic income is included in the means-test of other benefits also matters for the amount of poverty-reduction that can be achieved. Even the tax structure matters. A basic income accompanied by a flat tax would for example overall be far less redistributive compared to a progressive tax. As De Wispelaere and Stirton

(2004) rightly put it, 'There is no such thing as a preferred basic income scheme independent of the overall institutional and policy context.'

In conclusion, the microsimulation exercises we have at present show that some of the most vulnerable sections of the population would lose out from replacing existing benefits with a basic income, except if social expenditure and thus tax levels were to be vastly increased. This is less the case in countries with large coverage gaps in their existing social protection systems or extremely bad targeting of benefits. Basically, the hard truth is that despite the noblest of intentions, a full basic income replacing existing benefits essentially involves taking from the unemployed, sick, and financially needy to give to people with jobs, good health, and money. The story is somewhat different for a partial basic income. This type of scheme is potentially more complementary with existing benefits, which are usually far more targeted towards the most needy. While a partial basic income can help to 'lift the floor', it cannot bring the sizeable improvement in work incentives a basic income proper can bring, at least for those with the lowest earnings potential. A full basic income, on the other hand, does have that potential but it will bring a dramatically higher effective tax rates for high earners, making it politically unrealistic.

## 6.4 What We Do Not Know Yet (But Still Have Reasonable Guesses About)

The key limitation of virtually all existing simulation studies of basic income is that they only consider first-round effects. That is to say: the effective assumption is that a basic income does nothing to people's behaviour. This assumption says that a basic income, however small or large, would have no impact on whether people will work or not, and how hard they would choose to work. Of course basic income proponents will argue that behavioural change is *exactly* why they advocate a basic income (Van Parijs & Vanderborght, 2017). The argument is that it would radically alter behaviour, especially for people trapped in dire situations. For example, people who do not have enough to make ends meet on their current meagre benefit but cannot find sufficiently stable and well-paying jobs to make an exit from the little they have really worthwhile.

Take people currently living on social assistance. A large share of them live in financial poverty because the benefit they receive tends to be below the poverty threshold as we have illustrated at length in Chapter 2. In theory they find themselves in a situation where any additional income they earn is deducted from their social assistance benefit. Until the total income they earn exceeds their benefit, they effectively face a 100% marginal tax rate. In reality many countries have earnings disregards to avoid this situation, as we demonstrated in Chapter 4. That is to say: people on social assistance are sometimes allowed to earn some extra money, but usually not very much or indefinitely. Also, rules tend to be complex and administrative procedures tedious and discouraging. In part this stems from an understandable concern that people already in low-paid jobs will enter social assistance.

Now, the cruel thing is that some extra money would of course make a world of difference for people on social assistance. If they could complement their social assistance benefit with only a couple of hundred euro (or an equivalent amount in other currencies) they would in many cases escape financial poverty by commonly used thresholds. But at present they cannot because they would see their social assistance support curbed.

Here is where basic income, even a partial basic income, could make a vast difference. Remember that people can complement their basic income at will. If we assumed that most people currently on social assistance were in fact capable of earning some additional income, aided or not by labour market liberalization friendly to part-time and gig work, the outcome of any micro-simulation exercise could look dramatically different. This is the big unknown.

Birnbaum and De Wispelaere (2020) make the case that a basic income-induced exit strategy effectively amounts to a hollow threat. Given how labour markets operate in reality and how the opportunities of disadvantaged workers are structured, a basic income-centred exit option might as well become an exit trap rather than an empowered fallback position.

A crucial point at any rate is that the segments who would see their labour incentives potentially (again: details matter!) improved under basic income are relatively small in size. Essentially we are talking about people currently on social assistance and in long-term unemployment, especially if they are in means-tested unemployment assistance schemes. Perhaps we should also count in a portion of people in sickness and disability schemes. Altogether these groups make up a small minority in most countries.

It is in this context that the experiments that have been conducted are particularly instructive. At the risk of oversimplification, it seems fair to say that a reduction in conditionality and less punitive treatment of additional earnings does not yield wonder outcomes among those facing the worst work incentives. The municipal experiments in the Netherlands involving more generous earnings disregards for social assistance recipients and reduced monitoring of conditions and sanctioning in case of non-compliance did not very significantly impact on work and mobility outcomes (Verlaat & Zulkarnain, 2022). Simply allowing social assistance recipients to work without tapering their benefit has a limited impact on their work effort. Similarly, the much publicized Finnish 'basic income' study, which basically involved a reduction of conditionality for long-term unemployment beneficiaries, found very small employment effects leading the researchers to conclude 'the problems related to finding employment are not related to bureaucracy or to financial incentives' (Ministry of Social Affairs and Health, 2020).[4]

This points to a problem perhaps that has marred 'making work pay' efforts for a long time: the idea that people are rational utility optimizers combined with the notion that long-term benefit entrapment is mainly a problem of financial incentives. Since psychologists and economists started working together the naivety of that reductionist conception has become clear. Social work research has also documented that people's realities are far removed from the work incentive graphs that have been so central to activation efforts (Bertrand, Mullainathan, & Shafir, 2004; Mani et al., 2013; Mullainathan & Shafir, 2013). They are loved by economists and policy wonks but there is increasing evidence that they matter less than we thought. People on social assistance often face multiple hurdles to work, financial incentives being only one and not necessarily the most important.

The idea that a basic income by and of its own will propel people into new orbits of self-realization simply amounts to wishful thinking. There is no reason to believe that a basic income will help people overcome the multiple problems and challenges they are facing: a lack of qualifications and work experience, social isolation, lack of self-esteem, addiction issues, physical separation from jobs, bad housing, problematic indebtedness, etc. That is not to say, of course, that this applies to all long-term social assistance recipients but there is no denying that such problems are more prevalent among this group of people.

By contrast, the population that would likely see their work incentives deteriorate is much larger in relative size, especially for higher amounts of basic income. Those on higher incomes would see their marginal tax rates rise, unless sizeable alternative sources of revenue are available, which is very rarely the case, unless in countries with vast precious natural resources (think Norway). The idea that a sizeable basic income could be financed in full from taxing the wealthy or wealthy corporations is completely illusory, at least within reasonable limits.[5]

A full basic income would almost inevitably imply higher personal income tax rates on higher incomes. Some segments of the population do respond fairly strongly to financial incentives, as a sizeable empirical labour economics literature shows (Ashenfelter & Card, 2010). The employment rate of single persons and men in cohabiting couples is relatively insensitive to financial incentives but the work effort of mothers with young children is.

It is quite possible for that reason that people already in work would reduce their work effort if a sizeable basic income were introduced, especially women with working partners. This is in effect what macro-economic modelling for the Netherlands shows. The Dutch Central Planning Bureau has sophisticated models that estimate aggregate labour supply effects, among other outcomes. Those models predict that a basic income would have a very sizeable negative impact on employment, especially second-earner work effort (see also Box 6.1). It would, in effect, reduce women's employment (see Olsthoorn et al., 2020; Goderis & Vlekke, 2023).

## 6.5 Political Feasibility

This brings us to the issue of political feasibility. There is quite a bit of political science research on support for basic income (Laenen, 2023). Surveys have at times suggested people like the idea of basic income in great numbers. A Eurobarometer question gauging support for basic income in 2001 found massive support levels, upwards of 70%, but the question was distinctly vague: 'The government should provide everyone with a guaranteed basic income.'

There is a big difference between people instinctively warming to a vague idea superficially presented to them in a survey and actually supporting a basic income once they are made aware of what it exactly entails. The more precisely one seeks to gauge people's attitudes to basic income the more complex and for basic income enthusiasts encouraging the picture becomes.

The European Social Survey took a more refined approach in 2016, quizzing people about a hypothetical scheme that involved a monthly income to cover essential living costs while replacing many other social benefits. They were told the purpose is to guarantee everyone a minimum standard of living, that everyone receives the same amount regardless of whether or not they are working, and that people also keep the money they earn from work or other sources. They were informed that the scheme itself was paid for by taxes.

Support levels remained quite significant if people were presented with a concrete proposal like this. The weakest support came from respondents in Sweden, Switzerland, and Norway. In the UK and the Netherlands, support was split almost 50/50. More than half the respondents in Slovenia, Belgium, Poland, Ireland, and the Czech Republic supported universal basic income.

Levels of support were below 50% in France, Estonia, Austria, Iceland, and Germany.

Those are very substantial support levels indeed but keep in mind that the level of the BI remained unspecified in the question posed by the survey. There was no clear indication of whether, how and by how much taxes would have to raised. Moreover, it was not clear which social benefits would have been replaced (Vlandas, 2019). As we show in Aerts, Marx, and Verbist (2023) such issues are absolutely crucial. It is almost useless to gauge support for a basic income unless one is very specific indeed about how it funded and what the impact would be on other benefits and tax advantages.

All the available BI simulations reveal that the policy switch would result in a substantial amount of losers, some incurring very heavy losses. Patterns are diverse across countries but they all confirm that simple observation (Browne & Immervoll, 2017; Martinelli, 2017a). Basically, the higher the basic income, the more polarized the outcomes in terms of winners and losers (Aerts, Marx, & Verbist, 2023). This matters because we know that voters are particularly averse to losses. Political turmoil has erupted over reforms that in terms of impact pale in significance compared to what a basic income would entail.

The simulation by Brown and Immervoll for Finland, Italy, France, and the UK suggests that approximately 30–40% of the working age population would be net losers. Around one in five people would experience a more than 5% drop in income. Around 15% of the working age population would face a 10% drop or more. Early retirees would be particularly hard hit. On the flip side, there would be many gainers too. In the order of 20 to 30% of working age adults would gain more than 10%. At any rate, the outcomes are so uneven that it is hard to envisage a broad coalition naturally emerging under any scenario. In scenario's where a basic income replaces existing social benefits the almost inevitable consequence is that the unemployed, sick, and elderly lose out, unless the basic income were set at a very high level. But that of course would imply many higher income losers and near punitive marginal tax rates.

There is an interesting paradox here. In-depth analysis of the ESS data shows that low-income individuals, the unemployed, workers in elementary occupations and left-leaning individuals are more likely to support a BI (Vlandas, 2021). Presumably these people do so because they think that they will be better off with a BI. But in reality a BI would likely make many of them worse off. Would they still support a BI if they were aware of this? That is a very big if.

This points to a key weakness in much of the sophisticated research crunching the ESS data on support for BI. There appears to be a large gap between what a BI would actually do and what people believe it would do (for them). Would people still support a BI if they were made aware that introduction of a BI would drive up inequality and poverty and make them personally worse off?

Qualitative research also gives reason to doubt that the public is actually ready for BI.

In-depth interviews conducted in the Netherlands suggest that people there still adhere to the well-known deservingness criteria of control, need and reciprocity (Rossetti et al., 2020). Even in the case of a BI, people still distinguish between those who are considered 'unable' to reciprocate to society and those who are 'able' to earn an income for themselves. The latter are judged undeserving and should be encouraged if not forced to participate in the labour market. Interviewees often indicate that benefit recipients, if they can, should do something (useful) in return. People cannot get 'something for nothing', and they have a duty to engage in work. Support for conditionality in terms of job seeking, training and social obligations seems to triumph over the unconditionality of a UBI.

Rossetti et al. (2020) conclude, 'In their strong reliance on the deservingness criteria, it seems that our respondents generally reject the idea of equal redistribution, in the sense that everybody should receive the same. In this way, they also reject an important foundation of a UBI as unconditional in terms of assessed financial need, a person's present or past contributions and/or their willingness to work.'

Research also shows that insofar that there is support for BI among both left-wing and right-wing voters, their motives are different (Roosma & van Oorschot, 2020; Vlandas, 2021). Mixed support among the left means a pro-BI coalition has to draw on right-wing voters who may support it only with lower taxes (which is quite unlikely) and market liberalization. That is unlikely to appeal to the left. Add to that the fact that support among unions and organized labour remains lukewarm to say the least (Vanderborght, 2006; Van Parijs & Vanderborght, 2017). That is perhaps not surprising given claims that basic income would empower individual workers and reduce their need for union representation. Moreover, organized labour played a large role in bringing about many of the existing income maintenance provisions—think unemployment insurance, sickness benefits, pensions, and so much more. In some countries they remain involved in the governance of social security and even in some cases in the actual provision of benefits, notably unemployment insurance benefits in the so-called Ghent systems found in the Nordic countries and Belgium. It would require quite an altruistic commitment to social justice—if that is what basic income brings—for unions to give up what they historically fought for and hold dear.

All this having been said, Van Parijs and Vanderborght are certainly right that 'political feasibility must not be treated as a parameter to be taken as a given. It is something that can be shaped by opinion and is indeed our job to help shape' (Van Parijs & Vanderborght, 2017, p. 170). Whether a universal basic income, especially as a lock, stock, and barrel replacement for existing income protection provisions, is a good idea remains highly doubtful, to say the least. Partial basic incomes may make more sense, although even that is unsure. Yet that social and economic progress sometimes comes from radically new ideas that require a lot of relentless convincing before these to take hold, that we can agree on.

### Box 6.1 Basic income in the Netherlands: the ultimate test case?

The Netherlands is an interesting case to examine the potential benefits of a basic income because on a range of measures it already ranks among the best performing welfare states in the world. On the EU's Social Scoreboard, for example, the Netherlands shows up as a top performer on a host of indicators. Especially relevant in this context is that the Netherlands is among the best performers in Europe when it comes to poverty prevention. While it has lost some of its lustre over recent years—poverty has gone up—it still does better than many countries with higher levels of social spending. In addition, the Netherlands is also one of the best performing countries on a range of work-related outcomes. More than 80% of the working age population has a job, close to the highest score in Europe. Long-term unemployment is very low.

All this matters because basic income advocates see inherent trade-offs between minimum income adequacy under conventional provisions and incentives for work and self-sufficiency. If anything, the Netherlands seems to illustrate that, contrary to often repeated claims, there is no such thing as an inescapable trade-off between comparatively generous social protection and a dynamic, well-performing economy, including a well-functioning labour market that provides work for people who need it. This is especially relevant because a basic income is often presented as an innovative and radical solution to overcome exactly such a trade-off.

When it comes to poverty reduction the Dutch approach can be summed up as 'targeting within universalism'. That is to say: relatively generous universal benefits and services are supplemented by a range of income and household situation tested

*continued*

**Box 6.1** *continued*

supplements. As a consequence, minimum income protection levels are among the highest in Europe, both for working as non-working people. (The focus here is on the working aged population but it is worth noting that the Netherlands has in effect a basic pension, making a full-blown basic income perhaps less incongruous than in other contexts.) In fact, the Netherlands ranks as one of the few countries where the guaranteed level of minimum income protection exceeded the relative poverty threshold for a while, a feat matched or exceeded by very few countries. As Chapter 2 shows, the level of minimum income protection there still ranks among the most generous in Europe.

The Netherlands is also an interesting case to look at because of its in many ways atypical labour market, seen sometimes as a precursor to what post-industrial economies are heading towards. Part-time employment is so common that it has almost become the norm. With about half of all women working part-time and close to one in four men, the Netherlands has been dubbed the 'first part-time economy in the world'. There is also a lot of temporary and temp agency work. In addition, many people already combine earned income and transfer income. This is in major part because activation into work has been a priority of successive Dutch governments. Benefit systems have thus been reformed to stimulate and accommodate such combinations.

Critics will however argue that the situation in the Netherlands looks much rosier on paper than in reality. This is perhaps best illustrated by the 'Toeslagenaffaire' (supplements affair) which has rocked Dutch society and politics to its core. This affair erupted after it had come to light that households holding double nationality and characteristics indicating that they belonged to an ethnic minority were being withheld child care supplements by the Dutch tax authorities. Apparently the tax authority was running algorithms to that effect, illegally denying people benefits to which they were eligible. The affair brought accusations of institutionalized racism. The 'Toeslagenaffaire' thrusted the issue of targeting to the front pages of the newspapers, prompting parliamentary enquiries and resignations of senior civil servants, ministers, and eventually the entire government in 2021.

It is in this context that basic income retains much traction in Dutch society. Basic income proponents like publicist Rutger Bregman, a best-selling author, sway significant influence over the public debate. A number of political parties have embraced basic income ideas.

Consequently, several studies have sought to model the potential first-order ('morning after') effects of a basic income on poverty and inequality levels in the Netherlands. A report for the Dutch GAK foundation we did (cf. Boone et al., 2018) followed the approach taken by Browne and Immervoll (2017). The results are thus comparable to those generated by the OECD for Finland, France, Italy, and the UK.

Three different Basic Income scenarios are examined. The main (or 'Medium') scenario sets the Basic Income at the level of the GMI for an individual on active working age with a partner and no children (then around €702 per month). Children receive a lower Basic Income of €165 per month. To finance this reform social and fiscal benefits are abolished and the Basic Income is made taxable. A 'Low BI' scenario gives each adult €415 per month and children €80. These monthly benefits can be financed by abolishing most existing social and fiscal benefits. Finally, a 'High BI' scenario gives €982 per month to adults. This corresponds to the amount that a single person with no children received from social assistance at the time of the study. The child Basic Income remains unchanged. This reform is financed by abolishing most existing social benefits and tax benefits and by making the Basic Income taxable. Personal income tax rates would need to rise by 24% to get the whole reform financed.

The number of winners and losers is almost '50–50' in the three scenarios, but their profile is completely different. The gains and losses become more polarized as the basic income increases. Winners are mainly found among students and the economically active population. Losers are mainly found among the unemployed and others relying heavily on benefits, especially in the Low and Medium scenarios. This should not come as a surprise. Basically, implementing a basic income by abolishing or curbing existing benefits effectively amounts to taking away from the unemployed, sick, and financially needy to give to people with jobs, good health, and money.

Poverty and inequality levels would increase significantly in the 'Low BI' and 'Medium BI' scenarios. Only in the 'High BI' scenario do poverty and inequality levels decrease but the effect is limited compared to the size of the reform. Recall that a basic income would require a very substantial increase in personal income tax rates. The highest tax bracket would go up from 52% to 65%.

A similar microsimulation exercise by the Dutch Social and Cultural Planning bureau in cooperation with the Central Planning Bureau of an even more generous variant yields a stronger reduction against the poverty line as the SCP defines it. This is a reference budget-based poverty line that differs from the relative one used throughout this book. The most interesting and unique feature of this particular simulation is that it also looks at the macro impact of the reform, notably on overall employment (CPB/SCP, 2020).

The simulation shows that the impact on taxes is massive. In the SCP calculation the lowest tax rate would go from 37.1% to 52.7% and the highest from 49.5% to 70.2%. In addition, and importantly, the CPB/SCP study, which also involves macro general equilibrium modelling, estimates a strong negative impact on employment. That is due to both the extra non-earned income a basic income brings and to the higher tax rates needed to pay for it. The expected impact in terms of reduced

*continued*

**Box 6.1** *continued*

employment is strongest for second earners, in couples with children under 12. To a lesser extent this applies to second earners in couples with older children and couples without children. The effect is smallest for singles (both with and without children). An earlier study found a milder impact on employment for the reason that it assumed a lower basic income, which meant that tax rates had to be raised less.

In conclusion, the Dutch would have to be very adventurous if not more than a tad reckless to give up a system that demonstrably yields comparatively good if not exemplary outcomes on a host of social and economic indicators with a system that in terms of its projected initial effects has little going for it. Under most scenarios modelled thus far employment decreases (especially among women), taxes increase and poverty is not significantly or at least commensurately reduced. Of course, the existing models mostly give us an idea of the 'morning after' effects. But one would have to be very optimistic indeed to believe that the further round effects would eventually bring a complete reverse of the projected first round effects.

## 6.6 Basic Income Advocates, Sober Up

In conclusion, what we know so far should sober up basic income advocates. There is no denying the appeal and power of a simple, radical idea like basic income. The idea that everybody, rich or poor, smart or not so gifted, thrifty or lazy, has the right to one vote was quite radical at one time. It took a long time and many a struggle but the principle of one person, one vote has not only become widely accepted, it has become an unshakable cornerstone of Western democracy. Perhaps we will see the day when, in addition to equal rights before the law and equal political rights, every person has a basic economic right. Still, the idea that an identical money transfer every month or so to every citizen is the best way of realizing such a basic economic right is an altogether different matter.[6]

We have been concerned here mainly with the question of whether a basic income would be a superior way of ensuring adequate protection against financial poverty. The available research allows us to think in an empirically informed way about the (partial) first-round effects of a sizeable basic income. Neither the insights we get from (quasi-)experimental research nor those from simulation modelling are exactly very encouraging.

True, we can only make informed speculations about the 'day after' effects of a basic income. It requires an enormous leap of faith to assume that the effects further down the road would miraculously better. Also, we can actually make empirically informed speculations about at least some potential next-round effects. But as these dynamically interact to produce new outcomes—work patterns, wages, prices, etc.—things become more uncertain. It is hard to model with any degree of scientific accuracy how a sizeable basic income would affect an economy, even under ceteris paribus conditions.

Of course ceteris paribus is very unlikely. A basic income is likely to trigger political and institutional change. It is likely to make employers and unions behave differently. Central banks and so many other relevant actors would behave differently if a basic income was in place. On top of that, one can well imagine that some of the societal and economic changes that a basic income is said to remedy or buffer will themselves be reinforced by a basic income.

Efforts to automate human labour might shift into even higher gears, driven by fears that people will not want to do certain jobs any more or demand higher wages to do certain jobs. Unions and political parties representing workers may become less resistant to robotization and automation.

Deregulation of labour markets might well intensify if a substantial basic income were to be introduced. Remember that basic income advocates argue that a basic income would be good for the poor because it would allow them to acquire any additional earned income they can get at will. Presumably the logical step then is to make sure that such additional income is available even if it comes in the form of part-time work, gig, and platform work. What else would be the point of having a basic income?

In short, a basic income might well precipitate exactly the many transformations it is presented as an answer to. Philippe Van Parijs and Yannick Vanderborght along with other advocates present a basic income as something akin to an economic life vest protecting people against the ever rougher currents of change. Even if it is not a very high amount, the fact that it is guaranteed and unconditional will help people to keep afloat. True perhaps, but not drowning is not quite the same as an existence in dignity, as a surfer or in any other capacity.

# 7
# Moving Forward

## 7.1 Why Adequate Minimum Income Protection Matters More than Ever

### 7.1.1 First Comes Poverty Prevention but That Is Not Enough

This final chapter sums up and sets out what we think can be done to provide people more adequate shelter against financial poverty. Of course, poverty prevention requires a far wider set of policies than the ones that make up the core focus of this book. It is important that we acknowledge this, even if many of these policies are outside the scope of this book.

One could legitimately argue that poverty reduction is first and foremost about prevention. That it is about nurturing talent from an early age, so that people develop the capacity to earn a decent living. One could add that it is also about policies enabling people to fully realize and maintain their earnings potential, for example in the shape of child care or lifelong learning. Social investment scholars have made forceful cases for such policies. Indeed, it is fair to say that over the past decades pleas for more 'social investment' have been far more forceful and louder than the ones for more adequate wages and social transfers.

Already more than 20 years ago, in an influential report to the Presidency of the European Union, Esping-Andersen et al. (2002) called for a radical overhaul of welfare state architectures in Europe stating: 'As the new social risks weigh most heavily on the younger cohorts, we explicitly advocate a reallocation of social expenditures towards family services, active labour market policy, early childhood education and vocational training, so as to ensure productivity improvement and high employment for both men and women in the knowledge-based economy.' The OECD around the same time started to stress the crucial importance of human capital investments in the fight against growing inequality and poverty, while stating that 'redistribution strategies based on government transfers and taxes alone would be neither

*Zero Poverty Society*. Sarah Marchal and Ive Marx, Oxford University Press. © Sarah Marchal and Ive Marx (2024).
DOI: 10.1093/9780191967771.003.0007

effective nor sustainable' (OECD, 2011). By the same token, the European Commission launched in 2013 a 'Social Investment Package' emphasizing human capital investment. Publicly provided or subsidized services of various kinds, and particularly education and care services, were seen as key instruments in this package.

Meanwhile, the term social 'social investment' has become ubiquitous in EU discourse. A recent report by the High-Level Group on the future of social protection and the welfare state in the EU, chaired by former European Commissioner Anna Diamantopoulou, again puts social investment front and centre (Directorate General for Employment Social Affairs and Inclusion, 2023). Likewise, scholars like Anton Hemerijck, Nathalie Morel, Bruno Palier, and Joakim Palme, among many others, have continued to make impassioned cases for social investment (Morel et al., 2012; Hemerijck, 2018, 2017; Garritzman et al., 2022). Still, how much social progress, especially poverty reduction, we can really expect from social investment remains contentious. Not everybody is equally convinced that it has the potential yields its advocates claim.[1]

This is not the place to rehash, let alone expand, that debate. What matters here is that we know for certain that social investment does not suffice if we care about poverty and social inclusion. Not every child has the chance to pursue a good education, sometimes because parents lack decent minimum incomes. Even the best educated, most diligent, hardworking people encounter accidents in life that hamper or even destroy their earnings capacity. Social security has a crucial role to play in compensating people affected by social risks but it is also a reality that many people do not have full access to such social protection. Young people often do not have entitlements, nor do new immigrants. Non-standard workers are still at risk of lacking adequate coverage. People often have to wait a considerable time before they get the social insurance benefits they are entitled to or until they receive privately arranged compensations, for example from a former partner or employer. People deplete social insurance entitlements after a while. Unemployment insurance benefits, for example, tend to be limited in time. In all such cases, minimum income protection has a key role to play in protecting people against destitution.

And crucially, we know that being in work does not protect against poverty in and of itself. Even full-year, full-time workers, doing their utmost to be economically self-sufficient, can find themselves struggling financially. Sole earners with dependent children or other dependents are at a particularly high risk of poverty. They need adequate wage floors, appropriate, poverty-conscious fiscal policies and adequate direct transfers to supplement their earned incomes up to a level allowing for a life in dignity, including for their children. The policy levers within the scope of this book thus clearly matter.

### 7.1.2 Social Insurance: More Gaps, Less Adequacy

Social security remains the most important income maintenance provision by far in most rich welfare states, usually dwarfing social assistance and related final safety net provisions in terms of caseloads and expenditure levels.

The social insurance systems nowadays in place in rich economies emerged and came to maturity in different times. Those systems have adapted for sure, in some cases almost beyond recognition, but change has also been slow, erratic, and imperfect, resulting in gaps in coverage and in some cases a decline in adequacy. In a social insurance system, the level of protection is a function of accumulated rights. Without exemptions, a precarious work situation automatically results in precarious protection (Schoukens et al., 2018; Spasova & Wilkens, 2018; OECD, 2019). The broad umbrella of precarious employment shelters an assortment of non-standard work forms: part-time work, temporary work, (bogus) self-employment and, most recently, gig and platform work. Meanwhile, the forces of globalization and technological change are not exactly grinding to a halt. New technologies destroy distance as a cost factor and make it easier and cheaper to offer and find work online. Gig and platform work is expected to expand, although its significance should not yet be overstated (Prassl, 2018).

There are adaptations to these new realities. Social insurance schemes have been adapted to grant more if not equal rights to part-time workers and temporary workers. Some countries have introduced (voluntary) unemployment insurance schemes for self-employed workers (Spasova & Wilkens, 2018; OECD, 2019). But important gaps in terms of coverage remain in many countries, an issue starkly highlighted first by the Great Recession of 2008 and then the COVID-19 crisis.

Against this backdrop, safety nets of last resort, as well as in-work income support, have almost automatically gained in importance. Figure 7.1 shows increases in beneficiary count in 18 out of 28 countries. On average, the number of beneficiaries rose by 17% (and 11% if we leave out developments in outlier Lithuania).

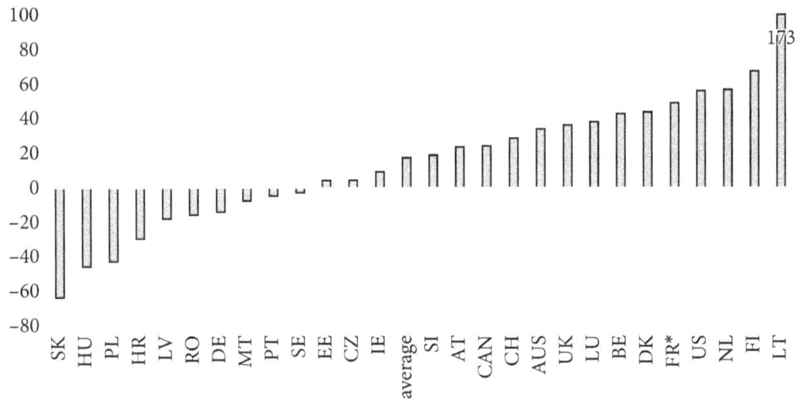


**Figure 7.1** Percentage change increase in beneficiaries of the means-tested minimum income protection schemes for the non-working active age population, 2007–2018

*Note:* Data for France refer to the increase from 2009 to 2018.
*Source:* OECD SOCR database.

## 7.1.3 Two Crises, Two Wake-Up Calls

By the turn of the century the belief that having more people in paid work was the key to better poverty and broader social inclusion outcomes had become common currency in OECD countries. The notion that work had a near magical potential to cure social ills, not in the least poverty, was at the core of influential new policy doctrines at the time, notably the 'Third Way' and the 'Active Welfare State'. Disproving fears of a future characterized by 'jobless growth' and 'the end of work', the 15 years prior to the crisis of 2008 were marked by strong net employment gains so that, just prior to the crisis, employment rates had reached historically high levels in many countries. Yet exactly that fact exposed the fallacy of the idea that more people in work would automatically bring less people in poverty. Employment growth in and of itself had not produced the expected social improvements. Marked increases in employment rates had for the most part gone accompanied with rising or stagnant relative poverty rates for the working-age population (Gábos et al., 2019; Akarçeşme et al., 2023; Marx & Verbist, 2014).

When the banking crisis of 2008 morphed into a full-fledged economic recession, causing job loss not seen in a generation, social safety nets in most European countries were not in the best of shape. Minimum income provisions had by and large deteriorated during the two decades preceding the crisis as social policy in many EU countries had come to rest on the idea that work offered the best way out of poverty (Van Mechelen & Marchal, 2013a). Confronted with soaring unemployment levels, be it to varying degree, the relevance of adequate protection arrangements acquired a new level of significance (Marchal et al., 2014). At the EU level a more acute awareness developed that the ad nauseam repeated platitude that 'a job is the best protection against poverty' did not hold true in the best of times and certainly not in the worst of times.

In earlier work, we asked whether the Great Recession triggered a revaluation and restoration of social safety nets (Marchal et al., 2014). We found a general pattern of increases in minimum income benefits levels across the EU, especially in the years 2008 and 2009, before fiscal considerations took centre stage. Yet the size of the increases did not point to marked breaks in long-term trends. Some countries took measures to boost the net income packages of households reliant on social assistance or equivalent minimum income support, usually in the form of hikes in child-related benefits. Although supportive measures were the general pattern during the initial phase of the crisis from 2010 onwards most countries did not issue further expansionary measures (Marchal et al., 2016). In some countries there was (gradual) retrenchment. Whereas the expansionary measures generally involved increases in benefits, retrenchment measures were more often enacted through less visible, apparently technical changes. Examples include: skipping indexation, tightening the means-test, abolishment or decrease of additional benefits (for instance child benefits). Countries that introduced retrenchment measures were mainly those where the crisis hit the hardest (Hay & Wincott, 2012).

The Great Recession brought no decisive breaks in policy relating to minimum income protection. Neither the size of the increases nor the choice of instruments (i.e., temporary one-off allowances) added up to anywhere near pathbreaking ruptures towards more adequate social safety nets.

Preliminary assessments of the impact of the COVID-19 crisis on social safety nets point towards a similar pattern (Aidukaite et al., 2021; Béland, Cantillon, et al., 2021; Béland, Dinan, et al., 2021; Moreira et al., 2021). This was even more so as the non-working population was in many countries not immediately recognized as a target group in need of additional non-discretionary support during the first COVID-19 lockdowns. Immediate efforts were concentrated on employees—including non-standard workers—at risk of dismissal for lack of work and the self-employed who had to halt their activities (Bonoli et al., 2022; Cantó et al., 2022). However, by summer 2020 the first additional support measures to either minimum income beneficiaries, or, more broadly, people living in low income households, were noticeable. Again, the size of this additional support does not point towards structural improvements in the adequacy of minimum income protection packages for those out of work, as it generally concerned one-off or temporary lump sum increases. The introduction of the Spanish national minimum income scheme is a notable exception. However, this large scale reform was already under preparation before the onset of the COVID-19 crisis. Rather, it was the actual implementation that was pushed forward (see also Box 2.3 in Chapter 2).

### 7.1.4 Finally a Real Push from Europe? Realizing the Pillar of Social Rights

If words offer good guidance, the European Union has long cared deeply about poverty. At the Lisbon summit in 2000, leaders of the European Union proclaimed that 'Steps must be taken to make a decisive impact on the eradication of poverty.'

Progress has however been frustratingly disappointing. Responding to criticism that the EU was too much of an economic project and its 'social dimension' too weak, the 2015 Five Presidents' report stated the ambition that the EU needed to be 'Triple A' on social issues (Juncker et al., 2015). That culminated in the European Pillar of Social Rights, a common declaration of principles. It was signed by every EU Member State (European Commission, 2017). Particularly relevant in the context of this book are principles 6 and 14, calling for fair and adequate wages, and adequate minimum income benefits respectively.

These principles were later reiterated in the Action Plan on the implementation of the European Pillar of Social Rights, which, among other things, says (European Commission, 2021): 'Minimum income schemes are essential to ensure that no one is left behind. While in place in all Member States, minimum income schemes vary significantly in their adequacy, coverage, take-up and articulation with labour market activation measures and enabling goods and services, including social services. In many cases, the eligibility criteria and the levels of benefits would deserve to be modernised.'

The Von der Leyen Commission translated these two principles in legislative instruments. Importantly, the European Parliament voted on 14 September 2022 with a large majority in favour of the so-called 'minimum wage directive', adopted by the Council on 4 October (European Council, 2022). The directive hinges on two key points: First, it aims to ensure that adequate minimum wages protect EU workers, allowing for a decent living.

Second, the directive aims to strengthen collective bargaining as the main instrument to ensure fair wages and working conditions (European Commission, 2020c). Importantly, countries that have statutory minimum wages are required to identify whether the applicable levels are adequate, for which they need to develop clear and transparent reference values, taking account of socio-economic conditions, purchasing power, and long-term national productivity levels and developments (for more information, see Box 3.1 in Chapter 3).

Regarding means-tested minimum income schemes, the Commission published on 28 September 2022 a proposal for a council recommendation, which was adopted by the Council in January 2023. This recommendation focuses on a transparent methodology for setting and reviewing the level of income support. Again, reference values are proposed to guide the assessment of adequacy and annual adjustments. Also, the proposal mentions 2030 as the year by which adequate income support (against national benchmarks proposed by the member states) should be reached.

Importantly, the recommendation also mentions a number of more specific measures, including highlighting the benefits of an individual benefit payment (rather than on the household level), and the importance of simple application procedures and accessible information. It also stresses the importance of the current benchmarking framework set out by the European Commission and the Social Protection Committee, in which adequacy is effectively operationalized as 60% of median equivalent household income, and relative to the income of a low-wage earner. Member States should regularly report on their progress (European Commission, 2022a, 2022b; European Commission and Social Protection Committee, 2022).

In spite of the relative detail comprised in this recommendation, critics may argue that its non-binding nature still leaves too much leeway to the Member States. Van Lancker et al. (2020) argue that a legal instrument on out-of-work minimum income protection should be in the form of a 'framework' that sets core standards at the EU level but that allows Member States enough flexibility to develop minimum income schemes that fit their contexts, they cautioned against the lack of bite of soft law. For that reason, they advocate a binding legal instrument, in the form of a framework directive.

Still, the introduction of a binding EU-level instrument on adequate national minimum income schemes raises questions of European solidarity. The cost of bringing minimum income benefits to adequate levels differs a lot between Member States (Vandenbroucke et al., 2013). The poorer Member States would have to do most effort to close the poverty gap while lacking the money to do so, or fearing the loss of their comparative advantage within the

Single Market. The poorer member states will naturally only accept a binding EU directive if they get support from the richer Member States.

Whether such solidarity can be mustered remains a big if but it is not unthinkable. COVID-19 proved a catalyst for taboo breaking change. Next Generation EU, the economic recovery package to support member states adversely impacted by the COVID-19 pandemic, is not only unparalleled in sheer size but is financed by collective EU debt. Similarly, the temporary Support to mitigate Unemployment Risks in an Emergency (SURE) mechanism materialized faster than anyone imagined.

## 7.2 How to Improve Minimum Income Support? The Case for a Layered Approach

Throughout this book, we have identified and discussed a range of policy instruments that can be deployed to make sure people have an adequate minimum in financial resources. These include minimum wages and other forms of wage regulation, child benefits, tax credits, social assistance top-ups, and other allowances. If well-designed, these instruments can complement and reinforce each other. We have demonstrated here that there is substantial variation in the levels and design of minimum income protection provided to people in advanced welfare states.

Overall, we have shown that it is clearly possible to make sure that households where the adults present put in full work effort have minimally adequate incomes, even though there is still a long way to go in some countries, especially in the case of single parent households. The plight of jobless households or households with only limited labour market attachment remains extremely worrisome. Minimum income provisions largely fail to ensure an acceptable minimum living standard, usually by a wide margin.

Although optimal policy mixes cannot be readily defined—economic context, budget constraints and other country-specific factors matter—our results reveal four vital steps towards improving minimum income adequacy.

*First, raise wage floors*—Wage floors are key to adequate minimum income protection. That they matter for people mostly reliant on earnings for their livelihood is obvious. But they matter to everybody in need of adequate minimum income protection. That is because minimum wages, or more specifically net incomes at or around the minimum wage (including possible in-work and other benefits) effectively constrain out-of-work benefits, as policymakers are concerned with safeguarding financial incentives to work and honouring the principle that work should bring greater reward than not being in work. Moreover, institutionally determined wage floors ensure that employers (and consumers) bear an equitable share of the cost.

*Second, have universal child benefits as a first layer of direct income support*—Our analysis reveals that in the countries that manage to ensure minimum income protection packages at or above the poverty threshold, especially for households with dependent children, the child benefit package plays a particularly significant role in doing so. Universal child benefits provide immediate and stable income support at low administrative cost. They bring no disincentive to work or to move up the earnings ladder. Moreover, there exists a widely accepted rationale for child benefits as a cost compensation to parents for raising children, who have major collective benefits. In addition, overall child benefit packages—including more targeted supplements—for those on the lowest incomes tend to be higher in countries with (quasi-)universal cash benefits.

*Third, have a legally anchored, adequate, accessible social safety net*—There is a reason why social assistance schemes have existed for a long time and why they have proliferated in Europe and elsewhere in the world. Almost every European country now has a minimum income scheme codified in national law. For all their shortcomings and limitations, social assistance schemes have a demonstrated capacity for protecting people against severe material hardship. They provide an absolutely essential final safety net, at relatively low budgetary cost.

*Fourth, have more mildly targeted income supplements for lower income households, whether working or not*—Social assistance benefits, even in combination with generous child benefits, rarely suffice for non-working households in need of minimum income support. Similarly, even the highest minimum wages, combined with the lowest taxes and other levies, do not tend to provide single parents or single earners with other dependents with sufficient income for a living standard above the poverty line. Low-income targeted income supplements of various kinds can provide the final layers of additional support needed to lift otherwise poor households above the poverty line, tailored by need. Such benefits, for example child benefit or housing supplements, are ideally tapered at a more gradual rate than social assistance benefits so as to include the low-paid. Less severe tapers also help to dampen disincentives to work (more hours). Benefits restricted to those in work can make a transition to work financially extra attractive.

In short, we advocate a **multi-instrumental** and **multi-layered approach** and a redistributive approach that builds on the principle of **targeting within universalism.** We have at times compared this to a richly layered lasagne to contrast it to the silver bullet approaches advocated by others. Let us elaborate on the essential layers.

## 7.3 An Essential Precondition: Lift Wage Floors

It is hard to overstate how much this issue matters. Wage floors, as set through minimum wages or collective bargaining, obviously matter for workers. But as we discussed in Chapter 4 they also matter for the level of protection that can be provided to those out of work without compromising work incentives and violating the principle that work should bring greater reward than not being in work. If effective wage floors are low, then out-of-work benefits are almost inevitably low too, unless in-work benefits bring a significant net financial gain. In-work benefits at a significant level tend to be expensive, even if they are targeted at relatively low-paid workers. That is simply because so many people will qualify for them. If work intensity and promotion incentives are a concern, tapers have to be mild, further increasing the cost of in-work benefits, especially in settings with comparatively compressed wage distributions. The question of how to set wage floors is thus of crucial importance, as others have also forcefully stressed (Cantillon et al., 2020).

This brings to the issue of what is nowadays often referred to as 'predistribution'. The term is a bit of misnomer and seems to have been invented to avoid the word 'regulation' but that is, at least in part, what predistribution is about. It is about the institutions and regulations shaping market incomes. The notion, at one time the dominant one, that high wage floors—set through minimum wages or collective bargaining—are incompatible with good employment outcomes (high employment, low structural unemployment) does not fit the empirical evidence. It is hard to overstate the extent to which the simple trade-off ideas that dominated thinking for decades have been proven to be erroneous. A pile of labour economics research, some of it reviewed in Chapter 3, has long debunked the notion that decent wage floors are necessarily incompatible with good employment outcomes. That is not to say that wage floors are not harmful to employment from some level on—they are—but things are clearly more nuanced than once held.

The introduction of an ambitious minimum wage in Germany in 2015 has been particularly influential in solidifying the change in appreciation, especially among policy makers. This daring political move at the time brought real stakes to debates that had been raging among labour economists for decades. These essentially pitted the faithful to the neoclassical orthodoxy ('minimum wages destroy jobs') against the growing adherents of the 'new economics' of the minimum wage ('it's more complicated').

As the plan was being debated prior to 2015, there remained a very influential and vocal camp of German economists insisting that a significant minimum wage would come at the cost of job destruction, especially to the detriment of the low-skilled. It did not happen. The studies on the impact of the German minimum wage, and there are many, are relatively unambiguous on this point. Some studies have unearthed other effects, for example on working time, but it seems fair to say that the neoclassical orthodoxy was delivered an if not mortal then at the very least consequential blow, especially in the perception of policy agents, also at the European level.

By that time, influential think tanks like the OECD had already totally abandoned the neoclassical orthodoxy as it was once espoused in countless reports and recommendations. The OECD is now fully on board with the idea that 'minimum wages set at an appropriate level' do more good than bad. A study of prevailing opinions among members of the American Economic Association found that in 1990, 63% of economists agreed that: 'A minimum wage increases unemployment among young and unskilled workers.' In 2020 that was only 30%. That shift in the prevailing opinion (which admittedly remains far from a consensus opinion) has also trickled down into the political sphere, as is again evidenced by what is happening in the United States. Emboldened by accumulating and ever more sophisticated evidence that minimum wage hikes are not necessarily detrimental to employment, some states and cities have taken bold steps to increase minimum wages far above the national minimum. Increasing numbers of firms appear to be committing themselves towards paying 'living wages'.

There are of course still those who see harmful effects, especially in the longer term. And of course nobody will argue that there are no limits to lifting wage floors. At a certain point, jobs—or job growth—will be lost. They may force more people into the shadow economy or into (bogus) self-employment.

From a review of research looking into the employment effects of minimum wage increases, in preparation for a reassessment of the national living wage level in the UK, Dube (2019) concludes that past minimum wage increases of up to 60% of the median wage usually had no substantial adverse overall employment effects. Currently, very few of the countries discussed in Chapter 3 actually have such elevated minimum wage levels. Our analysis demonstrates that most minimum wages in the European countries find themselves in the ranges of 47–57% of the median wage, and 40–45% of the national average wage. For the best-performing countries in terms of providing adequate in-work income protection packages, in combination with modest poverty rates, minimum wages are generally at least around 50% of the median wage. In these countries, the minimum wage translates to over 130% of the at-risk-of-poverty threshold for a single person household. This is a level guaranteeing a decent living standard to a single person working full-time and it is also a level that in theory allows for an out-of-work minimum for a single person while maintaining a significant work incentive. Once there are multiple children and/or other dependents a single minimum wage income at that level will not suffice on its own to guarantee a decent living standard, even if taxed at a minimal rate. Income supplements will be needed as an additional layer of support.

## 7.4 Universal Benefits Can Provide an Important Layer of Support, but Only a Layer

Universal benefits, such as universal child benefits, have many advantages. A universal benefit is relatively easy to determine eligibility and once determined the payment can be made in a simple, timely manner. There is little bureaucracy involved, take-up rates tend to be high and there are no issues of stigma. People are sure that they can spend the money—they are not at risk of refund claims because of overpayments. There are no incentive issues, apart from a potential and presumably small income effect.[2] When everybody gets the same benefit it does not matter whether or not one works, and how much. Income or household changes will not affect the benefit. All that simplicity and predictability brings immense advantages.

But of course universal benefits are also quite costly, at least in a budgetary sense. From a poverty reduction perspective universal benefits are immensely wasteful since the bulk of the money goes to households not in poverty. Even a small amount has sizable public finance implications.

Universal child benefits tend to enjoy wide and robust political support in the countries which have them. They also seem to bring a level of unease among parts of the better off population receiving them. Some among the better off middle classes in countries with generous or at least sizeable (quasi-)universal child benefits wonder aloud why they are receiving government money that 'they do not really need' while there are still children growing up in poverty.

Now, a level of (self-) justification can be found in the fact that child benefits are not only there to prevent poverty but also to compensate for the cost of raising children. Children are public goods, as Nancy Folbre (1994) once argued. They will pay for the pensions of the generation raising them and they will provide them the goods, services, and care they need when they retire. Yet the costs of raising and educating children to become productive workers, taxpayers, and carers are of course largely private. That cost of child raising comes in a double form: a direct and an indirect one, notably in the form of reduced parental earnings over the lifetime. That mothers in particular can have very significant career and earnings penalties has been abundantly documented. People who do not have children and who devote no or little time to child-rearing are, at least in an economist's eye, essentially free-riding on parental labour, investment, and career self-sacrifice. That provides a very strong rationale for socializing part of the cost of raising children. Indeed, child benefits are in some countries very explicitly regarded as a cost compensation and not as an income supplement.

Basic income advocates have proposed rationales for extending such universality beyond children. These rationales are varied, some cleverly argued. But that is not to say that they have as yet much traction beyond intellectuals engaged in such debates. That means that while universal benefits, notably in the form of child benefits, can provide an important and crucial layer of minimum income protection, it can only be a layer. This is not to say that such a layer cannot be quite substantial indeed. Universal child benefits represent on average across the countries included in our analyses nearly 10% of the at-risk-of-poverty threshold for a lone parent with two children (and nearly 14% when excluding the seven countries that do not have a universal child benefit). Some of the better performing countries in terms of guaranteeing adequate income protection packages to lone parents with two children, have universal child benefits as high as 15% of the at-risk-of-poverty threshold.

Child benefits, entrenched and popular as they are in many countries, do lend themselves to a strategy of targeting within universalism whereby benefits (and services) are provided to all but where more goes to the most needy. Targeting can take the form of income tested or categorical supplements awarded on top of the (quasi-) universal entitlements. Such as an approach has the advantage of embedding targeted benefit within a bigger system. Indeed, analysis suggests that countries that employ a strategy of 'targeting within universalism' tend to do best (Aerts et al., 2022).

## 7.5 Social Assistance: A Time-Tested Provision

Poverty relief based on demonstrated need, modulated by criteria of deservingness and subject to conditions and sanctions has existed for hundreds of years. Some of the schemes in existence today have origins that can be traced well back to the middle ages, making them among the most enduring collective welfare arrangements in existence. In the present day needs-based income support mostly takes the form of rights-based social assistance, legally codified, regulated, and monitored at the national level but in many countries operated in a decentralized way, still leaving much scope for local autonomy (Janssens & Marchal, 2022).

Social assistance schemes remain relatively 'cheap'. They tend to account for less than 1 percentage of GDP in most—if not all—EU Member States (European Commission, 2022a), their cost usually dwarfed by expenditures for pensions, social insurance benefits, health care, etc. Social assistance may usually be small in spending terms but is among the most redistributive provisions even within extensive welfare states, as we demonstrated in Chapter 5. Insofar that social transfers are strongly redistributive towards the poor, it is usually social assistance driving the brunt of these transfers, even if they make up only a fraction of total expenditure.

Social assistance has its limits. Currently, there is not a single country where social assistance levels alone provides adequate protection against poverty. The most generous social assistance benefit levels for single persons are around 80–99% of the at-risk-of-poverty threshold. The most generous social assistance benefits for lone parent households are somewhat lower, and find themselves in the range of 50–80% of the at-risk-of-poverty threshold for a three-person household. Additional support measures bring the net minimum income protection packages for this household type well into the 80–90% of the at-risk-of-poverty threshold range in the more generous countries.

There are well-known downsides, which we have discussed at length in this book, but we should not forget that social assistance remains very important in offering a crucial buffer against extreme hardship. If it was not for this final safety net, extreme hardship would be very visible in the streets. The scores of undocumented migrants sleeping roughly in the streets of Europe and elsewhere serve as a daily reminder of the extreme hardship that not being entitled to final safety net provisions can bring.

There is somewhat of a tendency to overstate the problems with social assistance. Social assistance schemes have turned out to be remarkably durable and popular despite the many problems they are associated with. For all their (alleged) shortcomings, there has been a steady expansion of social assistance schemes in Europe and elsewhere. Italy and Spain are notable examples of countries having introduced nation-wide social assistance schemes fairly recently. There has been an even more impressive proliferation of social assistance schemes outside the developed world, in Latin America and parts of Africa and Asia (Barrientos, 2013, 2018, 2019; Leisering & Barrientos, 2013). Over recent decades, minimum income rights have become ever more strongly enshrined into law, even to some extent into constitutional law (Vonk & Olivier, 2019).

### 7.5.1 Work Incentives Are an Issue but Complexity, Low Take-Up and Inadequacy May Be the Bigger Problem

Work incentives in social assistance schemes are not good. After all, for every euro minimum income beneficiaries earn they lose in theory a euro in benefit, making the effective payoff to work zero until they earn enough to move off social assistance. That is theoretically true although many countries now have earnings disregards in one form or another, as we documented in Chapter 4. Still, there is no denying that work incentives in social assistance schemes generally do not look good.

But do they effectively trap people in dependence, thus worsening their capacity for self-reliance, as is widely feared? Researchers have a hard time isolating the causal effects of work incentives from other mechanisms influencing how long people remain dependent on benefits. Other factors appear to play a larger role in understanding dependence dynamics than the undeniably worrisome work incentives characteristic of social assistance schemes. As we have demonstrated in this book, minimum income benefits are highly inadequate in most countries. That raises the concern that people and their children may become severely impoverished and deprived after longer spells on minimum income support. The stress caused by deprivation, debts and constant money worries may progressively hamper them in regaining self-reliance. The way poverty hampers people's ability to function may for that reason well outweigh the isolated effect of any high marginal effective tax rates they are facing.

Policy makers may well have to worry more about the more impactful dysfunctional behavioural consequences of impoverishment than about work discouraging impact of severe benefit tapers. To put it more simply: the bigger problem may well be that benefits are too low than that they are too high (and too steeply tapered).

Still, activation policies in many countries are strongly predicated on the idea that financial incentives to 'make work pay' matter a lot. Policy analysts, and as a consequence policy makers, usually think and talk about work incentives on the basis of quite stylized representations of the realities of life on benefits. The work incentive graphs that adorn many a policy report usually assume a stable pre- and post- employment income situation. In reality, however, people's lives are unpredictable and that is particularly true for those on the fringes of the labour market.

Real life rarely conforms to such stylized assumptions. Temporary contracts, part-time work, or even flexible hour contracts, make it hard to predict the income for persons working in low-skilled, low-wage jobs. Also, there is the sheer complexity of many schemes. Income support and maintenance provisions in most rich countries are patchworks of different schemes introduced and reformed over time to cater to different needs and circumstances. They are sometimes administered by different agencies and at different levels of government. These subsystems sometimes cater to specific groups, such as families with children. Usually, there is the additional layer of complexity imposed by the tax system, especially when benefits are subject to taxation. All these systems together can make effective work incentives at various (potential) wage levels and work intensities very complicated indeed. It usually takes a highly educated policy analyst quite some time to figure out what the combined net pay-off to any transition into work really adds up to. The fact that entitlements of other household members may be affected adds yet another level of complexity, especially when work incentives are gauged at the household and not just the individual level.

Complex interactions between all these components and layers create 'bureaucratic traps', where rule complexity sometimes combined with opaque administrative practices and interpretations create a real or perceived risk of losing eligibility or delayed benefit payments. In addition to the work disincentives 'on paper', bureaucratic complexity can discourage risk-adverse, often cash-strapped, individuals from taking up work.

For all those reasons, simplicity and transparency are of the essence. This brings us to some specific recommendations.

### 7.5.2 Above All, Make Sure that People Get What They Are Entitled To

Adequate minimum income provisions are only helpful if they actually reach the intended target groups. Research shows that this is easier said than done. Non-take-up rates of means-tested benefits of last resort can be as high as 60%. Such low take-up obviously limits the expected effectiveness of the scheme in terms of poverty reduction.

Standard economic theory sees non-take-up as the result of a cost-benefit analysis, that rational prospective beneficiaries deem to be unfavourable: expected benefits are deemed too low to make a real difference in their lives, especially in relation to the process and hassle costs people have to go through when filing a claim, even more so when this claiming process can feel overly intrusive and stigmatizing.

Still, we know by now that many of the risk factors related to non-take-up surpass the individual level but are in fact for large part influenced by the design and implementation of benefits. Policy design can make sure that benefits are predictable and that claiming procedures are not overly taxing. At the implementation level, minor actions can already substantially reduce hassle costs that may lead people to postpone their claim. Extended opening hours, easily understandable information leaflets, or follow-up calls during a claiming process can make a real difference. Reforms like the ones that were undertaken in Finland and Austria, and discussed in Chapter 4, show that substantial improvements are possible. Finland has moved towards online applications and eligibility determination no longer involves meeting a social worker as a standard step in the procedure. Austria has made the claiming process more anonymous, also boosting effective take up.

### 7.5.3 Accept Spillover: There Are Limits to Targeting Minimum Income Support

As we have argued throughout this book, the better one tries to target minimum income protection on those in financial need and only on those in need, from exactly the moment that situation of need arises until it ends, the more complex a policy execution challenge it becomes.

'Real time' adjustment of benefits to changing incomes and household conditions in order to increase the 'target-efficiency' of social spending sounds appealing. But it remains much easier said than done. In theory, higher target efficiency holds the attractive prospect of being able to award more generous benefits to those in effective need for a given budget. In reality, attempts to adjust benefits at high frequency to changes in need have so far largely proved disappointing.

Social assistance schemes tend to operate means-tests that gauge current (monthly) incomes. Respondents are generally required to report changes in incomes and other circumstances immediately. In a volatile context in terms of incomes or household composition, such requirements often do more harm than good. Continuously reporting changes, which often also represent highly stressful periods in claimant's lives, adds to the burden placed on beneficiaries. To the extent that (conscious or unconscious) delays in such reporting are heavily sanctioned, such a requirement may further impede access to adequate support for needy families. Additionally, if benefits become less predictable due to their swift reactions to changing circumstances, budgeting challenges can become very pressing. Intensive means-testing will prevent beneficiaries to accumulate savings, for example from short work engagements, which could act as a buffer for the incomes of future months.

Policy makers are at their peril if they underestimate the complexity and fluidity of people's lives and if they overestimate the power of information technologies to deal with this complexity. A minimum income support system that reacts as fast as a thermostat does to changing temperatures probably remains illusory for some time to come. And it may not even be desirable either: people need a certain predictability when budgeting.

Erring on the side of generosity and forgiveness, especially at first, brings people a shock absorber for unexpected expenses and also some margin for error in the way they spend their money. In a later phase there is perhaps more scope to give higher priority to other objectives, such as stimulating steps towards more self-reliance. While there is a legitimate expectation that welfare beneficiaries live soberly and frugally, this is easier said than done. A shoe-string budget in combination with unpredictable real-life circumstances may well lead to suboptimal survival strategies, including debts. So it seems advisable to accept a level of redundancy. If our bigger concern is that people do not fall between the cracks or have to face hurtful delays (rather than maximum spending efficiency) then one has to accept some level of spill-over.

### 7.5.4 Do Not Obsess about Control

Similarly, do not obsess about control. A degree of monitoring and sanctioning is needed, if only to make schemes palatable to electorates. But fears that generous minimum income protection will inevitably breed a sizeable class of chronically dependent slackers have been much overblown. There is not much hard evidence to suggest that tight monitoring and intense sanctioning is a necessary precondition for close to adequate levels of minimum income support.

That is not to say that monitoring and sanctioning practices do not matter. They do, even if the effects are hard to disentangle from internalized norms of behaviour that are socialized through other, more subtle channels than formal bureaucratic procedures. But avoiding chronic or repeated dependency on minimum benefits clearly requires more than tight monitoring and sanctioning regimes. Research on social assistance dynamics shows that exit rates from social assistance are not simply reflective of activation zeal on the part of governments.

That is very clear in the case of new immigrants for example. The fact that there is high and often longer-term dependency among this demographic is largely a consequence of the multiple and often formidable hurdles they face in getting access to labour markets (especially decent jobs), affordable quality housing, social security rights, and so on. It is not that governments are not doing enough to 'activate' these people—it is simply the case that the opportunities for economic self-sufficiency and progression are often not sufficiently there. Harsh monitoring and sanctioning have limited effectiveness in such a context.

Workfare programmes, whereby people are required to perform certain jobs or duties in order to remain eligible, have yet to show any demonstrable purpose. Public or subsidized jobs, well-intentioned though they may be, are rarely effective in keeping people in employment after the subsidy ends. There is even evidence that employers are reluctant to recruit people with subsidized employment in their CV. This is not necessarily good enough reason not to deploy such programmes, but it is important to keep in mind that such programmes may have the reverse from the intended consequence.

The countries that manage to combine relatively adequate minimum income protection with good employment outcomes, including low levels of long-term or repeated dependency, do not do 'one thing right'. They do many things right. First and foremost, they have vibrant economies and open societies offering opportunities for economic improvement. The essential precondition for people not to become chronically and exclusively dependent on income support by the state is that there are better opportunities available than life on a minimum benefit, even if it just allows for a life in dignity. Most people aspire to more than that. But for that they need better alternatives. Concretely, that requires that decent jobs are sufficiently plentiful and that people effectively have access to such jobs, also if they have a migration background, if they have health issues, if they have been detached from the labour force for a while, if they are older or if they have other issues complicating their lives and capacity for self-reliance.

That requires that (decent) jobs are available and accessible and that people who are not readily equipped to take up work are assisted to do so. The countries that do well in terms of jobs and poverty have good public education as well as extensive arsenals of training and active labour market policies. They have accessible, good-quality services of various kinds to assist people in need of help in other areas than education, work, and income, be it for mental, physical, or other reasons.[3] They have flexible labour markets. They have institutions and policies that foster economic growth and dynamism.

This is not an exhaustive and perhaps in practical terms not even very helpful list ('so what do we need to be doing concretely?' one might legitimately ask) but the point here is that countries managing to combine comparatively adequate minimum income protection with good employment outcomes do not stand out in terms of their formalized monitoring and sanctioning practices. It is their broader socio-economic policy and institutional context which matters more.[4]

## 7.6 Have Layers of Mildly Targeted Supplements for Low Income Households

Targeted supplements allow for additional financial support on top of social assistance (or indeed social insurance) benefits or on top of earnings for those who need them to get to a decent income level. We know that social assistance benefits alone rarely suffice to bring people to the poverty line. Similarly, even the highest prevailing minimum wages (or effective wage floors) do not bring a single earner with dependent children or others to the poverty line.

Income supplements can take various forms and can be targeted by category, for instance to single parent households, by income, or by a combination of both. Such low-income and/or categorically targeted benefits are ideally tapered at a more gradual rate than social assistance benefits so as to include the low-paid. More gradual tapering also helps to dampen disincentives to work and to move up the earnings ladder, i.e. to seek promotion. Specific in-work benefits, for example relating to the costs associated with work, may make a transition to work financially extra attractive.

Many of the countries discussed in Chapters 2 and 3 have supplements to cover specific costs, or additional needs. These take the forms of means-tested child benefits, housing or heating allowances, or cash-like tax credits and in-work benefits. Evidently, means-tested child benefits are intended to support low-income families with the cost of raising children. In some countries, (part of) the means-tested component of their child benefits is even explicitly termed an education allowance, or disbursed at the start of the school year. Housing and heating allowances often depend on the housing costs that are actually paid by beneficiaries. Usually, a percentage of these housing costs are paid out as allowance. Generally, a cap applies to the share of housing costs that is compensated for in this way to discourage housing overconsumption. In some countries high housing costs may disqualify for the housing allowance altogether. Elsewhere, overconsumption is prevented by only compensating for housing costs of dwellings with specific characteristics (see also Chapter 2). In-work benefits are usually designed as top-ups to low wages, what is not ideal from a redistributive viewpoint since the low paid are not always working poor. In fact, in that they are secondary or tertiary earners in the household they may well be far above the poverty line. The actual level of in-work benefits may depend on the hours worked, the actual income level, but also of the presence and number of children in the household. While they can be disbursed through the tax system as tax allowances or tax credits, the terms are certainly not interchangeable. Some countries have cash-like tax credits that mirror (means-tested or universal) child benefits, elsewhere in-work benefits are implemented through a separate benefit scheme, necessitating separate claiming procedures.

To the extent that such targeted supplements are less stigmatizing and more generally available than means-tested minimum income support, they may offer a form of income protection to vulnerable households when they have not (yet) filed a claim for social assistance support. Individuals may also find it easier to identify themselves as entitled to benefits that are designed and 'marketed' as a way to support households with the cost of raising children, high housing cost burdens or to make work pay, rather than as needs-based social assistance. Self-identification as a potential beneficiary may come even more easily when these are more well-known and more broadly available schemes, that are not exclusively targeted towards the poorest.

Indeed, these benefits often cater to far wider target groups than pure social assistance benefits. The Dutch housing allowance system for instance, has recipiency rates that are three times as high as the number of social assistance beneficiaries (OECD SOCR, 2022). The design of its means-test ensures that also households with lower paid jobs, or more piecemeal labour market attachment, are eligible for relatively sizable benefits. Often, such targeted supplements have a very real impact on guaranteed net minimum income protection packages. In Ireland, the Netherlands, and France, for instance, targeted income supplements make up well over 30% of the guaranteed minimum income package for a full-time working single parent with children, bringing this family type's income above the at-risk-of-poverty threshold. As we further demonstrated in Chapter 3, and more specifically in Section 3.8.3, targeted supplements also bring persons with very piecemeal labour market attachment above or near the poverty threshold, more so than high minimum wages do. Here we should note that, the brunt of additional support to individuals with piecemeal labour market attachment still goes through social assistance top-ups, that, through earnings disregards in the means-test, allow for some combination of social assistance benefits and income from work. Such a design requires individuals to apply to social assistance benefits specifically, a step they may be less inclined to take if they perceive their needy situation as only temporary. Moreover, non-take-up is usually (even) higher among smaller social assistance top-up benefits, as the expected arduous claiming process compares unfavourable to the expected duration and amount of benefits. More automatic and less-stigmatizing broadly targeted cost-compensations or supplements, might remedy this situation.

It bears repeating that targeting comes at the cost of bureaucratic complexity and sometimes a level of stigma, resulting in potentially significant levels of non-take-up or incomplete take-up. Timeliness is also a serious issue: people do not always get the support when they need it. We therefore qualify this recommendation by pleading for mildness in targeting (see also Section 7.5.2). Income supplements can operate weaker tapers and milder means-tests than social assistance schemes, making them perhaps also less stigmatizing.

To make this concrete, some countries apply income tests on quarterly or previous years' incomes (with the possibility to get access if your current income is projected to be substantially below last year's). (Parts of) application procedures are more and more getting automated. Advances in information technology may make accurate, timely targeting more achievable than in the past. After all, governments nowadays have far richer and far more up to date information about people's circumstances and incomes. That, combined with advances in data processing capacity and artificial intelligence, may well improve the accurate and timely provision of well-targeted benefits.

Still, as we have argued in Chapter 4, overreliance on ICT brings news dangers. Automated Decision Making systems can compound the effects of simple errors. This is never trivial but even more so in the case of decisions that affect people's ability for economic survival. Also, existing patterns of prejudice, however subtle, can get incorporated into algorithms, effectively reproducing them with perhaps greater consistency than humans. Automation may thus reinforce existing forms of exclusion of, e.g., low-income families, minorities, or other persons at risk of exclusion. Mild targeting, already in the benefit design, may in turn also allow for more administrative simplification and increase the scope for less hazardous automation.

## 7.7 Final Reflections

### 7.7.1 Are Fully Integrated Systems the Next Step?

It seems to make a lot of sense to fully integrate schemes of minimum income protection for people who are not (yet) working and for people who are working but are having difficulties making ends meet on their earned income. Why have social assistance and then also a whole range of income targeted income supplements? Why not integrate everything into one scheme? Integrated schemes could after all help reduce complexity, bureaucratic redundancy, and improve work incentives, especially because people remain within the same system, working or not.

All that is true but there are drawbacks. The experience with the French RSA Activité or the German Arbeitlosengeld II—the means-tested part of German unemployment benefit system—shows that working people are reluctant to take up means-tested benefits primarily aimed at non-working people because of the associated stigma of being a 'welfare recipient'. So while on paper integrating systems makes sense, certainly from the perspective of transparency and alignment of incentives and bureaucratic ease, psychology may stand in the way. From that perspective it seems better to keep out-of-work and in-work benefits apart, although on-line procedures and even automatized allocation may help to reduce stigma.

Another drawback is that a fully integrated system, as exemplified by the UK's Universal Credit, for all its potential benefits of transparency, internal consistency, and bureaucratic efficiency, exposes people to a situation of all or nothing. If that single, integrated provision fails, people are left with nothing. In the case of a final safety net the consequences may well be disastrous, with potential further round effects worsening an already challenging situation. Think for example of potential eviction and a descent into problematic indebtedness. For children experiencing traumatic deprivation and upheaval due to a failing safety net the effects may well be long-lasting. From that perspective, multiple provisions reduce the chance of catastrophic failure, even if they bring administrative duplication and complex interactions. As we documented at some length in Chapter 4, the experience with the UK's Universal

Credit serves as sober reminder that there can be a big gap between what looks like a sound design on paper and what effectively works.

### 7.7.2 The Fiscalization of Minimum Income Protection Is Not the Future

Traditionally taxes serve to finance the functions of the state. But the personal tax system can also be used to do the reverse and to actually channel money to people. That has several potential advantages. It avoids unnecessary duplication of bureaucracy. Instead of having one bureaucracy to collect money and another to hand out transfers, you merge both into one. That also reduces the chance that people will be given with one hand while another hand takes from them later. It thus also opens up the possibility to design work incentives in smarter and more transparent ways. Add to that the fact that there is far more administrative data on people's incomes and living arrangements available and that ICT capacity to process that data fast has taken enormous strides, aided in part by sophisticated automated algorithms and artificial intelligence. The potential to use the tax system to get money to people in an efficient and accurate way seems to hold promise.

Let us remind us of what Lane Kenworthy wrote in 2011 in *Progress for the Poor*, 'Given the importance of employment and working hours for the market incomes of low-end households, policy makers must guard against programs that provide attractive benefits without encouraging or requiring employment. An ideal transfer would be one that both boosts the incomes of low-earning households and promotes employment by able working-aged adults. As it happens such a program exists. Referred to variously as "in-work benefit" or "employment-conditional earnings subsidy", it is best exemplified by the Working Tax Credit (WTC) in the United Kingdom and the Earned Income Credit (EITC) in the United States' (Kenworthy, 2011, p. 44). Around the same time the OECD's Herwig Immervoll and Mark Pearson (2009) wrote that while such schemes were for a long time seen as 'interesting but unusual' they were destined to become mainstream policies.

For a time EITC/Working Tax Credit type schemes did seem very promising. But that promise has not quite materialized. Few countries have introduced an EITC type scheme of any serious magnitude. The UK has moved away from the tax credits that got expanded as part of Tony Blair's Third Way. Why is this? There are many reasons.

A first reason is that such schemes essentially rest on the idea that there is work for everybody. Perhaps not stable, full-time let alone well-paid work but at least some work, even if it is temporary, part-time, and badly remunerated. But once someone puts in some minimum amount of work, the tax systems kicks in and it supplements that earned income, as a 'reward' and as channel of direct minimum income support. The obvious downside of course is that this keeps people who are unable to find any work out in the cold. That is certainly what the US experience has taught us. While the EITC is of demonstrable help to those who find (relatively steady) employment, it does nothing for those unable to work or unable to find work. That has left many of the poor in the US completely destitute, especially since the expansion of EITC there came at the cost of draconian cuts in what is there called 'welfare', i.e. means-tested minimum income protection.

If the concern is primarily with work incentives and 'making work pay' then an EITC type scheme has much to be said for it. But if the primary concern is with providing adequate protection against poverty than such a scheme cannot be relied upon. It just does not reach the most vulnerable, those most in need, those furthest away from the labour market. That is not to say that EITC type schemes have no role to play as a potential channel of minimum income support, especially for those who cannot make ends meet on work alone, but they cannot substitute for schemes that reach the most needy.

What then about the role of such working tax credits as channels of income support for those in work? In-work poverty was for a long time an ignored reality, in Europe especially. That has changed. There is a full awareness nowadays that a sizeable section of the working age population living in poverty or at risk of poverty is actually for the most part working. That more needs to be done for the working poor is an accepted tenet of policy. Indeed, principle 6 of the European Pillar of Social Rights explicitly acknowledges this.

Refundable tax credits seem a very sensible way of supporting the working poor. Indeed, this is what the EITC in the US does well to a significant extent. But there are important problems too. First, there are quite serious issues of non-take up. EITC, as a provision within the already complex personal tax system, is not sufficiently widely known and understood. That leads to take up rates far below the number of people entitled. Even if people apply and qualify, the tax refund arrives only after a long delay, possibly much later than when people actually need the income support. Second, an EITC type scheme discourages work effort in the phase-out zone of the benefit. After people receive the maximum they only have a limited financial pay-off to working longer hours or to seeking a promotion and higher earnings. Finally, there are concerns that systems like EITC may be exacerbating the actual underlying problem of inadequate pay. EITC is thought to make workers more reluctant to bargain for higher wages and employers less inclined to pay higher wages, knowing that the state will bail them out. The subsidy to workers is thus in effect—at least partially—captured by employers through reduced wages. Those are some of the reasons why EITC is seen as a qualified success even in the US, where it is now the largest anti-poverty programme by far.

There are additional reasons why an EITC type scheme as a main anti-poverty transfer is unlikely to take hold in much of Europe. Earnings inequality tends to be far smaller in most European countries and so to be affordable within reasonable limits, an EITC type tax credit would have to be strongly targeted because otherwise too many households would qualify. However, such strong targeting may create prohibitive mobility traps which can only be avoided if taper-off rates are made sufficiently flat. But that comes at a very considerable cost if the lower end of the (household) earnings distribution is densely populated, as is the case in many European countries. This cost can only be avoided by making the amount of the tax credit itself smaller, but in that case the anti-poverty effect is reduced.

Moreover, many European countries have moved away from joint taxation of couples towards more individualized taxation. In order to be effective as an anti-poverty measure it is absolutely crucial that refundable tax credits are targeted towards low earning households and not low earning individuals. Individualized taxation does not preclude household income based (refundable) tax credits but makes it less straightforward.

### 7.7.3 Basic Income Is Likely to Remain a Mirage

As we discussed in Chapter 6, it is hard to imagine a more ironclad guarantee against poverty than a universal basic income, if set high enough. Basic income has gained remarkable traction in societal debates. That is encouraging in many ways. It shows that people can warm to the idea of basic economic rights for every citizen, without conditions or restrictions, regardless of circumstance or personal responsibility.

But the reality is also that very few people grasp what a basic income would actually mean, for themselves, their households and the societies they live in. A basic income of some significance (in the order of 10% or 20% of GDP, as some propose) would not only be an intervention of monumental proportions, it would also be far more complicated that many people, including BI advocates, seem to realize.

Below that gleaming, appealing tip of simplicity, there is a murky mass of complex choices to be made and interactions to be accounted for. The exact specification of the BI matters a great deal. Which parts of the existing tax/benefit system are maintained? What is abolished, modified, or replaced? Is a BI made taxable? Is eligibility to other benefits affected by a BI, for example through a means-test? All these choices matter for outcomes, even apparently 'minor' choices matter. Depending on how exactly a BI is specified, the effects may vary a lot. What people get in a society with a significant basic income may be very different from what they wish for.

For one, a higher BI will not necessarily bring fewer people living in poverty than a more modest one. This would be the case when much of that BI was financed through personal income taxation, which would be the most realistic way of financing the bulk of a substantial basic income in most countries.

Microsimulations invariably show basic income schemes bringing substantial to large losses to important segments of the population, including disadvantaged groups falling deeper into poverty under some scenarios. The higher the basic income, the more polarized the distributional outcomes tend to be, with some sections of the population incurring big losses and other sections having large gains. That makes political feasibility if not doubtful than at the very least far from straightforward let alone conflict-free.

Partial schemes which retain the existing benefits, taxes, and tapers largely avoid such losses but fail to achieve many of BI's broader goals—including drastic reductions in bureaucratic complexity and the minimization of poverty and unemployment traps. Martinelli (2017b) has rightfully concluded that 'an affordable UBI would be inadequate, and an adequate UBI would be unaffordable'.

Add to this that the longer-term effects remain highly uncertain. It is certainly true that the wealth of (quasi-)experimental and econometric evidence that has been gathered does not support fears of a collapse in work effort. Some simulations do however suggest that a substantial basic income would have a negative impact on labour participation among some segments of the workforce, especially among women in multi-earner households, which is not irrelevant from a gender perspective. Even so, if fewer people do jobs that they do not want to do that could be seen as a societal gain. Yet, while fears of people quitting jobs in great numbers may be overblown, there is also not much hard evidence that a BI would make people more entrepreneurial, more caring or more civic, even if it brings them a greater peace of mind and sense of security.

### 7.7.4 The Answer Is Layers and Bold Incrementalism

To conclude, let us just reiterate that we do not believe that improved minimum income protection and eventually a society largely free from poverty will come from silver-bullet approaches in the shape of a Basic Income, a Universal Credit type integrated provision, or another all-encompassing solution. Rather, we believe in a multi-layered and multi-instrumental approached, tailored to context. We believe that incremental steps towards more decent and eventually adequate income floors is the way forward. Even if it does not quite get us to a Zero Poverty Society, it should bring us far.

The way forward is to draw from what actually, demonstrably works in some countries and to build on that. There is no reason for holding back taking steps in that direction. Some of the best performing countries when it comes to providing adequate protection against poverty also have exemplary economic outcomes, sustainable public finances, and well-functioning labour markets.

Yet it is also true that even if policy makers are not facing some gloomy, inescapable trade-off between 'Equity and Efficiency', to use Arthur Okun's famed expression, the conditions under which adequate social protection and a thriving economy go hand in hand are not necessarily easily emulated everywhere. But we never said that social progress comes easy, risk-free, and overnight. It does, however, lie in our own hands.

# Notes

## Chapter 1

1. For discussions on minimum income protection for other target groups, such as the disabled or the elderly, we refer the reader to Bahle et al. (2011); Marx and Nelson (2013); and Goedemé and Marchal (2016).
2. Note that this is a fairly weak interpretation of a legal guarantee. In fact, we focus here on legally guaranteed as a matter of intent rather than outcome. In contrast, Panican and Ulmestig (2016) identify the following aspects in order to be considered a social right: (i) a clear legislative basis; (ii) a right and power to appeal; and (iii) legal enforceability of this right. According to these strict rules, that not only look at 'de jure' social rights, but also how they are translated 'de facto', they argue that social assistance is not a strong social right in Sweden, a fact they explain by referring to its poor-relief roots. They argue that social rights are far more at risk than civil and political rights, as they follow a different logic (protection from the state vis-à-vis social protection provided by the state). An echo of this attention to actual implementation is found in Leibetseder et al. (2017), who argue that social assistance only contributes to social citizenship if territorial subsidiarity and social worker discretion is restricted, and social assistance is part of a well-functioning broader welfare state. Whereas we do acknowledge the importance of taking actual implementation into account, we do consider minimum income protection that is only guaranteed de jure already a clear departure from traditional charity relief, meriting the inclusion of such schemes in this analysis. Still, and as we will consider in the remainder of this book, the actual implementation of these schemes is evidently key, in order to assess their practical relevance.
3. Note that in some countries there is no reference to social rights in the constitution (or there did not use to be), and specific legislation is the only legal basis available for guaranteeing certain minimum income provisions.
4. Clearly, there are important differences in constitutions (and their use and interpretation) between countries. In Germany, for instance, two principles mentioned in the Base Law are consistently interpreted by the Federal Constitutional Court as together constituting a right to a subsistence minimum: the definition of Germany as a Social state, and the right to human dignity. Over time, the Federal Constitutional Court has played an active role in invoking these principles in court cases questioning the legality of certain reforms in the German minimum income protection schemes for the non-working or for asylum seekers. In its jurisprudence, the Court has sometimes ruled existing benefit values inadequate in light of these two principles and made reference to the elements a subsistence minimum would need to cover, urging the Government to make adjustments within a certain time period, rather than putting forward an actual monetary value (Leijten, 2015; Eichenhofer, 2016). Recently, the Federal Constitutional Court has ruled that certain sanctions in the minimum income scheme for the non-working are not in line with the constitutional principles (Bundesverfassungsgericht, 2019).

5. The identification of Rowntree with the absolute approach seems to have been based on a misunderstanding of his work, see Veit-Wilson (1986), but this does not matter very much for the argument at this point.
6. In its action plan for the implementation of the European Pillar of Social Rights, the European Commission aims to reduce the number of people at risk of poverty or social exclusion by at least 15 million by 2030, 5 million of which should be children (European Commission, 2021). Among the measures proposed to actually reach these targets are the promotion of adequate wages and working conditions. Minimum income schemes are considered essential to ensure that no one is left behind.
7. This official poverty threshold used by the Central Bureau of Statistics is equal to the indexed value of the social assistance benefit level in 1979 (https://www.cbs.nl/nl-nl/onze-diensten/methoden/begrippen/lage-inkomensgrens).
8. Do note that this more absolute poverty concept still requires the identification of individuals and households who fail to reach 'adequate social participation in the relevant national societies' (Menyhert et al., 2021, p. 171).

## Chapter 2

1. We discuss country trajectories until Autumn 2022, unless otherwise indicated.
2. However, note that Van Lancker et al. (2020) analyse the scope of various sources of primary EU legislation, and conclude that a legal basis for a binding framework directive on minimum income can be found.
3. Since the time of writing, Germany substantially overhauled its minimum income scheme through the introduction of the Bürgergeld (Federal Ministry of Labour and Social Affairs, 2023).
4. Self-evidently, there are limits to these pre-post analyses. The EU SILC survey that is commonly used to carry out a pre-post analysis does not clearly distinguish between minimum income protection and other benefits. In addition, the counterfactual situation of no social assistance protection does not have a clear relation to reality. Likely, potential beneficiaries would modify their behaviour if there would be no benefit of last resort at all.
5. In addition van de Ven et al. (2017) also calculate tax implicit equivalence scales for higher incomes, and they track how tax implicit equivalence scales change with rising incomes.
6. Similarly, the original OECD scale, with additional adults valued at 0.7, and additional children at 0.5, was proposed by the OECD for cases where no national equivalence scales were available, and for international comparisons. An alternative equivalence scale that is commonly used in international research is the square root scale, where household incomes are made comparable by dividing the income by the square root of the number of household members (Immervoll, 2009).
7. The empirical basis is relatively limited: it is a middle way between relatively low subjective scales calculated by Hagenaars, De Vos, and Zaidi (1994) and the old OECD equivalence scale. Still, it is commonly used due to its transparency. However, its common use may lead us to lose sight of their pragmatic nature. Similarly, as the differences between the countries under investigation widen, the use of a single equivalence scale may confound rather than enlighten results. (See for instance Brandolini, 2006 for a comparison of EU15 and EU12 countries based on the old and modified OECD scale.)

8. Marchal and Van Mechelen (2017) found for instance that more punitive activation measures, such as sanctions and workfare requirements, were more common in the Eastern European countries.
9. This is for instance the case in Denmark, both before and after the January 2023 reform. In spite of the recommendations made by the Minimum Income Benefit Commission in preparation of the reform, benefit ceilings were not abolished, although policy makers did take efforts to simplify the application of the benefit ceiling (Kvist, 2022).
10. Hence, the hypothetical household simulations in Figure 2.1 ultimately give a very rosy picture of the actual generosity of minimum income protection.
11. Please note that this is not a unique feature. Eight more countries have similar schemes for all considered family types in MIPI-HHoT.
12. This is sometimes coped with by the existence of 'passport benefits'. Means-tested minimum income receipt can then immediately, and ideally also automatically, lead to eligibility for related benefits, such as housing cost related parts of social assistance, or heating allowances.
13. Again, we must note that these four countries are not exceptional in this regard. Rather, we focus here on the commonalities between these four countries, expecting that the *combined* implementation of these practices aids in securing relatively generous minimum income protection packages.
14. In the general social assistance scheme, that does not explicitly focus on those able to work, and is therefore not shown in Figure 2.1, family benefits are included in the means-test.
15. In 2021, the Danish minimum income scheme does not allow assets higher than around 1300 euro for a single person. In the Netherlands the threshold is at 6295 euro, with (rather atypically) the possibility to also partially assess the family home. In Finland, distinction is made between the (non-asset-tested) labour market subsidy, and the actual social assistance benefit, that may additionally be relevant for those who are in dire need. The latter only disregards the permanent residence, households goods, and goods used at work or in study. However, there is an important discretionary component in this assessment. Finally, Austria requires assets to be depleted until a threshold of around 4700 euro (de Vos, 2021; Greve & Azhar Hussain, 2021; Premrov & Fuchs, 2021; Räsanen & Simanainen, 2021).

## Chapter 3

1. High collective bargaining coverage may result from high levels of union membership but also from extension mechanisms ('erga omnes' clauses) being in place.
2. At its introduction the German minimum wage affected around one in 10 workers (Bruttel, 2019).
3. Research has speculated on the reasons behind the enormous cross-national variation in wage dispersion, even in countries with comparable employment rates. It appears puzzling, for example, that European workers in the bottom wage decile sometimes earn more than twice as much as Americans in a similar position while they are hardly more likely (or even less likely) to be unemployed or non-employed. One hypothesis is that many European countries have education and training systems that succeed better in educating wide sections of the population and giving them productive skills. The thesis

that cross-national differences in earnings inequality are in large part reflective of skill formation differences has some empirical backing but is not uncontested (see for example Paccagnella, 2015).

4. Note that the wage concepts are not fully comparable. The average and median wage concepts also include overtime pay and bonuses, which are not included in the minimum wage.
5. The correlation between the relative minimum wage level and the share of employees earning below 90% is only 0.2, whereas it is around 0.45 for those paid around the minimum wage.
6. Note that the hypothetical household simulations assume that when a household is eligible to a certain benefit, they will successfully take all the actions needed to also receive this benefit. Studies on non-take-up have shown that such behaviour is not self-evident. This is especially the case when the expected benefits are small. This may very well be so in the case of working households, where benefits may only represent small top-ups (see also Chapter 2). The information in Figure 3.2 therefore represents a 'best-case' scenario.
7. The value under the means-tested child benefit for the United States in Figure 3.2, panel B shows the impact of the child tax credit.
8. Wilson (2017) highlights the importance of this argument in the policy debate in liberal welfare states.
9. In Section 3.4, we referred to Schmitz (2019) who found that the minimum wage introduction in Germany effectively led to fewer welfare recipients, because of this mechanism. Note that Germany is not included in Figure 3.5, as the minimum wage was not yet introduced in 2009.
10. In a research note focusing on the situation in Ireland, McGuinness et al. (2020) benefit from a specific question in the Labour Force Survey that asks below minimum wage earners why their wage does not reflect the statutory minimum wage. They find that in the brunt of cases legally valid reasons—i.e. because of the various exemptions allowed under the minimum wage law—are responsible for below minimum wage rates. Evidently, these findings only relate to the situation in Ireland. Still, one could expect that also in other countries, exemptions may explain at least some part of the observed non-compliance with the minimum wage.
11. This wage rate is derived from the most common earnings of platform workers reported in Piasna et al. (2022). In reality, such earnings will most often be combined with earnings from other sources. We therefore provide here merely an illustration of the workings of the tax benefit system in what could be considered a 'worst case' scenario. For technical reasons, we also have to assume that this situation lasts for a full year (in order to be able to calculate personal income taxes), whereas in reality, the earnings of persons in non-standard work forms may be far more volatile. While this may increase their annual incomes, it also poses additional challenges in terms of the claiming and correct calculation of eligibility to additional supportive benefits. We refer readers who would be interested in estimates of net disposable income under different wage and working time assumptions to the appendix of the report by the European Commission and Social Protection Committee (2022).
12. The graph also includes non-minimum wage countries. For these countries we assume the total working time to be the EU average of 17 hours per week.
13. It should additionally be noted that the Romanian and Greek minimum wage are far less outstanding relative to the alternative benchmarks of median and average wages (see

Table 3.2). Similarly, the Spanish minimum wage is relatively low, when compared to the overall Spanish wage distribution. Median equivalent incomes are indeed driven by far more elements than solely median wages, including non-wage incomes, household composition, and labour market participation (Nolan, 2020). A number of countries, in particular Romania and Greece and Croatia, have surprisingly high minimum wages when expressed as a percentage of the poverty threshold, a fact that stems from very low median equivalent incomes and poverty lines, relative to the median wage. This is partially due to a combination of high minimum wage levels (often in a context of a large grey economy and multiple exceptions for specific target groups), but mainly stems from low median equivalent incomes relative to median wages, due to the factors described above. Indeed, there are indications that the EU at-risk-of-poverty threshold might for certain countries do less well in capturing real poverty. A comparison with needs-based reference budgets shows that incomes at the 60% at risk of poverty threshold would only cover a fraction of the needed budget to fully participate in society (see Goedemé et al., 2019). This observation is in line with the large share of minimum wage earners in Greece and Croatia (and other Southern and Eastern EU Member States) that indicate that they have trouble making ends meet (see Eurofound, 2020b), despite the relatively high minimum wage and net minimum wage levels reported for those countries in Figure 3.2.

## Chapter 4

1. Laenen, Marchal, and Van Lancker (forthcoming) report in their study on the relationship between targeting design, targeting outcomes and targeting preferences widely varying preferences regarding the targeting of unemployment benefits and income taxes. Using data from the European Social Survey, they show that, on average across the 31 European countries included in their study, around 12% is in favour of higher benefits for previously low earners when becoming unemployed, 56% is in favour of a flat-rate benefit, and 32% supports higher benefits for previously higher earnings. In addition, while most respondents are in favour of a progressive tax system, on average, 42.6% of the population supports proportional taxes, and a further 7% is even in favour of a lump-sum tax. Clearly, respondents have different views and preferences regarding optimal targeting design.
2. In fact, the book was dismissed in the New York Times by one reviewer as 'right-wing polemic masquerading as dispassionate social science', echoing a widely held sentiment among social scientists. Nevertheless the book spent 15 weeks on the *New York Times* Bestseller list.
3. This has led some to rather strong conclusions. Beaulier and Caplan (2007), to take one example, have argued: 'Existing literature provides good reasons to think that the deviations of the poor from the standard neoclassical model are especially pronounced. Their judgmental biases are more extreme, and their self-control problems more severe, than those of the rest of the population. Standard neoclassical theory is unusually likely to mislead us when we analyze policies intended to assist the disadvantaged' (p. 494).
4. Some studies find much more severe consequences of stigma. One American study (Pak, 2020) found welfare stigma to be as a risk factor for major depressive disorder. The study found that Food stamp participation in the US was associated with significant increases in depressive symptoms and higher odds of major depression, especially among men,

middle-aged adults, Whites, and those without disability. In other words, among those most likely to be stigmatized by the social norm for not being able to rise above poverty.

5. There are many qualitative studies on the experience of being a welfare applicant, see for instance Jun (2022) and Baumberg (2016) for overviews.
6. In part by design. Under the design of UC new claimants must wait for five weeks for their first payment.
7. Clinton said about Murray in 1993, 'He did the country a great service. I mean, he and I have often disagreed, but I think his analysis is essentially right' (NBC News interview 12/3/93, Clinton Library).
8. See inter alia Biegert (2017); Brady (2019); and Biegert et al. (2022).
9. Most countries have a general scheme, which means that people end up in social assistance for various reasons. Some countries do make a distinction between people able to work, or not. Or they have even separate schemes for groups as specific as asylum seekers or single parents, but these are in fact the minority of countries.
10. Specifically, they omit business cycle controls and broaden the sample to include all unmarried women. The study uses a different outcome variable: whether single mothers overall reported working in the previous week as opposed to during the year. They argue that this empirical approach is preferable because the business cycle likely affects single women with children differently than those without children, and because it is preferable to investigate the impact of the EITC on individuals with low levels of education, as it is the EITCs main target population. Including individuals with high education levels, who generally earn too much to be eligible for the EITC, is claimed to attenuate the true policy effect.
11. Microsimulation exercises conducted a decade ago, for example by Bargain and Orsini (2007) for Germany, France, and Finland, by Figari (2010) for four southern European countries (Italy, Spain, Portugal, and Greece) and by Marx et al. (2012) and Vandelannoote and Verbist (2019) for Belgium all shed doubt over the feasibility of sizeable refundable tax credits similar to EITC.

## Chapter 5

1. Indeed, it seems impossible to fit together the trajectories of any of the Southern European in a single narrative, cf. Aguilar-Hendrickson and Arriba González de Durana (2020b); Aguilar-Hendrickson and Arriba González de Durana (2020a); Matsaganis (2020).
2. One criticism was that Korpi and Palme gauged redistributive impact by comparing the observed income distribution with a very rudimentary counterfactual 'pre-transfer' distribution whereby that pre-transfer distribution was simply approximated by deducting observed social transfers and re-adding observed taxes. Such an approach, which is still widely used by scholars of inequality, clearly makes abstraction of any behavioural effects that a change in the tax/benefit benefits may entail. Unemployed people might well look harder for work or accept less appealing jobs if their benefit was taken away from them. People might well retire later and save more if public pensions ceased to exist. While such criticisms are perfectly valid, the reality is that no satisfactory method exists to model such behavioural effects with any degree of validity, except perhaps for very marginal deviations.

3. Cash assistance allocations from Temporary Assistance for Needy Families (TANF) and its predecessor programme fell from $34.3 billion to $7.4 billion in real value from 1993 to 2016, a 78% decrease (Parolin, 2021).

## Chapter 6

1. Laín (2022) reports that experiments have taken place in places such as Namibia, Finland, Barcelona, the Netherlands, Canada, Iran, and India. Others are still running in the USA, Kenya, Uganda, Macau, Brazil, and South Korea, while others are being designed in Germany, France, Wales, Scotland, and Catalonia, and that list is not exhaustive.
2. That depends on the exact specification of the Basic Income and its interaction with existing benefits. In the case of a partial basic income means-tested top-ups are likely to remain necessary (see Aerts et al. 2022).
3. In the Brown and Immervoll exercise the BI amount is also adjusted up or down to make the reform budget-neutral.
4. Note also that the Finnish basic income experiment was not a pure RCT because in the second experiment year (2018), the government introduced a punitive labour market activation reform that forced the standard UB recipients in the control group to seek work or have their benefits cut. The year before the ALMP reform (2017) no statistically significant difference in employment between control and treatment group could be found. The year after the ALMP reform (2018), the control group (standard UB recipients under punitive ALMP) worked less than treatment group (basic income recipients). Basic income did not have substantive employment effects but increasing the conditionality of standard unemployment benefit apparently made things worse for that group. Comparing the effect of two policy changes at the same time makes it very hard to establish any causality which is also why the Finnish BI reports tend to be so careful in their conclusions.
5. Even the most ambitious, progressive proposals on wealth taxes do not raise anywhere near enough to finance a substantial basic income, see for example Landais et al. (2020).
6. We refer here to the thoughtful analysis by Daniel Dumont (2022), who contrasts principles in contemporary social protection systems with an ideal typical basic income. He concludes that while the difficulties of contemporary social protection systems identified by basic income proponents are relevant, a basic income cannot be considered 'the most convincing solution' to these ailments. Rather, he proposes to use some of the main basic income claims as inspiration to update social insurance systems.

## Chapter 7

1. See among other scholars Cantillon and Van Lancker (2013); Nolan (2013); and Parolin and Van Lancker (2021). See also the reply by Parolin and Van Lancker (2021).
2. This has been an important point of contention in debates over the effects of the Biden Child Tax Credit expansion during the COVID19 pandemic. Powerful political forces opposed the extension of the measure on grounds that it would reduce labour supply. Yet little evidence was found for that, see Enriquez et al. (2023) and references therein.

3. Not all of these points are elaborated in this volume. This is based on our reading of the expansive empirical welfare state literature we have today. For good overviews we refer to the writings of Lane Kenworthy (Kenworthy, 2004, 2008, 2011, 2014, 2020, 2022).
4. There is an enormous literature on this topic of course. Perhaps the most comprehensive analysis of what sets successful welfare states apart from less successful ones is to be found in Lane Kenworthy series of books on the topic. See Kenworthy 2004, 2008, 2011, 2014, 2020, 2022.

# References


Adema, W. (2012). Setting the scene: The mix of family policy objectives and packages across the OECD. *Children and Youth Services Review*, *34*(3), 487–498. doi:10.1016/j.childyouth.2011.10.007.

Aerts, E., Marx, I., & Parolin, Z. (2022). Income support policies for single parents in Europe and the U.S.: What works best? *The ANNALS of the American Academy of Political and Social Science*, *702*(1), 55–76. doi:10.1177/00027162221120448.

Aerts, E., Marx, I., & Verbist, G. (2023). Not that basic: how level, design, and context matter for the redistributive outcomes of universal basic income. *Journal of Social Policy*. Published online 2023: 1–23. doi:10.1017/S0047279423000582.

Aguilar-Hendrickson, M., & Arriba González de Durana, A. (2020a). Out of the wilderness? The coming back of the debate on minimum income in Spain and the Great Recession. *Social Policy & Administration*, *54*(4), 556–573. doi:10.1111/spol.12605.

Aguilar-Hendrickson, M., & Arriba González de Durana, A. (2020b). The politics of safety net reform in Southern Europe during the Great Recession: Introduction to the regional issue. *Social Policy & Administration*, *54*(4), 533–538. doi:10.1111/spol.12609.

Aidukaite, J., Saxonberg, S., Szelewa, D., & Szikra, D. (2021). Social policy in the face of a global pandemic: Policy responses to the COVID-19 crisis in Central and Eastern Europe. *Social Policy & Administration*, *55*(2), 358–373. doi:10.1111/spol.12704.

Akarçeşme, S., Aranguiz, A., Lemmens, A., & Cantillon, B. (2023). Reaching the European Social Targets: The Need for Better Balanced Power Resources (EUSOCIALCIT Working Paper D5.5). Amsterdam: UvA.

Alesina, A., Glaeser, E., & Glaeser, E. L. (2004). *Fighting poverty in the US and Europe: A World of Difference*. Oxford: Oxford University Press.

Alm, S., Nelson, K., & Nieuwenhuis, R. (2020). The diminishing power of one? Welfare state retrenchment and rising poverty of single-adult households in Sweden 1988–2011. *European Sociological Review*, *36*(2), 198–217.

Alsos, K., Nergaard, K., & Van Den Heuvel, A. (2019). Collective bargaining as a tool to ensure a living wage. Experiences from the Nordic countries. *Transfer: European Review of Labour and Research*, *25*(3), 351–365.

Anderson, S. G. (2002). Ensuring the stability of welfare-to-work exits: The importance of recipient knowledge about work incentives. *Social Work*, *47*(2), 162–170.

Andor, L. (2020). EU minimum wage: Why now? *The progressive post*. Retrieved from https://progressivepost.eu/progressive-page/eu-minimum-wage-why-now.

Anne, D., & L'Horty, Y. (2012). The RSA (Revenu de solidarité active) and back-to-work incentives in France. *International Social Security Review*, *65*(3), 77–100. doi:10.1111/j.1468-246X.2012.01437.x.

Aprea, M., Gallo, G., & Raitano, M. (2022). Why Social Benefits Fail to Target Poverty. Empirical Evidence on Target Efficiency of the Italian Minimum Income Scheme. Paper presented at the 2022 ESPANET conference, Vienna.

Aranguiz, A. (2022). *Combating Poverty and Social Exclusion in European Union Law*. Abingdon/New York: Routledge Taylor and Francis Group.

Arlotti, M., & Sabatinelli, S. (2017). Assessing income support where no national minimum income scheme exists. Is it possible to apply the model family method to the Italian case? *International Review of Sociology*, *27*(1), 142–159. doi:10.1080/03906701.2016.1259125.

Arriba, A., & Ibáñez, Z. (2002). Minimum Income Guarantee and Social Assistance (Unidad de Políticas Comparadas Working Paper 02–12). Madrid: Unidad de Políticas Comparadas (CSIC). Retrieved from https://digital.csic.es/bitstream/10261/1526/1/minimum_social_assistance.pdf.

Arriba, A., & Moreno, L. (2005). Spain—poverty, social exclusion and 'safety nets'. In M. Ferrera (ed.), *Welfare State Reform in Southern Europe: Fighting Poverty and Social Exclusion in Italy, Portugal, Spain and Greece* (pp. 141–160). Abingdon, Oxon: Routledge.

Ashenfelter, O., & Card, D. (2010). *Handbook of Labor Economics*. North Holland: Elsevier.

Atkinson, A. B. (2015). *Inequality: What Can Be Done?* Cambridge, MA: Harvard University Press.

Atkinson, A. B., & Bourguignon, F. (2014). *Handbook of Income Distribution*. New York: Elsevier Science.

Atkinson, A. B., Leventi, C., Nolan, B., Sutherland, H., & Tasseva, I. (2017). Reducing poverty and inequality through tax-benefit reform and the minimum wage: The UK as a case-study. *The Journal of Economic Inequality*, *15*(4), 303–323. doi:10.1007/s10888-017-9365-7.

Atkinson, A. B., Piketty, T., & Saez, E. (2011). Top incomes in the long run of history. *Journal of Economic Literature*, *49*(1), 3–71. doi:10.1257/jel.49.1.3.

Atkinson, A. B., Rainwater, L., & Smeeding, T. M. (1995). Income Distribution in Advanced Economies: Evidence from the Luxembourg Income Study (LIS). *LIS Working papers*.

Attree, P. (2004). Growing up in disadvantage: A systematic review of the qualitative evidence. *Child Care Health and Development*, *30*(6), 679–689. doi:10.1111/j.1365-2214.2004.00480.x.

Attree, P. (2006). The social costs of child poverty: A systematic review of the qualitative evidence. *Children & Society*, *20*, 54–66. doi:10.1002/CHI.854.

Aust, A., & Arriba, A. (2005). Towards activation? Social assistance reforms and discourses. In P. Taylor-Gooby (ed.), *Ideas and Welfare State Reform in Western Europe* (pp. 100–123). London: Palgrave Macmillan UK.

Avram, S. (2016). Social assistance performance in Central and Eastern Europe: A pre-transfer post-transfer comparison. *Journal of European Social Policy*, *26*(5), 428–441. doi:10.1177/0958928716664296.

Ayala, L., Arranz, J. M., Garcia-Serrano, C., & Martinez-Virto, L. (2021). The effectiveness of minimum income benefits in poverty reduction in Spain. *International Journal of Social Welfare*, 30: 152–169. doi:10.1111/ijsw.12447.

Ayala, L., Martinez, R., & Ruiz-Huerta, J. (2003). Equivalence scales in tax and transfer policies. *Investigacions Economicas*, *XXVII*(3), 593–614.

Ayala, L., & Rodriguez, M. (2013). Evaluation social assistance reforms under programme heterogeneity and alternative measures of success. *International Journal of Social Welfare*, *22*, 406–419. doi:10.1111/ijsw.12008.

Badenes Plá, N., & Gambau-Suelves, B. (2020). The New 'Minimum Vital Income' in Spain: Distributional and Poverty Effects in the Presence and Absence of Regional Minimum Income Schemes (Euromod Working paper Series EM 22/20). Colchester: ISER, University of Essex

Bahle, T., Hubl, V., & Pfeifer, M. (2011). *The Last Safety Net. A Handbook of Minimum Income Protection in Europe*. Bristol: Policy Press.

Baicker, K., Congdon, W. J., & Mullainathan, S. (2012). Health insurance coverage and take-up: Lessons from behavioral economics. *The Milbank Quarterly*, *90*(1), 107–134.

Bakker, W., & Mulder, C. H. (2013). Characteristics of post-separation families in the Netherlands: Shared residence versus resident mother arrangements. *Geojournal*, 78(5), 851–866. https://doi.org/10.1007/s10708-012-9470-x.

Baldini, M., Casabianca, E. J., Giarda, E., & Lusignoli, L. (2018). The impact of REI on Italian households' income: A micro and macro evaluation. *Politica Economica/Journal of Economic Policy*, *24*(2), 103–134.

Bargain, O., Immervoll, H., & Viitamäki, H. (2012). No claim, no pain. Measuring the non-take-up of social assistance using register data. *Journal of Economic Inequality*, *10*, 375–395.

Bargain, O., & Orsini, K. (2007). Beans for breakfast? How exportable is the British workfare model? In O. Bargain (ed.), *Microsimulation in Action: Policy Analysis in Europe Using EUROMOD* (pp. 165–198). Oxford: Elsevier.

Barr, N. (2001). *The Welfare State as Piggy Bank: Information, Risk, Uncertainty, and the Role of the State*. Oxford: Oxford University Press.

Barrientos, A. (2013). *Social Assistance in Developing Countries*. Cambridge: Cambridge University Press.

Barrientos, A. (2018). *Pension Reform in Latin America*. Abingdon, UK: Routledge.

Barrientos, A. (2019). The role of social assistance in reducing poverty and inequality in Asia and the Pacific. *Asian Development Bank Sustainable Development Working Paper Series* (62). https://www.adb.org/sites/default/files/publication/525401/sdwp-062-social-assistance-asia-pacific.pdf.

Bartholomae, S., Fox, J. J., & McKenry, P. C. (2004). The legacy of welfare. Economic endowments or cultural characteristics? *Journal of Family Issues*, *25*(6), 783–810. doi:10.1177/0192513X03259145.

Bastian, J. (2020). The rise of working mothers and the 1975 earned income tax credit. *American Economic Journal: Economic Policy*, *12*(3), 44–75. doi:10.1257/pol.20180039.

Baumberg, B. (2016). The stigma of claiming benefits: A quantitative study. *Journal of Social Policy*, *45*(2), 181–199.

Beaulier, S., & Caplan, B. (2007). Behavioral economics and perverse effects of the welfare state. *Kyklos*, *60*(4), 485–507.

Becher, M., & Pontusson, J. (2011). Whose interests do unions represent? Unionization by income in Western Europe. In *Comparing European Workers Part B: Policies and Institutions* (Vol. 22, pp. 181–211). Bingley: Emerald Group Publishing Limited.

Bekckmannshagen, M., & Schröder, C. (2020). Earnings Inequality and Working Hours Mismatch. Retrieved from https://papers.ssrn.com/sol3/papers.cfm?abstract_id=3584328.

Béland, D., Cantillon, B., Hick, R., & Moreira, A. (2021). Social policy in the face of a global pandemic: Policy responses to the COVID-19 crisis. *Social Policy & Administration*, *55*(2), 249–260. doi:10.1111/spol.12718.

Béland, D., Dinan, S., Rocco, P., & Waddan, A. (2021). Social policy responses to COVID-19 in Canada and the United States: Explaining policy variations between two liberal welfare state regimes. *Social Policy & Administration*, *55*(2), 280–294. doi:10.1111/spol.12656.

Belman, D., Wolfson, P., & Nawakitphaitoon, K. (2015). Who is affected by the minimum wage? *Industrial Relations: A Journal of Economy and Society*, *54*(4), 582–621.

Benassi, C., & Vlandas, T. (2022). Trade unions, bargaining coverage and low pay: A multilevel test of institutional effects on low-pay risk in Germany. *Work, Employment and Society*, *36*(6), 1018–1037.

Bergh, A. (2005). On the counterfactual problem of welfare state research: How can we measure redistribution? *European Sociological Review*, *21*(4), 345–357. doi:10.1093/esr/jci024.

Bertrand, M., Mullainathan, S., & Shafir, E. (2004). A behavioral-economics view of poverty. *The American Economic Review*, *94*(2), 419–423.

Bertrand, M., Mullainathan, S., & Shafir, E. (2006). Behavioral economics and marketing in aid of decision making among the poor. *Journal of Public Policy & Marketing*, *25*(1), 8–23. doi:10.1509/jppm.25.1.8.

Bhuller, M., Moene, K. O., Mogstad, M., & Vestad, O. L. (2022). Facts and fantasies about wage setting and collective bargaining. *Journal of Economic Perspectives*, *36*(4), 29–52.

Biegert, T. (2017). Welfare benefits and unemployment in affluent democracies: The moderating role of the institutional insider/outsider divide. *American Sociological Review*, *82*(5), 1037–1064. doi:10.1177/0003122417727095.

Biegert, T., Brady, D., & Hipp, L. (2022). Cross-national variation in the relationship between welfare generosity and single mother employment. *The ANNALS of the American Academy of Political and Social Science*, *702*(1), 37–54. doi:10.1177/00027162221120760.

Birnbaum, S., & De Wispelaere, J. (2020). Exit strategy or exit trap? Basic income and the 'power to say no' in the age of precarious employment. *Socio-Economic Review*, *19*(3), 909–927. doi:10.1093/ser/mwaa002.

Blank, R. M. (2002). Evaluating welfare reform in the United States. *Journal of Economic Literature*, *40*(4), 1105–1166.

Bonoli, G., Fossati, F., Gandenberger, M., & Knotz, C. (2022). Sometimes needs change minds: Interests and values as determinants of attitudes towards state support for the self-employed during the COVID-19 crisis. *Journal of European Social Policy*, *32*(4), 407–421 doi:10.1177/09589287221106977.

Bonoli, G., Minas, R., & Trein, P. (2015). Cost-shifting in multitiered welfare states: Responding to rising social assistance caseloads in Sweden, Germany and Switzerland. *Publius: The Journal of Federalism*, *46*(4), 596–622. doi:10.2139/ssrn.2638814.

Boockmann, B., L. Thomsen, S., & Walter, T. (2014). Intensifying the use of benefit sanctions: An effective tool to increase employment? *IZA Journal of Labor Policy*, *3*, 1–19.

Boone, J., Marchal, S., Marx, I., Van Cant, L., Van Lancker, W., & Verbist, G. (2018). *Feit en fictie omtrent het basisinkomen in Nederland: een wetenschappelijke verkenning mogelijk gemaakt door instituut GAK.* Antwerpen: Universiteit Antwerpen.

Booth, A. L., Francesconi, M., & Frank, J. (2002). Temporary jobs: Stepping stones or dead ends? *The Economic Journal*, *112*(480), 189–213. doi:10.1111/1468-0297.00043.

Bosch, G. (2018). The making of the German minimum wage: A case study of institutional change. *Industrial Relations Journal*, *49*(1), 19–33.

Boschman, S., Maas, I., Kristiansen, M. H., & Vrooman, J. C. (2019). The reproduction of benefit receipt: Disentangling the intergenerational transmission. *Social Science Research*, *80*, 51–65. doi:10.1016/j.ssresearch.2019.02.009.

Boschman, S., Maas, I., Vrooman, J. C., & Kristiansen, M. H. (2021). From social assistance to self-sufficiency: Low income work as a stepping stone. *European Sociological Review*, *37*(5), 766–782. doi:10.1093/esr/jcab003.

Bothfeld, S., Eydoux, A., & Leibetseder, B. (2022). Minimum Income Schemes in Continental Welfare States—Poor Cousins or Innovative Supportive Social Security Schemes? Paper presented at the 2022 ESPANET, Vienna.

Bouckaert, N., & Schokkaert, E. (2011). Een eerste berekening van non-take-upgedrag bij leefloon. *Belgisch Tijdschrift voor Sociale Zekerheid*, *53*(4), 603–627.

Bouvard, L. (2021). France (FR)—2018–2021 (EUROMOD working paper series). Sevilla: JRC.

Bradbury, B. (2014). Pensions for singles and couples. *Review of Income and Wealth*, *60*(3), 480–498. doi:10.1111/roiw.12106.

Brady, D. (2019). Theories of the causes of poverty. *Annual Review of Sociology*, *45*(1), 155–175. doi:10.1146/annurev-soc-073018-022550.

Brady, D., & Bostic, A. (2015). Paradoxes of social policy: Welfare transfers, relative poverty, and redistribution preferences. *American Sociological Review, 80*(2), 268–298.

Brandolini, A. (2006). *Measurement of Income Distribution in Supranational Entities* (452). Luxembourg: Luxembourg Income Studies.

Bratberg, E., Nilsen, Ø. A., & Vaage, K. (2014). Assessing the intergenerational correlation in disability pension recipiency. *Oxford Economic Papers, 67*(2), 205–226. doi:10.1093/oep/gpu028.

Bray, J. R. (2013). *Reflections on the Evolution of the Minimum Wage in Australia: Options for the Future* (1/2013). Canberra: Crawford School of Public Policy.

Brink, B., & Bouwmeester, M. (2022). The Household as a Constraint on Social Assistance: Analysing the Household-Notion in the Netherlands' Parliamentary History on Social Assistance. Paper presented at the 2022 ESPANET Conference, Vienna.

Browne, J., & Immervoll, H. (2017). Mechanics of replacing benefit systems with a basic income: Comparative results from a microsimulation approach. *The Journal of Economic Inequality, 15*(4), 325–344. doi:10.1007/s10888-017-9366-6.

Bruttel, O. (2019). The effects of the new statutory minimum wage in Germany: A first assessment of the evidence. *Journal for Labour Market Research, 53*(1), 10. doi:10.1186/s12651-019-0258-z.

Bubonya, M., & Cobb-Clark, D. A. (2021). Pathways of disadvantage: Unpacking the intergenerational correlation in welfare. *Economics of Education Review, 80*, 102066.

Bundesverfassungsgericht. (2019). Sanctions imposed on recipients of unemployment benefits to enforce their cooperation obligations are in part unconstitutional [Press release]

Burauel, P., Caliendo, M., Fedorets, A., Grabka, M. M., Schröder, C., Schupp, J., & Wittbrodt, L. (2017). *Minimum Wage Not Yet for Everyone: On the Compensation of Eligible Workers Before and After the Minimum Wage Reform from the Perspective of Employees* (49.2017). Berlin: DIW.

Burgoon, B., & Rooduijn, M. (2021). 'Immigrationization'of welfare politics? Anti-immigration and welfare attitudes in context. *West European Politics, 44*(2), 177–203.

Buysse, L., Goedemé, T., Janssens, J., Nisen, L., & Van Mechelen, N. (2017). De automatische toekenning van rechten in de Belgische sociale bescherming. Stand van zaken en kritische reflectie. In W. Lahaye (ed.), *Armoede in België. Federaal Jaarboek.* (pp. 73–99). Gent: Skribis.

Caliendo, M., Fedorets, A., Preuss, M., Schröder, C., & Wittbrodt, L. (2018). The short-run employment effects of the German minimum wage reform. *Labour Economics, 53*, 46–62. doi:10.1016/j.labeco.2018.07.002.

Callan, T., & Nolan, B. (1991). Concepts of poverty and the poverty line. *Journal of Economic Surveys, 5*(3), 243–261.

Calnitsky, D. (2016). 'More normal than welfare': The Mincome experiment, stigma, and community experience. *Can Rev Sociol, 53*(1), 26–71. doi:10.1111/cars.12091.

Calnitsky, D. (2020). The employer response to the guaranteed annual income. *Socio-Economic Review, 18*, 493–517. doi:10.1093/ser/mwy009.

Calnitsky, D., & Latner, J. P. (2017). Basic income in a small town: Understanding the elusive effects on work. *Social Problems, 64*(3), 373–397. doi:10.1093/socpro/spw040.

Cantillon, B. (2011). The paradox of the social investment state: Growth, employment and poverty in the Lisbon era. *Journal of European Social Policy, 21*(5), 432–449. doi:10.1177/0958928711418856.

Cantillon, B. (2019). The European Pillar of Social Rights. In M. Ferrera (ed.), *Towards a European Social Union: The European Pillar of Social Rights and the Roadmap for a Fully-fledged Social Union—A Forum Debate* (pp. 54–63). Torino: Centro Einaudi.

Cantillon, B. (2022). Poverty and the Tragedy of the Welfare State. Seven Terms for a New Social Contract (CSB Working paper 22/06). Antwerp: University of Antwerp.

Cantillon, B., & Buysse, L. (2016). *De staat van de welvaartstaat [The State of the Welfare State]*. Leuven/Den Haag: Acco.

Cantillon, B., Goedemé, T., & Hills, J. (eds). (2019). *Decent Incomes for the Poor? Improving Policies in Europe*. Oxford: Oxford University Press.

Cantillon, B., Marchal, S., & Luigjes, C. (2019). Towards adequate minimum incomes: Which role for europe? In B. Cantillon, T. Goedemé, & J. Hills (eds), *Decent Incomes for the Poor? Improving Policies in Europe* (pp. 269–288). Oxford: Oxford University Press.

Cantillon, B., Marchal, S., Peeters, N., Penne, T., & Storms, B. (2020). *Huishoudbudgetten en sociale minima in lockdown* (COVIVAT policy note 2). Leuven/Antwerpen: Universiteit Antwerpen/KULeuven.

Cantillon, B., Parolin, Z., & Collado, D. (2020). A glass ceiling on poverty reduction? An empirical investigation into the structural constraints on minimum income protections. *Journal of European Social Policy*, *30*(2), 129–143. doi:10.1177/0958928719880500.

Cantillon, B., & Van Lancker, W. (2013). Three shortcomings of the social investment perspective. *Social Policy and Society*, *12*(4), 553–564. doi:10.1017/S1474746413000080.

Cantillon, B., & Van Mechelen, N. (2014). Cracks in a policy paradigm—poverty reduction and social security: The case of Belgium. *International Review of Sociology*, *24*(2), 270–290. doi:10.1080/03906701.2014.933026.

Cantillon, B., Van Mechelen, N., Frans, D., & Schuerman, N. (2014). *Het glazen plafond van de actieve welvaartsstaat: twee decennia ongelijkheid, armoede en beleid in België* (CSB Bericht xx). Antwerpen: Centrum voor Sociaal Beleid Herman Deleeck, Universiteit Antwerpen.

Cantillon, B., Van Mechelen, N., Marx, I., & Van den Bosch, K. (2004). *The Evolution of Minimum Income Protection in 15 European Countries, 1992–2001* (CSB-berichten D/2004/6104/02). Antwerp: Herman Deleeck Centre for Social Policy, University of Antwerp.

Cantillon, B., Van Mechelen, N., & Schulte, B. (2008). Minimum income policies in old and new EU member states. In J. Alber, T. Fahey, & C. Saraceno (eds), *Handbook of Quality of Life in the Enlarged European Union* (pp. 218–234). London/New York: Routledge.

Cantillon, B., & Vandenbroucke, F. (2015). *Reconciling Work and Poverty Reduction: How Successful Are European Welfare States?* Oxford: Oxford University Press.

Cantillon, B., Parolin, Z., & Collado, D. (2020). A glass ceiling on poverty reduction? An empirical investigation into the structural constraints on minimum income protections. *Journal of European Social Policy*, *30*(2), 129–143. doi:10.1177/0958928719880500.

Cantó, O., Figari, F., Fiorio, C. V., Kuypers, S., Marchal, S., Romaguera-de-la-cruz, M., ... Verbist, G. (2022). Welfare resilience at the onset of the COVID-19 pandemic in a selection of European countries: Impact on public finance and household incomes. *Review of Income and Wealth*, *68*, 293–322. doi:10.1111/roiw.12530.

Card, D., & Cardoso, A. R. (2022). Wage flexibility under sectoral bargaining. *Journal of the European Economic Association*, *20*(5), 2013–2061.

Card, D., Kluve, J., & Weber, A. (2010). Active Labor Market Policy Evaluation: A Meta-analysis (NBER Working Paper Series 16173). Cambridge: National Bureau of Economic Research.

Card, D., & Krueger, A. B. (1994). Minimum wages and employment: A case study of the fast-food industry in New Jersey and Pennsylvania. *American Economic Review*, *84*(4), 772–793. doi:10.3386/w4509.

Carpentier, S., Neels, K., & Van den Bosch, K. (2017). Exit from and re-entry into social assistance benefit in Belgium among people with migration background and the native-born. *International Journal of Social Welfare*, *26*(4), 366–383.

Cengiz, D., Dube, A., Lindner, A., & Zipperer, B. (2019). The effect of minimum wages on low-wage jobs*. *The Quarterly Journal of Economics, 134*(3), 1405–1454. doi:10.1093/qje/qjz014.

Centraal Bureau voor de Statistiek. (2023). Lage-inkomensgrens. Retrieved from https://www.cbs.nl/nl-nl/onze-diensten/methoden/begrippen/lage-inkomensgrens.

Centre for Parliamentary History. (2014). Het minimumloon in de periode-De Jong [The minimum wage in the De Jong Period]. Retrieved from https://www.ru.nl/cpg/@941500/minimumloon-periode/.

Chaveyron, S., Gray, D., & L'Horty, Y. (2018). Raising take-up of social assistance benefits through a simple mailing: Evidence from a French field experiment. *Revue d'économie politique, 128*(5), 777–805. doi:10.3917/redp.285.0777

Cheetham, M., Moffatt, S., Addison, M., & Wiseman, A. (2019). Impact of universal credit in north east England: A qualitative study of claimants and support staff. *BMJ open, 9*(7), 1–9. doi:10.1136/bmjopen-2019-029611.

Chemla, E. (2016). France: The French social security system. In M. Wujckzyk (ed.), *The Right to Social Security in the Constitutions of the World: Broadening the Moral and Legal Space for Social Justice* (pp. 61–71). Geneva: ILO.

Chetty, R., & Saez, E. (2013). Teaching the tax code: Earnings responses to an experiment with EITC recipients. *American Economic Journal: Applied Economics, 5*(1), 1–31.

Christelis, D., Jappelli, T., Paccagnella, O., & Weber, G. (2009). Income, wealth and financial fragility in Europe. *Journal of European Social Policy, 19*(4), 359–376. doi:10.1177/1350506809341516.

Chzhen, Y., & Bradshaw, J. (2012). Lone parents, poverty and policy in the European Union. *Journal of European Social Policy, 22*(5), 487–506. doi:10.1177/0958928712456578.

Cingano, F. (2014). Trends in Income Inequality and Its Impact on Economic Growth (OECD Social, Employment and Migration Working Papers 163). Paris: OECD Publishing. doi:10.1787/5jxrjncwxv6j-en

Clasen, J., & Clegg, D. (2007). Levels and levers of conditionality: Measuring change within welfare states. In J. Clasen & N. A. Siegel (eds), *Investigating welfare state change. The 'dependent variable problem' in comparative analysis* (pp. 166–197). Cheltenham: Edward Elgar.

Clegg, D. (2015). The Demise of Tax Credits. *The Political Quarterly, 86*(4), 493–499. doi:10.1111/1467-923X.12203

Coady, D., Jahan, S., Matsumoto, R., & Shang, B. (2021). Guaranteed Minimum Income Schemes in Europe: Landscape and Design (Working paper WP/21/179). International Monetary Fund.

Collado, D., Cantillon, B., Van den Bosch, K., Goedemé, T., & Vandelannoote, D. (2019). The end of cheap talk about poverty reduction: The cost of closing the poverty gap while maintaining work incentives. In B. Cantillon, T. Goedemé, & J. Hills (eds), *Decent Incomes for All: Improving Policies in Europe* (pp. 223–242). Oxford: Oxford University Press.

Concialdi, P. (1999). SMIC report calls for continued social contribution cuts on low-paid jobs. Retrieved from https://www.eurofound.europa.eu/publications/article/1999/smic-report-calls-for-continued-social-contribution-cuts-on-low-paid-jobs.

Conen, W., & Schippers, J. (2019). *Self-employment as Precarious Work. A European perspective.* Cheltenham: Edward Elgar.

Consolidated version of the Treaty on the Functioning of the European Union. Part Three - Union Policies and Internal Actions Title X - Social Policy. Article 153 (ex Article 137 TEC), (2016).

Conte, A., & Mazza, J. (2019). Migrants and welfare dependency: Evidence from the EU. *JRC, Ispra, JRC116591*. https://migrant-integration.ec.europa.eu/sites/default/files/2019-10/tr_final_after_last_revision_21052019.pdf.

Cooper, K., & Stewart, K. (2021). Does household income affect children's outcomes? A systematic review of the evidence. *Child Indicators Research*, *14*(3), 981–1005. doi:10.1007/s12187-020-09782-0.

Corcoran, M., & Adams, T. (1995). Family and neighborhood welfare dependency and sons' labor supply. *Journal of Family and Economic Issues*, *16*(2), 239–264. doi:10.1007/BF02353710.

Council (2023), Council Recommendation of 30 January 2023 on adequate minimum income ensuring active inclusion 2023/C 41/01, (2023).

Council of the EU. (2022). Council adopts EU law on adequate minimum wages [Press release]. Retrieved from https://www.consilium.europa.eu/en/press/press-releases/2022/10/04/council-adopts-eu-law-on-adequate-minimum-wages/.

Council of the European Communities. (1992). Council Recommendation of 24 June 1992 on common criteria concerning sufficient resources and social assistance in social protection systems (92/441/EEC, OJ L 245, 26/08/1992).

CPB/SCP. (2020). *Kansrijk armoedebeleid [Oppportunity Rich Poverty Policy]*. Den Haag: Centraal Planning Burea/Sociaal Cultureel Planning Bureau.

Crepaldi, C., Da Roit, B., Castegnaro, C., & Pasquinelli, S. (2017). *Minimum Income Policies in EU Member States*. Brussels: European Parliament, Directorate General for Internal Policies. Policy Department A: Economic and Scientific Policy.

Crettaz, E. (2013). A state-of-the-art review of working poverty in advanced economies: Theoretical models, measurement issues and risk groups. *Journal of European Social Policy*, *23*(4), 347–362.

Cronert, A., & Forsén, R. (2023). Like worker, like union? Labor market risk exposure, white-collar predominance and trade unions' policy advocacy. *Socio-Economic Review*, *21*(1), 367–395.

D'Arcy, C., & Finch, D. (2019). The calculation of a living wage: The UK's experience. *Transfer*, *25*(3), 301–317. doi:10.1177/1024258919847313.

Dahl, G. B., Kostøl, A. R., & Mogstad, M. (2014). Family Welfare Cultures*. *The Quarterly Journal of Economics*, *129*(4), 1711–1752. doi:10.1093/qje/qju019.

Daly, M., & Kelly, G. (2015). *Families and Poverty: Everyday Life on a Low Income*. Bristol: Policy Press.

Davidescu, A. A., & Schneider, F. (2017). *Nature of the Relationship between Minimum Wage and the Shadow Economy Size: An Empirical Analysis for the Case of Romania* (IZA Discussion Paper Series 11247). Bonn: IZA. Retrieved from http://hdl.handle.net/10419/177051.

De Becker, E., Schoukens, P., Spasova, S., Haapanala, H., & Marenco, M. (2023). Improving Access to Social Protection in the European Union: A Proposal for Further Action: Paper providing expertise to the future Belgian Presidency of the Council of the European Union (January–June 2024).

De Stefano, V. (2016). *The Rise of the 'Just-in-Time Workforce': On-demand Work, Crowdwork and Labour Protection in the 'Gig-economy'* (ILO Conditions of work and employment series 71). ILO.

de Vos, K. (2021). *Netherlands (NL): 2018–2021* (EUROMOD Country Report). Sevilla: JRC of the European Commission.

de Vos, K., & Zaidi, A. (1997). Equivalence Scale Sensitivity of Poverty Statistics for the Member States of the European Community. *Review of Income and Wealth*, *43*(3), 319–333.

De Wilde, M. (2016). Het gebruik van de discretionaire ruimte door Vlaamse OCMW-medewerkers. In M. De Wilde, B. Cantillon, F. Vandenbroucke, & M. De Bie (eds), *40 jaar OCMW en bijstand* (pp. 104–120). Leuven: Acco.

De Wilde, M. (2018). *Between Legislation and Realisation Comes Implementation: The Effect of the Multi-layered Implementation Process on Social Policy Outcomes.* Antwerpen: Universiteit Antwerpen, Faculteit Sociale Wetenschappen.

De Wilde, M., Cantillon, B., Vandenbroucke, F., & De Bie, M. (2016). *40 jaar OCMW en bijstand.* Leuven: Acco.

De Wilde, M., Hermans, K., & Cantillon, B. (2020). *Meer vragen om hulp bij OCMW's en voedselbanken: eerste resultaten van een grootschalige bevraging* (COVIVAT Beleidsnota 4).

De Wilde, M., & Marchal, S. (2016). De voorwaardelijkheid van de bijstand: de werkbereidheidseis. In M. De Wilde, B. Cantillon, F. Vandenbroucke, & M. De Bie (eds), *40 jaar OCMW en bijstand* (pp. 85–105). Leuven: Acco.

De Wilde, M., & Marchal, S. (2019). Weighing up work willingness in social assistance: A balancing act on multiple levels. *European Sociological Review*, *35*(5), 718–737. doi:10.1093/esr/jcz028.

De Wispelaere, J., & Stirton, L. (2004). The many faces of universal basic income. *Political Quarterly*, *75*(3), 266–274. doi:10.1111/j.1467-923X.2004.00611.x.

Dingeldey, I., Grimshaw, D., & Schulten, T. (2021). *Minimum Wage Regimes: Statutory Regulation, Collective Bargaining and Adequate Levels.* Abingdon, UK: Routledge.

Diop-Christensen, A. (2015). Is 'making work pay' effective for the 'unemployable'? The impact of benefit sanctions on social assistance recipients in Denmark. *Journal of European Social Policy*, *25*(2), 210–224. doi:10.1177/0958928715573484.

Directorate General for Employment Social Affairs and Inclusion. (2023). *The Future of Social Protection and of the Welfare State in the EU.* Brussels: Publications Office of the European Union. Retrieved from https://data.europa.eu/doi/10.2767/35425.

Dobbins, T. (1999). National minimum wage debate gathers pace. Retrieved from https://www.eurofound.europa.eu/publications/article/1999/national-minimum-wage-debate-gathers-pace.

Dolls, M., Fuest, C., & Peichl, A. (2012). Automatic stabilizers and economic crisis: US vs. Europe. *Journal of Public Economics*, *96*(3), 279–294.

Doorley, K., & McTague, A. (2021). *Ireland (IE), 2018–2021* (EUROMOD country report). Sevilla: JRC.

Dube, A. (2019). *Impacts of Minimum Wages: Review of the International Evidence.* London: HM Treasury.

Duflo, E. and Banerjee, A. (2019). Economic incentives don't always do what we want them to do. *New York Times Opinion*, published 26 October 2019: https://www.nytimes.com/2019/10/26/opinion/sunday/duflo-banerjee-economic-incentives.html.

Dumont, D. (2022). Universal basic income as a source of inspiration for the future of social protection systems? A counter-agenda. *European Journal of Social Security*, *24*(4), 299–318.

Duncan, G., Magnuson, K., Kalil, A., & Ziol-Guest, K. (2012). The importance of early childhood poverty. *Social Indicators Research—SOC INDIC RES*, *108*, 1–12. doi:10.1007/s11205-011-9867-9.

Duncan, G. J., Hill, M. S., & Hoffman, S. D. (1988). Welfare dependence within and across generations. *Science*, *239*(4839), 467–471. doi:10.1126/science.3277267.

Eardley, T., Bradshaw, J., Ditch, J., Gough, I., & Whiteford, P. (1996). *Social Assistance in OECD Countries: Synthesis Report* (Research Report 46). London: HSMO Department of Social Security.

Edwards, P. (1999). The UK's first national minimum wage. Retrieved from https://www.eurofound.europa.eu/publications/article/1999/the-uks-first-national-minimum-wage.

Eichenhofer, E. (2016). The right to social security in the German constitution. In M. Wujckzyk (ed.), *The Right to Social Security in the Constitutions of the World: Broadening the Moral and Legal Space for Social Justice* (pp. 72–78). Geneva: ILO.

Eichhorst, W., Bonin, H., Krause-Pilatus, A., Marx, P., Dolls, M., & Lay, M. (2023). *Minimum Income Support Systems as Elements of Crisis Resilience in Europe—Final Report.* Bonn/München: Federal Ministry of Labour and Social Affairs.

Eichhorst, W., & Konle-Seidl, R. (2008). Contingent Convergence: A Comparative Analysis of Activation Policies (IZA Discussion Paper 3905). Bonn: IZA.

Eissa, N., & Hoynes, H. W. (2006). Behavioral responses to taxes: Lessons from the EITC and labor supply. *Tax Policy and the Economy, 20*, 73–110. doi:10.1086/tpe.20.20061905.

Eissa, N., & Liebman, J. B. (1996). Labor supply response to the earned income tax credit. *The Quarterly Journal of Economics, 111*(2), 605–637.

Eleveld, A. (2016). Work-related Sanctions in European Welfare States: An Incentive to Work or a Violation of Minimum Subsistence Rights? (Research paper 2016/01). Retrieved from https://ssrn.com/abstract=2802656.

Enriquez, B., Jones, D., & Tedeschi, E. V. (2023). The Short-term Labor Supply Response to the Expanded Child Tax Credit (NBER working paper 31110). National Bureau of Economic Research.

Esping-Andersen, G., Gallie, D., Hemerijck, A., & Myles, J. (2002). *Why We Need a New Welfare State.* Oxford: Oxford University Press.

ETUC. (2020). ETUC Reply to the First Phase Consultation of Social Partners under Article 154 TFEU on a Possible Action Addressing the Challenges Related to Fair Minimum Wages. Brussels: ETUC.

EU China Social Protection Reform Project. (2015). *EU-China Social Protection Reform Project Component 3. Volume on 2015 Research Topics.* Bejing: EU China Social Protection Reform Project.

Eurofound. (2015). *Access to Social Benefits: Reducing Non-take-up.* Luxembourg: Publications Office of the European Union.

Eurofound. (2017a). Austria: Social partners agree on €1,500 monthly minimum wage for all sectors. Retrieved from https://www.eurofound.europa.eu/publications/article/2017/austria-social-partners-agree-on-eu1500-monthly-minimum-wage-for-all-sectors.

Eurofound. (2017b). *Statutory Minimum Wages in the EU 2017.* Dublin: Eurofound.

Eurofound. (2018). *Concept and Practice of a Living Wage.* Luxembourg: Publications Office of the European Union.

Eurofound. (2019a). *Minimum wages in 2019: Annual review.* Luxembourg: Publications Office of the European Union.

Eurofound. (2019b). To have or have not: A statutory minimum wage. Retrieved from https://www.eurofound.europa.eu/publications/article/2019/to-have-or-have-not-a-statutory-minimum-wage.

Eurofound. (2020a). *Minimum Wages in 2020: Annual Review.* Luxembourg: Publications Office of the European Union.

Eurofound. (2020b). Proportion of minimum wage workers who find it difficult to make ends meet. Retrieved from https://www.eurofound.europa.eu/data/proportion-of-minimum-wage-workers-who-find-it-difficult-to-make-ends-meet.

Eurofound. (2022). *Minimum Wages in 2022: Annual Review.* Luxembourg: Publications Office of the European Union.

European Commission. (2008). Commission Recommendation of 3 October 2008 on the active inclusion of people excluded from the labour market 2008/867/EC CFR.

European Commission. (2010). *Industrial Relations in Europe 2010.* Luxembourg: Publications Office of the European Union.

European Commission. (2017). Pillar of social rights. Retrieved from http://ec.europa.eu/social/main.jsp?catId=1226&langId=en.

European Commission. (2020a). *Consultation Document: First Phase Consultation of Social Partners under Article 154 TFEU on a Possible Action Addressing the Challenges Related to a Fair Minimum Wage* (C(2020) 83 final). Brussels: European Commission.

European Commission. (2020b). *Consultation Document: First Phase Consultation of Social Partners under Article 154 TFEU on a Possible Action Addressing the Challenges Related to Fair Minimum Wages.* (C(2020) 83 final). Brussels: European Commission.

European Commission. (2020c). *Proposal for a Directive of the European Parliament and of the Council on Adequate Minimum Wages in the European Union.* (COM/2020/682 final). Retrieved from https://eur-lex.europa.eu/legal-content/EN/TXT/?uri=CELEX%3A52020PC0682&qid=1653568164152.

European Commission. (2021). *The European Pillar of Social Rights Action Plan.* Luxembourg: Publications Office of the European Union. Retrieved from https://op.europa.eu/webpub/empl/european-pillar-of-social-rights/downloads/KE0921008ENN.pdf.

European Commission. (2022a). *Commission Staff Working Document Accompanying the Document Proposal for a Council Recommendation on Adequate Minimum Income Ensuring Active Inclusion* (SWD(2022) 313 final). Brussels: European Commission.

European Commission. (2022b). *Proposal for a Council Recommendation on Adequate Minimum Income Ensuring Active Inclusion* (COM(2022) 490 final). Brussels: European Commission.

European Commission and Social Protection Committee. (2022). *The 2022 Minimum Income Report. Joint Report Prepared by the Social Protection Committee and the European Commission (DG EMPL).* Luxembourg: Publications Office of the European Union.

European Council. (2010). *European Council 17 June 2010 Conclusions.* Brussels: European Council.

European Council. (2021). The Porto Declaration [Press release]. Retrieved from https://www.consilium.europa.eu/en/press/press-releases/2021/05/08/the-porto-declaration/.

European Council. (2022, 6 August 2022). Adequate minimum wages in the EU. Retrieved from https://www.consilium.europa.eu/en/policies/adequate-minimum-wages/.

European Parliament. (2000). *Lisbon European Council 23 and 24 March 2000. Presidency Conclusions.* Retrieved from http://www.europarl.europa.eu/summits/lis1_en.htm.

European Parliament (2010). European Parliament resolution of 20 October 2010 of the European Parliament on the role of minimum income in combating poverty and promoting an inclusive society in Europe.

European Parliament (2017a). European Parliament resolution of 24 October 2017 on minimum income policies as a tool for fighting poverty (2016/2270(INI)

European Parliament (2017b). European Parliament resolution of 19 January 2017 on a European Pillar of Social Rights.

European Parliament. (2022a). Deal reached on new rules for adequate minimum wages in the EU [Press release]. Retrieved from https://www.europarl.europa.eu/news/en/press-room/20220603IPR32188/deal-reached-on-new-rules-for-adequate-minimum-wages-in-the-eu.

European Parliament. (2022b). Parliament adopts new rules on adequate minimum wages for all workers in the EU [Press release]. Retrieved from https://www.europarl.europa.eu/news/en/press-room/20220909IPR40138/parliament-adopts-new-rules-on-adequate-minimum-wages-for-all-workers-in-the-eu.

The European Parliament and the Council (2022). Directive (EU) 2022/2041 of the European Parliament and of the Council of 19 October 2022 on adequate minimum wages in the European Union. (2022).

Eurostat. (2020). Minimum wage statistics. *Statistics Explained.* Retrieved from https://ec.europa.eu/eurostat/statistics-explained/index.php/Minimum_wage_statistics.

Eurostat. (2022a). Minimum wage statistics. Retrieved 23 August 2022 https://ec.europa.eu/eurostat/statistics-explained/index.php?title=Minimum_wage_statistics.

Eurostat. (2022b). Monthly minimum wages—bi-annual data (EARN_MW_CUR). Retrieved 23 August 2022, from Eurostat https://ec.europa.eu/eurostat/databrowser/view/EARN_MW_CUR__custom_3240356/default/table?lang=en.

Eurostat. (2022c). Structure of earnings survey. Retrieved from https://ec.europa.eu/eurostat/web/microdata/structure-of-earnings-survey.

Eurostat. (2022d). Structure of earnings survey: Annual earnings (EARN_SES_ANNUAL). Retrieved 23 August 2022, from Eurostat https://ec.europa.eu/eurostat/databrowser/view/EARN_SES_ANNUAL__custom_3240339/default/table?lang=en.

Eurostat. (2023). In-work at-risk-of-poverty rate by age and sex—EU-SILC survey. Retrieved 15/03/2023 https://ec.europa.eu/eurostat/databrowser/view/ILC_IW01__custom_5397071/default/table?lang=en.

FEBA. (2021). *COVID 19: A Unique Opportunity for a Real Change* (European Food Banks Federation Report). FEBA. Retrieved from https://lp.eurofoodbank.org/wp-content/uploads/2021/09/FEBA_Report_Survey_COVID_Sept2021.pdf.

Federal Ministry of Labour and Social Affairs. (1999). *Lonen en arbeidsduur [Wages and Hours Worked].* Brussels: Federaal Ministerie van Tewerkstelling en Arbeid,. Retrieved from https://werk.belgie.be/sites/default/files/nl/modules_pages/publicaties/document/214fd05270a6492590ce1fcec55f93d92.pdf?id=4170.

Federal Ministry of Labour and Social Affairs. (2023, 15 February 2023). The Citizen's Benefit Act (Bürgergeld-Gesetz). Retrieved from https://www.bmas.de/EN/Services/Press/recent-publications/2023/the-citizens-benefit-act.html.

Ferge, Z., & Juhász, G. (2004). Accession and social policy: The case of Hungary. *Journal of European Social Policy, 14*(3), 233–251.

Ferrarini, T., Nelson, K., & Höög, H. (2012). From universalism to selectivity: Old wine in new bottles for child benefits in Europe en other countries. In I. Marx & K. Nelson (eds), *Minimum Income Protection in Flux,* (pp. 137–160). Basingstoke: Palgrave Macmillan.

Figari, F. (2010). Can in-work benefits improve social inclusion in the southern European countries? *Journal of European Social Policy, 20*(4), 301–315. doi:10.1177/0958928710374375.

Figari, F., & Fiorio, C. V. (2020). Welfare Resilience in the Immediate Aftermath of the COVID-19 Outbreak in Italy (EUROMOD Working Paper EM06/20). Colchester: University of Essex.

Figari, F., Matsaganis, M., & Sutherland, H. (2013). Are European social safety nets tight enough? Coverage and adequacy of minimum income schemes in 14 EU countries. *International Journal of Social Welfare, 22*(1), 3–14.

Figari, F., Paulus, A., & Sutherland, H. (2015). Microsimulation and policy analysis. In A. B. Atkinson & F. Bourguignon (eds), *Handbook of Income Distribution* (Vol. 2, Chapter 24, pp. 2141–2221). New York: Elsevier.

Filomena, M. (2023). Unemployment scarring effects: An overview and meta-analysis of empirical studies. *Italian Economic Journal,* 1–60. doi:10.1007/s40797-023-00228-4.

Financial Mirror. (2021, 20th November 2021). Minimum wage possible next year. *Financial Mirror.* Retrieved from https://www.financialmirror.com/2021/11/20/minimum-wage-possible-next-year/.

Folbre, N. (1994). Children as public goods. *The American Economic Review, 84*(2), 86–90.

Fortuna, N., & Neto, A. (2021). The impact of labour market institutions on income inequality: Evidence from OECD countries. *Applied Economics Letters, 28*(13), 1110–1113.

Foster, R., Adams, L., Svabaes, S., O'Driscoll, C., & Thomson, D. (2018). Universal Credit Full Service Survey. In: IFF Research. https://assets.publishing.service.gov.uk/media/5b1a4f9eed915d2cc380163f/universal-credit-full-service-claimant-survey.pdf.

Frazer, H., & Marlier, E. (2016). *Minimum Income Schemes in Europe. A Study of National Policies.* Brussels: European Union.

Frericks, P., & Höppner, J. (2019). Self-responsibility readdressed: Shifts in financial responsibility for social security between the public realm, the individual, and the family in Europe. *American Behavioral Scientist, 63*(1), 65–84. doi:10.1177/0002764218816805.

Frericks, P., Och, R., & Höppner, J. (2020). The family in minimum income benefits in Europe: An institutional analysis. *Social Politics: International Studies in Gender, State & Society, 27*(3), 615–642. doi:10.1093/sp/jxz003.

Fuchs, M. (2009). *Social Assistance—No, Thanks? The Non-Take-up Phenomenon and Its Patterns in Austria, Germany and Finland after 2000.* Vienna: European Centre.

Fuchs, M., Gasior, K., Premrov, T., Hollan, K., & Scoppetta, A. (2020). Falling through the social safety net? Analysing non-take-up of minimum income benefit and monetary social assistance in Austria. *Social Policy & Administration, 54*, 827–843.

Gábos, A., Branyiczki, R., Binder, B., & Tóth, I. G. (2019). Employment and poverty dynamics before, during, and after the crisis. In B. Cantillon, T. Goedemé, & J. Hills (eds), *Decent Incomes for All: Improving Policies in Europe* (pp. 34–55). Oxford: Oxford University Press.

Garnero, A. (2021). The impact of collective bargaining on employment and wage inequality: Evidence from a new taxonomy of bargaining systems. *European Journal of Industrial Relations, 27*(2), 185–202.

Garritzman, J. L., Hausermann, S., & Palier, B. (eds). (2022). *The World Politics of Social Investment: Volume I: Welfare States in the Knowledge Economy.* Oxford: Oxford University Press.

Gelber, A. M., & Mitchell, J. W. (2012). Taxes and time allocation: Evidence from single women and men. *The Review of Economic Studies, 79*(3), 863–897.

Genettian, L., & Millar, C. (2004). How welfare reform can affect marriage: Evidence from an experimental study in Minnesota. *Review of Economics of the Household, 2*, 275–301.

Gerbery, D., & Miklošovič, T. (2018). Poor support for poor people? Assessing the impacts of improving adequacy in minimum income scheme in Slovakia. *Sociológia, 50*(3), 246–267.

Ghuesquière, F. (2020). *Prendre, occuper et quitter le statut d'indépendant en Wallonie. Analyse des trajectoires professionnelles d'indépendants et réflexion sur leurs déterminants sociaux* (Rapport de recherche n° 39). Namur: IWEPS.

Gilman, M. (1998). Youth income and expenditure: Will the National Minimum Wage help? Retrieved from https://www.eurofound.europa.eu/publications/article/1998/youth-income-and-expenditure-will-the-national-minimum-wage-help.

Goderis, B., Hulst, B. v., Wilderboer Schut, J. M., & Ras, M. (2018). *De SCP methode voor het meten van armoede.* Den Haag: Sociaal en Cultureel Planbureau.

Goderis, B., & Vlekke, M. (2023). Tax and benefit policies to reduce poverty in the Netherlands: A microsimulation analysis. doi:10.34196/ijm.00277.

Goedemé, T., & Marchal, S. (2016). Exploring a blind spot in comparative pension reform research: Long-term trends in non-contributory pensions in Europe. *International Journal of Social Welfare, 25*(2), 161–175. doi:10.1111/IJSW.12189.

Goedemé, T., Penne, T., Hufkens, T., Karakitsios, A., Bernát, A., Franziskus, A., ... Storms, B. (2019). What does it mean to live on the poverty threshold? Lessons from reference budgets. In B. Cantillon, T. Goedemé, & J. Hills (eds), *Decent Incomes for the Poor? Improving Policies in Europe* (pp. 13–33). Oxford: Oxford University Press.

Goedemé, T., Storms, B., Penne, T., & Van den Bosch, K. (2015). Pilot project for the development of a common methodology on reference budgets in Europe. *Final Report.*

Golightley, M., & Holloway, M. (2016). Daring to speak out. *The British Journal of Social Work*, 46, 1149–1157.
Goodin, R., & Le Grand, J. (1987). Not Only the Poor; The Middle Classes and the Welfare State. London: Unwin Hyman.
Goodin, R. E., & Ware, A. (1990). *Needs and Welfare*. SAGE Publications.
Gottschalk, P. (1996). Is the correlation in welfare participation across generations spurious? *Journal of Public Economics*, *63*(1), 1–25. doi:10.1016/S0047-2727(96)01585-X.
Gough, I., Bradshaw, J., Ditch, J., Eardley, T., & Whiteford, P. (1996). Social assistance in OECD countries. *Journal of European Social Policy*, *7*(1), 17–43.
Gray, M., & Stanton, D. (2010). Costs of children and equivalence scales: A review of methodological issues and Australian estimates. *Australian Journal of Labour Economics*, *13*(1), 99–115.
Greiss, J., Schoneville, H., Adomavičienė, A., Baltuté, R., Bernat, A., Cantillon, B., ... Van der Horst, H. (2022). Food Aid in Europe in Times of the COVID-19 Crisis. An International Survey Project. (CSB Working Paper 22/05). Antwerp: Centre for Social Policy.
Greve, B., & Azhar Hussain, M. (2021). *Denmark (DK): 2018–2021* (EUROMOD country report). Sevilla: JRC of the European Commission.
Grimshaw, D., Bosch, G., & Rubery, J. (2014). Minimum wages and collective bargaining: What types of pay bargaining can foster positive pay equity outcomes? *British Journal of Industrial Relations*, *52*(3), 470–498.
Gruen, C., Mahringer, H., & Rhein, T. (2011). Low-wage Jobs: A Means for Employment Integration of the Unemployed? Evidence from Administrative Data in Germany and Austria. IAB-Discussion Paper.
Haapanala, H., Marx, I., & Parolin, Z. (2023). Decent wage floors in Europe: Does the minimum wage directive get it right? *Journal of European Social Policy*, *33*(4), 421–435. doi:10.1177/09589287231176977.
Hagenaars, A., de Vos, K. & Zaidi, A. (1994). *Poverty statististics in the late 1980s: research based on microdata*. Luxembourg: Eurostat
Hall, M. (2015). UK: TUC calls for stronger enforcement of national minimum wage. Retrieved from https://www.eurofound.europa.eu/publications/article/2015/uk-tuc-calls-for-stronger-enforcement-of-national-minimum-wage.
Hardy, B. L. (2017). Income instability and the response of the safety net. *Contemporary Economic Policy*, *35*(2), 312–330. doi:10.1111/coep.12187.
Harnisch, M. (2019). Non-take-up of Means-Tested Social Benefits in Germany (DIW Discussion papers 1793, V, 41 S.). Berlin: DIW.
Hay, C., & Wincott, D. (2012). *The Political Economy of European Welfare Capitalism*. Basingstoke: Palgrave Macmillan.
Heggebø, K., Dahl, E., & van der Wel, K. A. (2020). Disentangling the dynamics of social assistance: A linked survey-Register data cohort study of long-term social assistance recipients in Norway. *PLoS One*, *15*(3), e0230891. doi:10.1371/journal.pone.0230891.
Heggebø, K., & West Pedersen, A. (2022). The Norwegian Welfare State Adjusting to Crisis—Temporary Changes in Unemployment Benefit Regulations during the COVID-19 Pandemic and Their Long-Term Implications. Paper presented at the 2022 ESPANET conference, Vienna.
Hemerijck, A. (2018). Social investment as a policy paradigm. *Journal of European Public Policy*, *25*(6), 810–827. doi:10.1080/13501763.2017.1401111.
Hemerijck, A. (ed.) (2017). *The Uses of Social Investment*. Oxford: Oxford University Press.
Herke, B., & Janky, B. (2023). The role of the deservingness criteria in the case of single mothers' perceived welfare deservingness in Hungary. *Journal of Social Policy*, *52*(3), 560–580.

Hermans, K., Cantillon, B., Bernat, A., Carillo Alvarez, E., Cussó Parcerisas, I., Makinen, L., ... Szivós, P. (forthcoming). Methodological Working Paper: Using Cross-country Comparable Food Baskets to Price Charitable Food Aid Packages in Four European Countries (CSB Working paper). Antwerp: Herman Deleeck Centre for Social Policy.

Hermans, K., Cantillon, B., & Marchal, S. (forthcoming). Shifts at the Margin of the European Welfare States: How Important and Desirable Is Food Aid in Complementing Inadequate Minimum Incomes? (CSB Working Paper). Antwerp: University of Antwerp.

Hernández, A., Picos, F., & Riscado, S. (2022). Moving towards fairer regional minimum income schemes in Spain. *Journal of European Social Policy*, *32*(4), 452–466

Hernanz, V., Malherbet, F., & Pellizzari, M. (2004). Take-Up of Welfare Benefits in OECD Countries: A Review of the Evidence (OECD Social Employment and Migration Working Papers). OECD Publishing.

Herrnstein, R. J., & Murray, C. (2010). *The Bell Curve: Intelligence and Class Structure in American Life*. New York: Free Press.

Herwartz, H., Tafenau, E., & Schneider, F. (2015). One share fits all? Regional variations in the extent of the shadow economy in Europe. *Regional Studies*, *49*(9), 1575–1587. doi:10.1080/00343404.2013.848034.

Hick, R., & Marx, I. (2022). Poor Workers in Rich Democracies: On the Nature of In-Work Poverty and Its Relationship to Labour Market Policies (IZA Discussion Paper Series 15163). Bonn: IZA Institute for Labor Economics. Retrieved from https://docs.iza.org/dp15163.pdf.

Hiilamo, H., & Lehmus-Sun, A. (2020). Tuleeko ongella kaloja: Etuoikeutetun tulon ja toimeentulotuen saajien työssäkäynti [Will there be a problem with the fish: Employment of privileged income and subsistence allowance recipients]. *Kansantaloudellinen aikakauskirja*.

Hillmann, K., & Hohenleitner, I. (2012). Impact of Benefit Sanctions on Unemployment Outflow: Evidence from German Survey Data. HWWI Research Paper.

Hills, J. (2015). *Good Times, Bad Times: The Welfare Myth of Them and Us*. Bristol: Policy Press.

Hills, J., Smithies, R., & McKnight, A. (2006). *Tracking Income: How Working Families' Incomes Vary through the Year* (CASEreport 32). London: ESRC Research Centre for Analysis of Social Exclusion.

Hoff, S., Soede, A., Vrooman, C. J., Van Gaalen, C., Luten, A., & Lamers, S. (2010). *The Minimum Agreed Upon. Consensual Budget Standards for the Netherlands*. The Hague: The Netherlands Institute for Social Research SCP.

Holcomb, S., Hetling, A., & Yeo, V. (forthcoming). A multi-country systematic review of research on sanctions and equity in social welfare programs. *Social Policy & Administration*, 1–14. doi:10.1111/spol.12880.

Horemans, J. (2016). *Half a job, twice the poverty risk: Empirical investigations into the role of earnings, family composition, and institutions as factors underlying the higher in-work poverty risk of part-timers across Europe*. (PhD), Antwerp: University of Antwerp.

Horemans, J., & Marx, I. (2017). *Poverty and material deprivation among the self-employed in Europe: An exploration of a relatively uncharted landscape* (IZA DP No. 11007). Bonn: IZA.

Horemans, J., & Marx, I. (2018). Doesn't anyone else care? Variation in poverty among working single parents across Europe. In R. Nieuwenhuis & L. Maldonado (eds), *The Triple Bind of Single Parent Families: Resources, Employment and Policies to Improve Well-being* (pp. 195–221). Policy Press.

Hotz, V. J., & Scholz, J. K. (2006). Examining the Effect of the Earned Income Tax Credit on the Labor Market Participation of Families on Welfare (NBER Working Paper Series 11968). NBER.

Howard, M. W., Pinto, J., & Schachtschneider, U. (2019). Ecological Effects of Basic Income. In M. Torry (ed.), *The Palgrave International Handbook of Basic Income* (pp. 111–132). Cham: Springer International Publishing.

Howell, D. R. (2021). Low Pay in Rich Countries: Institutions, Bargaining Power and Earnings Inequality in the US, UK, Canada, Australia and France. Working Paper. Washington Center for Equitable Growth.

Howell, D. R., & Kalleberg, A. L. (2022). *Labour market inequality: |A comparative political economy perspective.* London: Institute for Fiscal Studies.

Hoynes, H. W., & Patel, A. J. (2018). Effective policy for reducing poverty and inequality? The earned income tax credit and the distribution of income. *Journal of Human Resources, 53*(4), 859–890.

Hufkens, T., Leventi, C., Rastrigina, O., Manios, K., Van Mechelen, N., Verbist, G., ... Goedemé, T. (2016). *HHoT: A New Flexible Hypothetical Household Tool for tax-benefit simulations in EUROMOD.* Leuven: HIVA. Retrieved from http://anet.uantwerpen.be/docman/irua/3d2c38/132957.pd.

Hungerford, T. L., & Thiess, R. (2013). *The earned income tax credit and the child tax credit* (Economic policy institute issue bried 370).

ILO. (2021). *Global wage report 2020–21. Wages and minimum wages in the time of COVID-19.* Geneva: International Labour Office. Retrieved from https://www.ilo.org/wcmsp5/groups/public/—dgreports/—dcomm/—publ/documents/publication/wcms_762534.pd.

Imbens, G. W., Rubin, D. B., & Sacerdote, B. I. (2001). Estimating the effect of unearned income on labor earnings, savings, and consumption: Evidence from a survey of lottery players. *American Economic Review, 91*(4), 778–794. doi:10.1257/aer.91.4.778.

Immervoll, H. (2009). Minimum-Income Benefits in OECD Countries: Policy Design, Effectiveness and Challenges (IZA Discussion Paper 4627). Bonn: IZA.

Immervoll, H., Hyee, R., Fernandez, R., & Lee, J. (2022). How Reliable Are Social Safety Nets?: Value and Accessibility in Situations of Acute Economic Need (OECD Social, Employment and Migration Working Papers, No. 252). OECD Publishing, Paris, https://doi.org/10.1787/65a269a3-en.

Immervoll, H., S. Jenkins, and S. Königs (2015). *Are Recipients of Social Assistance 'Benefit Dependent'?: Concepts, Measurement and Results for Selected Countries* (OECD Social, Employment and Migration Working Papers, No. 162). OECD Publishing, Paris, https://doi.org/10.1787/5jxrcmgpc6mn-en.

Immervoll, H., & Knotz, C. (2018). How Demanding Are Activation Requirements for Jobseekers (OECD Social, Employment and Migration Working Papers 215). Paris: OECD.

Immervoll, H., & Pearson, M. (2009). *A Good Time for Making Work Pay? Taking Stock of In-Work Benefits and Related Measures across the OECD* (OECD Social, Employment and Migration Working Papers 81). Paris: OECD Publishing.

Immervoll, H., & Scarpetta, S. (2012). Activation and employment support policies in OECD countries. An overview of current approaches. *IZA Journal of Labor Policy, 1*(9), 1–20.

Insitute of Medicine, & National Research Council (Eds.). (2013). *Supplemental Nutrition Assistance Program: Examining the Evidence to Define Benefit Adequacy.* Washington DC: The National Academies Press.

International Labour Organization. (2008). *Global Wage Report 2008/09: Minimum Wages and Collective Bargaining—Towards Policy Coherence.* Geneva: International labour organization.

International Labour Organization (2012). Recommendation concerning National Floors of Social Protection, 202 CFR. (2012).

International Labour Organization. (2016). *The Right to Social Security in the Constitutions of the World. Broadening the Moral and Legal Space for Social Justice* (ILO Global Study). Geneva: ILO.

International Monetary Fund. (2012). *Greece: Request for Extended Arrangement under The Extended Fund Facility—Staff Report* (IMF Country Report 12/57). Washington: International Monetary Fund.

ISTAT, Grassi, D., & Pannuzi, N. (2009). *La misura della poverta assoluta* (Argomenti Istat series 24).

Iversen, T., & Soskice, D. (2009). Distribution and redistribution: The shadow of the nineteenth century. *World Politics, 61*(3), 438–486.

Jacques, O., & Noël, A. (2021). Targeting within universalism. *Journal of European Social Policy, 31*(1), 15–29. doi:10.1177/0958928720918973

James, K. (2007). German minimum wage debate exposes deep left-right divide. Retrieved from https://www.dw.com/en/german-minimum-wage-debate-exposes-deep-left-right-divide/a-2509258.

Janssens, J. (2023). *Gaps in Belgium's Final Safety Net: towards a Better Measurement and Understanding of Non-take-up of Social Benefits in Belgium.* University of Antwerp.

Janssens, J., & Marchal, S. (2022). When do municipalities smooth access for new social assistance claimants? Local determinants of municipal welfare agency's implementation practices in Belgium. *Journal of Social Policy*, 1–20. doi:10.1017/S0047279422000253.

Janssens, J., & Van Mechelen, N. (2022). To take or not to take? An overview of the factors contributing to the non-take-up of public provisions. *European Journal of Social Security, 24*(2), 95–116. doi:10.1177/13882627221106800.

Jessoula, M., & Natili, M. (2020). Explaining Italian exceptionalism and its end: Minimum income from negltect to hyper-politicization. *Social Policy & Administration, 2020*(54), 599–613. doi:10.1111/spol.12608.

Jørgensen, C. (2015). Denmark: Heated debate about introducing minimum wage. Retrieved from https://www.eurofound.europa.eu/publications/article/2015/denmark-heated-debate-about-introducing-minimum-wage.

Jun, M. (2022). Stigma and shame attached to claiming social assistance benefits: Understanding the detrimental impact on UK lone mothers' social relationships. *Journal of Family Studies, 28*(1), 199–215.

Juncker, J.-C., Tusk, D., Dijsselbloem, J., Draghi, M., & Schulz, M. (2015). *The Five Presidents' Report: Completing Europe's Economic and Monetary Union.* Brussels: European Commission.

Kakoulidou, T., Konstantinou, P., & Moutos, T. (2020). Abolishing the Marital Wage Premium in Greece: Employment and Participation Effects on Minimum Wage Workers (CESifo Working Paper 8591). Munich: Center for Economic Studies and Ifo Institute. Retrieved from https://www.econstor.eu/bitstream/10419/226293/1/cesifo1_wp8591.pdf.

Kalíšková, K., Münich, D., & Pavel, J. (2021). *Czechia (CZ), 2018–2021* (EUROMOD country report). Sevilla: JRC.

Kangas, O., Jauhiainen, S., Simanainen, M., & Ylikanno, M. (2021). *Experimenting with Unconditional Basic Income.* Cheltenham, UK: Edward Elgar Publishing.

Karamessini, M., & Grimshaw, D. (2017). Minimum wages and the remaking of the wage-setting systems in Greece and the UK. In D. Grimshaw, C. Fagan, G. Hebson, & I. Tavora (eds), *Making Work More Equal: A New Labour Market Segmentation Approach* (pp. 330–356). Manchester: Manchester University Press.

Kazepov, Y., & Barberis, E. (2013). Social assistance governance in Europe: Towards a multilevel perspective. In I. Marx & K. Nelson (eds), *Minimum Income Protection in Flux* (pp. 217–248). Houndmills: Palgrave Macmillan.

Kenworthy, L. (2004). *Egalitarian Capitalism. Jobs, Incomes and Growth in Affluent Countries.* New York: Russel Sage Foundation.

Kenworthy, L. (2008). *Jobs with Equality.* Oxford: Oxford University Press.

Kenworthy, L. (2011). *Progress for the Poor.* Oxford: Oxford University Press.

Kenworthy, L. (2014). *Social Democratic America.* Oxford: Oxford University Press.

Kenworthy, L. (2020). *Social Democratic Capitalism.* Oxford: Oxford University Press.

Kenworthy, L. (2022). *Would Democratic Socialism Be Better?* Oxford: Oxford University Press.

Kenworthy, L., & Marx, I. (2018). In-work poverty in the United States. In H. Lohmann & I. Marx (eds), *Handbook on In-work Poverty* (p. 528). Cheltenham: Edward Elgar.

Kilhoffer, Z., De Groen, W. P., Lenaerts, K., Smits, I., Hauben, H., Waeyaert, W., . . . Robin-Olivier, S. (2019). *Study to Gather Evidence on the Working Conditions of Platform Workers.* Brussels: European Commission.

Kleven, H. (2019). *The EITC and the Extensive Margin: A Reappraisal.* National Bureau of Economic Research.

Kleven, H. J., & Kopczuk, W. (2011). Transfer program complexity and the take-up of social benefits. *American Economic Journal: Economic Policy*, *3*(1), 54–90.

Knijn, T., & Van Berkel, R. (2003). Again revisited: Employment and activation policies for lone parents on social assistance in the Netherlands. In J. Millar & M. Evans (eds), *Lone Parents and Employment: International Comparisons of What Works. Report prepared for the Department of Work and Pensions* (pp. 87–108). Bath: CASP Centre for the Analysis of Social Policy, University of Bath.

Knotz, C. (2018). A rising workfare state? Unemployment benefit conditionality in 21 OECD countries, 1980–2012. *Journal of International and Comparative Social Policy*, *34*(2), 91–108. doi:10.1080/21699763.2018.1472136.

Ko, W., & Moffitt, R. (2022). Take-up of Social Benefits (NBER Working Paper w30148). National Bureau of Economic Research.

Königs, S. (2018). Micro-level dynamics of social assistance receipt: Evidence from four European countries. *International Journal of Social Welfare*, *27*(2), 146–156.

Kopczuk, W., & Pop-Eleches, C. (2007). Electronic filing, tax preparers and participation in the Earned Income Tax Credit. *Journal of Public Economics*, *91*(7), 1351–1367. doi:10.1016/j.jpubeco.2006.11.003.

Korpi, W. (2006). Power resources and employer-centered approaches in explanations of welfare states and varieties of capitalism: Protagonists, consenters, and antagonists. *World Politics*, *58*(2), 167–206.

Korpi, W., & Palme, J. (1998). The paradox of redistribution and strategies of equality: Welfare state institutions, inequality, and poverty in the Western countries. *American Sociological Review*, *63*(5), 661–687.

Koutsampelas, C. (2016). The Cypriot CMI scheme and comparisons with other European countries. *Cyprus Economic Policy Review*, *10*(1), 3–26.

Kuypers, S., & Marx, I. (2019). The truly vulnerable: Integrating wealth into the measurement of poverty and social policy effectiveness. *Social Indicators Research*, *142*(1), 131–147. doi:10.1007/s11205-018-1911-6.

Kvist, J. (2022). *Denmark: A Minimum Income Benefit Reform Is Underway, Which Includes an Innovative Child Leisure Allowance* (ESPN Flash report 2022/62). Brussels: European Social Policy Network.

Laatu, M., Airio, I., & Mattila, H. (2020). Perustoimeentulotukiasiakkaiden käsityksiä ja kokemuksia toimeentulotukiuudistuksesta ja Kelan palveluista. *Teoksessa Tuija Korpela & Hanna-Mari Heinonen & Markku Laatu & Simo Raittila & Minna Ylikännö (toim.) Ojista allikkoon*, 116–150.

Laenen, T. (2018). Do institutions matter? The interplay between income benefit design, popular perceptions, and the social legitimacy of targeted welfare. *Journal of European Social Policy, 28*(1), 4–17. doi:10.1177/0958928718755777.

Laenen, T. (2020). *Welfare Deservingness and Welfare Policy: Popular Deservingness Opinions and Their Interaction with Welfare State Policies.* Cheltenham: Edward Elgar Publishing.

Laenen, T. (2023). *The Popularity of Basic Income: Evidence from the Polls.* New York: Springer.

Laenen, T., Marchal, S. & Van Lancker, W. (forthcoming). Policy feedback and income targeting in the welfare state. *Journal of Social Policy.* Forthcoming.

Lafleur, J.-M., & Vintila, D. (2020). *Migration and Social Protection in Europe and Beyond (volume 1): Comparing Access to Welfare Entitlements.* New York: Springer Nature.

Laín, B. (2022). Between epistemic necessity and political utility: The role of basic income experiments. *Journal of Policy Analysis and Management, 41*(2), 633–639. doi:10.1002/pam.22384

Laird, J., Parolin, Z., Waldfogel, J., & Wimer, C. (2018). Poor state, rich state: Understanding the variability of poverty rates across US States. *Sociological Science, 5*, 628–652.

Lalioti, V. (2015). The curious case of the guaranteed minimum income (GMI): Highlighting Greek 'exceptionalism' in a Southern European context. *Journal of European Social Policy, 26*(1), 80–93. doi:10.1177/0958928715608795.

Landais, C., Saez, E., & Zucman, G. (2020). A progressive European wealth tax to fund the European COVID response. In CfEP Research (ed.), *Europe in the Time of COVID19* (pp. 113–118).

Lecerf, M. (2016). *At a Glance. What Is 'Social Triple A'?* Brussels: European Parliament. Retrieved from https://www.europarl.europa.eu/RegData/etudes/ATAG/2016/577996/EPRS_ATA(2016)577996_EN.pdf.

Lee, M. A., Singelmann, J., & Yom-Tov, A. (2008). Welfare myths: The transmission of values and work among TANF families. *Social Science Research, 37*(2), 516–529. doi:10.1016/j.ssresearch.2007.09.005.

Leibetseder, B., Gubrium, E., Dierckx, D., Fluder, R., Hauri, R., & Raeymaeckers, P. (2017). Subsidiarity and social citizenship: Social assistance schemes in Austria, Belgium, Switzerland and Norway. *International Journal of Social Welfare, 26*(4), 353–365. doi:10.1111/ijsw.12241.

Leibfried, S. (1992). Towards a European welfare state? On integrating poverty regimes into the European Community. In Z. Ferge & J. E. Kolberg (eds), *Social Policy in a Changing Europe* (pp. 245–279). Frankfurt am Main: Campus Verlag.

Leigh, A. (2010). Who benefits from the earned income tax credit? Incidence among recipients, coworkers and firms. *The BE Journal of Economic Analysis & Policy, 10*(1).

Leijten, I. (2015). The German right to an existenzminimum, human dignity, and the possibility of minimum core socioeconomic rights protection. *German Law Journal, 16*(1), 23–48.

Leisering, L., & Barrientos, A. (2013). Social citizenship for the global poor? The worldwide spread of social assistance. *International Journal of Social Welfare, 22*, S50–S67.

Lemieux, T., & Milligan, K. (2008). Incentive effects of social assistance: A regression discontinuity approach. *Journal of Econometrics, 142*(2), 807–828.

Lens, D., Marx, I., & Vujić, S. (2019). Double jeopardy: How refugees fare in one European labor market. *IZA Journal of Development and Migration, 10*(1), 1–29.

Lepianka, D., Gelissen, J., & Van Oorschot, W. (2010). Popular explanations of poverty in Europe: Effect of contextual and individual characteristics across 28 European countries. *Acta Sociologica*, *53*(1), 53–72.

Living Wage Foundation. (2016). For the real cost of living. Retrieved from http://www.livingwage.org.uk/what-living-wage.

Lohmann, H. (2009). Welfare states, labour market institutions and the working poor: A comparative analysis of 20 European countries. *European Sociological Review*, *25*(4), 489–504. doi:10.1093/esr/jcn064.

Lohmann, H. (2018). The concept and measurement of in-work poverty. In H. Lohmann & I. Marx (eds), *Edward Elgar Handbook of Research on In-work Poverty* (pp. 7–25). Cheltenham: Edward Elgar.

Lohmann, H., & Marx, I. (2008). The different faces of in-work poverty across welfare state regimes In H.-J. Andreβ & H. Lohmann (eds), *The Working Poor in Europe* (pp. 17–46). London: Edward Elgar.

Lohmann, H., & Marx, I. (2018). *Handbook on In-work Poverty*. Cheltenham: Edward Elgar Publishing.

Løken, K. V., Lommerud, K. E., & Holm Reiso, K. (2018). Single mothers and their children: Evaluating a work-encouraging welfare reform. *Journal of Public Economics*, *167*, 1–20. doi:10.1016/j.jpubeco.2018.09.003.

Lorentzen, T., & Dahl, E. (2021). Social assistance dynamics in Norway revisited: A two-decade prospective study of trajectories of young social assistance recipients. *International Journal of Social Welfare*, *30*(3), 291–304.

Loukanova, P., & Tzanov, V. (2011). *Bulgaria*. (EEO ad hoc request April 2011).

Low Pay Commission. (2020). National Minimum Wage. Low Pay Commission Report 2019. Presented to Parliament by the Secretary of State for Business, Energy and Industrial Strategy by Command of Her Majesty. Retrieved from https://assets.publishing.service.gov.uk/government/uploads/system/uploads/attachment_data/file/856590/LPC_Report_2019.pdf.

Luzar, B. (2015). Slovenia: Around 6% of workers are on the minimum wage. Retrieved from https://www.eurofound.europa.eu/publications/article/2015/slovenia-around-6-of-workers-are-on-the-minimum-wage.

Machin, S., & Manning, A. (1997). Minimum wages and economic outcomes in Europe. *European Economic Review*, *41*(3–5), 733–742.

Machin, S., & Manning, A. (1999). The causes and consequences of longterm unemployment in Europe. In O. C. Ashenfelter & D. Card (eds), *Handbook of Labor Economics* (Vol. 3, pp. 3085–3139). New York: Elsevier.

Madama, I., Jessoula, M., & Natili, M. (2014). Minimum Income: The Italian Trajectory—One, No One and One Hundred Thousand Minimum Income Schemes. Working Paper-LPF. Centro Einaudi, Laboratorio di Politica Comparata e Filosofia Pubblica. Torino.

Malmberg-Heimonen, I., & Vuori, J. (2005). Activation or discouragement—the effect of enforced participation on the success of job-search training [Aktivointi vai lannistaminen—Työnhakuryhmään velvoittamisen vaikutukset]. *European Journal of Social Work*, *8*(4), 451–467.

Mani, A., Mullainathan, S., Shafir, E., & Zhao, J. (2013). Poverty impedes cognitive function. *Science*, *341*(6149), 976–980.

Manning, A. (2021). Monopsony in Labor Markets: A Review. *ILR Review*, *74*(1), 3–26. doi:10.1177/0019793920922499.

Marchal, S. (2020). An EU minimum wage target for adequate in-work incomes? *European Journal of Social Security*, *22*(4), 452–466. doi:10.1177/1388262720968118.

Marchal, S., & Cantillon, B. (2022). Poverty and multi-layered social assistance in Europe. In Y. Kazepov, E. Barberis, R. Cucca, & E. Mocca (eds), *Handbook of Urban Social Policy* (pp. 269–288). London: Edward Elgar Publishing.

Marchal, S., & De Wilde, M. (2019). De bijstand: wat als het maatwerk achter de feiten aanholt? [Social assistance: what if tailored policies lag behind?]. In M. Somers (ed.), *Fundamenten: sociale zekerheid in onzekere tijden. [Foundations: Social Security in Insecure Times]* (pp. 278–301). Sint-Gillis: Denktank Minerva.

Marchal, S., Kuypers, S., Marx, I., & Verbist, G. (2018). The Impact of Asset Tests in Two European Minimum Income Schemes. Paper presented at the 16th Annual ESPANET conference, Vilnius, Lithuania.

Marchal, S., Kuypers, S., Marx, I., & Verbist, G. (2021). But what about that nice house you own? The impact of asset tests in minimum income schemes in Europe: An empirical exploration. *Journal of European Social Policy*, *31*(1), 44–61.

Marchal, S., & Marx, I. (2018). Stemming the tide: What have European Union countries done to support low-wage workers in an era of downward wage pressures? *Journal of European Social Policy*, *28*(1), 18–33. doi:10.1177/0958928717704747.

Marchal, S., Marx, I., & Van Mechelen, N. (2014). The great wake-up call? Social citizenship and minimum income provisions in Europe in times of crisis. *Journal of Social Policy*, *43*(2), 247–267. doi:10.1017/s0047279413000950.

Marchal, S., Marx, I., & Van Mechelen, N. (2016). Minimum income schemes in the austerity tide. *IZA Journal of European labor studies*, *5*(4), 1–20. doi:10.1186/s40174-016-0052-7.

Marchal, S., & Siöland, L. (2019). A Safety Net That Holds? Tracking Minimum Income Protection Adequacy for the Elderly, the Working and the Non-working of Active Age (CSB Working Paper 19/09). Antwerp: Centre for Social Policy Herman Deleeck, University of Antwerp.

Marchal, S., Siöland, L., & Goedemé, T. (2018). Methodological Working Paper: Using HHoT to Generate Institutional Minimum Income Protection Indicators (18/20). Antwerp: Centre for Social Policy Herman Deleeck.

Marchal, S., Storms, B., Cantillon, B., Delanghe, H., Frederickx, M., Lemmens, A., ... Penne, T. (2022). *Onderzoek naar de haalbaarheid van het ontwikkelen en het gebruik van een bijkomende inicator om armoede te monitoren op Vlaams niveau [Feasibility Study into the Development and Use of an Additional Flemish Poverty Indicator]* (2022/06a). Leuven: Steunpunt Welzijn, Volksgezondheid en gezin. Vlaanderen.

Marchal, S., & Van Lancker, W. (2019). The measurement of targeting design in complex welfare states: A proposal and empirical applications. *Social Indicators Research*, *143*(2), 693–726.

Marchal, S., & Van Mechelen, N. (2013). Activation Strategies within European Minimum Income Schemes (GINI Discussion paper 87). Amsterdam: Aias.

Marchal, S., & Van Mechelen, N. (2014). A New Kid in Town? Active Inclusion in European Minimum Income Schemes. *Improve Discussion Paper*, *14*, 1–33.

Marchal, S., & Van Mechelen, N. (2017). A new kid in town? Active inclusion elements in European minimum income schemes *Social Policy & Administration*, *51*(1), 171–194. doi:10.1111/spol.12177.

Martin, J. P., & Immervoll, H. (2007). *The Minimum Wage: Making It Pay*. OECD Observer.

Martin, S., Murray, S., Marston, G., Chalmers, J., & Murphy, J. (2020). *Half a Citizen: Life on Welfare in Australia*. Abingdon, UK: Routledge.

Martinelli, L. (2017a). *The Fiscal and Distributional Implications of Alternative Universal Basic Income Schemes in the UK*. London: Institute for Policy Research.

Martinelli, L. (2017b). *Assessing the Case for a Universal Basic Income in the UK. (IPR Policy Brief)*. London: Institute for Policy Research.

Martinelli, L. (2020). A basic income trilemma: Affordability, adequacy, and the advantages of radically simplified welfare. *Journal of Social Policy*, *49*(3), 461–482. doi:10.1017/S0047279419000424.

Marx, A., & Peeters, H. (2008). An unconditional basic income and labor supply: Results from a pilot study of lottery winners. *The Journal of Socio-Economics*, *37*(4), 1636–1659. doi:10.1016/j.socec.2007.08.007.

Marx, I. (2007). The Dutch 'miracle'revisited: The impact of employment growth on poverty. *Journal of Social Policy*, *36*(3), 383–397.

Marx, I. (2019) The working poor. In B. Greve (ed.), *Routledge International Handbook of Poverty* (pp. 245–255). London: Routledge

Marx, I., Marchal, S., & Nolan, B. (2013). Mind the gap: Net incomes of minimum wage workers in the EU and the US. In I. Marx & K. Nelson (eds), *Minimum Income Protection in flux* (pp. 54–80). Houndmills: Palgrave.

Marx, I., & Nelson, K. (eds). (2013). *Minimum Income Protection in Flux*. Houndmills: Palgrave Macmillan.

Marx, I., & Nolan, B. (2014). In-work poverty. In B. Cantillon & F. Vandenbroucke (eds), *Reconciling Work and Poverty Reduction* (pp. 133–156). Oxford: Oxford University Press.

Marx, I., Salanauskaite, L., & Verbist, G. (2016). For the poor, but not only the poor: On the optimal design of redistributive policy. *Social Forces*, *95*(1), 1–24.

Marx, I., Vanhille, J., & Verbist, G. (2012). Combating in-work poverty in continental Europe: The potential impact of higher minimum wages and targeted tax relief. *Journal of Social Policy*, *41*(1), 19–41. doi:10.1017/s0047279411000341.

Marx, I., & Verbist, G. (1998). Low-paid work and poverty: A cross-country perspective. In S. Bazen (ed.), *Low-wage Employment in Europe* (pp. 63–86). Cheltenham: Elgar.

Marx, I., & Verbist, G. (2014). The policy response: Boosting employment and social investment. In *Changing Inequalities in Rich Countries: Analytical and Comparative Perspectives* (pp. 265–293). Oxford: Oxford University Press.

Matsaganis, M. (2018). The Contorted Politics of Guaranteed Minimum Income in Greece. DAStU Working Papers. Politechnico di Milano. Milano.

Matsaganis, M. (2020). Safety nets in (the) crisis: The case of Greece in the 2010s. *Social Policy & Administration*, *54*(4), 587–598. doi:10.1111/spol.12614.

Matsaganis, M., Ferrera, M., Capucha, L., & Moreno, L. (2003). Mending nets in the South: Anti-poverty policies in Greece, Italy, Portugal and Spain. *Social Policy and Administration*, *37*(6), 639–655.

McGuinness, S., Redmond, P., & Delaney, J. (2020). *Minimum Wage Non-Compliance: Evidence from Ireland* (12884). Bonn: IZA.

Mead, L. (1986). *Beyond Entitlement: The Social Obligations of Citizenship*. New York: Free Press.

Menyhert, B., Cseres-Gergely, Z., Kvedaras, V., Mina, B., Pericoli, F., & Zec, S. (2021). *Measuring and Monitoring Absolute Poverty (ABSPO)—Final Report* (EUR 30924 EN). Luxembourg: Publications Office of the European Union. Retrieved from https://publications.jrc.ec.europa.eu/repository/handle/JRC12744.

Mesiäislehto, M., Moisio, P., & Ilmakunnas, I. (2022). Do red-flagged clients exit social assistance earlier than others? The case of the Finnish social assistance system. *Social Policy and Society*, 1–15. doi:10.1017/S1474746422000380.

Meulders, D., & Jepsen, M. (2002). *The Individualisation of Rights in Social Protection Systems*. ULB—Universite Libre de Bruxelles.

Meyer, B. D., & Rosenbaum, D. T. (2001). Welfare, the earned income tax credit, and the labor supply of single mothers. *The Quarterly Journal of Economics*, *116*(3), 1063–1114.

Michalopoulos, C., Robins, P. K., & Card, D. (2005). When financial work incentives pay for themselves: Evidence from a randomized social experiment for welfare recipients. *Journal of Public Economics*, *89*(1), 5–29.

Mikloš, M. (2021). *Slovak Republic (SK), 2018–2021*. Sevilla: JRC.

Milanovic, B. (2016). *Global Inequality: A New Approach for the Age of Globalization*: Cambridge, MA: Harvard University Press.

Millar, J., & Bennett, F. (2017). Universal Credit: Assumptions, contradictions and virtual reality. *Social Policy and Society*, *16*(2), 169–182.

Millar, J., & Whiteford, P. (2020). Timing it right or timing it wrong: How should income-tested benefits deal with changes in circumstances? *Journal of Poverty and Social Justice*, *28*(1), 3–20.

Millar, M., & Crosse, R. (2018). Lone parent activation in Ireland: Putting the cart before the horses? *Social Policy & Administration*, *52*(1), 111–129. doi:10.1111/spol.12296.

Minas, R., Bäckman, O., Jakobsen, V., Korpi, T., Lorentzen, T., & Kauppinen, T. (2014). Rescaling inequality? Welfare reform and local variation in social assistance payments. In K. Farnsworth, Z. Irving, & M. Fenger (eds), *Social Policy Review 26* (pp. 239–258). Bristol: Policy Press.

Minas, R., & Øverbye, E. (2010). The territorial organization of social assistance schemes in Europe. In Y. Kazepov (ed.), *Rescaling Social Policies: Towards Multilevel Governance in Europe* (pp. 31–67). Surrey: Ashgate.

Minas, R., Wright, S., & Van Berkel, R. (2011). Decentralization and centralization: Governing the activation of social assistance recipients in Europe. *International Journal of Sociology and Social Policy*, *32*(5), 286–298.

Ministry of Social Affairs and Health. (2020). Results of the basic income experiment: Small employment effects, better perceived economic security and mental wellbeing [Press release]. Retrieved from https://stm.fi/en/-/perustulokokeilun-tulokset-tyollisyysvaikutukset-vahaisia-toimeentulo-ja-psyykkinen-terveys-koettiin-paremmaksi.

MISSOC. (2017). MISSOC Comparative Tables Database. Retrieved April 2019 from http://www.missoc.org/MISSOC/comparativeTables.

MISSOC. (2020). https://www.missoc.org/.

MISSOC. (2022). MISSOC Comparative Tables. Retrieved October 2022 from www.missoc.org.

Mood, C. (2010). Neighborhood social influence and welfare receipt in Sweden: A panel data analysis. *Social Forces*, *88*(3), 1331–1356.

Moreira, A. (2008). *The Activation Dilemma: Reconciling the Fairness and Effectiveness of Minimum Income Schemes in Europe*. Bristol: The Policy Press.

Moreira, A., Léon, M., Coda Moscarola, F., & Roumpakis, A. (2021). In the eye of the storm ... again! Social policy responses to COVID-19 in Southern Europe. *Social Policy & Administration*, *55*(2), 339–357. doi:10.1111/spol.12681.

Morel, N., Palier, B., & Palme, J. (2012). *Towards a Social Investment Welfare State? Ideas, Policies and Challenges*. Chicago: The University of Chicago Press.

Mullainathan, S., & Shafir, E. (2013). *Scarcity: Why Having Too Little Means so Much*. New York: Times Books.

Müller, T., & Schulten, T. (2020). *The European Minimum Wage on the Doorstep* (ETUI policy brief 1/2020). Brussels: ETUI.

Müller, T., & Schulten, T. (2022, August 22, 2022). *Minimum-Wages Directive—History in the Making*. Retrieved from https://socialeurope.eu/minimum-wages-directive-history-in-the-making.

Murgia, A., & Pulignano, V. (2021). Neither precarious nor entrepreneur: The subjective experience of hybrid self-employed workers. *Economic and Industrial Democracy*, *42*(4), 1351–1377. doi:10.1177/0143831x19873966.

Murray, C. (2008). *Losing Ground: American Social Policy, 1950–1980.* New York: Basic Books.

Murray, C., & Kneebone, E. (2017). The earned income tax credit and the white working class. Retrieved from https://www.brookings.edu/blog/the-avenue/2017/04/18/the-earned-income-tax-credit-and-the-white-working-class/.

NAO. (2018). *Rolling out Universal Credit.* London: Department for Work and Pensions.

Natili, M. (2018). Explaining different trajectories of minimum income schemes: Groups, parties and political exchange in Italy and Spain. *Journal of European Social Policy*, *28*(2), 116–129. doi:10.1177/0958928717707272.

Natili, M. (2019). *The Politics of Minimum Income: Explaining Path Departure and Policy Reversal in the Age of Austerity.* New York: Springer.

Natili, M. (2020). Worlds of last-resort safety nets? A proposed typology of minimum income schemes in Europe. *Journal of International and Comparative Social Policy*, *36*(1), 57–75. doi:10.1080/21699763.2019.1641134.

National Conference of State Legislatures. (2023). *Earned income tax credit overview.* Retrieved from https://www.ncsl.org/human-services/earned-income-tax-credit-overview.

Nautet, M., & Piton, C. (2019). An analysis of non-standard forms of employment in Belgium. *NBB Economic Review*, 1–28.

Navas Román, M., & Villazán Pellejero, N. (2021). *SPAIN (ES), 2018–2021* (EUROMOD Country report). Sevilla: JRC.

Navicke, J., Avram, S., & Demmou, L. (2016). The Effects of Reform Scenarios for Unemployment Benefits and Social Assistance on Financial Incentives to Work and Poverty in Lithuania (OECD Economics Department Working Papers). Paris: OECD Publishing.

Nelson, K. (2007). *Introducing SaMip: The Social Assistance and Minimum Income Protection Interim Dataset* (S-WpPEc 11/2007). Stockholm: Swedish institute for Social Research.

Nelson, K. (2008). Minimum income protection and european integration: Trends and levels of minimum benefits in comparative perspective. *International Journal of Health Services*, *38*(1), 103–124.

Nelson, K. (2012). Counteracting material deprivation: The role of social assistance in Europe. *Journal of European Social Policy*, *22*(2), 148–163. doi:10.1177/0958928711433658.

Nelson, K., & Fritzell, J. (2015). *ESPN Thematic Report on Minimum Income Schemes: Sweden.* Brussels: European Commission.

Nichols, A., & Rothstein, J. (2016). 2. The earned income tax credit. In R. Moffitt (ed), *Economics of Means-Tested Transfer Programs in the United States, Volume I* (pp. 137–218). Chicago: University of Chicago Press.

Nieuwenhuis, R., & Maldonado, L. (2018a). Single-parent families and in-work poverty. In H. Lohmann & I. Marx (eds), *Handbook on In-work Poverty* (pp. 171–192). Cheltenham: Edward Elgar Publishing.

Nieuwenhuis, R., & Maldonado, L. (eds.). (2018b). *The Triple Bind of Single-Parent Families: Resources, Employment and Policies to Improve Well-being.* Bristol: Policy Press.

Niscimento, R. (1997). Legislation increases national minimum wage. Retrieved from https://www.eurofound.europa.eu/publications/article/1997/legislation-increases-national-minimum-wage.

Noël, A. (2019). The politics of minimum income protection in OECD countries. *Journal of Social Policy*, *48*(2), 227–247. doi:10.1017/S0047279418000351.

Nolan, B. (2013). What use is social investment? *Journal of European Social Policy*, *23*, 459. doi:10.1177/0958928713499177.

Nolan, B. (2018a). *Generating Prosperity for Working Families in Affluent Countries*. Oxford: Oxford University Press.

Nolan, B. (2018b). *Inequality and Inclusive Growth in Rich Countries: Shared Challenges and Contrasting Fortunes*. Oxford: Oxford University Press.

Nolan, B. (2020). The median versus inequality-adjusted GNI as core indicator of 'ordinary' household living standards in rich countries. *Social Indicators Research, 150*(2), 569–585. doi:10.1007/s11205-020-02311-0.

Nolan, B., Salverda, W., Checchi, D., Marx, I., McKnight, A., Tóth, I. G., & van de Werfhorst, H. G. (2014). *Changing Inequalities and Societal Impacts in Rich Countries: Thirty Countries' Experiences*. Oxford: Oxford University Press.

OECD. (2004). *OECD Employment Outlook*. Paris: OECD.

OECD. (2008). *Growing Unequal?: Income Distribution and Poverty in OECD Countries*. Paris: OECD.

OECD. (2011). *Divided We Stand: Why Inequality Keeps Rising*. Paris: OECD.

OECD. (2015). *Minimum Wages after the Crisis: Making them Pay*. Paris: Directorate for Employment, Labour and Social Affairs. Retrieved from www.oecd.org/social/Focus-on-Minimum-Wages-after-the-crisis-2015.pdf.

OECD. (2017). *Minimum Wages per Country*. Paris: OECD.

OECD. (2019). *OECD Employment Outlook 2019*. Paris: OECD.

OECD. (2020). *OECD Employment Outlook 2020*. Paris: OECD.

OECD. (2022). *Tax Policy and Gender Equality: A Stocktake of Country Approaches*. Paris: OECD Publishing.

OECD. (2023a). *Benefits and Wages: Country Specific Files*. Retrieved from https://www.oecd.org/els/soc/benefits-and-wages/tax-benefit-web-calculator/#d.en.500997.

OECD. (2023b). Social Benefit Recipients (SOCR) Database. Retrieved from https://www.oecd.org/social/social-benefit-recipients-database.htm.

Official Journal of the EU (2016). Consolidated version of the Treaty on the Functioning of the European Union. Part Three – Union Policies and Internal Actions Title X – Social Policy. Article 153 (ex Article 137 TEC), (2016).

Olsthoorn, M., Koot, P., Ras, M., Hulst, B., Hoff, S., Wildeboer Schut, J. M., ... Verkade, E. (2020). *Kansrijk Armoedebeleid*. Den Haag: CPB/SCP.

Overstreet, D. (2019). The effect of minimum wage on per capita income in Arizona: Empirical analysis. *Poverty & Public Policy, 11*(1–2), 156–168. doi:10.1002/pop4.249.

Paccagnella, M. (2015). Skills and Wage Inequality: Evidence from PIAAC (OECD Education working papers 114). Paris: OECD Publishing.

Page, B. I., & Jacobs, L. R. (2009). *Class War?: What Americans Really Think about Economic Inequality*. Chicago: University of Chicago Press.

Pak, T.-Y. (2020). Welfare stigma as a risk factor for major depressive disorder: Evidence from the Supplemental Nutrition Assistance Program. *Journal of Affective Disorders, 260*, 53–60. doi:10.1016/j.jad.2019.08.079.

Palier, B. (2004a). French welfare reform in comparative perspective. *Revue française de sociologie, 45*(5), 93–120. doi:10.3917/rfs.455.0093.

Palier, B. (2004b). *Social Protection Reforms in Europe: Strategies for a New Social Model*.

Palier, B. (2019). Work, social protection and the middle classes: What future in the digital age? *International Social Security Review, 72*(3), 113–133. doi:10.1111/issr.12218.

Palmer, E. (2016). A meaningful right to social security in the UK: Beyond the policies and politics of austerity? In M. Wujckzyk (ed.), *The Right to Social Security in the Constitutions of the World: Broadening the Moral and Legal Space for Social Justice* (pp. 296–316). Geneva: ILO.

Palviainen, H. (2023). Incentivizing last-resort social assistance clients: Evidence from a Finnish policy experiment. *International Tax and Public Finance, 30*(1), 1–19.
Panican, A., & Ulmestig, R. (2016). Social rights in the shadow of poor relief—social assistance in the universal Swedish welfare state. *Citizenship Studies, 20*, 1–15. doi:10.1080/13621025.2016.1139053.
Pape, M. (2022). *Directive on Adequate Minimum Wages.* Brussels: European Parliament Research Service. Retrieved from https://www.europarl.europa.eu/RegData/etudes/BRIE/2022/733535/EPRS_BRI(2022)733535_EN.pdf.
Parasuraman, R., & Manzey, D. H. (2010). Complacency and bias in human use of automation: An attentional integration. *Human Factors, 52*(3), 381–410.
Pareliussen, J., Hwang, H., & Viitamäki, H. (2018). Basic income or a single tapering rule? Incentives, inclusiveness and affordability compared for the case of Finland. (OECD Economics Department Working Papers No. 1464) doi: 10.1787/d8c0fbc4-en.
Parolin, Z. (2021). Decomposing the decline of cash assistance in the United States, 1993 to 2016. *Demography, 58*(3), 1119–1141. doi:10.1215/00703370-9157471.
Parolin, Z., & Luigjes, C. (2019). Incentive to retrench? Investigating the interactions of state and federal social assistance programs after welfare reform. *Social Service Review, 93*(2), 305–339. doi:10.1086/703118.
Parolin, Z., & Van Lancker, W. (2021). What a social investment 'litmus test' must address: A response to Plavgo and Hemerijck. *Journal of European Social Policy, 31*(3), 297–308. doi:10.1177/09589287211012974.
Penne, T., Cornelis, I., & Storms, B. (2019). *Reducing out-of-pocket costs to improve the adequacy of minimum income protection? Reference Budgets as an EU Policy Indicator: The Belgian Case* (Working Paper 4/19). Antwerpen: Herman Deleeck Centre for Social Policy.
Penne, T., Cornelis, I., & Storms, B. (2020). All we need is.... *Social Indicators Research, 147*(3), 991–1013. doi:10.1007/s11205-019-02181-1.
Penne, T., Hufkens, T., Goedemé, T., & Storms, B. (2020). To what extent do welfare states compensate for the cost of children? The joint impact of taxes, benefits and public goods and services. *Journal of European Social Policy, 30*(1), 79–94. doi:10.1177/0958928719868458.
Pennings, F. (2016). Constitutional and conventional protection of social security in the Netherlands. In M. Wujckzyk (ed.), *The Right to Social Security in the Constitutions of the World: Broadening the Moral and Legal Space for Social Justice* (pp. 172–179). Geneva: ILO.
Perez, S. A., & Matsaganis, M. (2017). The political economy of austerity in Southern Europe. *New Political Economy, 23*(2), 192–207. doi:10.1080/13563467.2017.1370445.
Perista, H., Carrilho, P., Lima, C., & da Paz, M. (2015). Portugal: Rise in number of workers on minimum wage. Retrieved from https://www.eurofound.europa.eu/publications/article/2015/portugal-rise-in-number-of-workers-on-minimum-wage.
Pesole, A., Urzí Brancati, M., Fernández-Macías, E., F, B., & Gonzálze Vázquez, I. (2018). *Platform Workers in Europe.* Luxembourg: Publication Office of the European Union.
Petersen, M. B. (2012). Social welfare as small-scale help: Evolutionary psychology and the deservingness heuristic. *American Journal of Political Science, 56*(1), 1–16.
Piasna, A., Zwysen, W., & Drahakoupil, J. (2022). *The Platform Economy in Europe. Results from the Second ETUI Internet and Platform Work Survey.* (2022.05). Brussels: European Trade Union Institute.
Piketty, T. (2014). *Capital in the Twenty-First Century.* Cambridge, MA: Harvard University Press.
Pingle, J. F. (2005). Welfare, intergenerational cohabitation penalties, and single mothers' employment. *Review of Economics of the Household, 3*, 123–144.
POD Maatschappelijke Integratie. (2018). PRIMABOOK. Retrieved from https://primabook.mi-is.be/nl/recht-op-maatschappelijke-integratie/berekening-van-de-bestaansmiddelen.

Prassl, J. (2018). *Humans as a Service: The Promise and Perils of Work in the Gig Economy.* Oxford: Oxford University Press.

Premrov, T., & Fuchs, M. (2021). *Austria (AT): 2018–2021* (Euromod country report). Sevilla: JRC of the European Commission.

Räsanen, T., & Simanainen, M. (2021). *Finland (FI): 2018–2021* (Euromod country report). Sevilla: JRC of the European Commission.

Rat, C. (2022). Social Minima and the Minimum Income Guarantee Program in Romania. Paper presented at the ESPANET, Vienna.

Rodríguez Cabrero, G. (2009). *Assessment of Minimum Income Schemes in Spain (Peer Review on Social Protection and Social Inclusion and Assessment in Social Inclusion).* Brussels: European Commission DG Employment, Social Affairs and Equal Opportunities.

Røed, K., & Westlie, L. (2012). Unemployment insurance in welfare states: The impacts of soft duration constraints. *Journal of the European Economic Association, 10*(3), 518–554.

Roosma, F., & van Oorschot, W. (2020). Public opinion on basic income: Mapping European support for a radical alternative for welfare provision. *Journal of European Social Policy, 30*(2), 190–205. doi:10.1177/0958928719882827.

Rossetti, F., Roosma, F., Laenen, T., & Abts, K. (2020). An unconditional basic income? How Dutch citizens justify their opinions about a basic income and work conditionality. *Journal of International and Comparative Social Policy, 36*, 1–17. doi:10.1017/ics.2020.15.

Rothstein, J. (2010). Is the EITC as good as an NIT? Conditional cash transfers and tax incidence. *American Economic Journal: Economic Policy, 2*(1), 177–208.

Ruge, M. (2010). Determinants and size of the shadow economy—a structural equation model. *International Economic Journal, 24*(4), 511–523. doi:10.1080/10168737.2010.525988.

Russell, H., & Whelan, C. T. (2004). *Low Income and Deprivation in an Enlarged Europe.* Dublin: European Foundation for the Improvement of Living and Working Conditions. Retrieved from https://www.esri.ie/publications/low-income-and-deprivation-in-an-enlarged-europe.

Ryckx, F., & Kampelmann, S. (2012). *Who Earns Minimum Wages in Europe? New Evidence Based on Household Surveys* (124). Brussels: European Trade Union Institute.

Sabatinelli, S. (2010). Activation and rescaling: Interrelated questions in social policy? In Y. Kazepov (ed.), *Rescaling Social Policies: Towards Multilevel Governance in Europe* (pp. 75–101). Farnham/Burlington: Ashgate.

Sainsbury, D. (2006). Immigrants' social rights in comparative perspective: Welfare regimes, forms in immigration and immigration policy regimes. *Journal of European Social Policy, 16*(3), 229–244. doi:10.1177/0958928706065594.

Sainsbury, R. (2014). Talking Universal Credit: In conversation with Lord Freud, Minister for Welfare Reform. *Journal of Poverty and Social Justice, 22*(1), 37–44.

Salverda, W. (2018). Low earnings and their drivers in relation to in-work poverty. In L. Henning (ed), *Handbook on In-work Poverty* (pp. 26–49). Cheltenham: Edward Elgar Publishing.

Salverda, W., & Checchi, D. (2014). Labour-Market Institutions and the Dispersion of Wage Earnings Labour-Market Institutions and the Dispersion of Wage Earnings. In A. B. Atkinson & F. Bourguignon (eds), *Handbook of Income Distribution* (pp. 1535–1728).

Salverda, W., & Rook, V. (2023). The Vicious Entanglement of Labour-Market and Income Inequalities in Europe (CSB Working Paper 23/02). Antwerp: Centre for Social Policy Herman Deleeck.

Schilbach, F., Schofield, H., & Mullainathan, S. (2016). The psychological lives of the poor. *American Economic Review, 106*(5), 435–440.

Schmitz, S. (2019). The effects of Germany's statutory minimum wage on employment and welfare dependency. *German Economic Review, 20*(3), 330–355. doi:10.1111/geer.12196.

Schoukens, P. (2016). Belgium: the right to social security in the Belgian constitution. In M. Wujckzyk (ed.), *The Right to Social Security in the Constitutions of the World: Broadening the Moral and Legal Space for Social Justice* (pp. 7–19). Geneva: ILO.

Schoukens, P., Barrio, A., & Montebovi, S. (2018). The EU social pillar: An answer to the challenge of the social protection of platform workers? *European Journal of Social Security*, *20*(3), 219–241.

Schulten, T., & Luebker, M. (2019). *WSI Minimum Wage Report 2019: Time for Substantial Minimum Wage Rises and a European Minimum Wage Policy* (46). Dusseldorf: WSI, Hans-Böckler-Stiftung.

Schuseil, P. (2013). Follow-up: The German minimum wage debate. Retrieved from https://www.bruegel.org/2013/09/follow-up-the-german-minimum-wage-debate/.

Scott, E. K., Edin, K., London, A. S., & Kissane, R. J. (2004). Unstable work, unstable income: Implications for family well-being in the era of time-limited welfare. *Journal of Poverty*, *8*(1), 61–88. doi:10.1300/J134v08n01_04.

Sen, A. (1983). Poor, relatively speaking. *Oxford Economic Papers*, *35*(2), 153–169. Retrieved from http://www.jstor.org/stable/2662642.

Seo, H. (2021). 'Dual' labour market? Patterns of segmentation in European labour markets and the varieties of precariousness. *Transfer: European Review of Labour and Research*, *27*(4), 485–503. doi:10.1177/10242589211061070.

Sheehan, B., & Geary, J. (1998). Ireland set to introduce a national minimum wage in 2000. Retrieved from https://www.eurofound.europa.eu/publications/article/1998/ireland-set-to-introduce-a-national-minimum-wage-in-2000.

Simonse, O., Vanderveen, G., van Dillen, L. F., van Dijk, W. W., & van Dijk, E. (2023). Social security or insecurity? The experience of welfare participation by financially vulnerable households in the Netherlands. *Social Policy & Administration*, 57(3), 255–271. https://doi.org/10.1111/spol.12849.

Skocpol, T. (1991). Targeting within universalism: Politically viable policies to combat poverty in the United States. In C. Jencks & P. E. Peterson (eds), *The Urban Underclass* (pp. 411–436). Washington, DC: The Brookings Institution.

Smedsvik, B., & Iacono, R. (2022). (In)visible Sanctions: Micro-level Evidence on Compulsory Activation for Young Welfare Recipients (INET Oxford Working paper 2022-24). Institute for New Economic Thinking, University of Oxford.

Snel, E., Reelick, F., & Groenenboom, N. (2013). Time and poverty revisited: A replication of Leisering and Leibfried. *Journal of European Social Policy*, *23*(2), 179–191.

Spasova, S., & Wilkens, M. (2018). The social situation of the self-employed in Europe: Labour market issues and social protection. In B. Vanhercke, D. Ghailani, & S. Sabato (eds.), *Social Policy in the European Union: State of Play 2019* (pp. 97–116). Brussels: European Trade Union Institute (ETUI) and European Social Observatory (OSE).

Standing, G. (1997). The folly of social safety nets: Why basic income is needed. *Eastern Europe Social Research*, *64*(4), 1339–1379.

Standing, G. (2011). *The Precariat: The New Dangerous Class*. London and New York: Bloomsbury Acadamic.

Standing, G. (2014). The Precariat. *Contexts*, *13*(4), 10–12. doi:10.1177/1536504214558209.

Standing, G. (2017). *Basic Income: And How We Can Make It Happen*. UK: Penguin.

Starr, G. (1981). *Minimum Wage Fixing: An International Review of Practices and Problems*. Geneva: ILO.

Steenssens, K., Hausmann, T., Lamberts, M., Van Regenmortel, T., & Cortese, V. (2016). *Aanpassing van de leeflooncategorieën aan de hedendaagse samenlevings- en woonvormen. Een mixed method verbeteronderzoek [Adjustment of the Living Wage Categories to New Cohabitation and Living Arrangements. A Mixed Method Improvement Study].* Brussels: POD MI.

Stenberg, S.-Å. (2000). Inheritance of welfare recipiency: An intergenerational study of social assistance recipiency in postwar Sweden. *Journal of Marriage and Family, 62*(1), 228–239.

Storms, B., Goedemé, T., Van den Bosch, K., Penne, T., Schuerman, N., and Stockman, S. (2014), *Review of current state of play on reference budget practices at national, regional, and local level,* Pilot project for the development of a common methodology on reference budgets in Europe. Contract no. VC/2013/0554, Brussels: European Commission, 150p.

Swank, D. (2020). The partisan politics of new social risks in advanced postindustrial democracies: Social protection for labor market outsiders. In R. Careja, P. Emmenegger, & N. Giger (eds), *The European Social Model under Pressure* (pp. 139–157). Wiesbaden: Springer.

Swedish Institute for Social Research. (2016). *SPIN (Social Policy Indicators) Dataset* Retrieved from: http://www.sofi.su.se/spin/data.

Taschwer, M. T. (2021). The political economy of minimum income benefits: How parties, unions and migration influence benefit adequacy. *Journal of European Social Policy, 31*(1), 30–43.

Tasseva, I. V. (2016). Evaluating the performance of means-tested benefits in Bulgaria. *Journal of Comparative Economics, 44*(4), 919–935. doi:10.1016/j.jce.2016.02.003.

Tervola, J., Mesiäislehto, M., & Ollonqvist, J. (2023). Smaller net or just fewer to catch? Disentangling the causes for the varying sizes of minimum income schemes. *International Journal of Social Welfare, 32*(2), 133–148.

Theodoulou, N. (2022, August 31, 2022). 'Historic' minimum wage set at €940 after six months of employment (update 4). *CyprusMail.* Retrieved from https://cyprus-mail.com/2022/08/31/minimum-wage-last-attempt-to-find-common-ground/.

Thewissen, S., Kenworthy, L., Nolan, B., Roser, M., & Smeeding, T. (2015). Rising Income Inequality and Living Standards in OECD Countries: How Does the Middle Fare? LIS Working Paper Series.

Torry, M. (2019). *The Palgrave International Handbook of Basic Income.* London: Palgrave Macmillan.

Townsend, P. (1979). *Poverty in the United Kingdom.* London: Allen Lane and Penguin Books.

Trade Union Congress. (2015). National minimum wage enforcement. Keeping up the pressure—what more needs to be done? TUC. Retrieved from https://www.tuc.org.uk/sites/default/files/ImprovingNationalMinimumWag%20Enforcement_0.pd.

Trlifajová, L., & Hurrle, J. (2019). Work must pay: Does it? Precarious employment and employment motivation for low-income households. *Journal of European Social Policy, 29*(3), 376–395.

van Berkel, R. (2007). Social assistance dynamics in the Netherlands: Exploring the sustainability of independence from social assistance via labour market inclusion. *Social Policy and Society, 6*(2), 127–139. doi:10.1017/S147474640600340X.

van de Ven, J., Hérault, N., & Azpitarte, F. (2017). Identifying tax implicit equivalence scales. *The Journal of Economic Inequality, 15,* 257–275. doi:10.1007/s10888-017-9354-x.

Van Gestel, R., Goedemé, T., Janssens, J., Lefevere, E., & Lemkens, R. (2022). Improving take-up by reaching out to potential beneficiaries. Insights from a large-scale field experiment in Belgium. *Journal of Social Policy,* 1–21. doi:10.1017/S004727942100088X.

Van Lancker, A., Aranguiz, A., & Verschueren, H. (2020). *Expert Study on a Binding EU Framework on Adequate National Minimum Income Schemes. Making the Case for an EU Framework Directive on Minimum Income.* Brussels: EAPN.

Van Lancker, W., Marchal, S., Schuerman, N., Van Mechelen, N., & Van Kerm, P. (2015). Leven aan de dop. De impact van werkloosheid op het inkomen in België in vergelijkend perspectief. In I. Pannecoucke, W. Lahaye, J. Vranken, & R. Van Rossem (eds), *Armoede in België—Jaarboek 2015* (pp. 191–214). Gent: Academia Press.

Van Lancker, W., & Van Mechelen, N. (2015). Universalism under siege? Exploring the association between targeting, child benefits and child poverty across 26 countries. *Social Science Research*, *50*, 60–75. doi:10.1016/j.ssresearch.2014.11.012.

Van Limberghen, G., Bertrand, O., Dumont, D., Fontaine, M., Tojerow, I., Cantillon, B., ... Marchal, S. (2020). *L'accès des travailleurs à la sécurité sociale en Belgique (Mission d'étude pour le SPF Sécurité sociale).* Bruxelles: SPF Sécurité sociale.

Van Mechelen, N. (2010). *Barriers to Adequate Social Safety Nets.* Antwerp: University of Antwerp.

Van Mechelen, N., & Bogaerts, K. (2008). *Aanvullende financiële steun in Vlaamse OCMW's.* Antwerpen: UA/Centrum voor Sociaal Beleid Herman Deleeck.

Van Mechelen, N., & Bradshaw, J. (2013). Child poverty as a government priority: Child benefit packages for working families, 1992–2009. In I. Marx & K. Nelson (eds), *Minimum Income Protection in Flux* (pp. 81–107). Houndmills: Palgrave Macmillan.

Van Mechelen, N., & Janssens, J. (2017). *Who Is to Blame? An Overview of the Factors Contributing to the Non-take-up of Social Rights* (17/08). Antwerp Herman Deleeck Centre for Social Policy.

Van Mechelen, N., & Marchal, S. (2013a). Struggle for life: Social assistance benefits, 1992–2009. In I. Marx & K. Nelson (eds), *Minimum Income Protection in Flux* (pp. 28–53). Houndmills: Palgrave Macmillan.

Van Mechelen, N., & Marchal, S. (2013b). Trends and Convergence of Europe's Minimum Income Schemes *(Improve working papers 13/11).* Antwerp: Herman Deleeck Centre for Social Policy.

Van Mechelen, N., Marchal, S., Goedemé, T., Marx, I., & Cantillon, B. (2011). The CSB-Minimum Income Protection Indicators Dataset *(CSB-MIPI)* (CSB Working Paper Series 11/05). Antwerp: Herman Deleeck Centre for Social Policy, University of Antwerp.

van Oorschot, W. (2000). Who should get what, and why? On deservingness criteria and the conditionality of solidarity among the public. *Policy & Politics*, *28*(1), 33–48. doi:10.1332/0305573002500811.

Van Oorschot, W. (2006). Making the difference in social Europe: Deservingness perceptions among citizens of European welfare states. *Journal of European Social Policy*, *16*(1), 23–42.

van Oorschot, W., Roosma, F., Meuleman, B., & Reeskens, T. (2017). *The Social Legitimacy of Targeted Welfare: Attitudes to Welfare Deservingness.* Cheltenham: Edward Elgar Publishing.

van Oorschot, W. J. H. (1994). *Take It or Leave It. A Study of Non-take-up of Social Security Benefits.* Tilburg: Tilburg University Press.

Van Parijs, P., & Vanderborght, Y. (2017). *Basic Income: A Radical Proposal for a Free Society and a Sane Economy.* Cambridge: Harvard University Press.

Van Parijs, P., & Vanderborght, Y. (2020). Basic Income: A Radical Proposal for a Free Society and a Sane Economy (excerpts). *Journal of Economic Sociology-Ekonomicheskaya Sotsiologiya*, *21*(1), 44–59.

Vandelannoote, D., & Verbist, G. (2019). The design of in-work benefits: how to boost employment and combat poverty in Belgium? In B. Cantillon, T. Goedemé, & J. Hills (eds), *Decent Incomes for All: Improving Policies in Europe* (pp. 244–268). Oxford: Oxford University Press.

Vandenbroucke, F. (2019). The European pillar of social rights: From promise to delivery. In M. Ferrera (ed.), *Towards a European Social Union: The European Pillar of Social Rights and the Roadmap for a Fully-fledged Social Union—A Forum Debate* (pp. 2–11). Torino: Centro Einaudi.

Vandenbroucke, F., Cantillon, B., Van Mechelen, N., Goedemé, T., & Van Lancker, A. (2013). *The EU and Minimum Income Protection: Clarifying the Policy Conundrum*. New York: Springer.

Vandenbroucke, F., & Diris, R. (2014). Mapping at-risk-of-poverty rates, Household Employment and Social Spending. In B. Cantillon & F. Vandenbroucke (eds), *Reconciling Work and Poverty Reduction: How Successful Are European Welfare States?* (pp. 1–59). Oxford: Oxford University Press.

Vandenbroucke, F., & Vleminckx, K. (2011). Disappointing poverty trends: Is the social investment state to blame? *Journal of European Social Policy*, *21*(5), 450–471. doi:10.1177/0958928711418857.

Vanderborght, Y. (2006). Why trade unions oppose basic income. *Basic Income Studies*, *1*, 5-5. doi:10.2202/1932-0183.1002.

Vaughan-Whitehead, D. (2010). *The Minimum Wage Revisited in the Enlarged EU*. Cheltenham: Edward Elgar.

Veale, M., Van Kleek, M., & Binns, R. (2018). Fairness and Accountability Design Needs for Algorithmic Support in High-Stakes Public Sector Decision-Making. Paper presented at the Proceedings of the 2018 Chi Conference on Human Factors in Computing Systems.

Veit-Wilson, J. H. (1986). Paradigms of poverty: A rehabilitation of BS Rowntree. *Journal of Social Policy*, *15*(1), 69–99.

Vella, S., Said, R., & Apap, W. (2021). *Malta (MT), 2018–2019*. Sevilla: Joint Research Center of the European Commission.

Ventry, D. (2000). The collision of tax and welfare politics: The political history of the Earned Income Tax Credit, 1969–99. *National Tax Journal*, *53*(4), 983–1026.

Verlaat, T., & Zulkarnain, A. (2022). *Evaluatie experimenten Participatiewet: effecten op brede baten*. Den Haag: Centraal Planbureau.

Vlandas, T. (2013). The politics of in-work benefits: The case of the active income of solidarity in France. *French Politics*, *11*(2), 117–142.

Vlandas, T. (2019). The politics of the basic income guarantee: Analysing individual support in Europe. *Basic Income Studies*, *14*. doi:10.1515/bis-2018-0021.

Vlandas, T. (2021). The political economy of individual-level support for the basic income in Europe. *Journal of European Social Policy*, *31*(1), 62–77. doi:10.1177/0958928720923596.

Vonk, G., & Olivier, M. (2019). The fundamental right of social assistance: A global, a regional (Europe and Africa) and a national perspective (Germany, the Netherlands and South Africa). *European Journal of Social Security*, *21*(3), 219–240.

Wang, J., & van Vliet, O. (2016). Social assistance and minimum income levels and replacement rates dataset. *Available at SSRN 2894471*.

Wang, J., van Vliet, O., & Goudswaard, K. (2018). Minimum income protection and EU coordination. *European Journal of Social Security*, *20*(3), 253–271. doi:10.1177/1388262718798896.

Watt, A. (2019). Towards a European Social Union: From spillovers to just transitions. In M. Ferrera & F. Vandenbroucke (eds), *European Social Union: A Public Forum Debate* (pp. 160–169). Torino: Centro Einaudi.

Watts, B., & Fitzpatrick, S. (2018). *Welfare Conditionality*. Abingdon, UK: Routledge.

Weisner, T. S., Gibson, C., Lowe, E. D., & Romich, J. (2002). Understanding working poor families in the New Hope Program. *Poverty Research Newsletter*, *6*(4), 3–5.

Whiteford, P., Mendelson, M., & Millar, J. (2003). Timing It Right? Tax Credits and Responding to Income Changes. (Discussion paper). York: Joseph Rowntree Foundation.

Whitmore, D. (2002). *What Are Food Stamps Worth?* Princeton: Princeton University.

Whitmore Schanzenbach, D., & Strain, M. R. (2021). Employment effects of the Earned Income Tax Credit: Taking the long view. *Tax policy and the economy*, *35*(1), 87–129.
Widerquist, K. (2018). *A Critical Analysis of Basic Income Experiments for Researchers, Policy-makers, and Citizens*. Houndmills: Palgrave Macmillan.
Wilson, S. (2017). The politics of 'minimum wage' welfare states: The changing significance of the minimum wage in the liberal welfare regime. *Social Policy & Administration*, *51*(2), 244–264. doi:10.1111/spol.12286.
Wright, S., & Dwyer, P. (2022). In-work universal credit: Claimant experiences of conditionality mismatches and counterproductive benefit sanctions. *Journal of Social Policy*, *51*(1), 20–38. doi:10.1017/S0047279420000562.
Zucman, G. (2015). *The Hidden Wealth of Nations*. Chicago: University of Chicago Press.
Zwysen, W. (2022). Global and institutional drivers of wage inequality between and within firms. *Socio-Economic Review*. doi:10.1093/ser/mwac054.

# Index

Please note that 'MIP' stands for 'minimum income protection'; references to Figures are followed by the letter *f*, to Tables by the letter '*t*'

*For the benefit of digital users, indexed terms that span two pages (e.g., 52–53) may, on occasion, appear on only one of those pages.*

The manufacturer's authorised representative in the EU for product safety is Oxford University Press España S.A. of el Parque Empresarial San Fernando de Henares, Avenida de Castilla, 2 – 28830 Madrid (www.oup.es/en or product.safety@oup.com). OUP España S.A. also acts as importer into Spain of products made by the manufacturer.

www.ingramcontent.com/pod-product-compliance
Lightning Source LLC
Chambersburg PA
CBHW051833040926
51016CB00004B/411
* 9 7 8 0 1 9 2 8 7 1 5 2 7 *